$49.50

CAREER OPPORTUNITIES IN LAW AND THE LEGAL INDUSTRY

CAREER OPPORTUNITIES IN LAW AND THE LEGAL INDUSTRY

Susan Echaore-McDavid

Ferguson

An imprint of ☑®Facts On File

Career Opportunities in Law and the Legal Industry

Copyright © 2002 by Susan Echaore-McDavid

All rights reserved. No part of this book may be reproduced or utilized in any form or by any means, electronic or mechanical, including photocopying, recording, or by any information storage or retrieval systems, without permission in writing from the publisher. For information contact:

Ferguson
An imprint of Facts On File, Inc.
132 West 31st Street
New York NY 10001

Library of Congress Cataloging-in-Publication Data

Echaore-McDavid, Susan.
  Career opportunities in law and the legal industry / by Susan Echaore-McDavid.
    p. cm.
  Includes bibliographical references and index.
  ISBN 0-8160-4552-6 (hc.: alk. paper)
  1. Lawyers—Vocational guidance—United States. 2. Lawyers—Employment—United States.
  3. Practice of law—United States. I. Title.

  KF297.E245 2002
  340′.023′73—dc21   2002004125

Ferguson books are available at special discounts when purchased in bulk quantities for businesses, associations, institutions, or sales promotions. Please call our Special Sales Department in New York at (212) 967-8800 or (800) 322-8755.

You can find Ferguson on the World Wide Web at http://www.fergpubco.com

Cover design by Nora Wertz

Printed in the United States of America

VB Hermitage 10 9 8 7 6 5 4 3 2

This book is printed on acid-free paper.

To Jennifer Ereno-Pasetta and her daughter
Franchesca Mae Cadelina.
Strength, wisdom, love, and joy.
That's what you two are all about!

CONTENTS

HOW TO USE THIS BOOK

Career Opportunities in Law and the Legal Industry covers 87 legal and legal-related professions. In this book, you'll read about a wide range of occupations that you may enter with or without law school training. You'll learn about various types of:

- attorneys in the private and public sectors
- judges in the U.S. court systems
- legal, office, and administrative support personnel found in law offices and courts
- professionals who provide litigation support to attorneys
- social services practitioners in the criminal justice system
- legal-related professionals in compliance, alternative dispute resolution, education, publishing, insurance, and other fields and industries

For each of the 87 occupations, you'll learn what the job is like. You'll learn what basic requirements are needed to enter the profession. You'll also learn what the salary, job market, and advancement prospects are like for each profession. Perhaps after reading about some, or all, of the professions in this book, you'll find one that is right for you.

Sources of Information
The information presented in *Career Opportunities in Law and the Legal Industry* comes from a variety of sources. Many professionals (attorneys, law professors, legal recruiters, legal support personnel), professional associations, and other organizations were contacted for information. The research process also included reading books, newspapers, journals, and other periodicals relating to the occupations in this book. Other sources of information included brochures, pamphlets, and other written materials from professional associations, federal agencies, businesses, and other organizations. Job descriptions, work guidelines, and other work-related materials for the different professions were also studied.

The World Wide Web was also a valuable source. A wide range of web sites were visited to learn about the 87 professions that are described in this book. These web sites include professional societies, trade associations, law schools, universities, government agencies, social service agencies, law firms, businesses, online professional periodicals, and so forth.

How This Book Is Organized
Career Opportunities in Law and the Legal Industry is designed to be easy to use and read. The 87 jobs are divided into 16 sections. A section may have as few as two profiles to as many as 13 profiles. Each profile is two or three pages long. The profiles follow the same format so that you may read the job profiles or sections in any order that you prefer.

The first four sections discuss attorneys and the professions that provide them with legal or litigation support. The next three sections cover occupations in the court systems, and the following section includes opportunities found in politics. The last eight sections describe legal-related professions in such fields as conflict resolution, compliance, and contract administration, as well as in such areas as education, career services, insurance, and publishing.

The Job Profiles
The job profiles give you basic information about 87 legal and legal-related careers. Each job profile starts with a *Career Profile,* a summary of the position's major duties, salary, job outlook, and promotion possibilities. It also sums up general requirements and special skills needed for a job, as well as any skills that successful professionals may share. The *Career Ladder* section is a visual presentation of a typical career path.

The rest of the occupational profile is divided into the following parts:

- The *Position Description* details a profession's major responsibilities and duties and provides information about working conditions.
- *Salaries* presents a general idea of the wages that professionals may earn.
- *Employment Prospects* provides a general idea of the job market for an occupation.
- *Advancement Prospects* discusses possible ways that professionals may advance in their careers.
- *Licensure/Certification* lists any professional license, certification, or registration that may be required.
- *Education and Training* describes the type of education and training that may be required to enter a profession.
- *Experience, Skills, and Personality Traits* generally covers the job requirements needed for entry-level positions. It also describes some basic employability qualities that

employers expect job candidates to have. In addition, this section describes some personality traits that successful professionals have in common.

- *Unions/Associations* provides the names of some professional associations and other organizations that professionals are eligible to join.
- *Tips for Entry* offers general advice for finding jobs and improving employability. It also suggests ways to find more career information on the World Wide Web.

The Appendixes

At the end of the book are six appendixes that provide additional resources for the 87 professions in *Career Opportunities in Law and the Legal Industry.* You can learn about resources for education and training for some professions. You can also find contact information for professional associations and other organizations that may provide you with

additional career information. Further, you can find a list of books, periodicals, and web site addresses that may give you further information and insight about the occupations that interest you.

The World Wide Web

Throughout *Career Opportunities in Law and the Legal Industry,* web site addresses for various professional organizations and other resources are provided so that you can learn more on your own. All the web sites were accessible as the book was being written. Please keep in mind that the web site owners may change URLs, remove the web pages to which you have been referred, or shut down their web sites completely. Should you come across a URL that does not work, try to find the new address by entering the name of the organization or person in a search engine.

ACKNOWLEDGMENTS

I could not have written this book without the help of the many people, professional associations, government agencies, and other organizations that were willing to answer a stranger's questions by phone and through e-mail. Nor could I not have written it without the help of my friends in legal and nonlegal professions who let me "pop up" with yet another question about their careers and jobs. To all of you, my sincere thanks!

In particular, I would like to express my gratitude to the following folks for taking so much time out of their busy schedule to help me:

Andrew Adkins, Director, Legal Technology Institute, Levin College of Law, University of Florida; Sally Andress, RP, Board Advisor, National Federation of Paralegal Associations; Ted Baker, Executive Vice President, American Society of Appraisers; Steve Bernheim, Litigation Specialist; Paul L. Biderman, Director, Rozier E. Sanchez Judicial Education Center of New Mexico, Institute of Public Law, University of New Mexico School of Law; Bill Brandt, Secretary/Treasurer, International Association of Accident Reconstruction Specialists.

Gina Viola Brown, Coordinator of ADR Research, Policy Analysis, and Law School Programs, ABA Section of Dispute Resolution; Christopher W. Bruce, Vice President of Administration, International Association of Crime Analysts; Mary E. Burns, PLS (on behalf of NALS . . . the Association for Legal Professionals).

Maureen E. Conner, Executive Director, JERITT Project; Dan Copfer, President, Demonstrative Evidence Specialists Association; Alan Crowe, Administrator, National Association of Professional Process Servers; Peter Davis, President, American Academy of Appellate Lawyers; Kevin Donahue, Public Relations Manager, The Affiliates; Marge Dover, CAE, Executive Director, National Association of Legal Assistants; Professor Robert J. Goldstein, Director, Environmental Programs, Pace Law School; Carol O'Brien English, PhD, ASA; Jennifer Ergina Ereno-Pasetta, BS, JD, Esquire.

Jaime Fatás, President, Judicial Interpreters of Massachusetts (The Translators and Interpreters Guild chapter); James R. Gripp, President, Legal Arts Multimedia, LLC; Bruce F. Hamm, JD, Board of Directors, American Association for Paralegal Education; Andrea Healy, Ethics Officer Association; John Horn, Founder, ADR International, Inc.; Marshall Jorpeland, Director of Communications, National Court Reporters Association; Joseph A. Marasco, Supervisory Patent Agent, Board of Directors, National Association of Patent Practitioners; Gayle Marquette, Founder/Administrator, American Guild of Court Videographers; Amy K. McDavid, JD, Clinical Instructor and Remington Fellow, University of Wisconsin Law School.

Patricia McEvoy, PhD, Trial Consultant, Zagnoli McEvoy Foley Ltd.; John L. Mellitz, Independent Legal Technology Consultant; Russell Gene Newman, Vice President, Industry Relations, Accredited Surety & Casualty Co., Inc.; Patricia A. Pap, Executive Director, Management Information Exchange; Mae Pittman, President, U.S. Court Reporters Association; Oliva Poole; Pat Prudhomme, Treasurer/Administrative Officer, Demonstrative Evidence Specialists Association.

Joyce A. Pratt, President, American Association for Affirmative Action; Lisa Shanholtzer Quirk, Director of Electronic Information Services, National Association of Law Placement (NALP) and the NALP Foundation; Barbara Rielly, Legal Support Professional Program Coordinator, Spokane Community College; Melissa Rosen, JD/MA, Division Director, The Affiliates.

Mary T. Sammon, Director, Court Executive Development Program, National Center for State Courts; Andrew Sheldon, JD, PhD, President, Sheldon Associates; Kathy Shimpock, Esquire, President, Juris Research; Dwayne Smith, Chair, Department of Criminology, University of South Florida; Sergeant Mark Stallo, Dallas Police Department; Judith A. Stein, Esquire, President (2000/2001), National Academy of Elder Law Attorneys; Ralph Thomas, Founder/Director, National Association of Investigative Specialists, Inc.; and Richard P. Zicari Jr., Operator of the International Process Servers Association.

My thanks also to James Chambers, my editor, for his confidence in me.

Lastly, thank you to my husband Richard McDavid for his willingness to read over my manuscript and catch my grammatical horrors.

INTRODUCTION

What professions come to mind when you think of the field of law? What kind of career options do you think are available in the legal industry?

Lawyers and judges: those are the two occupations—and career options—that people usually think of when it comes to law or the legal industry. Indeed, lawyers and judges are the major players, but they would not be able to perform their jobs without legal, office, and administrative assistance from paralegals, legal clerks, secretaries, document processors, administrators, technology specialists, and other professionals. All those support professionals in the law office and courtroom are part of the legal industry. You will learn about some of them in this book, as well as learning about lawyers and judges. In addition, you will discover that there are many other legal-related professions, some of which may surprise you. For instance, did you know that labor arbitrators, ethics officers, juvenile counselors, lobbyists, title examiners, process servers, legal reporters, law professors, and law library technicians are also part of the legal industry?

Traditionally, the legal industry covers professions in the areas of law, courts, law enforcement, and corrections and rehabilitation. (Law enforcement will not be covered in this book. See *Career Opportunities in Law Enforcement, Security and Protective Services* [Facts On File, 2000] for information about careers in law enforcement.) However, this industry also includes a wide range of legal-related occupations that are found in other fields and industries. Many of these professions offer different litigation services to attorneys, such as trial consulting, expert witness services, or private investigation. Some professionals perform legal-related work in such areas as compliance, conflict resolution, contract administration, patent prosecution, or human resource management. Other legal-related occupations are found in the areas of politics, publishing, education, career services, and library services.

So, as you can see, a variety of occupations and career options are available in the field of law and the legal industry. In this book, you will learn about 87 of them.

Your Options in the Field of Law

Anyone who is considering a career in law should know that there are many options. Attorneys usually narrow their practice of law to a few, or even one, substantive area—such as criminal law, elder law, or environmental law—depending on their interests. Attorneys also have a choice of different settings in which to work. They can work in the private sector as solo practitioners, as associates and partners in law firms, or as in-house counsel in private corporations. Opportunities are also available in the public sector, where attorneys work in government agencies, public-interest groups, and nonprofit organizations.

Alternative law careers are also available for those who do not want to become attorneys. You can combine your interest in law with your other interests and ambitions. For example, you might become a journalist who writes about the law; an educator who designs training programs for judges; a forensic psychologist who provides expert witness services; a legal administrator who runs a public-interest organization; a compliance officer who works for a health care provider; a technology specialist who provides consulting services specifically to law offices; or an administrative judge who rules on regulatory cases for a government agency such as the Environmental Protection Agency.

For many of these alternative careers, employers require that candidates possess law degrees and have some legal experience. In addition, employers may require that candidates hold a bachelor's or advanced degree in a field that is related to a particular profession. If you are interested in pursuing a career that involves law, you might consider enrolling in a joint JD (juris doctor) program as well as a graduate degree program in another field. Various law schools offer a variety of programs that award a JD as well as a master's degree in psychology, environmental science, business administration, nonprofit management, public administration, library science, or other discipline.

Growing Industries

Many of the occupations were chosen for this book because of the increasing need for qualified persons to fill positions. Since the 1990s, for example, there has been a particular demand for attorneys who specialize in such practice areas as intellectual property law, environmental law, elder law, employment law, and health care. Among the legal support positions that law offices seek to fill are qualified paralegals, legal secretaries, receptionists, calendar clerks, docket clerks, and legal technology support staff.

Some of the professions described in this book have grown since 1990 or so. For example, many legal-related occupations in the workplace, such as compliance officers, ethics officers, and contract administrators, have emerged due to the increasing number of complex employment and labor laws and regulations. Conflict resolution is another growth field because of the increasing number of disputing parties who are looking for quicker and less expensive alternatives to litigation.

The growing acceptance of technology in the law office and courtroom has also given rise to a number of new professions since 1980. These include legal technology consultants and legal support technicians. They also include such litigation support specialists as legal videographers and demonstrative evidence specialists.

Salary Information

The salary information provided in this book consists of estimated figures. The figures can give you an idea of what professionals may earn. As you read about salaries, be aware that they vary from region to region. An individual's salary is also dependent on such factors as the individual's experience and education, the job responsibilities and duties for a position, and the size and type of an employer.

Salary information for many of the occupations in this book comes from the Bureau of Labor Statistics, an agency in the U.S. Department of Labor. Each year it conducts an Occupational Employment Statistics (OES) survey to obtain estimates of occupational employment and wages across all industries for the United States, individual states, and selected metropolitan areas. As this book was being written, the national occupational employment and wage estimates for 2000 were available. For current information, visit the OES home page at *http://stats.bls.gov/oes/home.htm.*

Explore Your Career Options

The purpose of *Career Opportunities in Law and the Legal Industry* is to provide you with a useful tool for your career exploration. As you come across professions that interest you, take the time to learn more about them. Read books that explore a profession in more depth and read professional newspapers, magazines, and journals. If possible, talk with professionals about their jobs, and, perhaps, observe them at work.

The World Wide Web is also a valuable resource for career exploration. Visit web sites for professional associations and other organizations that are related to the occupations in which you're interested. Also go to web sites of employers—law firms, businesses, government agencies, and so forth—to get an idea of what it may be like to work in such a setting. At many web sites, you will find articles posted about occupations and the industry along with links that lead to other related web sites or web pages. Many employers and organizations also include career information and job listings on their web sites.

In addition, take advantage of the career center at your school or library. If there is a law school near you, visit its career services department and browse through its available resources. While you're at the law school, talk with career counselors and even law instructors.

Also get hands-on experience working in the fields and settings in which you're interested. If you are a high school student, find out if there is a work experience program for which you qualify. Talk about your interests with the program coordinator and see if you can be placed in a law firm, court office, social service agency, or other appropriate setting. If you are a college student, find out about available internships (or part-time jobs) in the fields and settings that interest you. If you are interested in a public interest career, learn about volunteer opportunities with nonprofit associations related to the areas (such as environmental law, legal assistance, or criminal justice social services) in which you're interested.

As you explore different career possibilities, you will discover the kind of careers you might like—and don't like. Furthermore, you will also be gaining valuable experience and building a network of contacts for future references.

Good luck with your career exploration!

ATTORNEYS

PRIVATE ATTORNEY

CAREER PROFILE

Duties: Manage clients' personal and business legal affairs; provide legal advice to clients; represent clients before court trials and administrative hearings

Alternate Titles: Lawyer, Associate, Senior Associate, Partner; Employment Lawyer, Appellate Lawyer, Criminal Lawyer, or other title that reflects a specific area of practice

Salary Range: $65,000 to $175,000 for law associates

Employment Prospects: Good

Advancement Prospects: Good

Prerequisites:

    Education/Training—A law degree; a bachelor's degree in any field

    Experience—Completion of a law clerkship is preferred by many employers

    Special Skills and Personality Traits—Research, writing, communication, interpersonal, and self-management skills; analytical, responsible, creative, persistent, flexible

    Licensure/Certification—An attorney's license

CAREER LADDER

```
┌─────────────────────────────────────┐
│ Partner (law firm) or Solo Practitioner │
└─────────────────────────────────────┘

┌─────────────────────────────────────┐
│      Senior Associate (law firm)      │
│        or Solo Practitioner           │
└─────────────────────────────────────┘

┌─────────────────────────────────────┐
│      Junior Associate (law firm)      │
└─────────────────────────────────────┘

┌─────────────────────────────────────┐
│             Law Student               │
└─────────────────────────────────────┘
```

Position Description

The majority of Attorneys, or lawyers, in the United States work in private practice, focusing on civil and criminal law. They handle personal and business legal affairs for their clients—individuals, businesses, nonprofit groups, institutions, and others. They perform a wide variety of legal services; for example, they draft wills, set up trust funds, review business contracts, negotiate settlements, and argue criminal or lawsuit cases before juries.

Attorneys advise clients of their legal rights and obligations, as well as suggest legal plans of action. They also represent clients in court trials as well as in arbitrations and administrative hearings. Attorneys establish a special relationship with each client and are obligated to put each client's interests above their own.

The practice of law covers a wide range of areas—criminal law, real estate law, family law, corporate law, immigration law, intellectual property law, and so on. Attorneys concentrate on providing services in one or a few practice areas.

Many Attorneys also specialize by being litigation or transactional lawyers. Litigation Attorneys, also known as trial lawyers, prepare lawsuits for court trials. Transactional Attorneys advise clients with legal transactions, such as estate planning, insurance claims, labor contracts, and corporate mergers.

A major part of an Attorney's job is performing legal research to learn what laws apply to the particular legal problems or situations that their clients face. Some other major duties that Attorneys perform are:

- review and analyze legal documents
- draft contracts, wills, court briefs, and other legal documents
- write legal correspondence
- supervise legal secretaries, paralegals, and other legal support staff
- keep up with the laws and regulations relating to their areas of practice

In addition to their paid work, Attorneys sometimes perform pro bono services. That is, they provide free legal services to economically disadvantaged individuals.

Many Attorneys work in law firms, which range from small offices with two lawyers to large firms with 2,000 or more lawyers. Attorneys are assigned to a practice area in their law firms according to their interests and their firm's needs. They work on projects alone or in teams, and sometimes are assigned to projects in other practice areas. In many law firms, Attorneys are under pressure to fulfill a minimum of billable hours—the number of working hours for which the law firm can bill a client.

Other private practice lawyers are solo practitioners, or self-employed. They have more flexible schedules than Attorneys in law firms. They can determine their own work hours, type of new cases they will take, and the size of their caseload. In addition to practicing law, solo practitioners may be responsible for their own office management. They supervise legal support staff, hire and fire staff, pay bills and taxes, generate new clients, and so on.

Attorneys work long and irregular hours, often working more than 40 hours per week.

Salaries

Salaries vary, depending on such factors as experience, job duties, type of employer, and location. Attorneys in the top law firms typically earn the highest wages. According to a 2001 salary survey by the National Association for Law Placement, the national median salaries for law associates ranged from $65,000 for first-year associates to $175,000 for eighth-year associates.

Attorneys in law firms generally receive annual bonuses in addition to their salaries.

Employment Prospects

In general, the employment for Attorneys should grow about as fast as the average for all occupations through 2010, according to the Bureau of Labor Statistics. Much of the growth is expected to be with salaried positions in private law firms, government agencies, and corporations.

Most job opportunities in law firms are found in urban areas. Competition is strong, particularly for positions in the top law firms.

Advancement Prospects

In most law firms, Attorneys start as junior associates. After five to 10 years, they may become partners, which gives them a share in the profits of their law firms.

Some Attorneys move from one firm to another to pursue positions with higher pay, more prestige, or more complex responsibilities. Others choose to continue their careers by becoming lawyers for corporations or government agencies.

For many Attorneys, their top career goal is to become successful solo practitioners.

Furthermore, Attorneys can pursue other careers; for example, they can become judges, law professors, law librarians, FBI special agents, lobbyists, politicians, and corporate executives.

Education and Training

Attorneys typically earn a bachelor's degree in any field, and then complete three years of law school, earning a juris doctor (J.D.) degree. Most state bars require that students graduate from law schools accredited by the American Bar Association. Admission requirements vary among the different law schools, but all schools require that applicants take the standardized Law School Admission Test (LSAT).

The first year in law school generally focuses on required courses such as contracts, torts, civil procedures, constitutional law, criminal law, and legal research. During the last two years, students choose elective courses in different areas of law and participate in legal clinics, moot courts, and practice trials to gain practical experience.

Most law firms provide their employees with in-house training and education programs. Many law firms have mentor programs that team new associates with senior members.

Experience, Skills, and Personality Traits

Law firms generally prefer to hire first-year associates who have completed law clerkships in law firms, court systems, government agencies, or corporate legal departments.

To succeed in their profession, Attorneys need excellent research, writing, and communication skills. Interpersonal skills are also essential, as lawyers must work well with colleagues, clients, judges, and others. In addition, Attorneys need strong self-management skills—the ability to prioritize and organize tasks, meet deadlines, work well under stress, and so forth. Being analytical, responsible, creative, persistent, and flexible are a few personality traits that successful Attorneys share.

Licensure and Certification

To practice law in any state (as well as the District of Columbia or a U.S. territory), Attorneys must hold a valid license. This generally requires passing a state bar examination and being sworn into the state bar. For licensure renewal, Attorneys may need to fulfill Continuing Legal Education (CLE) requirements. For specific information about licensure, contact the State Board of Bar Examiners in the jurisdiction where you wish to practice.

To practice before a federal court, Attorneys must be registered with that court. Each federal court has its own qualifications for admission.

Unions and Associations

Most Attorneys are members of local and state bar associations. (In some states, membership in the state bar association is mandatory.) Attorneys might join a national professional association such as the American Bar Association or the National Lawyers Association. They might also join special-interest organizations such as the Association of Trial Lawyers of America, the National Asian Pacific American Bar Association, or the National Association of Women Lawyers. By joining professional organizations, Attorneys can take advantage of education programs, networking opportunities, and other professional services and resources.

Tips for Entry

1. While in middle school and high school, you can start preparing for a career in law by developing good study habits.
2. Some Attorneys gain work experience by signing up with temporary agencies that place lawyers in short-term or temporary positions with law firms.
3. Use the Internet to explore different types of private practices. To get a list of relevant web sites, enter *law firm* or *solo practitioner.*

CORPORATE COUNSEL

CAREER PROFILE

Duties: Provide legal services to corporations that are their sole clients (and therefore their employers); may provide business advice

Alternate Titles: In-House Counsel, Staff Attorney, Deputy General Counsel, General Counsel, Chief Legal Officer

Salary Range: $63,000 to $264,000

Employment Prospects: Good

Advancement Prospects: Good

Prerequisites:

Education/Training—A law degree

Experience—Corporate law experience; knowledge of and general experience in business as well as in the corporation's particular industry

Special Skills and Personality Traits—Administrative, management, writing, communication, negotiating, interpersonal, and teamwork skills; self-starter, analytical, collaborative, flexible

Licensure/Certification—An attorney's license

CAREER LADDER

```
┌─────────────────────────────┐
│      Managing Counsel       │
└─────────────────────────────┘

┌─────────────────────────────┐
│   Senior Corporate Counsel  │
└─────────────────────────────┘

┌─────────────────────────────┐
│      Corporate Counsel      │
└─────────────────────────────┘
```

Position Description

Corporate Counsels are in-house lawyers for corporations—banks, insurance companies, hospitals, retail stores, oil firms, biotechnology companies, manufacturing companies, and so on. They are employed as staff members of corporate legal departments.

Unlike private lawyers, Corporate Counsels represent only one client—their employer, who is the corporation. Corporate Counsels serve the legal interests of the corporations, not the people who own the businesses nor those who run them.

Corporate Counsels provide legal assistance on various matters related to the business. They practice corporate law, as well as other related areas of law, such as trademarks, mergers and acquisitions, securities, tax law, bankruptcy, employment, real estate, or international commercial law.

Corporate Counsels typically work in a fast-paced environment. They meet with corporate board members and chief executive officers as well as with management and supervisory staff. They perform a wide range of legal duties, which vary from one employer to the next. The following are some legal duties that Corporate Counsels perform:

- review new business agreements for vendors and subcontractors
- negotiate employee contracts
- draft legal documents
- advise managers on regulatory and compliance matters
- prepare and file government reports
- conduct training workshops on compliance matters for managers and supervisors
- write employee handbooks
- review promotional materials
- identify legal issues relating to proposed products or offerings
- assist in the structuring of joint ventures with other organizations
- counsel managers and supervisors about employee disciplinary matters

- represent their clients before administrative boards and court trials
- supervise outside lawyers who are hired to provide specific legal services such as litigation

Many Corporate Counsels are also part of the management teams that provide strategy and planning advice for corporations. In providing business advice, Corporate Counsels must carefully watch that their business advice and legal advice do not mix.

Corporate Counsels may work alone or with other in-house lawyers. Small or new corporations usually have one or two lawyers on staff, while large corporations may have various lawyers, each specializing in one or more practice areas.

Corporate Counsels usually have a regular 40-hour work schedule. They occasionally put in additional hours to complete projects.

Salary

Salaries vary, depending on factors such as experience, type of employer, and geographical location. According to the *2002 Law Department Compensation Benchmarking Survey* (by Altman Weil, Inc.), the average annual salary for recent law graduates was $63,091; for attorneys, $107,350; for managing attorneys: $157,178; and for chief legal officers, $263,295.

Employment Prospects

According to some legal recruiters, the late 1990s have seen an increasing demand for Corporate Counsels nationwide. Opportunities are expected to continue as more businesses of all sizes realize the benefits of having legal advisors on staff. Some types of corporations that are especially looking for experienced Corporate Counsels are energy, biotechnology, and communications companies.

Advancement Prospects

Corporate Counsels who are interested in administrative and management positions can advance to become supervisory attorneys, managing attorneys, deputy chiefs (second in command), and eventually to general counsels or chief legal officers. Many Corporate Counsels move from one corporation to the next in pursuit of the top positions.

Education and Training

Employers require that Corporate Counsels have a juris doctor (J.D.) degree, preferably from a law school accredited by the American Bar Association.

Throughout their careers, Corporate Counsels enroll in training programs and continuing education programs to strengthen and build their legal skills and knowledge of substantial areas.

Experience, Skills, and Personality Traits

Requirements vary from one employer to the next. In general, employers look for candidates who have corporate law experience as well as experience in the particular areas of law (such as trademark or employment law) they would be practicing. Additionally, candidates are knowledgeable of and have general experience in business as well as in the particular industry—such as health care or technology—of which the corporation is part.

Along with their legal skills, Corporate Counsels have strong administrative and management skills. In addition they have excellent writing, communication, and negotiating skills, as well as interpersonal and teamwork skills.

Being a self-starter, analytical, collaborative, and flexible are some personality traits that successful Corporate Counsels share.

Licensure and Certification

Corporate Counsels are required to hold valid licenses in the states where they practice. To represent clients in federal courts, they must be admitted to practice in each federal court.

Unions and Associations

Many Corporate Counsels belong to local, state, or national bar associations to take advantage of networking opportunities, professional services, and professional resources. Many legal bars, such as the American Bar Association, have corporate counsel sections. In addition, Corporate Counsels might join the American Corporate Counsel Association, the Minority Corporate Counsel Association, and other such organizations that are devoted specifically to in-house counsels.

Tips for Entry

1. To enhance your employability, enroll in a few business administration courses.
2. Network with legal peers as well as other professionals in your chosen industry, as many Corporate Counsels have found jobs informally through their contacts.
3. Directly contact the corporate law departments where you would like to work. If vacancies are not available, you might ask for an informational interview with the general counsel or other key person in the department. This type of interview gives you a chance to learn more about a company as well as to let the company know about your skills.
4. You can learn more about the Corporate Counsel profession on the Internet. One place to start is at the American Corporate Counsel Association web site (*http://www.acca.com*). Or enter the keywords *corporate counsel* or *corporate law* in a search engine to view a list of relevant web pages.

GOVERNMENT LAWYER

CAREER PROFILE

Duties: Provide legal services to government agencies in the capacity of in-house attorneys; perform duties as required for a position

Alternate Titles: Staff Attorney, Attorney-Advisor, City Attorney, District Attorney, Attorney General, U.S. Attorney, Prosecutor, Public Defender

Salary Range: $33,000 to $152,000 for city and state attorneys; $41,000 to $107,000 basic pay for federal attorneys

Employment Prospects: Good

Advancement Prospects: Good

Prerequisites:

Education/Training—A law degree; a specific undergraduate or graduate degree may be required

Experience—May require one or more years of work experience as a practicing lawyer

Special Skills and Personality Traits—Legal research, writing, analytical, organizational, communication, interpersonal, and teamwork skills; intelligent, responsible, creative, dedicated, flexible

Licensure/Certification—An attorney's license

CAREER LADDER

```
┌─────────────────────────────────────┐
│  Supervising or Managing Attorney    │
└─────────────────────────────────────┘

┌─────────────────────────────────────┐
│          Senior Attorney             │
└─────────────────────────────────────┘

┌─────────────────────────────────────┐
│          Staff Attorney              │
└─────────────────────────────────────┘
```

Position Description

Hundreds of attorneys are employed by the government at the local, state, and federal levels. They provide legal assistance in the various departments of the executive, legislative, and judicial branches. All Government Lawyers serve only one client—the federal government or a local or state government. Thus they are charged with the duty of providing legal counsel and advocacy in the public interest.

Government Lawyers practice in all areas of law—criminal, appellate, social security, immigration, antitrust and trade regulation, tax, intellectual property, consumer protection, environmental, labor, malpractice, military, Indian, bankruptcy, worker's compensation, and so forth. They perform different roles for various government agencies. For example, they might:

- counsel government officials about the legal aspects relating to the diverse problems and issues that their offices must address

- develop governmental policies and procedures
- draft laws, regulations, and ordinances
- enforce laws and regulations governing public, health, environment, taxes and so on
- investigate criminal and civil cases
- prosecute individuals and institutions suspected of having committed criminal offenses
- serve as criminal lawyers for impoverished defendants
- represent the local, state, or federal government in civil lawsuits
- provide legal assistance to municipal, trial, and appellate courts

Like all attorneys, Government Lawyers perform the same general legal tasks. They review legal documents, conduct legal research, draft legal correspondence, documents, and other materials, and so on. They also perform various other duties that are specific to their positions.

Government Lawyers have a 40-hour work schedule; but many put in additional hours at night and on weekends to complete their assignments.

Salaries

Salaries vary and depend on factors such as experience, job responsibilities, and geographical location. Pay is typically higher in metropolitan areas due to their high cost of living.

Most federal attorneys are paid within the GS-11 and GS-15 levels of the General Schedule, the federal pay schedule. In 2002, the basic pay rate for these levels was between $41,684 and $107,357 per year.

According to a 2001 salary survey by the *National Law Journal,* the annual salaries for city attorneys and their assistants ranged from $33,407 to $159,661; for state attorney generals, $56,000 to $151,500; and for entry-level positions in state attorney general's offices $32,988 to $46,444.

Employment Prospects

At the federal level, many lawyer positions are concentrated in Washington, D.C. The largest number of attorneys is employed by the U.S. Department of Justice and the U.S. Armed Forces. At the state level, Attorney Generals' offices are typically the largest state government employer of attorneys. At the local level, most lawyer positions are found with the offices of the city attorney, district attorney, county counsel, and public defender.

In general, job opportunities for any government agency depend on staffing needs, turnover rates, and the agency's budget. Most opportunities become available as attorneys retire, resign, or transfer to other positions. New positions may be created when funding is available.

Advancement Prospects

Government Lawyers can advance to supervisory and administrative positions, based on their experience, abilities, and job availability. Government Lawyers who seek leadership positions are usually appointed for limited terms by executive or legislative officials. In some state and local governments, they are elected for limited terms by voters.

Many former Government Lawyers have used their positions as stepping stones to careers as private lawyers, in-house counsel, and public interest lawyers.

Education and Training

Government Lawyers have juris doctor (J.D.) degrees. (Most employers prefer graduates from law schools accredited by the American Bar Association.) Government agencies that serve particular interests may require or strongly prefer candidates with specific undergraduate or graduate degrees. For example, a government environmental regulatory agency usually prefers lawyers with science or engineering training.

Government agencies usually provide initial and ongoing training programs for their attorneys. In addition, Government Lawyers enroll in outside training and continuing education programs throughout their careers to develop and improve their legal skills and knowledge.

Experience, Skills, and Personality Traits

Qualifications vary and depend on the position that is being offered. Many positions, including entry-level ones, require one or more years of work experience as a practicing lawyer.

Like all attorneys, Government Lawyers need excellent legal research, writing, and analytical skills, as well as strong organizational and communication skills. Having effective interpersonal and teamwork skills is also important. Being intelligent, responsible, creative, dedicated, and flexible are a few personality traits that successful Government Lawyers share. Furthermore, they have a deep commitment to serve the best interests of the public welfare.

Licensure and Certification

Government Lawyers are required to be licensed attorneys. In addition, they must apply for admission to practice before a federal court.

Unions and Associations

Government Lawyers join professional bar associations to take advantage of networking opportunities, training programs, and other professional services and resources. Most Government Lawyers are members of local and state bar associations. (In some states, membership in the state bar association is mandatory.) Many Attorneys belong to a national trade association such as the American Bar Association. In addition, many join special-interest organizations such as the National Association of Women Lawyers, the Federal Bar Association, or the National District Attorneys Association.

Tips for Entry

1. Get an idea of what it's like to work in government. Many government agencies offer volunteer programs, student work experience programs, and internship programs to law students as well as to undergraduate and high school students.
2. For information about working for the U.S. Department of Justice, contact the Office of Attorney Personnel Management. Its address is Room 7254, Main Building, 950 Pennsylvania Avenue NW, Washington, DC 20530-0001. For recorded information, call (202) 514-3396. The TDD number is (202) 616-2113. Or visit its web page at *http://www.usdoj.gov/oapm.*

3. Contact each government agency, division, and bureau where you wish to work. Ask for information about job vacancies and hiring procedures.

4. You may be able to learn more about a particular government agency on the Internet. To find an agency, enter its name in a search engine (for example, *U.S. Department of Justice* or *Idaho Attorney General*). To find a state or government site, enter the name of the state, city, or county and the word *government*—for example: *New York government, Chicago government,* or *Alpine County government.*

MILITARY LAWYER

CAREER PROFILE

Duties: Provide various legal services to military officers and enlisted personnel; perform duties as required for a position; serve as a military officer

Alternate Title: Judge Advocate, Coast Guard Law Specialist

Salary Range: $26,000 to $45,000 for newly commissioned Military Lawyers

Employment Prospects: Good

Advancement Prospects: Good

Prerequisites:

Education/Training—A law degree; completion of officer training and military legal programs

Experience—Previous work experience generally not required

Special Skills and Personality Traits—Interpersonal, teamwork, and self-management skills; courageous, honest, respectful, open, humble, disciplined

Licensure/Certification—An attorney's license

CAREER LADDER

```
┌─────────────────────────────┐
│   Senior Military Lawyer    │
└─────────────────────────────┘

┌─────────────────────────────┐
│      Military Lawyer        │
└─────────────────────────────┘

┌─────────────────────────────┐
│          Recruit            │
└─────────────────────────────┘
```

Position Description

Hundreds of Military Lawyers serve in the U.S. Armed Forces, where they conduct various legal activities within the military's judicial system. In the army, air force, navy, and marine corps, Military Lawyers are called Judge Advocates and are part of their branch's Judge Advocate General's Corps (JAG Corps). In the Coast Guard, Military Lawyers are known as Coast Guard Law Specialists.

Military Lawyers practice in various areas of law—administrative law, tort claims, operational law, contract law, labor law, environmental law, international law, criminal law, and so on. Usually, at the start of their careers, Military Lawyers are assigned to the practice of military justice, or criminal law. They advise commanders of the most appropriate action to take in disciplinary matters. They also prosecute or defend court-martial cases that include criminal misdemeanors and felonies such as theft, assault, and murder, as well as military offenses such as failure to obey orders, absence without leave, desertion, and conduct unbecoming an officer.

Some other areas in which Military Lawyers may be assigned are:

- legal assistance—providing legal advice to military personnel and their families on personal matters such as estate planning, landlord-tenant disputes, taxes, divorces, and consumer law problems
- appellate litigation—drafting briefs and preparing oral arguments for civil and criminal appellate cases
- contract law—advising base officers on contracts for major construction, acquisition, and procurements
- tort claims—processing personal property claims made by military personnel as well as civilians
- administrative law—advising officers of the legal aspects related to operating installations
- international law—advising overseas commanders on agreements governing U.S. military forces
- operational law—providing legal counsel to commanders during military operations

All Military Lawyers are commissioned as officers. Hence their first duty is to serve as officers. For example, in the marine corps, Military Lawyers—like all marine officers—are trained to be combat leaders.

All members of the U.S. Armed Forces are required to serve eight years, which may be a combination of active and reserve duty. Depending on their branch, Military Lawyers' initial tour of duty is three or four years. They may be assigned to any location in the United States and, except for the Coast Guard, may be stationed overseas.

Salaries

The basic pay for Military Lawyers depends on their rank, length of service, and whether they are on active or reserve duty. In 2000, the basic pay for newly commissioned Military Lawyers ranged from about $26,000 to about $45,000.

Along with their pay, they receive money allowances for housing subsistence, military uniforms, and certain types of duty, such as foreign duty. They also get vacation leave, military supermarket and department store shopping privileges, use of recreational facilities, and other benefits. After completing 20 years of service, Military Lawyers are eligible for retirement benefits.

Employment Prospects

Military Lawyers are recruited each year by the different military branches, and competition for the positions is keen.

Each armed forces branch has its own set of eligibility requirements that candidates must meet. They must be U.S. citizens, meet certain age and physical requirements, possess high moral character, and demonstrate leadership potential.

Advancement Prospects

Depending on their prior military service, Military Lawyers start their legal career with an appointment at the lieutenant or captain rank. Promotions to higher ranks—major, colonel, and general grades—are based on experience, performance, and availability.

Experienced Military Lawyers are selected to complete a master of law (L.L.M.) degree in a specialized area of law. Also, Military Lawyers can become military judges.

Upon completion of their military service, many Military Lawyers continue their law careers as successful private lawyers, in-house counsel, government lawyers, and public-interest lawyers.

Education and Training

Military Lawyers are required to have earned a juris doctor degree from a law school accredited by the American Bar Association. Depending on the armed forces branch, they complete a two- to four-week basic officers training program followed by a nine- to 10-week legal training program. The legal training program provides new Military Lawyers with an overview of military law and other areas of law (such as administrative law, tort claims, and international law) as they pertain to the armed forces.

Military Lawyers also attend training and continuing education programs throughout their careers to build up their legal skills and expertise.

Experience, Skills, and Personality Traits

Previous lawyer experience is generally not required to apply for a commission as a Military Lawyer.

In addition to their legal skills and expertise, Military Lawyers have excellent interpersonal and teamwork skills, as well as superior self-management skills. Some personality traits that successful Military Lawyers share are being courageous, honest, respectful, open, humble, and disciplined. They are dedicated to the service of the military branch in which they serve.

Licensure and Certification

Military Lawyers are required to hold a valid license to practice before the highest court in any one of the 50 states, a U.S. territory, the District of Columbia, the Commonwealth of Puerto Rico, or a federal court.

Unions and Associations

Many Military Lawyers join the Judge Advocates Association to take advantage of networking opportunities and professional services and resources. Many belong to local and state bar associations, as well as national organizations such as the American Bar Association.

Tips for Entry

1. Get an idea if a military career may be for you. As a law student, obtain an internship with the military branch in which you are interested.
2. The different armed forces have several types of recruitment programs for Military Lawyers. For example, the navy has a law education program that enrolls qualified active-duty commissioned officers in law school. Upon earning a law degree, they can serve as a Military Lawyer.
3. You can learn more about military legal careers on the Internet. The web pages for the legal divisions are: U.S. Air Force JAG—*http://www.jagusaf.hq.af.mil;* U.S. Army JAG—*http://www.jagcnet.army.mil;* U.S. Navy JAG—*http://www.jag.navy.mil;* U.S. Marine Corps JAG—*http://www.mcrc.usmc.mil/section/o/index(ol).htm;* U.S. Coast Guard Direct Commission Lawyer Program—*http://www/uscg.mil/legal/recruit/dclinterinfo/htm.*

PUBLIC INTEREST LAWYER

CAREER PROFILE

Duties: Provide legal services to various public interest organizations such as social advocacy organizations, citizen action groups, and legal assistance programs; perform duties as required for a position

Alternate Titles: Staff Attorney; a title, such as Environmental Attorney, that reflects a particular practice area

Salary Range: $21,000 to $225,000

Employment Prospects: Good

Advancement Prospects: Fair

Prerequisites:

    Education/Training—A law degree; on-the-job training

    Experience—Previous work experience in public interest law is required or strongly preferred

    Special Skills and Personality Traits—Legal research, legal writing, communication, interpersonal, and self-management skills; enthusiastic, energetic, dedicated, compassionate, creative, flexible

    Licensure/Certification—An attorney's license

CAREER LADDER

```
┌─────────────────────────────────┐
│       Senior Staff Attorney     │
└─────────────────────────────────┘

┌─────────────────────────────────┐
│          Staff Attorney         │
└─────────────────────────────────┘

┌─────────────────────────────────┐
│  Lawyer, Law Clerk, or Law Student │
└─────────────────────────────────┘
```

Position Description

Public Interest Lawyers work in the field of public service, providing legal services to various nonprofit organizations, as well as to individuals on limited incomes. They practice in all areas of law, such as environmental, civil rights, consumer protection, health, human rights, administrative law, Indian law, family law, and education.

Public Interest Lawyers are employed in a wide variety of settings. Many work for public-interest law centers which advocate for legal reforms on behalf of the general public. These organizations work on social issues such as human rights, civil rights, women's issues, education, voting rights, and the environment. Public Interest Lawyers review proposed laws in legislation and advise organizations on how the laws may affect their particular cause. Public Interest Lawyers also draft legislation, as well as lobby legislators. In addition, these attorneys handle litigation. They take on civil action suits that affect the legal rights of a large group of people. The result of such a lawsuit may help in the advancement of a law (or social) reform.

Some Public Interest Lawyers work for citizen action groups, special-interest organizations, lobbying groups, or other nonprofit organizations that advocate specific social concerns. Attorneys in these organizations perform a variety of legal activities that include litigating, conducting legal research, lobbying legislators, organizing, and so on. Furthermore, lawyers are part of a team of organizers, scientists, social scientists, policy analysts, and others who work to promote the particular goals of an organization.

Many Public Interest Lawyers provide direct legal services to people. They mostly work for legal assistance programs that offer legal counsel and representation to those who cannot afford private counsel. Attorneys mostly handle civil cases, typically practicing in such areas as social security and disability benefits, health care issues, domestic relations, employment law, landlord-tenant relations, and consumer protection rights. Attorneys who work for legal aid programs sometimes handle criminal cases as well.

Public Interest Lawyers also work in other nonprofit settings. Some Public Interest Lawyers work in private or nonprofit law firms. Many of these lawyers do law reform litigation for nonprofit organizations. They might also provide low-fee legal services to people on limited incomes.

Salaries

Salaries vary, depending on experience, job duties, and other factors. A 2001 survey by the *National Law Journal* reported that the annual salary for staff attorneys in public interest organizations ranged from $30,000 to $225,000; and for staff attorneys in legal services $21,262 to $80,000.

Employment Prospects

Opportunities are available for Public Interest Lawyers in urban, suburban, and rural settings. But employers are able to hire only when they get funding through government grants and other development activities.

Advancement Prospects

Public Interest Attorneys generally measure success by winning cases for their clients and effecting social changes. For those who desire administrative or management responsibilities, opportunities are available but limited. The top goal for some lawyers is to start their own public interest law firm.

Other career paths lead to becoming lobbyists, elected officials, and executive directors of public interest organizations.

Education and Training

Public Interest Lawyers earn a juris doctor (J.D.) degree, usually from a law school accredited by the American Bar Association.

Throughout their careers, Public Interest Lawyers enroll in training and continuing education programs to strengthen their legal skills and learn about developments in their practice areas.

Experience, Skills, and Personality Traits

Because of their limited budgets, employers hire experienced lawyers who do not need extensive training. Employers may count experiences as law clerkships, clinical work, summer internships, and volunteer work with public interest organizations.

Public Interest Lawyers need excellent legal research and legal writing skills. Having strong communication and interpersonal skills is also important, as they must be able to work with many people from various backgrounds. In addition, Public Interest Lawyers need strong self-management skills—the ability to work independently, prioritize and organize tasks, solve problems, work well under stress, and so forth.

Being enthusiastic, energetic, dedicated, compassionate, creative, and flexible are a few personality traits that successful Public Interest Lawyers share.

Licensure and Certification

Public Interest Lawyers hold valid licenses in the states where they practice. To represent clients in federal courts, they must be admitted to practice in the individual federal courts.

Unions and Associations

Public Interest Lawyers join professional attorney's bars to take advantage of professional services and resources as well as networking opportunities. Most are members of local and state bar associations. (In some states, membership in the state bar association is mandatory.) Many join other associations such as the American Bar Association, the National Lawyers Guild, and the National Legal Aid and Defender Association. Many also join special-interest bars such as the American Immigration Lawyers Association or the National Employment Lawyers Association.

Tips for Entry

1. Participate in conferences sponsored by public interest organizations that interest you. Meet lawyers, directors, organizers, and others to begin building a network of contacts whom you can call when you are ready to do your job search.
2. Many public interest employers do not have the budget to advertise widely for job openings. Thus, take the initiative and contact employers for whom you would like to work.
3. Learn more about public interest law on the Internet. You might start by visiting the National Association of Public Interest Law web site at *http://www.napil.org*. (Note: In 2002, this organization changed its name to Equal Justice Works.) Or, to find a list of relevant web sites, enter the keywords *public interest law, public interest attorney,* or *legal services* in any search engine.

ELDER LAW ATTORNEY

CAREER PROFILE

Duties: Provide legal services to the elderly population; assess nonlegal needs of clients and refer them to appropriate service providers

Salary Range: $40,000 to $70,000 or more

Employment Prospects: Excellent

Advancement Prospects: Good

Prerequisites:

Education/Training—A law degree

Experience—Experience working with the elderly; familiarity with the various government programs in which the elderly participate

Special Skills and Personality Traits—Legal research, writing, communication, interpersonal, and teamwork skills; calm, trusting, respectful, sensitive, and compassionate

Licensure/Certification—An attorney's license

CAREER LADDER

```
┌─────────────────────────────────────────┐
│  Partner (law firm) or Solo Practitioner │
└─────────────────────────────────────────┘

┌─────────────────────────────────────────┐
│       Senior Associate (law firm)        │
│          or Solo Practitioner            │
└─────────────────────────────────────────┘

┌─────────────────────────────────────────┐
│       Junior Associate (law firm)        │
└─────────────────────────────────────────┘
```

Position Description

Elder Law Attorneys specialize in a practice that serves the legal needs of the older population, usually categorized as senior citizens or the elderly. They counsel elderly clients and their family members on a wide range of issues related to aging and death. Some of these issues include:

- estate planning—how clients wish to have their property and assets distributed to family members and others after their death.
- guardianships and conservatorships—who shall make financial and other decisions for clients in the event they become mentally or physically unable to make those decisions
- claims for public benefits such as Social Security, Medicare, veterans' benefits, and disability
- retirement benefits
- insurance claims against nursing homes or other service providers
- housing matters, such as home equity conversions or landlord-tenant problems
- financial planning for possible long-term care needs in nursing homes, as well as the transfer of assets so that a spouse would not become impoverished in the event the other must enter a nursing home
- tax planning
- civil rights matters, including age discrimination in the workplace
- consumer protection issues, including elder fraud
- elder abuse
- nursing home issues, including patients' rights and quality care

Much of these lawyers' work involves legal transactions. They draft legal documents such as wills, trusts, and durable powers of attorney. They review contracts in the areas of insurance, finance, nursing homes, and so forth, as well as advise clients on their content and legal rights. They complete applications for claims, benefits, appeals, and so on with government agencies, insurance companies, nursing homes, and other institutions. They also represent clients in administrative hearings before government agencies, as well as talk on their clients' behalf to nursing homes, employers, insurance companies, and others.

In addition, Elder Law Attorneys are trained to assess clients' nonlegal needs. For example, a client may be in need of affordable housing, another client could use financial assistance with utility bills, another client may be experiencing elder abuse, and still another client may be in need of mental health counseling. Elder Law Attorneys are typically part of a formal or informal network of social workers, psychologists, health care providers, financial advisors, clergy, and others who work with the elderly. Thus, Elder Law Attorneys can refer clients to the appropriate professionals for assistance.

Most Elder Law Attorneys are solo practitioners or work in small private firms.

Salaries

Salaries vary, depending on such factors as experience and geographical location. Annual salaries for Elder Law Attorneys generally range from $40,000 to $70,000 or more.

Employment Prospects

Although elder law practice is one of the newer types of practices, it is also one of the fastest growing. Opportunities are expected to continue to meet the legal needs of the ever-increasing number of individuals who are turning 65 years old. The U.S. Administration on Aging reports that by 2030, the number of senior citizens in the United States is predicted to double.

Advancement Prospects

In law firms, Elder Law Attorneys may advance to supervisory, administrative, or management positions, depending on the size of the firm. For many Elder Law Attorneys, their career goal is to become successful solo practitioners or partners in elder law practices.

Education and Training

Elder Law Attorneys are required to earn a juris doctor (J.D.) degree. Most state bars require that students graduate from law schools accredited by the American Bar Association.

Throughout their careers, Elder Law Attorneys enroll in continuing education and training programs to build up and strengthen their legal skills and expertise.

Experience, Skills, and Personality Traits

Employers generally look for candidates who have practical experience and knowledge about the social, health, and economic needs of the elderly. In addition, candidates should be familiar with the various government programs in which the elderly may participate.

Elder Law Attorneys must have superb legal research and writing skills. Having excellent communication, interpersonal, and teamwork skills is also important, as they must be able to work well with their clients as well as relatives, social workers, and others involved with their clients' needs. Being calm, trusting, respectful, sensitive, and compassionate are a few personality traits common to successful Elder Law Attorneys.

Licensure and Certification

To practice before a state court (or courts in District of Columbia and U.S. territories), Elder Law Attorneys must hold a valid license. To practice in federal courts, they must apply for admission to each court.

Unions and Associations

Elder Law Attorneys are typically members of local and state bar associations, as well as national organizations such as the American Bar Association. (In some states, membership in the state bar association is mandatory.) In addition, many join state or national organizations, such as the National Academy of Elder Law Attorneys, that serve their particular interests. By joining professional organizations, Attorneys can take advantage of networking opportunities as well as professional services and resources.

Tips for Entry

1. To get an idea if you might be interested in an elder law practice, volunteer at a senior center, nursing home, or agency such as the Alzheimer's Association or the American Association of Retired Persons (AARP) that serves the needs of older citizens.
2. To enhance their employability, many Elder Law Attorneys obtain the *Certified Elder Law Attorney* designation. For more information, write to the National Elder Law Foundation at 1604 North Country Club Road, Tucson, AZ 85716. Or call (520) 881-1076, or fax (520) 325-7925. Or visit its web site at *http://www.nelf.com.*
3. You can learn more about the elder law practice on the Internet. To get a list of web sites, enter any of these keywords in a search engine: *elder law, elder law attorney,* or *elder law practice.*

EMPLOYMENT LAWYER

CAREER PROFILE

Duties: Provide legal services to employers or employees regarding workplace issues and problems

Alternate Titles: A title, such as Employment Benefits Lawyer, that reflects a specialty

Salary Range: $65,000 to $175,000

Employment Prospects: Good

Advancement Prospects: Good

Prerequisites:

　Education/Training—A law degree

　Experience—One or more years practicing employment law

　Special Skills and Personality Traits—Research, writing, communication, interpersonal, and self-management skills; analytical, responsible, creative, persistent, flexible

　Licensure/Certification—An attorney's license

CAREER LADDER

```
┌─────────────────────────────────────┐
│ Partner (law firm) or Solo Practitioner │
└─────────────────────────────────────┘

┌─────────────────────────────────────┐
│      Senior Associate (law firm)      │
│         or Solo Practitioner          │
└─────────────────────────────────────┘

┌─────────────────────────────────────┐
│       Junior Associate (law firm)      │
└─────────────────────────────────────┘
```

Position Description

Employment Lawyers specialize in the practice of law which covers a wide variety of problems and issues that may arise in the workplace. Some areas that federal, state, and local employment laws cover are:

- wage and overtime standards
- termination of employment
- employee benefits, including leaves of absence and retirement benefits plans
- workers' compensation
- workplace safety
- discrimination against employees based on ancestry, color, creed, disability, marital status, medical condition, national origin, race, religion, sex, sexual orientation, or age
- sexual harassment
- privacy rights that employees may or may not have—for example, employers may request that their employees submit to random drug testing

Employment Lawyers typically focus their practice in a few areas of employment law. Some Employment Lawyers also handle legal matters that involve labor law, which covers the area of collective bargaining between management and employees.

Most Employment Lawyers specialize in providing legal services to either employers (also referred to as management) or employees. Attorneys who work with employers generally provide preventative lawyering. That is, they help clients create workplace policies and procedures that comply with federal, state, and local employment laws. In doing so, employers may lessen the risk of lawsuits by their employees.

As counsel to employers, Employment Lawyers perform a variety of legal tasks. For example, they review contracts with vendors and independent contractors. They advise on personnel matters such as employee disciplinary actions or harassment claims. They also represent their clients before government administrative boards relating to issues such as wage issues, discrimination claims, or workplace safety violations. Many Employment Lawyers perform litigation work for their clients, defending their clients in state and federal courts.

Employment Lawyers whose clients are employees perform a variety of legal transaction or litigation services. For example: They review employment contracts for clients. They advise clients of their legal rights regarding specific issues and suggest different legal actions that they could take to resolve the issues. They counsel clients on disciplinary matters. They mediate agreements between clients and their employers. They also represent individuals in civil lawsuits against employers.

Employment Lawyers are employed by private law firms or are solo practitioners. Many Employment Lawyers work in law departments of private and nonprofit corporations. Some work in public interest organizations that offer legal services to employees.

Salaries

Salaries vary, depending on factors such as experience, job responsibilities, type of employer, and geographical location. Attorneys typically earn higher wages in large national firms, as well as in metropolitan areas. According to a 2001 survey by the National Association for Law Placement, the median salaries for first- to eighth-year law associates ranged from $65,000 to $175,000. According to the *2002 Law Department Compensation Benchmarking Survey* (by Altman Weil, Inc.), the average annual salary for in-house attorneys was $107,350; and for recent law graduates, $63,091.

Employment Prospects

Because of the wide range of complex employment laws, there will continually be a need for attorneys who specialize in this area. Most opportunities become available to replace lawyers who retire, resign, or transfer to other positions. The creation of new positions depend on staffing needs as well as budgets.

Advancement Prospects

Many Employment Lawyers move from one law firm to another to pursue positions with higher pay, more prestige, or with more complex responsibilities. For many Employment Lawyers, their top career goal is to become successful law firm partners or solo practitioners.

Education and Training

Employment Lawyers earn bachelor's degrees in any field prior to earning a juris doctor degree. Most employers require or prefer lawyers who have graduated from a law school accredited by the American Bar Association.

Many employers provide their employees with in-house training and education programs. In addition, many Employment Lawyers voluntarily enroll in training and education programs sponsored by legal associations to improve their legal skills and knowledge.

Experience, Skills, and Personality Traits

Most employers require that candidates have one or more years experience as practicing lawyers, particularly in the area of employment law.

Employment Lawyers need excellent research, writing, and communication skills. Interpersonal skills are also essential, as lawyers must work well with colleagues, clients, judges, and others. In addition, attorneys need strong self-management skills—the ability to prioritize and organize tasks, meet deadlines, work well under stress, and so forth. Being analytical, responsible, creative, persistent, and flexible are a few personality traits that successful Employment Lawyers share.

Licensure and Certification

Employment Lawyers must hold valid licenses in the states where they practice. To represent clients in a federal court, they must be first admitted to practice in that court.

Unions and Associations

Most Employment Lawyers are members of local and state bar associations. (In some states, memberships in the state bar association is mandatory.) In addition, many Employment Lawyers join a national bar assoication such as the American Bar Association or the National Lawyers Guild. Those who counsel employees are eligible to join the National Employment Lawyers Association. By joining professional organizations, lawyers can take advantage of networking opportunities, education programs, job listings, and other professional services and resources.

Tips for Entry

1. Having experience working in human resources or personnel departments may enhance your employability with many employers.
2. Many bar associations offer memberships to law students. Consider joining at least one such association to begin networking with attorneys, judges, and other legal professionals.
3. You can learn more about the practice of employment law on the Internet. To find pertinent web sites, use any of these keywords in a search engine: *employment law, employment lawyer,* or *employment attorney.*

ENVIRONMENTAL LAWYER

CAREER PROFILE

Duties: Provide legal services to individuals, citizen action groups, nonprofit organizations, government agencies, businesses, or corporations

Alternate Title: Staff Attorney (in nonprofit organizations)

Salary Range: $30,000 to $225,000

Employment Prospects: Good

Advancement Prospects: Good

Prerequisites:

Education/Training—A law degree; a college degree in environmental studies, science, or engineering is preferable

Experience—Knowledge and skills in science or engineering; environmental law experience is preferred

Special Skills and Personality Traits—Research, writing, communication, negotiations, interpersonal, teamwork skills; intelligent, diplomatic, creative, flexible

Licensure/Certification—An attorney's license

CAREER LADDER

```
┌─────────────────────────────────────┐
│   Partner (law firm) or Managing     │
│  Attorney (nonprofit organization)   │
└─────────────────────────────────────┘

┌─────────────────────────────────────┐
│  Senior Associate (law firm) or Senior │
│ Staff Attorney (nonprofit organization) │
└─────────────────────────────────────┘

┌─────────────────────────────────────┐
│     Junior Associate (law firm) or   │
│  Staff Attorney (nonprofit organization) │
└─────────────────────────────────────┘
```

Position Description

Environmental Lawyers are experts in the many local, state, and federal laws that address the problems and issues related to air and water pollution, hazardous waste, and wilderness and wildlife protection. Some Environmental Lawyers also handle legal matters that extend into the areas of energy law and the conservation of natural resources. In general, Environmental Lawyers do three types of legal activites for their clients: transactions, environmental litigation, and the enforcement of environmental statutes and regulations.

Some Environmental Lawyers specialize in providing legal services to clients in the private sector. Private sector clients include small business owners, manufacturers, real estate developers, agricultural growers, logging companies, and so on. As their counsel, Environmental Lawyers perform a variety of legal services. They advise clients of environmental laws with which they must comply. They also review prospective environmental legislation and explain how it can affect their clients' business. In addition, they complete applications for regulatory approvals from government agencies, as well as represent their clients before government administrative boards. Environmental Lawyers may also handle litigation for civil lawsuits.

Other Environmental Lawyers specialize in providing legal counsel to individuals, citizen action groups, and environmental conservation groups. Their work generally involves environmental litigation, representing clients in civil lawsuits against the government or private sector. Some Environmental Lawyers also perform lobbying services and assist in the drafting of proposed legislation.

Many Environmental Lawyers are employed by government environmental regulatory agencies at the local, state, or federal level. Their duties include: advising agencies of their legal obligations to the public; drafting proposed laws and regulations; counseling staff on legal matters related to new policy that is being made; preparing civil lawsuits; and so forth.

Environmental Lawyers work long and irregular hours, often working more than 40 hours per week.

Salaries

Salaries vary, depending on such factors as experience, employer, and geographical location. According to a 2001 survey by the National Association for Law Placement, the median salaries for first- to eighth-year law associates ranged from $65,000 to $175,000. In a 2001 salary survey completed by the *National Law Journal,* annual salaries for public interest lawyers ranged from $30,000 to $225,000.

Employment Prospects

Environmental Lawyers work in private and nonprofit law firms, government agencies, nonprofit organizations, and law departments in corporations and institutions.

Jobs are highly competitive in all work settings—law firms, public interest groups, in-house corporate law departments, and government. Opportunities for entry-level positions are more favorable in the public sector, especially at the local and state levels.

Advancement Prospects

Many Environmental Lawyers start their careers working with a government agency or public interest group, then transfer to private law firms. In any work setting, Environmental Lawyers can advance to administrative and management positions.

Environmental Lawyers can also pursue other related careers, such as law professors, corporate environmental compliance managers, environmental organizers, lobbyists, or environmental policy advisors to government agencies.

Education and Training

Environmental Lawyers have Juris Doctor (J.D.) degrees. Most employers require or prefer candidates who have graduated from a law school accredited by the American Bar Association. In addition, they look for candidates who hold a college degree in environmental studies, science, or engineering.

Throughout their careers, Environmental Lawyers enroll in training and continuing education programs to increase their legal skills and knowledge in environmental law.

Experience, Skills, and Personality Traits

Employers generally look for candidates who have knowledge and skills in science or engineering. They should also have experience in the particular areas of environmental law in which they will be working.

To succeed in their profession, Attorneys need excellent research, writing, communication, and negotiation skills.

Interpersonal and teamwork skills are also essential, as lawyers must work well with colleagues, clients, and others. Being intelligent, diplomatic, creative, and flexible are a few personality traits that successful Environmental Lawyers share.

Licensure and Certification

Environmental Lawyers must hold valid licenses in the states where they practice. To represent clients in a federal court, they must be first admitted to practice in that court.

Unions and Associations

Many Environmental Lawyers join professional organizations to take advantage of networking opportunities, education programs, and other professional services and resources. They join local and state bar associations, as well as national bar associations such as the American Bar Association and the National Lawyers Guild. Some bar associations have environmental divisions or sections.

Tips for Entry

1. You can start gaining valuable experience in middle school or high school by getting involved with an environmental group.
2. To gain environmental law experience, obtain an internship or a part-time job (or volunteer) with an environmental law firm or public interest organization. Contact these firms and groups directly.
3. Contact local and state environmental regulatory agencies for available job openings. Law enforcement agencies and natural resources departments may also have opportunities for Environmental Lawyers. At the federal level, two agencies you might check are the U.S. Department of Justice *(http://www.doj.gov)* and the Environmental Protection Agency *(http://www. epa.gov).*
4. You can learn more about environmental law on the Internet. Using any of these keywords in a search engine can bring up relevant web sites: *environmental law, environmental law careers,* or *environmental lawyer.* You might also check out web sites of environmental law groups such as the National Resources Defense Council *(http://www.nrdc.org)* or the Environmental Law Institute *(http://www.eli.org).*

INTELLECTUAL PROPERTY (IP) ATTORNEY

CAREER PROFILE

Duties: Provide legal services to artists, inventors, or other owners of intellectual property

Alternate Titles: Patent Lawyer, Trademark Lawyer, or other title that reflects a specific intellectual property area

Salary Range: $65,000 to $175,000 (for private lawyers)

Employment Prospects: Excellent

Advancement Prospects: Good

Prerequisites:

Education/Training—A law degree; for patent lawyers, a college degree in engineering, physics, or science preferred

Experience—General knowledge and experience in the disciplines of their clients; business knowledge and skills

Special Skills and Personality Traits—Legal research, writing, communication, and negotiation skills; analytical, responsible, creative, persistent, flexible

Licensure/Certification—An attorney's license

CAREER LADDER

```
┌─────────────────────────────────────────┐
│  Partner (law firm) or Solo Practitioner │
└─────────────────────────────────────────┘

┌─────────────────────────────────────────┐
│        Senior Associate (law firm)       │
│            or Solo Practitioner          │
└─────────────────────────────────────────┘

┌─────────────────────────────────────────┐
│         Junior Associate (law firm)      │
└─────────────────────────────────────────┘
```

Position Description

Intellectual Property (IP) Attorneys practice in areas of law that protect the exclusive rights of clients who own property that has been created by the human mind. Intellectual property includes artistic and scientific work such as poetry, stories, plays, music, lyrics, paintings, sculptures, illustrations, cartoons, software, inventions, chemical formulations, manufacturing processes, advertising, and trade secrets. All forms of intellectual property are assets that can be sold, licensed, exchanged, or given away like real and personal property. Therefore, intellectual property laws have been created to prevent the sale or use of such property without the authorization of the owners. To ensure that their rights are protected, the owners must register their property with the appropriate federal agencies.

Intellectual property law is divided into four distinct areas. Typically, IP Attorneys specialize in one of those areas. Many specialize in patent law, which protects inventions as well as scientific and medical discoveries. (These lawyers are sometimes known as Patent Lawyers.) Some IP Attorneys specialize in copyright law, which protects the authorship of books, drawings, sound recordings, movies, maps, choreographic works, computer programs, and so on. Some lawyers handle cases involving trademark law, which protects brand names and symbols that stand for a particular good or service. Still other IP Attorneys specialize in trade secret law. This body of laws protects formulas, patterns, devices, strategies, and any other confidential information that a business develops to have an advantage over its competitors. Furthermore, IP Attorneys also practice in licensing laws, unfair competition laws, as well as statutes that regulate against counterfeiting and piracy of intellectual property.

IP Attorneys counsel individuals (authors, musicians, artists, inventors, scientists, and so on) as well as small-business owners, corporations, educational institutions, and other organizations. They may handle transactional and litigation work, depending on the needs of their clients. They perform various duties for their clients. For example, they might:

- advise clients of their rights and procedures for legally protecting their property
- counsel clients on issues such as whether their patents, trademarks, or copyrights are being infringed or whether

they may be infringing on the intellectual property rights of another
- draft legal documents such as licensing agreements
- prepare and file applications with the appropriate government agencies
- review business agreements and other legal contracts
- negotiate sales of rights for their clients
- represent clients before administrative agencies or courts regarding clients' rights of copyright, patent, or trademark
- defend or prosecute in civil suit trials

IP Attorneys work in private law firms, government agencies, and educational institutions. Many are also employed as in-house counsels by businesses and companies in all industries.

Salaries
Salaries vary, depending on such factors as experience, job responsibilities, type of employer, and geographical location. According to a 2001 salary survey by the National Association for Law Placement, the median salaries for first- to eighth-year law associates ranged from $65,000 to $175,000.

Employment Prospects
Intellectual property law practice has been one of the fastest-growing areas, and many legal recruiters see no end to the nationwide demand for IP Attorneys. Particularly in high demand are IP Attorneys (especially patent lawyers) with engineering or science backgrounds.

Advancement Prospects
IP Attorneys can advance to administrative and management positions in any work setting. Many IP Attorneys pursue positions with different employers to earn higher pay and receive more complex responsibilities. Private lawyers also pursue advancement by becoming law partners, which gives them a share in the profits of their law firms.

Education and Training
Employers require or prefer that IP Attorneys obtain a juris doctor degree from a law school accredited by the American Bar Association. IP Attorneys earn college degrees in different fields.

Employers require (or strongly prefer) that patent lawyers have a college degree or a strong academic background in engineering, physics, or natural sciences.

Many IP Attorneys receive ongoing training from their employers. In addition, many IP Attorneys continually develop and strengthen their legal skills and knowledge through training and continuing education programs.

Experience, Skills, and Personality Traits
IP Attorneys have general knowledge and experience in the particular discipline of art, technology, or science in which they work. In addition they have basic business knowledge and skills. Like all lawyers, IP Attorneys need excellent legal research and writing skills, as well as communication and negotiation skills. Being analytical, responsible, creative, persistent, and flexible are a few personality traits that successful IP Attorneys share.

Licensure and Certification
IP Attorneys are required to hold valid licenses in the states where they practice. To represent clients in federal courts, they must be admitted to practice in each federal district court.

To practice patent law before the U.S. Patent and Trademark Office, IP Attorneys must first apply for admission.

Unions and Associations
IP Attorneys join local, state, and national bar associations to take advantage of education programs and other professional services and resources, as well as networking opportunities. Many also become members of organizations that serve their particular interests such as the American Intellectual Property Law Association, International Trademark Association, Copyright Society of the USA, and the Licensing Executive Society.

Tips for Entry
1. Have work experience and extensive knowledge in the field—science, arts, business, technology, and so on—where you think you may be specializing in IP law. To have credibility among inventors, artists, and other creators, you must be able to understand their worlds and communicate with them on their own terms.
2. Take advantage of the Internet to find job openings in your field. Check out general job bank web sites such as America's Job Bank (http://www.ajb.org/seeker). For federal employment opportunities, visit the Office of Personnel Management website at http://www.usajobs.opm.gov. In addition, many law schools, legal associations, and legal publications post job listings on their web sites.
3. You can learn more about intellectual property law on the Internet. To get a list of relevant web sites, enter the keywords intellectual property attorney or intellectual property law in any search engine. For general information about patents or trademarks, visit the U.S. Patent and Trademark Office web site at http://www.uspto.gov.

PROSECUTOR

CAREER PROFILE

Duties: Conduct criminal proceedings on behalf of the government; enforce laws; may handle civil litigation

Alternate Titles: Prosecuting Attorney, City Attorney, Assistant City Attorney, City Prosecutor, District Attorney, Assistant District Attorney, County Prosecutor, Assistant Attorney General, State Prosecutor, Assistant U.S. Attorney

Salary Range: $29,000 to $150,000

Employment Prospects: Good

Advancement Prospects: Good

Prerequisites:

Education/Training—A law degree

Experience—One or more years of experience as a practicing lawyer; previous litigation experience preferred

Special Skills and Personality Traits—Research, writing, communication, interpersonal, self-management skills; enthusiastic, intelligent, responsible, creative, persistent, flexible

Licensure/Certification—An attorney's license

CAREER LADDER

```
┌─────────────────────────────────┐
│       Senior Prosecutor         │
└─────────────────────────────────┘

┌─────────────────────────────────┐
│      Assistant Prosecutor       │
└─────────────────────────────────┘

┌─────────────────────────────────┐
│ Law Student, Law Clerk, or Attorney │
└─────────────────────────────────┘
```

Position Description

Prosecutors are government lawyers who enforce criminal laws. They participate in legal proceedings that involve adults or juveniles who are charged with a crime—theft, vandalism, assault, manslaughter, drug possession, kidnapping, murder, fraud, white collar crime, or other misdemeanor or felony offense. On behalf of the government, Prosecutors are responsible for proving that criminal defendants are in fact guilty. (Under the U.S. Constitution, accused criminals are presumed innocent until proven guilty, and it is the responsibility of the government to prove their guilt.)

The job of Prosecutors is complex and demanding. They carry a heavy caseload, and must make sure that the legal process is followed for every case. They might work on a case alone or with other Prosecutors.

Prosecutors are responsible for issuing criminal charges against suspects. They base their decisions on investigations they conduct to discover the facts of a crime. If they believe that they can prove a suspect guilty beyond a reasonable doubt, they issue a criminal charge against the suspect. In

some jurisdictions, Prosecutors present the information to grand juries, which decide whether there is sufficient proof to charge suspects.

Prosecutors perform various tasks while preparing cases for trial. For example, they review law enforcement reports and previous criminal records. They interview witnesses. They develop strategies to build up the best case against the defendants. In addition, they attend arraignment hearings and pretrial conferences, as well as prepare pretrial motions.

Criminal cases may be heard before either judges or juries. In a jury trial, the Prosecutor and the defense lawyer are responsible for selecting the jurors. All criminal trials follow the same procedure. The Prosecutor and defense lawyer each present their opening statements, describing what each side expects to prove in the trial. Both the Prosecutor and defense lawyer present their cases through direct examination of their witnesses. (The Prosecutor introduces physical evidence through a witness's testimony.) Each side may cross-examine the other side's witnesses. Prosecutors make appropriate objections to offending testimony, evidence, jury instructions and summations by the defense. When both sides have presented their cases, the lawyers make their closing statements.

Generally most criminal cases do not reach the trial stage. Plea bargains are usually made between Prosecutors and the defense lawyers. Prosecutors offer to issue a lesser charge, if a defendant agrees to plead guilty to that charge. The defendant then receives a lesser form of punishment, such as a shorter jail or prison sentence.

Many Prosecutors are also assigned to perform other duties. For example, they might:

- handle appeals cases in appellate court
- defend or prosecute civil lawsuits
- review legal documents such as business contracts
- draft proposed ordinances or laws

Prosecutors are employed at the local, state, and federal levels of government. Many cities employ Prosecutors to handle criminal misdemeanors and violations against city ordinances. They are usually called Assistant City Attorneys and work under the leadership of the City Attorney, who is appointed by the mayor or city council.

At the county level, Prosecutors are part of the District Attorney or County Prosecuting Attorney offices. These offices prosecute defendants who have committed state offenses within their jurisdictions. District Attorneys are usually elected by the voters in their counties. Working under their leadership are Assistant District Attorneys or Assistant Prosecuting Attorneys.

At the state government level, Prosecutors work out of the state Attorney General's office. State Attorney Generals are elected to four-year terms by state voters. Working under their leadership are the Assistant State Attorneys who handle criminal or civil litigation for their states.

Federal prosecution is done by the U.S. Attorneys' Office, a division of the Department of Justice. There are 93 district offices in the country, each headed by a U.S. Attorney, who is appointed for a four-year term by the president of the United States. Handling both criminal and civil litigation are the Assistant U.S. Attorneys, who are not appointed. The federal Prosecutors try criminal cases that are violations of the U.S. Criminal Code, such as bank robberies, counterfeiting, public corruption, firearms violations, civil rights violations, hate crimes, narcotics trafficking offenses, health care fraud, interstate child support cases, immigration violations, certain violent crimes, and arson.

Staff prosecuting attorneys in all government offices are selected through regular hiring processes, so their jobs are not affected when new head Prosecutors have been elected or appointed.

Salaries

Salaries vary and depend on such factors as experience, job duties, employer, and geographical location. According to a 2001 salary survey by the *National Law Journal*, the annual salary for state Prosecutors ranged from $29,000 to $150,000; and for assistant U.S. attorneys, $40,000 to $125,700.

Employment Prospects

Most job openings become available as Prosecutors retire, resign, or transfer to other positions. An agency may create new positions when funding is available. More opportunities are available at the local level, where the turnover rate is higher.

Employers may require candidates to be U.S. citizens. Candidates must also submit to a selection process that may include written exams, oral interviews, drug testing, background checks, polygraph examinations, and so on.

Advancement Prospects

Prosecutors can advance to supervisory and administrative positions, depending on the size and needs of the office. Top Prosecutors are either appointed or elected for limited terms.

Many Prosecutors seek advancement in terms of being assigned more complex cases, earning higher pay, and receiving recognition from peers and the public. This may involve obtaining positions in other government offices.

Prosecutors can also pursue careers in private law firms, corporate law departments, or with other government agencies. In addition, they can pursue other legal-related career paths by becoming judges, law librarians, FBI special agents, and politicians.

Education and Training

Employers require that Prosecutors have a juris doctor degree from a law school accredited by the American Bar Association.

All new Prosecutors receive orientation training as well as learn on the job. Employers provide in-house or other training programs.

Experience, Skills, and Personality Traits

Many employers require or prefer candidates who have one or more years of experience after graduation from law school. They also look for candidates with previous litigation experience. In addition, they show an interest in public service as well as in the practice of criminal law.

To succeed in their profession, Prosecutors need excellent research, writing, and communication skills. Interpersonal skills are also essential, as lawyers must work well with colleagues, clients, judges, and others. In addition, they need strong self-management skills—the ability to prioritize and organize tasks, work well under stress, and so forth. Being enthusiastic, intelligent, responsible, creative, persistent, and flexible are a few personality traits that successful Prosecutors share.

Licensure and Certification

Prosecutors are required to have current attorney's licenses. To practice in a federal court, they must first apply for admission. Each federal court has its own set of admission requirements.

Unions and Associations

Prosecutors join professional associations to take advantage of professional services and resources as well as opportunities to network with peers. They become members of local and state attorney bars, as well as a national professional association such as the American Bar Association. Many also join state and national prosecutor bars such as the National District Attorneys Association or the National Criminal Justice Association.

Tips for Entry

1. To begin exploring a career as a Prosecutor, contact the city or county Prosecutor's office in your area.

Some offices sponsor education programs for high school and middle school students.

2. Gain experience by interning in a Prosecutor's office. Contact local, state, and federal Prosecutor offices for internship possibilities and how to apply.

3. To learn more about working for the U.S. Attorneys' Office, visit these web sites: the U.S. Attorneys' Office *(http://www.usdoj.gov/usao/eousa/usaos.html)* and the Office of Attorney Personnel Management *(http://www.usdoj.gov/oapm)*.

4. Many local and state Prosecutor offices have web pages on the Internet. To find some web pages, use such keywords as *prosecuting attorney, city prosecuting attorney, county prosecutor, district attorney,* or *state attorney general.*

CRIMINAL LAWYER

CAREER PROFILE

Duties: Counsel clients who have been accused of committing criminal offenses; defend clients in court hearings and trials; put together a defense case that proves their clients' innocence

Alternate Title: Criminal Defense Lawyer

Salary Range: $45,000 to $130,000

Employment Prospects: Fair

Advancement Prospects: Fair

Prerequisites:
    Education/Training—A law degree
    Experience—Experience in the practice of criminal law
    Special Skills and Personality Traits—Research, writing, analytical, presentation, communication, and self-management skills; aggressive, smart, brave, flexible, creative
    Licensure/Certification—An attorney's license

CAREER LADDER

```
┌─────────────────────────────────────────┐
│  Partner (law firm) or Solo Practitioner  │
└─────────────────────────────────────────┘

┌─────────────────────────────────────────┐
│       Senior Associate (law firm)         │
│          or Solo Practitioner             │
└─────────────────────────────────────────┘

┌─────────────────────────────────────────┐
│       Junior Associate (law firm),        │
│    Prosecutor, or Public Defender         │
└─────────────────────────────────────────┘
```

Position Description

Under the U.S. Constitution, accused criminals have the right to a lawyer to defend them in court. Thus, many criminal defendants hire private Criminal Lawyers to represent them in the criminal court system, which includes arraignments, pretrial hearings, settlement conferences, trials, and sentence hearings. Criminal Lawyers are experts in the practice of criminal law and criminal court procedures. They defend adults and juveniles in local, state, and federal courts.

Private Criminal Lawyers typically manage several criminal cases at a time, each at different stages of the criminal process. They handle a wide range of criminal cases involving misdemeanor or felony charges—petty theft, public nuisance, vandalism, burglary, armed robbery, assault, rape, kidnapping, manslaughter, murder, driving under the influence of alcohol, drug possession, fraud, embezzlement, counterfeiting, treason, and so on.

As the attorneys for criminal defendants, Criminal Lawyers are obligated to provide their clients with legal counsel that is in their best interest. It is also their duty to ensure that defendants' constitutional rights are not being compromised. All final decisions on any matter, however, are made by the defendants. For example, a defendant may choose to plead guilty at the arraignment or to waive the right to a jury trial.

At the start of each case, Criminal Lawyers obtain copies of all police reports, evidence, eyewitness testimony, and all other information that the prosecution has on the case. Criminal Lawyers assess the facts and advise their clients about what they would most likely be charged in legal fees, and their chances of being found guilty. They also work with their clients to develop defense strategies that fit the truth of what happened according to their clients' point of view.

Criminal litigation involves various complex tasks. Criminal Lawyers usually use the services of paralegals, private investigators, litigation consultants, and others to help them. Some of these tasks are:

- gathering additional evidence to support their case or dispute the prosecution's charges
- examining the crime scene
- interviewing witnesses
- conducting legal research
- locating expert witnesses who can testify on issues that support the defense or dispute the prosecution's charges
- developing demonstrative exhibits

Criminal Lawyers devote a lot of time and energy to prepare the best defense case that would produce a verdict of not guilty, or a verdict of guilt of a lesser charge, or an acceptable plea bargain. Most cases, in fact, do not reach the trial stage. Criminal Lawyers and prosecutors are often able to agree on a plea bargain in which the defendants receive lesser sentencing by pleading guilty to lesser criminal charges.

With cases that go to trial, the defendants decide whether to have their case tried before a judge or jury. In a jury trial, the Criminal Lawyer and prosecutor are responsible for selecting the jurors. All criminal trials follow the same procedure. They start with the Criminal Lawyer and prosecutor each presenting their opening statements. Each describes what his or her side expects to prove in the trial. The two sides then present their case through direct examination of their witnesses. (The Criminal Lawyer introduces physical evidence through a witness's testimony.) Each side may cross-examine the other side's witnesses. The Criminal Lawyer makes appropriate objections to offending testimony, evidence, jury instructions, and prosecutorial summations. When both sides have presented their cases, the lawyers make their closing statements. The Criminal Lawyer's closing statement covers a summary of the evidence from the defense's point of view. The Criminal Lawyer also explains why the defendant should be found not guilty.

The judge or jury deliberates on all the facts presented to them and decides on the verdict. If a verdict is guilty, the defendant may petition for appeals in state or federal appellate courts. These are requests for the higher courts to overturn the decisions because errors in the trials or applications of law had been made. If a Criminal Lawyer does not practice appellate law, he or she recommends an experienced appellate attorney to his or her client.

Private Criminal Lawyers work long and irregular hours, often working more than 40 hours per week.

Salaries

Private Criminal Lawyers generally make the lowest earnings among lawyers. Salaries vary, depending on factors such as experience and geographical location. According to the Bureau of Labor Statistics the majority of lawyers in 2000 earned an estimated annual salary between $44,590 and $130,170.

Employment Prospects

Private Criminal Lawyers work in law firms of all sizes, but most are solo practitioners or part of small firms. Besides private practices, Criminal Lawyers are also employed by public interest organizations and government agencies that serve individuals on limited incomes.

Competition is keen for available positions in law firms.

Advancement Prospects

Most Criminal Lawyers realize success by earning higher wages, being highly recognized for their work, and getting very complex cases.

Criminal Lawyers might pursue other careers by becoming law professors, criminal investigators, FBI special agents, or judges.

Education and Training

Criminal Lawyers, like all lawyers, hold a juris doctor (J.D.) degree. Throughout their careers, many enroll in training and continuing education programs to build and strengthen their legal skills.

Experience, Skills, and Personality Traits

Employers (and clients) typically choose candidates who have experience in the practice of criminal law. A recent law graduate with significant clinical experience may be considered.

Criminal Lawyers have excellent research, writing, and analytical skills. They also have superior presentation and communication skills, being able to think quickly and to clearly articulate complex ideas off the top of their heads. In addition, they have strong self-management skills—the ability to prioritize and organize multiple tasks, meet deadlines, work well under stress, and so forth.

Being aggressive, smart, brave, flexible, and creative are a few personality traits that successful Criminal Lawyers share.

Licensure and Certification

Criminal Lawyers are required to hold valid licenses in the states where they practice. To represent clients in a federal court, they must first apply for admission to practice in that court.

Unions and Associations

Most Criminal Lawyers are members of local and state bar associations. (In some states, membership in the state bar association is mandatory.) Many also join a national bar association such as the American Bar Association or the National Lawyers Association. Many join state and national special interest associations such as the National Association of Criminal Defense Lawyers and the Association of Trial Lawyers of America. By joining professional organizations, Criminal Attorneys can take advantage of networking opportunities, education programs, and other professional services and resources.

Tips for Entry

1. In law school, get experience by obtaining internships, volunteer positions, or part-time jobs with public

defender and prosecutor offices, as well as in private firms that have practices in criminal law.

2. Many private Criminal Lawyers started their careers as prosecuting attorneys and public defenders.

3. You can learn more about criminal law on the Internet. Enter the keyword *criminal law* or *criminal lawyer* in any search engine to get a list of relevant web sites.

PUBLIC DEFENDER

CAREER PROFILE

Duties: Provide legal counsel and representation for indigent defendants; prepare for court trials; defend clients in court trials

Alternate Title: Federal Defender

Salary Range: $29,000 to $126,000

Employment Prospects: Good

Advancement Prospects: Limited

Prerequisites:
  Education/Training—A law degree
  Experience—One or more years as a practicing lawyer; criminal trial experience preferred; commitment to public service
  Special Skills and Personality Traits—Legal writing, advocacy, communication, presentation, and self-management skills; optimistic, determined, aggressive, independent, creative, sympathetic
  Licensure/Certification—An attorney's license

CAREER LADDER

```
┌─────────────────────────────┐
│   Supervising or Managing    │
│      Public Defender         │
└─────────────────────────────┘

┌─────────────────────────────┐
│   Assistant Public Defender  │
└─────────────────────────────┘

┌─────────────────────────────┐
│    Law Student or Lawyer     │
└─────────────────────────────┘
```

Position Description

Public Defenders are criminal lawyers employed by the government to represent indigent (or poor) defendants. In the United States, persons who are accused of committing a crime that is punishable by prison or jail have the constitutional right to be defended by a lawyer. If they cannot afford to hire a private lawyer, the judge may appoint a lawyer—a Public Defender—to represent them.

Public Defenders carry heavy caseloads that include clients charged with misdemeanor and felony crimes. They may be appointed to serve adult or juvenile offenders. In some jurisdictions, Public Defenders are also assigned to represent the mentally ill and the developmentally disabled in civil commitment proceedings. For example a Public Defender might represent a developmentally disabled woman who was involuntarily placed in a residential facility and wishes to be released.

Like private criminal lawyers, Public Defenders are obligated to provide each of their clients with the best legal defense that they can. They also ensure that their clients' constitutional rights are not being compromised.

Throughout their workdays, they handle various cases that are at different stages of the criminal process. For example, Public Defenders:

- assess newly assigned cases
- attend arraignments and hearings
- negotiate plea bargains with the prosecuting attorneys
- prepare for trials, which includes tasks such as interviewing clients and witnesses, visiting crime scenes, preparing exhibits, developing defense strategies, and so on
- perform legal research
- participate in the selection of jury members for trials
- try court cases

In large offices, Public Defenders may be assigned to handle different stages of the criminal procedure for all cases. For example, new Public Defenders may be responsible for arraignment hearings or assessing cases, while experienced appellate lawyers handle appeals cases.

Government public defender programs are established at local, state, and federal levels. In large metropolitan areas, the public defender office may be part of the city or county government. In rural areas and small counties, solo practitioners or private law firms are contracted to provide public defender services.

The head of public defender programs is actually called the Public Defender. They oversee the day-to-day administration and management of their programs. They also educate the public about the role of the Public Defender. Depending on their staffing needs, they may or may not represent indigents. Chief Public Defenders are either appointed or elected into office. They serve a limited term upon which they may be reappointed or reelected.

Serving under the chief Public Defender are the staff attorneys, often known as Assistant Public Defenders or Deputy Public Defenders. Their positions are rarely in jeopardy when new Public Defenders are appointed or elected.

Salaries

Salaries vary, depending on experience, geographical locations, and other factors. According to a 2001 survey by the *National Law Journal,* annual salaries for county Public Defenders ranged from $29,000 to $107,000; for state Public Defenders, $38,163 to 123,255; and for federal Public Defenders, $41,000 to $125,700.

Employment Prospects

Most opportunites become available as Public Defenders resign, transfer to other positions, or retire. Employers create new positions from time to time as funding becomes available.

At the federal level, federal district courts may establish new defender organizations in a district if at least 200 persons in the district require a Public Defender each year.

Advancement Prospects

Public Defenders can advance to a limited number of supervisory and administrative positions. Those in top positions typically spend less time in litigation. Many career Public Defenders pursue advancement by seeking more complex assignments, earning higher wages, and receiving professional recognition.

The Public Defender position has been the starting point of many lawyers' careers. After working in a Public Defender's office for a few years, many lawyers seek employment with private firms, corporate legal departments, or other government agencies. Some start practices in criminal law as solo practitioners or as heads of small firms.

Education and Training

Employers require that Public Defenders have a juris doctor (J.D.) degree, preferably from a law school accredited by the American Bar Association. New Public Defenders receive initial training on the job. Many employers also have ongoing training programs.

Experience, Skills, and Personality Traits

Many employers require or strongly prefer candidates with one or more years of experience in the practice of law. They particularly look for lawyers with criminal trial experience. In addition, good candidates demonstrate a commitment to public service.

Public Defenders have excellent legal writing and advocacy skills, as well as superior communication and presentation skills. In addition, they have strong self-management skills—the ability to manage heavy caseloads, prioritize and organize tasks, work well under stress, and so forth.

Being optimistic, determined, aggressive, independent, creative, and sympathetic are a few personality traits that successful Public Defenders share. Furthermore, they are dedicated to the concept of the right to counsel for all people.

Licensure and Certification

Public Defenders are required to hold attorney licenses to practice in state courts. To practice in federal courts, they must first apply for admission. Each federal court has its own set of admission requirements.

Unions and Associations

Public Defenders are typically members of their state bar associations as well as local bars and national groups such as the American Bar Association. Many belong to local, state, and national associations that specifically serve the interests of criminal defense lawyers or Public Defenders. Some national organizations are the National Association of Criminal Defense Lawyers, the National Legal Aid and Defender Association, or the Association of Federal Defense Attorneys. By joining professional associations, Public Defenders take advantage of professional services, professional resources, and networking opportunities.

Tips for Entry

1. To gain experience as an undergraduate or a law student, obtain internship or volunteer positions in a Public Defender office.
2. Attend conferences and meetings for Public Defenders and network with participants.
3. Contact Public Defender offices directly for information about vacancies and hiring procedures.
4. Use the Internet to learn more about a Public Defender career. To get a list of relevant web sites, enter the keywords *public defender* or *federal defender* in any search engine.

APPELLATE ATTORNEY

CAREER PROFILE

Duties: Handle cases in state and federal appellate courts; counsel clients; prepare legal briefs; present oral arguments before appellate judges

Alternate Title: Appeals Lawyer, Federal Appellate Defender

Salary Range: $65,000 to $175,000, for private lawyers

Employment Prospects: Good

Advancement Prospects: Good

Prerequisites:

Education/Training—A law degree

Experience—Trial experience; appellate law experience preferred

Special Skills and Personality Traits—Legal writing, legal research, legal analysis, organizational, communication, presentation, and interpersonal skills; intelligent, analytical, adaptable, good-natured

Licensure/Certification—An attorney's license

CAREER LADDER

```
┌──────────────────────────────────┐
│   Senior Associate, Partner, or   │
│        Solo Practitioner          │
└──────────────────────────────────┘

┌──────────────────────────────────┐
│        Appellate Attorney         │
└──────────────────────────────────┘

┌──────────────────────────────────┐
│       Attorney or Law Clerk       │
└──────────────────────────────────┘
```

Position Description

Appellate Attorneys are experienced in the process of appealing cases in the state or federal higher courts called appellate courts. These courts may overturn decisions that are made in the trial courts if they find that errors had occurred in the trial procedure or in the application of the law, and such errors affected the decisions. However, Appellate Attorneys do not retry cases, nor do they introduce new evidence at appellate hearings. They present arguments either for or against appealing the decision of trial cases.

Appellate Attorneys handle appeals for criminal or civil cases. They may represent the appellant (the party petitioning for a appeal) or the respondent (the other party).

The appellate process begins after a court trial is ended. The Appellate Attorneys obtain and review all court transcripts and court records, or legal documents, that have been filed in a trial to determine whether a case can be appealed. An appeal can only be made on issues that have been brought up and challenged at the trial. After a thorough review, Appellate Attorneys advise clients of their chances for filing an appeal, as well as give them an idea of how long the appeal can take and the estimated cost of the total appeals

procedure. During the appeals process, they keep their clients informed of the status of their cases. Appellate Attorneys also represent their clients in settlement negotiations.

Appellate Attorneys are responsible for following the appellate procedures of each state or federal appellate court precisely. For example, they file motions and briefs by the established deadlines, attach the appropriate statements and forms, and follow the required formats for writing legal statements.

Unlike trial judges, judges in appellate courts make their decisions based on legal briefs, or written legal statements. Thus, Appellate Attorneys have the challenge of writing clear and concise legal arguments that address only the particular issues and include appropriate case precedents that support their appeal or response. Altogether, three briefs will be filed for a case. The attorney for the appellant files an opening brief that explains the facts and procedural history of the case and the reasons why the decision should be reversed. The attorney for the respondent then files a responsive brief, explaining why the trial court made the correct decision and presenting their arguments why the decision should not be reversed. The attorney for the appellant files the final brief, presenting arguments why the respondent's claims are wrong.

Appellate Attorneys may have the opportunity to also present oral arguments before a panel of appellate judges. But they are usually given a time limit of 10 to 30 minutes. Often the time is used to answer questions from the judges or to clarify points in their written briefs.

If a party is unhappy with the results of an appeal, Appellate Attorneys can petition to a higher appellate court to review the case. In most states, the state supreme court is the highest appeals court. In the federal judicial system, the highest court of appeals is the U.S. Supreme Court. Appellate Attorneys can appeal a state case all the way to the U.S. Supreme Court if the case involves a constitutional or federal issue.

Appellate Attorneys work long and irregular hours, often more than 40 hours per week.

Salaries

Salaries vary, depending on factors such as experience, employer, and geographical location. For example, private lawyers typically earn higher salaries than government or public interest lawyers. Also, lawyers who live in metropolitan areas usually earn higher wages.

Most federal attorneys are paid within the GS-11 and GS-15 levels of the General Schedule, the federal pay schedule. In 2002, the basic pay rate for these levels was between $41,684 and $107,357 per year. The annual salary in 2001 for many city and state attorneys and their assistants ranged from $32,988 to $151,500, according to a survey by the *National Law Journal*. A survey by the National Association for Law Placement reports that the median salaries in 2001 for first- to eighth-year law associates ranged from $65,000 to $175,000.

Employment Prospects

Appellate Attorneys work for government agencies, public interest organizations, and private law firms. Some are solo practitioners.

Most opportunities become available as lawyers resign, retire, or transfer to other positions.

Advancement Prospects

Administrative and management positions are available, but limited. Many Appellate Attorneys pursue advancement in terms of earning higher pay, being assigned to more complex cases, or receiving professional recognition.

Appellate Attorneys might pursue other career paths such as becoming judges, law professors, or elected officials.

Education and Training

Appellate Attorneys hold a juris doctor (J.D.) degree. Most state bars require that students graduate from law schools accredited by the American Bar Association.

Throughout their careers, many Appellate Attorneys regularly enroll in continuing education and training programs to strengthen their legal skills and expertise.

Experience, Skills, and Personality Traits

Employers generally look for candidates who have trial experience. They also prefer to hire lawyers who have appellate law experience.

Appellate Lawyers must have superior legal writing skills, being able to explain complex ideas clearly and succinctly. In addition, they have excellent legal research and legal analysis skills. Furthermore, they have strong organizational, communication, presentation, and interpersonal skills.

Some personality traits that successful Appellate Lawyers share are being intelligent, analytical, adaptable, and good-natured.

Licensure and Certification

To practice law in any state (as well as the District of Columbia or a U.S. territory), Attorneys must hold a valid license. To practice before a federal court, attorneys must first apply for admission.

Some state bars grant special certification to Appellate Lawyers who meet a particular level of expertise in appellate law. The certification, however, is not required to practice in this area of law. Many attorneys choose to obtain special board certification to enhance their employability.

Unions and Associations

Appellate Attorneys join professional organizations to take advantage of networking opportunities, training, and other professional services and resources. Most lawyers belong to their local and state bar associations, as well as join national bar associations such as the American Bar Association and the National Lawyers Association. Experienced Appellate Attorneys are eligible to join the American Academy of Appellate Lawyers.

Tips for Entry

1. The U.S. Attorneys' Office (USAO), in the U.S. Department of Justice, is one of the larger employers of Appellate Attorneys. There are 93 USAO offices in the country, and each office handles its own recruitment. You can get more information about USAO on the Internet by going to *http://www.usdoj.gov/usao/eousa/usaos.html.*

2. To gain appellate experience while in law school, you might obtain a clerkship with an appellate court, or a part-time or summer job as a law clerk in a private firm. Also participate in your school's moot court as well as its law review or other law journal.

3. Enroll in training programs that are sponsored by appellate professionals. One such resource is the Appellate Practice Institute. For more information, contact the American Bar Association Judicial Division, 541 N. Fairbanks Court, Chicago, IL 60611. Or call (312) 988-5705, fax (312) 988-5709, or e-mail: abajd@abanet.org.

4. Learn more about appellate law on the Internet. To get a list of relevant web sites, enter the keywords *appellate law* or *appellate attorney* in a search engine.

LEGAL SUPPORT PROFESSIONALS

LEGAL SUPPORT PROFESSIONAL

CAREER PROFILE

Duties: Provide general office, administrative, and/or legal support; perform duties as assigned

Alternate Titles: Legal Specialist; may be called Legal Clerk, Legal Technician, or Legal Administrative Clerk in government agencies; a title that reflects specific duties such as Legal Secretary, Paralegal, Case Clerk, Records Clerk, Mail Clerk, Office Clerk, Bookkeeping Clerk, Personnel Clerk, or Legal Word Processor

Salary Range: $22,000 to $84,000

Employment Prospects: Good

Advancement Prospects: Good

Prerequisites:

Education/Training—Requirements vary from high school diploma to college degree, depending on the occupation; on-the-job training

Experience—Requirements vary, depending on the occupation; previous experience in law office preferred

Special Skills and Personality Traits—Communication, interpersonal, teamwork, self-management, writing, and computer skills; ability to operate office equipment; enthusiastic, positive, dependable, hard-working, organized, detail-oriented

Licensure/Certification—None required

CAREER LADDER

```
┌─────────────────────────────────┐
│   Assistant Law Office Manager   │
│     or Supervising Paralegal     │
└─────────────────────────────────┘

┌─────────────────────────────────┐
│     Legal Specialist (such as    │
│   Records Clerk), Legal Secretary,│
│          or Paralegal            │
└─────────────────────────────────┘

┌─────────────────────────────────┐
│  Legal Receptionist, Legal Word  │
│  Processor, or Legal Assistant Clerk │
└─────────────────────────────────┘

┌─────────────────────────────────┐
│   General Office Clerk (Law Office) │
└─────────────────────────────────┘
```

Position Description

Various types of Legal Support Professionals help lawyers run their offices efficiently and effectively. In general, Legal Support Professionals perform duties in one or more of three areas—office, administrative, or substantial legal support. There are many job titles in this category; each title represents specific responsibilities. The following are some of the more common occupations found in law firms and law departments in corporations, government agencies, and other organizations.

Office Clerks perform a variety of routine office tasks. For example, they distribute mail, photocopy papers, do filing, set up conference rooms, run errands, answer telephones, and type correspondence.

Legal Receptionists are responsible for greeting clients and visitors to the law office in person, and sometimes by phone. They direct clients and visitors to the appropriate staff member in the office.

Legal Word Processors produce legal documents, correspondence, and other materials on word processors or computer systems. They make sure that the finished products are correct, accurate, and have been properly formatted.

Records Clerks or *Records Specialists* set up and maintain clients' case files for lawyers. They prepare new files, index legal documents, track files in computer databases, photocopy documents, update clients' files, access files for specific information as requested by lawyers, and so on.

Information Technology Specialists provide law offices with various types of technical support. Their duties include maintaining and upgrading hardware, software, databases, and networks. They also analyze specific legal and nonlegal needs, and troubleshoot technical problems.

Case Clerks or *Case Assistants* provide litigation support to paralegals and attorneys. Case Clerks are responsible for maintaining and organizing case files. They perform such tasks as coding legal documents, keeping documents in alphabetical and chronological order, and preparing indexes for documents and pleadings.

Calendar Clerks maintain the court calendar that shows the court dates (court filings, hearings, and trials) for all lawyers in their offices. These clerks also keep the office up to date with new court rules and procedures, and provide lawyers with regular calendar reports. In addition, the clerks make sure that legal documents being filed are in compliance with court procedure and rules.

Docket Clerks provide support to lawyers. They keep track of all transactions filed for clients' patents or trademarks. Their tasks include updating databases, preparing progress reports, monitoring attorney deadlines, opening and sorting mail, processing invoices, and so on.

Legal Secretaries provide support directly to one or more lawyers. Their primary duties are preparing legal correspondence and documents, maintain lawyers' schedules, and maintain legal files. Many also conduct legal research.

Paralegals or *Legal Assistants* are specially trained to assist lawyers with a variety of substantial legal tasks. Under the direction and supervision of attorneys, they interview clients, prepare legal documents, conduct legal research, draft documents, and prepare clients for trials.

Legal Administrators oversee the daily nonlawyer operations of the law office. They are in charge of all management functions, including administrative policies and procedures, human resources, marketing, financial management, information systems, and facilities management.

Legal Support Professionals work full time or part time. In large firms, they may work different shifts. Some, such as Paralegals, Legal Secretaries, and Legal Word Processors, may be required to work overtime.

Salaries

Salaries vary, depending on factors such as the position and employee's job duties, experience, size and type of employer, and geographical location. *The Affiliates 2001 Salary Guide* (by the Affiliates, a national legal staffing business) reports the average annual salary ranges for these positions:

- legal receptionist—$22,250 to $30,250
- office clerk—$23,250 to $29,250
- legal word processor—$33,500 to $43,500
- records clerk—$23,250 to $30,000
- docket/calendar clerk—$25,000 to $33,000
- legal secretary—$28,750 to $52,750
- paralegal—$28,000 to $66,250
- administrative/office manager—$50,000 to $83,750

Employment Prospects

In general, most positions for Legal Support Professionals become available as individuals resign, retire, or transfer to other positions. Law offices will create additional positions to fit staffing needs.

Currently, paralegals are in great demand throughout the United States. Opportunities are also good for highly experienced legal secretaries and legal administrators.

Advancement Prospects

Legal Support Professionals can advance in any number of ways, depending on their interests and ambitions. With additional experience and training, general office clerks can advance to specialized clerical positions such as legal receptionists, legal word processors, records clerks, and legal secretaries. Or they can obtain positions as legal assistant clerks, providing support to paralegals and lawyers. They can also become legal secretaries and paralegals. Those who are interested in pursuing legal administrative and management careers can become department coordinators (such as records coordinators) and legal administrators (such as human resource managers and office managers). Still another option for many is to earn a college degree and then continue on to law school to eventually become lawyers.

Education and Training

Requirements vary, depending on the position. A high school diploma or general equivalency diploma is needed for entry-level office positions. For higher office and administrative positions, employers generally prefer or require at least an associate degree or equivalent education and experience. For paralegal and some legal specialist positions, some employers require or prefer a bachelor's degree.

Legal Support Professionals receive on-the-job training. Many employers also provide in-house training programs to help support staff develop and build their skills.

Experience, Skills, and Personality Traits

Specific requirements for the different positions vary. In general, employers prefer to hire candidates with previous experience in a law office or who have general knowledge of legal terminology and procedures.

In general, Legal Support Professionals, regardless of their position, should have excellent communication, interpersonal, and teamwork skills. Additionally, they need strong self-management skills—the ability to perform several tasks at a time, be punctual, handle stressful situations, and so on. Legal Support Professionals also need good writing and computer skills, and should be able to operate office equipment such as fax machines and copiers.

Being enthusiastic, positive, dependable, hardworking, organized, and detail-oriented are some personality traits that successful Legal Support Professionals share.

Unions and Associations

Many Legal Support Professionals join different local, state, and national associations that support legal office and administrative professions. Some associations are NALS ... the association for legal professionals, the National Association of Legal Assistants, and the Association of Legal Administrators. By joining professional associations, Legal Support Professionals can take advantage of networking with peers, training and education programs, and other professional services and resources.

Tips for Entry

1. Such high school courses as English, speech, math, typing or keyboarding, computer, and business can help you prepare for a career as a Legal Support Professional.

2. Many community colleges have certification or degree programs in legal studies that prepare graduates for various Legal Support Professional positions. Graduation from such a program, or at least completion of several courses, may enhance your employability.

3. To gain experience, you might sign up with temporary agencies that work specifically with law offices.

4. Contact law firms and legal departments in corporations, government agencies, and other institutions directly about current and future vacancies.

5. You can learn more about the various legal support occupations on the Internet. Use a job title, such as *paralegal* or *legal records clerk,* as the keyword to enter in any search engine.

LEGAL RECEPTIONIST

CAREER PROFILE

Duties: Meet and greet clients and visitors to the law office; answer phones; perform other duties as required

Salary Range: $22,000 to $30,000

Employment Prospects: Good

Advancement Prospects: Good

Prerequisites:

Education/Training—A high school diploma; on-the-job training

Experience—Previous office or customer service experience is preferred

Special Skills and Personality Traits—Interpersonal, teamwork, communication, self-management skills; typing or keyboarding skills and familiarity with office machines; friendly, tactful, composed, organized, reliable, flexible

Licensure/Certification—None required

CAREER LADDER

```
┌─────────────────────────────────────┐
│  Legal Secretary, Paralegal, or Other │
│      Legal Support Professional       │
└─────────────────────────────────────┘

┌─────────────────────────────────────┐
│         Legal Receptionist           │
└─────────────────────────────────────┘

┌─────────────────────────────────────┐
│     Legal Receptionist Trainee       │
│      or Legal Office Clerk            │
└─────────────────────────────────────┘
```

Position Description

Legal Receptionists are responsible for greeting visitors and clients to law offices. They are often the first employees that the public meets, so they are expected to make a good first impression for their law office.

They usually sit at desks in lobbies or front offices. They provide information to visitors who come in with general questions about the law firm. They inform attorneys and other staff members of clients and visitors who have arrived for their appointments. Legal Receptionists then direct visitors and clients to their proper destinations. If they must wait for their appointments, receptionists invite them to sit down and rest, and may provide them with coffee or tea.

Legal Receptionists also help provide their offices with security, as they monitor who enters the offices. In some offices, Legal Receptionists request that visitors sign in and sign out on visitor logs. Many Legal Receptionists also oversee the receipt and distribution of legal documents from delivery services.

Many Legal Receptionists are responsible for answering incoming calls, often handling multiline phones or switchboards. They direct calls to the appropriate personnel in the offices. They take phone messages for staff who are absent or unable to answer the phone, and make sure the staff members receive messages.

In some law offices, Legal Receptionists keep track of conference room assignments, as well as prepare conference rooms for meetings and order food for meetings. Some are also assigned the task of maintaining the office kitchen.

Legal Receptionists may also be assigned clerical support tasks in addition to their reception duties. For example, they may complete fax transmittals, do filing, photocopy documents, type correspondence, open and sort mail, update appointment calendars, and purchase office supplies.

In some offices, Legal Receptionists are hired to perform additional roles, such as those of an office clerk, legal word processor, or legal secretary.

Legal Receptionists work full time or part time. In some offices, Legal Receptionists work evening shifts.

Salaries

Salaries vary, depending on a Legal Receptionist's experience, education, job duties, size of employer and other factors. According to *The Affiliates 2001 Salary Guide* (by the Affiliates, a national legal staffing business), the average salary for Legal Receptionists ranged between $22,250 and $30,250.

Employment Prospects

The Bureau of Labor Statistics reports that the employment of receptionists in all industries is expected to grow faster than the average for all occupations through 2008. The increase in jobs will come mostly from service industries, which includes the legal industry.

Most opportunities for Legal Receptionists become available as individuals resign or as they advance or transfer to other positions. Experienced Legal Receptionists are generally sought by large law firms, while smaller and midsize law firms usually look for Legal Receptionists who are also willing to perform the duties of legal secretaries.

Advancement Prospects

Legal Receptionists can advance in any number of ways, depending on their interests and ambitions. With further training and experience, they can become legal word processors, legal secretaries, legal assistant clerks, paralegals, and law office managers. Another path is to continue their education to earn their law degree and become lawyers.

Education and Training

Employers typically require that Legal Receptionists have at least a high school diploma or general equivalency diploma. Some employers prefer candidates who have some college or postsecondary training, particularly in business or office skills. Employers provide new employees with on-the-job training.

Experience, Skills, and Personality Traits

Work experience requirements vary from employer to employer. Many employers prefer applicants who have previous receptionist or customer service work experience, or who have general office experience in law settings. They look for candidates who have a clear speaking voice and a professional appearance.

Legal Receptionists need excellent interpersonal, teamwork, and communication skills, as they are constantly interacting with visitors, clients, attorneys, and other legal staff. They also need strong self-management skills—such as the ability to be punctual, handle several tasks at the same time, and be self-motivated. In addition, they must have solid typing or keyboarding skills and are familiar with computers, duplicating machines, and other office machines.

Successful Legal Receptionists share several personality traits, such as being friendly, tactful, composed, organized, reliable, and flexible.

Unions and Associations

Many Legal Receptionists join local, state, and national professional associations to take advantage of networking opportunities, training programs, job listings, and other professional services and resources. One national organization that they might join is NALS . . . the association for legal professionals.

Tips for Entry

1. If your high school has a work-experience program, talk with the program director about the possibility of being placed in a law office as a general office clerk.

2. Consider taking clerical training programs at community colleges or other postsecondary programs to develop and improve your office skills. Many community colleges offer certificate or degree programs for various legal support occupations such as Legal Receptionists.

3. Many law offices have web sites on the Internet. Check out some of them to get an idea of what different law offices do and how they are organized. To get a list of relevant web sites, enter the keywords *law office* or *law firm* in a search engine.

LEGAL WORD PROCESSOR

CAREER PROFILE

Duties: Use computers or other machines to produce complex legal documents, correspondence, and other materials; perform other duties as required

Alternate Titles: Legal Document Processor

Salary Range: $34,000 to $44,000

Employment Prospects: Good for highly skilled individuals

Advancement Prospects: Fair

Prerequisites:
  Education/Training—High school diploma; some college background preferred
  Experience—Previous word processing work experience is required
  Special Skills and Personality Traits—Typing or keyboarding skills; reading comprehension, grammar, proofreading, communication, and self-management skills; reliable, flexible, detail-oriented, hard-working
  Licensure/Certification—None required

CAREER LADDER

```
┌─────────────────────────────────┐
│   Legal Secretary or Paralegal  │
└─────────────────────────────────┘

┌─────────────────────────────────┐
│      Legal Word Processor       │
└─────────────────────────────────┘

┌─────────────────────────────────┐
│         Word Processor          │
└─────────────────────────────────┘
```

Position Description

Legal Word Processors operate computers or other machines to produce legal documents, correspondence, memorandums, reports, tables, and other materials. Because of the legal content of the materials, they are knowledgeable about legal terminology as well as about the required legal formatting for different materials. Their job requires typing at fast and accurate speeds. In fact, many Legal Word Processors type at 80 words or more per minute.

Legal Word Processors typically handle large volumes of work each day, working under heavy deadlines. Lawyers, paralegals, legal administrators, and other legal staff give them rough drafts or dictation tapes from which to transcribe notes. They enter the notes by keyboarding or using other devices, such as optical scanners. If there are any questions or concerns about the notes, Legal Word Processors check back with the proper staff member.

Most Legal Word Processors use complex word processing systems to create and edit documents, tables, and so forth. Many also use spreadsheet, presentation, and graphic software to produce graphics and exhibits.

Legal Word Processors are responsible for performing quality checks on printed documents before giving them to attorneys or other staff. They make sure that documents follow the required formats and standards. They proofread materials, locating and correcting errors in spelling, grammar, and punctuation.

In smaller offices, Legal Word Processors may provide other office support, such as filing, reception work, and mail distribution. Some Legal Word Processors perform additional support roles such as those of a legal secretary or legal receptionist.

Legal Word Processors work full time or part time. In large law firms, Legal Word Processors might work different shifts that may include evening, night, and weekend shifts.

Salaries

Salaries vary, depending on a Legal Word Processor's experience, job duties, size of employer, geographical location, and other factors. According to *The Affiliates 2001 Salary Guide,* the average salary for Legal Word Processors ranges from $33,500 to $43,500. (The Affiliates is a well-known national legal staffing business.)

Employment Prospects

Legal Word Processors are employed by law firms as well as by law departments in corporations, government agencies, and other institutions. Many word processors prefer to take short-term assignments with temporary office staffing agencies.

Most jobs become available as Legal Word Processors resign, or transfer to other jobs or positions. Opportunities are best for those with highly technical skills.

Advancement Prospects

Legal Word Processors can advance to senior and supervisory positions. Most pursue advancement by receiving higher wages and professional recognition.

Depending on their ambitions, Legal Word Processors can obtain additional education and experience to become legal secretaries, legal administrators, and even lawyers.

Education and Training

Legal Word Processors should have at least a high school diploma or a general equivalency diploma. Many employers also require or prefer that word processors have some college background.

Employers typically provide new Legal Word Processors with on-the-job training.

Experience, Skills, and Personality Traits

Employers require that applicants for entry-level positions have word processing experience. For higher-paying positions, employers generally hire Legal Word Processors with one or more years of work experience in law offices or other legal settings.

Candidates need outstanding typing or keyboarding skills; minimum speed requirements vary with the different employers. They also need reading comprehension, grammar, and proofreading skills, as well as good communication skills. In addition, they need excellent self-management skills—such as the ability to handle pressure, meet deadlines, and work independently.

Successful Legal Word Processors share several common personality traits, such as being reliable, flexible, detail-oriented, and hardworking.

Unions and Associations

Many Legal Word Processors join professional associations to take advantage of networking opportunities, continuing education programs, and other professional services and resources. Two national legal organizations that they might join are Legal Secretaries International, Inc. and NALS . . . the association for legal professionals.

Tips for Entry

1. High school courses that can help you prepare for this occupation are keyboarding or typing, word processing, English, math, and business.
2. To gain experience, you might sign up with temporary office placement agencies.
3. Being familiar with legal terminology and procedures can enhance your employability. You may find appropriate courses at community colleges or in continuing education programs.
4. You can learn more about the legal field on the Internet. Some web sites to explore are:
   - Findlaw for Legal Professionals, *http://library.lp. findlaw. com/index.html*
   - America's Law Links, *http://www.lawlinks.com*
   - Law.com, *http://www.law.com*

INFORMATION TECHNOLOGY (IT) PROFESSIONALS

CAREER PROFILE

Duties: Maintain all computer systems, equipment, software, networks, and so on; provide technical support; perform duties as required

Alternate Titles: A title that reflects a specialty such as Systems Analyst, Financial Analyst, Database Administrator, Technical Trainer, or Desktop Support Technician

Salary Range: $21,000 to $89,000

Employment Prospects: Good

Advancement Prospects: Fair

Prerequisites:

Education/Training—A college degree or college background required or preferred

Experience—Previous experience in legal settings required or preferred, or familiarity with particular needs of law offices

Special Skills and Personality Traits—Customer service, interpersonal, communication, writing, problem-solving, and self-management skills; patient, friendly, analytical, resourceful, organized, flexible, self-motivated

Licensure/Certification—None required

CAREER LADDER

```
┌─────────────────────────────────────┐
│      Legal Technology Manager        │
└─────────────────────────────────────┘

┌─────────────────────────────────────┐
│      IT Professional (Law Office)    │
└─────────────────────────────────────┘

┌─────────────────────────────────────┐
│              Trainee                 │
└─────────────────────────────────────┘
```

Position Description

Lawyers and their staff use technology to help them complete a wide range of legal and nonlegal tasks more efficiently and effectively. For example, they use various applications to draft legal documents, invoice clients, monitor budgets, organize litigation cases, and so on. Or, for example, they conduct legal research on databases found on CD-ROMs and the Internet, as well as communicate electronically with clients. Hence, many law offices employ staff Information Technology (IT) Professionals to maintain all computer systems and ensure that the equipment, software, and networks function smoothly each day. In addition, they provide technical support to lawyers and staff as needed.

IT Professionals have various responsibilities (such as technical support or systems analysis), and so perform different tasks. Depending on a law office's budgets and specific needs, there may be one or more IT Professionals on staff. The following are a few of the IT Professionals that are more commonly found in law offices:

Systems Analysts configure computer systems to meet the specific needs of lawyers and their staff. They continually look at ways to enhance computer systems so that they serve law offices more efficiently. Additionally, they are responsible for resolving problems with the systems. Large law offices may employ several systems analysts to support the separate needs of finance, practice, and other departments.

Database Administrators develop and maintain the various database systems used in the law office, such as accounting, practice management, and case management systems. They monitor systems, archive and back up information, update systems, troubleshoot problems, make necessary repairs, and perform other tasks. They are also responsible for making sure that all confidential information stored in the databases is safe and secure.

Network Administrators maintain and support various types of networking systems for communicating between computers inside and outside the law offices. These include local area networks (LANs) for intraoffice communication; wide area networks (WANs) that connect office computers to computers outside the office; and internetworks, such as the Internet, that connect office computers to various networks at the same time. Network Administrators also provide technical support to lawyers and staff, such as upgrading required software on individual computers, setting up e-mail accounts, troubleshooting new applications, and responding to security problems such as viruses and hacker attacks.

Computer Support Specialists, also known as *Desktop Support Technicians,* provide technical support to lawyers and staff regarding their individual computers. Computer Support Specialists troubleshoot problems with equipment and applications on an individual basis, in person or on the phone. They also upgrade and install hardware and software for individuals as well as answer questions about using computers and software.

Technical Trainers are responsible for providing technical instruction to lawyers and staff. Their duties also include developing training programs and preparing training materials.

All IT Professionals are responsible for keeping up with developments in technology. They also maintain their skills by obtaining necessary training to learn new skills.

IT Professionals work part time or full time. In large firms with nationwide offices, IT Professionals may work different shifts, including evening, night, and weekend hours. On occasion, IT Professionals work longer hours to complete their tasks. Some law offices require IT Professionals to be on call to assist lawyers and staff for system emergencies.

Salaries

Salaries vary, depending on the position, job duties, experience, employer, geographical location, and other factors. According to the Bureau of Labor Statistics, the estimated 2000 annual salary ranges for most workers in these positions were:

- $37,460 to $89,040 for systems analysts
- $29,400 to $89,320 for database administrators
- $21,260 to $63,480 for computer support specialists
- $32,450 to $81,150 for network administrators

Employment Prospects

IT Professionals work in private law firms, law departments of corporations and government agencies, nonprofit legal service programs, and other legal organizations.

The use of technology in the legal industry has been continually growing as more lawyers set up sophisticated computer systems. Law offices will create new technical support positions as they are needed.

Advancement Prospects

Depending on the size of the law office, IT Professionals can advance to senior and supervisory positions. With additional education and experience, they can become legal technology managers.

Education and Training

Education requirements vary, depending on the position. In general, many employers prefer candidates with associate or bachelor's degrees, or who have some college background. Some employers prefer that candidates have degrees in computer science.

Most employers provide technical training programs, which may also include sending IT Professionals to outside workshops, seminars, and classes.

Experience, Skills, and Personality Traits

Requirements vary, depending on the position and its job description. Generally, employers require or prefer candidates who have previous experience in legal settings. They must also be familiar with the types of legal and nonlegal needs particular to lawyers and law offices.

IT Professionals require excellent customer service, interpersonal, and communication skills, as they must be able to explain technical concepts in clear and nontechnical language to lawyers and other employees. Additionally, IT Professionals need good writing and problem-solving skills as well as self-management skills—the ability to prioritize tasks, handle stressful situations, follow directions, work independently, and so on.

Some personality traits that successful IT Professionals share are being patient, friendly, analytical, resourceful, organized, flexible, and self-motivated.

Unions and Associations

Many law office IT Professionals join professional associations at local, state, and national levels to take advantage of networking opportunities, training programs, and other professional services and resources. Two organizations to which many IT Professionals belong are the Association for Computing Machinery and the Association of Support Professionals.

Tips for Entry

1. While in college, participate in internship programs. Try to obtain placements in law firms or legal departments.
2. Enroll in training and continuing education programs to pick up new technical skills.
3. Computer specialists often enhance their credibility by obtaining professional certification. Many obtain the *Certified Computing Professional* (CCP) or the *Associate Computing Professional* (ACP) granted by

the International Certification of Computing Professionals (ICCP). For information, contact ICCP at 2350 East Devon Avenue, Suite 115, Des Plaines, IL 60018-4610. Or call (847) 299-4227, or fax (847) 299-4280. Or visit its web site at *http://www.iccp.org.*

4. You can learn more about the area of legal technology on the Internet. To find relevant web sites to browse, enter the keywords *legal technology* or *law office technology* in a search engine.

LEGAL SECRETARY

CAREER PROFILE

Duties: Prepare legal correspondence and documents; maintain lawyers' schedules; maintain legal files; perform other duties as required

Alternate Titles: Lawyer's Assistant, Administrative Assistant, Executive Assistant

Salary Range: $18,000 to $50,000 or more

Employment Prospects: Good

Advancement Prospects: Good

Prerequisites:

Education/Training—At least a high school diploma

Experience—Previous experience in law office settings or several years of general secretarial experience

Special Skills and Personality Traits—Typing, shorthand, computer, writing, communication, organizational, time management, and interpersonal skills; diplomatic, conscientious, flexible, adaptable, trustworthy

Licensure/Certification—None required

CAREER LADDER

```
┌─────────────────────────────────┐
│  Senior Legal Secretary, Law Office │
│  Manager, or Paralegal          │
└─────────────────────────────────┘

┌─────────────────────────────────┐
│  Legal Secretary                │
└─────────────────────────────────┘

┌─────────────────────────────────┐
│  Junior Legal Secretary         │
└─────────────────────────────────┘
```

Position Description

Legal Secretaries provide attorneys with clerical and administrative support as well as ensure the smooth and efficient delivery of legal services. They are specially trained secretaries who are versed in legal terminology and procedures. They are also familiar with a wide variety of legal documents, including contracts and such court papers as pleadings and motions.

Some Legal Secretaries work directly with one attorney, while others provide support to several lawyers in a law office or legal department. Their work involves contact with clients, attorneys, court personnel, and the general public. They perform a wide variety of tasks, usually working with minimal supervision. Their duties vary from office to office, depending on the particular needs of the attorneys.

One major duty that all Legal Secretaries perform is the preparation of highly confidential written materials—legal documents, correspondence, memorandums, reports, and so on. They take dictation directly from lawyers or transcribe lawyers' handwritten or taped notes, then process final documents on typewriters, word processors, or computers. Secretaries check materials for completeness and accuracy of information, bringing any facts or data that may be incorrect

to the attention of the attorneys. Secretaries also edit materials for correct sentence construction, grammar, spelling, and punctuation.

Another major responsibility for Legal Secretaries is the maintenance of lawyers' daily schedules and court-appearance calendars. They arrange appointments and meetings for attorneys and often make travel arrangements for them. Secretaries are also aware of deadlines, depositions, and other significant events, and remind lawyers of their commitments, as well as the need for any preparation for particular cases.

Most Legal Secretaries are also in charge of setting up and maintaining legal file systems—administrative as well as case files. This includes both paper and electronic files and records. They might also handle bookkeeping duties, such as keeping a record of time, money, or services rendered by attorneys. On occasion, they may be asked to record and transcribe minutes of meetings and conventions. Legal Secretaries also perform routine clerical tasks. They answer telephones; greet visitors; screen calls and visits; open, review, and distribute incoming mail; maintain office supplies; and so on.

In some offices, Legal Secretaries act as office managers or as supervisors of the legal clerical staff. Their duties might then include supervising and training staff, making daily work assignments, setting up office policies and procedures, and approving vacation or other leave.

Legal Secretaries might also perform paralegal duties for attorneys. For example, they might do legal research, compile documents or data to support pleadings, prepare questions for initial client interviews, prepare exhibits for court cases, file legal documents with the courts, or maintain law libraries.

Successful Legal Secretaries pursue their professional growth as well as keep up with developing issues and new technology that may affect their work. They read professional journals, network with colleagues, participate in professional conferences, enroll in continuing education programs, and so on.

Legal Secretaries work part time or full time. They often work overtime to in order to help lawyers meet their deadlines.

Salaries

Salaries vary and depend on such factors as education, experience, type of employer, and location. Annual salaries generally range from $18,000 for entry-level positions to $50,000 or more for experienced secretaries, according to NALS . . . the association for legal professionals.

Employment Prospects

Legal Secretaries work for private law firms and nonprofit law offices, as well as in legal departments of corporations, government agencies, educational institutions, and nonprofit organizations. Some Legal Secretaries are freelancers or independent contractors. Others work for temporary employment agencies.

The Bureau of Labor Statistics reports average growth in the field through 2010. Most opportunities become available as Legal Secretaries retire, resign, or transfer to other positions. Highly qualified and experienced Legal Secretaries are normally in demand by employers.

Advancement Prospects

With additional training and experience, Legal Secretaries can advance to positions such as paralegals and legal office administrators. Many Legal Secretaries seek advancement by earning higher pay and receiving more complex responsibilities, which may require seeking positions with other employers.

Legal Secretaries also have the option to earn law degrees and become practicing lawyers. They might also pursue other career paths by becoming patent agents, abstractors, title examiners, or medical secretaries.

Education and Training

The minimum education requirement is a high school diploma or general equivalency diploma. Some employers require two-year or four-year college degrees. Many employers prefer candidates who have completed a legal secretary program (or related program) in business schools, vocational-technical institutes, or community colleges.

Employers usually provide orientation training to new employees.

Experience, Skills, and Personality Traits

For entry-level positions, employers look for candidates who show the ability to learn quickly and work independently. They generally prefer candidates who have worked previously in law office settings or have several years of general secretarial experience, performing complex tasks.

Legal Secretaries have strong typing and shorthand skills, as well as computer skills, particularly with word processing, spreadsheets, and database applications. They also have superior writing, communication, organizational, time management, and interpersonal skills. Furthermore, they have excellent judgment, which is needed to make critical decisions in their work. Being diplomatic, conscientious, flexible, adaptable, and trustworthy are a few personality traits that successful Legal Secretaries share.

Unions and Associations

Many Legal Secretaries join professional associations to take advantage of networking opportunities, continuing education programs, and other professional services and resources. Two national organizations are NALS . . . the association for legal professionals and Legal Secretaries International, Inc.

Tips for Entry

1. To prepare for the Legal Secretary profession in high school, take courses in business and computers. If available, take a shorthand class and basic law class.
2. To enhance your employability, obtain voluntary certification, such as the *Accredited Legal Secretary* designation that is granted by NALS.
3. One way to gain work experience in legal settings is through work assignments with temporary employment agencies.
4. Use the Internet to learn more about legal secretaries. You might start by visiting the web site for NALS (*http://www.nals.org*).

PARALEGAL

CAREER PROFILE

Duties: Perform a variety of substantial legal tasks, such as legal research and interviewing clients, under the direction and supervision of an attorney

Alternate Titles: Legal Assistant; Paralegal Specialist (in government agencies); Corporate Paralegal or other title that reflects a law specialty

Salary Range: $28,000 to $66,000

Employment Prospects: Excellent

Advancement Prospects: Good

Prerequisites:

Education/Training—College degree or certificate in paralegal studies

Experience—Varies with the different employers

Special Skills and Personality Traits—Research, writing, communication, organizational, interpersonal, teamwork, and computer skills; analytical, detail-oriented, trustworthy, self-motivated, flexible, compassionate

Licensure/Certification—None

CAREER LADDER

```
┌─────────────────────────────────────┐
│  Legal Assistant Manager of Lawyer   │
└─────────────────────────────────────┘

┌─────────────────────────────────────┐
│              Paralegal               │
└─────────────────────────────────────┘

┌─────────────────────────────────────┐
│   Student (paralegal program),       │
│   Legal Secretary, or other          │
│   Legal Support Professional         │
└─────────────────────────────────────┘
```

Position Description

Paralegals assist lawyers with routine legal tasks so that lawyers can provide legal services more smoothly and effectively. Although Paralegals have substantial understanding of legal concepts and have the training and experience to do a wide variety of legal work, they are not lawyers. They cannot practice law. That is, Paralegals cannot perform certain legal duties, such as accept new clients for a law office, set legal fees, offer legal advice, or represent clients in court trials.

The paralegal profession is relatively new, having emerged in the 1960s. Traditionally, Paralegals worked in private law firms. Today, they are also employed by court systems, government agencies, and legal aid services. Additionally, they work in legal departments of corporations, financial institutions, nonprofit organizations, educational institutions, and other organizations. Depending on the setting or region, Paralegals may be known as *Legal Assistants* or *Paralegal Specialists*.

The ultimate responsibility for their work belongs to the lawyers under which Paralegals receive direction and supervision. In general, Paralegals assist attorneys in preparing for legal proceedings or transactional matters (contracts, trust instruments, and so on). Some tasks that Paralegals might perform are:

- conducting legal research in law libraries and on such electronic databases as CD-ROMs, software programs, and the Internet
- analyzing and summarizing materials and legal documents (such as contracts, wills, legal briefs, pleadings, or motions)
- drafting correspondence and legal documents for lawyers to review
- investigating the facts in a case or a legal matter
- interviewing clients to obtain background information
- preparing clients for court hearings or other administrative proceedings
- performing various clerical tasks, such as photocopying and compiling files

Paralegals work in all areas of the law, including litigation, corporate law, criminal law, family law, immigration law, and so forth. After five years or more, Paralegals usually specialize in one or more law areas. (For example, Litigation Paralegals help prepare cases for trial.) Corporate Paralegals perform tasks related to the legal needs of corporations, such as drafting employee benefits plans. Paralegal Specialists who work for government agencies have various duties, such as collecting evidence for agency hearings or preparing information guides on the law. Paralegals in community legal services programs often work as counselors or advocates for their clientele. They might perform such tasks as obtaining government benefits for clients. In certain circumstances, they can represent clients at administrative agency proceedings.

Some Paralegals play a dual role in law offices, performing duties of a Paralegal and legal secretary for attorneys. Paralegals in supervisory positions oversee paralegal staff. And in some offices, supervisors may provide direction to other legal support staff as well.

Paralegals are responsible for keeping current with changes in the law, technology, and other developments that may affect their work, as well as for pursuing their professional growth. They read legal and professional journals, network with colleagues, participate in professional conferences, enroll in continuing education programs, and so on.

Paralegals work part time or full time. They may be required to work overtime to help attorneys meet deadlines.

Salaries

Salaries vary, and depend on such factors as education, experience, job duties, type of employer, and geographic location. Paralegals who work for large law firms in metropolitan areas usually earn the highest wages. According to the *The Affiliates 2001 Salary Guide* (by the Affiliates, a national legal staffing business), the average salaries for Paralegals in law firms range from $28,000 to $66,250.

Employment Prospects

The Bureau of Labor Statistics reports that employment for paralegals is expected to increase by 21 to 35 percent through 2010. Many job opportunities are expected to be created to meet the legal support needs of employers in all settings.

Advancement Prospects

Paralegals can advance to supervisory and managerial positions. Many realize advancement by receiving higher pay and greater responsibilities, which may require seeking positions with other employers.

They can pursue other legal-related careers such as litigation support managers, real estate brokers, compliance inspectors, and mediators. They also have the option to earn a law degree and become practicing lawyers.

Education and Training

Education requirements vary among the different employers. Many employers prefer candidates who have four-year degrees. The National Federation of Paralegal Associations recommends that future Paralegals complete a paralegal program, consisting of 24 semester credits, in addition to holding a four-year college degree.

Paralegal programs are available through two-year colleges, four-year colleges, universities, business schools, proprietary schools, and continuing education programs. One can earn an associate degree, bachelor's degree, or a professional certificate in paralegal studies.

To learn more about various paralegal programs, contact the American Association for Paralegal Education. Write to: 2965 Flowers Road South, Suite 105, Atlanta, GA 30341. Or call (770) 452-9877. Or visit its web site at *http://www. aafpe.org*.

Experience, Skills, and Personality Traits

Experience qualifications vary from employer to employer. For example, some employers prefer to train Paralegals, so they hire candidates without any legal experience. However, all Paralegals must have excellent research, writing, and communication skills as well as organizational, interpersonal, and teamwork skills. Increasingly, more employers require that Paralegals have computer skills in legal research, word processing, spreadsheets, and database management. Being analytical, detail-oriented, trustworthy, self-motivated, flexible, and compassionate are some personality traits that successful Paralegals share.

Unions and Associations

Most Paralegals join professional organizations to take advantage of their services and resources, such as continuing education programs, professional certification, and networking opportunities. Along with local and state organizations, Paralegals might belong to national organizations such as the National Association of Legal Assistants, the National Paralegal Association, and the American Bar Association.

Tips for Entry

1. To enhance your employability, you might obtain one of the following voluntary certifications: the *Certified Legal Assistant* (CLA) designation, granted by the National Association of Legal Assistants *(http://www. nala.org),* or the *Registered Paralegal* (RP) designation, granted by the National Federation of Paralegal Associations *(http://www. paralegals. org).*
2. One source for learning about job openings is professional associations. Many local and state groups maintain job listings.

3. To learn about Paralegal Specialists openings in the federal government, contact the U.S. Office of Personnel Management (OPM). You might call the local office in your area. Or visit the OPM web site at *http://www. usajobs.opm.gov.*

4. Learn more about the Paralegal profession on the Internet. To get a list of relevant web sites, enter the keywords *paralegal* or *legal assistant* in any search engine.

LEGAL ADMINISTRATOR

CAREER PROFILE

Duties: Oversee the daily nonlegal management functions in law offices; make sure all business operations run smoothly and efficiently; perform a variety of duties and tasks as required

Alternate Titles: Office Manager, Law Office Administrator, Law Department Administrator, Program Administrator, Chief Office Administrator, Executive Director

Salary Range: $50,000 to $84,000

Employment Prospects: Good

Advancement Prospects: Fair

Prerequisites:

Education/Training—A college degree is preferred

Experience—Three to 10 years of office management experience, preferably in a law office; experienced or knowledgeable in business services, human resources, financial management, technology, facilities management, and marketing

Special Skills and Personality Traits—Supervisory, leadership, administrative, management, team building, interpersonal, communication, writing, and computer skills; energetic, composed, organized, hardworking, loyal, creative

Licensure/Certification—None required

CAREER LADDER

```
┌─────────────────────────────────┐
│    Chief Office Administrator    │
│      or Executive Director       │
└─────────────────────────────────┘

┌─────────────────────────────────┐
│       Legal Administrator        │
└─────────────────────────────────┘

┌─────────────────────────────────┐
│   Assistant Law Office Manager   │
│  or other legal management position │
└─────────────────────────────────┘
```

Position Description

Legal Administrators oversee the nonlegal management functions in law offices and departments so that lawyers can focus on helping their clients. They make sure that all administrative operations run smoothly and efficiently each day. They also identify changing needs for the office and plan for them accordingly. They troubleshoot problems and issues as they arise; these may include a staff conflict, the need for a new telephone system, loss of reliable delivery service, or the creation of a more effective filing system. In addition, they provide supervision and guidance to office support staff within a friendly environment that fosters teamwork and motivates individuals.

Legal Administrators work in private law firms, law departments in corporations, and government agencies, as well as for legal services programs and other public interest organizations. They act as liaison between lawyers and administrative staff. Depending on their employers, they may go by other titles, such as *Office Manager, Law Office Administrator, Program Administrator, Chief Office Administrator,* or *Executive Director.*

In general, Legal Administrators are responsible for several areas:

- office services, which includes all office support (such as word processing, filing, mail distribution, greeting clients, and answering phones) needed by lawyers, paralegals, and other staff
- human resources, which includes the recruitment and selection of all staff; salary and benefits administration; employee relations; professional development; and so on

- financial management, which includes preparing and monitoring annual budgets; handling payroll, billing, and collections; tax reporting; and maintaining bank relations
- facilities management, which includes the planning and maintenance of physical space; purchasing equipment and office supplies; taking care of mail and records storage needs; and other functions
- information systems, which includes all technology and telecommunications systems

In smaller offices, Legal Administrators are responsible for overseeing all management functions. In larger offices, they may be responsible for one or a few major functions and supervise managers of other functions. For example, a Legal Administrator might directly manage all functions but human resources and technology.

Legal Administrators are responsible for executing the vision and philosophy of law partners, chief lawyers, or executive officers. They establish office rules and procedures accordingly. They make recommendations to lawyers about ways to make cost-effective improvements to operations. In some law firms, Legal Administrators participate in management meetings with lawyers to make plans and strategies for developing further business.

Legal Administrators might work beyond their 40-hour week in order to complete necessary tasks.

Salaries

Salaries vary, depending on such factors as experience, education, employer, and geographical location. Some law firms give their Legal Administrators annual bonuses in addition to their salaries. According to the *2001 Salary Guide* (by the Affiliates, a national legal staffing business), legal administrative/office managers earn between $50,000 and $83,750.

Employment Prospects

Most opportunities become available as Legal Administrators retire, resign, or transfer to other positions.

Advancement Prospects

Legal Administrators pursue advancement by seeking positions with higher salaries, more complex responsibilities, or by being employed in the top law firms.

Depending on their interests and ambitions, Legal Administrators can pursue other legal professions by becoming lawyers or legal management consultants.

Education and Training

Most employers require or prefer that candidates have an associate or bachelor's degree or have some college

background. They especially look for candidates who have completed course work in business administration or management, finance, human resources, technology, or marketing.

Throughout their careers, Legal Administrators enroll in training and continuing education programs to develop and maintain their skills and expertise.

Experience, Skills, and Personality Traits

Depending on the employer, Legal Administrators need three to 10 years of office management experience, preferably in a law office. They have experience or are knowledgeable in the different areas of business operations, including business services, human resources, financial management, technology, facilities management, and marketing.

Legal Administrators need excellent supervisory and leadership skills along with superior administrative and management skills. They also need strong team building, interpersonal, and communication skills, as they must work well with attorneys, paralegals, and legal support staff. In addition, they must have competent writing and computer skills.

Being energetic, composed, organized, hardworking, loyal, and creative are a few personality traits that Legal Administrators share.

Unions and Associations

Many Legal Administrators join the Association of Legal Administrators and other national, state, and local legal organizations that serve their interests. By joining professional associations, they are able to take advantage of networking opportunities with peers as well as education programs, job listings, and other professional services and resources.

Tips for Entry

1. To enhance your employability, you might consider obtaining the *Legal Manager* designation, granted by the Association of Legal Administrators (ALA). For more information, contact ALA at 175 East Hawthorn Parkway, Vernon Hills, IL 60061-1428. Or call (847) 816-1212, or fax (847) 816-1213. Or visit its web site at *http://www.alanet.org.*
2. Build up a network of contacts from school, professional organizations, conferences, and so on. Call, write, or e-mail your contacts when doing your job search. Many of them may know of current or upcoming vacancies.
3. You can learn more about law office management on the Internet. To browse relevant web sites, enter keywords such as *legal administrator, legal management,* or *law office management* in any search engine.

HUMAN RESOURCES MANAGER (LAW FIRM)

CAREER PROFILE

Duties: Oversee all administrative functions relating to personnel, such as staff recruitment and training, compensation and benefits administration, and compliance with employment laws; perform duties as required

Alternate Titles: Director of Human Resources, Personnel Director

Salary Range: $33,000 to $104,000

Employment Prospects: Good

Advancement Prospects: Fair

Prerequisites:

   Education/Training—A bachelor's degree

   Experience—Previous work experience in law firms or other professional services; supervisory experience; knowledgeable about labor and employment laws

   Special Skills and Personality Traits—Leadership, administrative, management, interpersonal, teamwork, communication, writing, and computer skills; tactful, calm, fair-minded, ethical, persuasive, friendly, flexible

   Licensure/Certification—None required

CAREER LADDER

```
┌─────────────────────────────────┐
│   Director of Human Resources or │
│      Law Office Administrator    │
└─────────────────────────────────┘

┌─────────────────────────────────┐
│      Human Resources Manager     │
└─────────────────────────────────┘

┌─────────────────────────────────┐
│     Human Resources Specialist   │
└─────────────────────────────────┘
```

Position Description

Many law firms have Human Resources Managers who oversee all administrative functions relating to the employees of a law firm. These managers act as the link between top management (employers) and employees, and are responsible for executing their firm's personnel policies and requirements.

Human Resources Managers are responsible for a wide range of duties that may include any or all of the following:

* designing and administering compensation and benefits programs such as health insurance and pension plans
* developing and coordinating programs for the welfare of employees, such as programs promoting workplace safety and health practices, car pooling and transportation, child care, and counseling services
* overseeing the recruitment and selection process for new staff positions

* developing and coordinating staff training, including orientation programs for new employees and professional development programs
* coordinating job performance evaluations of lawyers and support staff
* assisting top management in the development of personnel policies and procedures
* making sure that their firm is in compliance with the appropriate local, state, and federal employment laws
* investigating workplace issues and concerns such as employee grievances

Human Resources Managers also provide supervision and guidance to support staff in their departments. In larger law firms, Human Resources Managers supervise specialists who are responsible for particular functions, such as compensation specialists, employee benefits specialists, affirmative action specialists, and training specialists.

Human Resources Managers generally work a standard 40-hour week. On occasion, they may work in the evenings and on weekends to complete projects.

Salaries

Salaries vary, depending on such factors as experience, education, employer, and geographical location. According to the Bureau of Labor Statistics most Human Resources Managers earned an estimated annual salary that ranged between $33,360 and $104,020 in 2000. (The survey includes responses from Human Resources Managers in all industries.)

Employment Prospects

Most opportunities for Human Resources Managers in law offices become available as individuals retire, resign, or transfer to other positions. New positions are usually created by small and medium-sized firms as they grow and require the need of experienced Human Resources Managers.

Advancement Prospects

Most Human Resource Managers pursue advancement by seeking positions with higher salaries and more complex responsibilities, or by being employed in the top law firms. The ultimate goal for some managers is to become human resources consultants, operating their own businesses.

Education and Training

Human Resources Managers have bachelor's degrees in various fields. For example, some have earned degrees in human resources or personnel administration, while others earned business or liberal arts degrees.

Most managers enroll in continuing education and training programs throughout their careers to develop and strengthen their skills and expertise.

Experience, Skills, and Personality Traits

In general, employers look for candidates who have previous work experience in law firms or with other professional services. They also have several years of supervisory experience. In addition, they have a thorough knowledge of labor and employment laws.

Human Resources Managers need excellent leadership, administrative, and management skills. They also require superb interpersonal, teamwork, and communication skills, as well as strong writing and computer skills. Furthermore, they must be able to work well with people of different backgrounds, abilities, and education.

Some personality traits that successful Human Resources Managers share are being tactful, calm, fair, ethical, persuasive, friendly, and flexible.

Unions and Associations

Many Human Resources Managers belong to local, state, and national professional associations in order to take advantage of professional services and resources as well as networking opportunities. One such national organization is the Society for Human Resource Management. Law office Human Resource Managers are also eligible to join the Association of Legal Administrators.

Tips for Entry

1. Obtain internships in human resources departments to gain experience.
2. Many Human Resources Managers got their start by working as human resources clerks while in college.
3. You may want to enhance your employability by obtaining professional certification granted by the Society for Human Resources Management (SHRM). For more information, write SHRM at 1800 Duke Street, Alexandria, VA 22314. Or call (703) 548-3440, or fax: (703) 535-6490. Or visit the SHRM web site at *http://www.shrm.org*.
4. You can learn more about the human resources field on the Internet. To find relevant web sites, enter keywords such as *human resources manager* or *human resources careers* in any search engine.

MARKETING MANAGER (LAW FIRM)

CAREER PROFILE

Duties: Assist law firms in developing marketing strategies and activities; oversee marketing activities; perform a variety of responsibilities and tasks as required

Alternate Titles: Marketing Coordinator, Marketing Director

Salary Range: $36,000 to $133,000

Employment Prospects: Good

Advancement Prospects: Limited

Prerequisites:

Education/Training—A bachelor's or advanced degree
Experience—Several years of marketing experience in law firms or other professional services
Special Skills and Personality Traits—Leadership, teamwork, interpersonal, communication, analytical, writing, and computer skills; positive, self-motivated, tactful, persuasive, decisive, persistent, creative, flexible
Licensure/Certification—None required

CAREER LADDER

```
┌─────────────────────────────────┐
│      Marketing Director or      │
│   Legal Marketing Consultant    │
└─────────────────────────────────┘

┌─────────────────────────────────┐
│       Marketing Manager         │
└─────────────────────────────────┘

┌─────────────────────────────────┐
│  Marketing Coordinator or Marketing │
│    Manager (non–law firm)       │
└─────────────────────────────────┘
```

Position Description

To succeed in business, private law firms must be able to continually bring in new clients. For this reason, many law firms hire Marketing Managers who are experts in the area of promoting legal services. They help law firms plan and execute marketing strategies and activities that would most effectively influence target audiences to hire their firms.

The responsibilities of Marketing Managers vary, depending on the needs of their employers as well as their levels of expertise. Legal Marketing Managers typically oversee the development of all promotional activities. They create promotional tools such as brochures, newsletters, and attorney biographies. They manage public relations tasks, such as writing and distributing press releases about their firm's activities to the media. They also coordinate advertising projects for print, radio, and other media. In addition, many Marketing Managers assist in the design of their law firm's web site as a promotional tool.

Another typical area of responsibility is the promotion of events, such as seminars, open houses, and conferences, where lawyers meet with potential clients, as well as current ones, to talk about the legal services they provide. Marketing Managers might also assist in the planning and coordination of these events.

Legal Marketing Managers are also responsible for conducting market research for different purposes. For example, they might survey current clients to measure their satisfaction with their lawyers' performance. Or, they might conduct research to find out the potential market for new legal services that lawyers would like to offer.

Many Marketing Managers also have the duty of developing education and training programs for attorneys and staff, covering topics such as client service, marketing, and presentation skills.

In law firms that have several practice areas, Marketing Managers may also have the responsibility of helping the different practice groups develop and execute marketing activities.

Most legal Marketing Managers are responsible for monitoring budget expenses throughout the year. This may also include budgets for practice groups and individual lawyers. In some law firms, Marketing Managers prepare, or help in the preparation of, the annual marketing budget.

In addition, Legal Marketing Managers perform a wide range of routine duties. Some of these tasks are:

- providing guidance and supervision to marketing staff
- managing relationships with outside vendors such as advertising agencies, graphic designers, or public relations consultants
- maintaining database systems for mail lists, referral sources, client and industry analysis, attorney biographies, and other information
- attending marketing meetings for different practice areas
- Preparing presentation materials, such as visual and handout materials, for attorneys' speaking engagements

Marketing Managers sometimes work evenings and weekends to complete their projects. Some of their tasks may involve traveling to different cities or states.

Salaries

Salaries vary, depending on job duties, experience, education, geographical location, and other factors. According to the Bureau of Labor Statistics, most marketing managers earned an estimated annual salary between $35,950 and $133,300 in 2000. (Note: The survey includes responses from Marketing Managers in all industries.) In a 1999 salary survey by the Legal Marketing Association (LMA), the average annual salary for full-time marketing directors was $85,900 for LMA members and $73,300 for non–LMA members.

Employment Prospects

The demand for experienced legal marketing professionals has been steadily growing in the last few years. Opportunities should increase as more and more law firms—from solo practitioners to large firms—realize the benefits of having experienced marketing professionals on staff.

Advancement Prospects

Legal Marketing Managers pursue advancement by earning higher salaries, receiving greater responsibilities, and gaining professional recognition. This generally requires moving from one law firm to the next. The top goal for some managers is to become legal marketing consultants, operating their own businesses.

Education and Training

Legal Marketing Managers have bachelor's or master's degrees in various fields. Some also have law degrees.

Throughout their careers, Legal Marketing Managers enroll in training and education programs sponsored by trade associations and colleges to develop and improve their skills.

Experience, Skills, and Personality Traits

Minimum requirements vary with the different employers. In general, they look for candidates who have several years of marketing experience in law firms or other professional services.

Legal Marketing Managers require the ability to see the big picture as well as pay attention to details. They should have strong leadership, teamwork, interpersonal, and communication skills as they must be able to work well with attorneys, staff, clients, media, and others. In addition, they need strong analytical, writing, and computer skills.

Some personality traits that successful Legal Marketing Managers share are being positive, self-motivated, tactful, persuasive, decisive, persistent, creative, and flexible.

Unions and Associations

Many Legal Marketing Managers join local, state, and national organizations that serve their field, such as the Legal Marketing Association and the American Marketing Association. They are also eligible to join the Association of Legal Administrators, an organization that serves all types of legal administrators. These different organizations offer various types of professional services and resources as well as opportunities for networking with colleagues.

Tips for Entry

1. Continue to build and develop your computer skills, particularly those related to the Internet. Many in the marketing field say that web marketing is a growing trend.
2. Talk with Legal Marketing Managers to learn more about their jobs. Also find out what courses you should take in college, and what types of work experiences might prepare you for their profession.
3. Possible sources for job listings are legal bars and professional associations. Many also post listings for nonlawyer positions.
4. You can learn more about the legal marketing field on the Internet. Enter the keywords *legal marketing* or *lawyer marketing* in any search engine to get a list of web sites.

LEGAL TECHNOLOGY CONSULTANT (INDEPENDENT)

CAREER PROFILE	CAREER LADDER

Duties: Provide technology consulting services to lawyers; perform assessments of office automation needs and make recommendations; oversee the purchase of new computer systems; manage the installation of new systems; perform other services as requested

Salary Range: $30,000 to $125,000

Employment Prospects: Good

Advancement Prospects: Limited

Prerequisites:

Education/Training—No standard requirements; ongoing professional development

Experience—Several years of technology expertise; understanding of the legal profession

Special Skills and Personality Traits—Interpersonal, communication, writing, presentation, and self-management skills; small business skills for business owners; patient, friendly, analytical, organized, self-motivated, flexible, creative

Licensure/Certification—None required

CAREER LADDER

Legal Technology Consultant

Technology Manager or Director (Law Office)

Law Office Technology Staff Member

Position Description

Legal Technology Consultants are experts in the area of office automation (or technology) for the law office. They help lawyers determine how technology can most effectively meet their legal, office, and administrative needs. In addition, Legal Technology Consultants educate their clients about unfamiliar technologies so that they can make informed decisions. Legal Technology Consultants are hired on a contractual basis by law firms as well as by corporate and government law departments. Independent consultants are not associated with any vendor or company.

Legal Technology Consultants provide several areas of service for lawyers. One area is making recommendations for improving a law office's automation systems. Consultants start by performing assessments of the lawyers' business management and practice management needs. They gather information about a law office's current automation systems, its problems and limitations, the office's immediate needs and long-range goals, and so forth. This involves talking with

lawyers, secretaries, legal administrators, information system administrators, and other staff members. Consultants then prepare an assessment report that defines the office's goals and objectives and summarizes problem areas and limitations of the automation systems. The report also includes recommendations for improving systems, detailing types of equipment and applications as well as networking and communications configurations. Consultants also provide a budget with estimated costs for the proposed system, as well as a rough schedule for completing the purchases and installations.

Coordinating the purchase of a law office's new information system is another service that Legal Technology Consultants provide. They contact prospective vendors, asking vendors to send them proposals, which include estimated costs and time schedules. Consultants review all proposals and prepare an evaluation report, providing comparisons of equipment and costs and a synopsis of strengths and weaknesses of each vendor.

Many Legal Technology Consultants also provide the service of overseeing the installation of new automation systems in the law office. Their tasks may include:

- negotiating prices, warranty provisions, and vendor performance obligations
- making sure vendors meet schedules and complete tasks for which they are paid
- managing the conversion of data from the old system to the new one
- developing or assisting in the development of training programs for the staff
- coordinating tests to ensure that everything works

Many law offices retain Legal Technology Consultants to advise lawyers on how to make changes to their systems as needed.

Independent Legal Technology Consultants may be self-employed or employees or owners of consulting firms. Business owners must handle such business responsibilities as setting fees, supervising staff, paying bills and taxes, invoicing clients, bookkeeping, maintaining office space, and so on.

Legal Technical Consultants may work part time or full time. Many Consultants travel to different cities and states to meet and work with clients.

Salaries

Annual earnings for business owners vary, depending on such factors as a consultant's experience and ambitions, fees, number of clients per year, and geographical location. In general, earnings run between $30,000 and $125,000 for Legal Technology Consultants.

Employment Prospects

Although law office technology is a young field, job opportunities are expected to grow in the coming years. Increasingly more law firms and law departments are seeing the need for setting up technology systems in their offices. Additionally, many law firms that are already technologically savvy are increasing their budgets to keep their systems up to date.

Advancement Prospects

As employees, advancement opportunities are usually limited to senior or supervisory positions. In general, Legal Technology Consultants realize advancement by earning higher wages and gaining professional recognition.

Education and Training

There are no standard educational requirements for Legal Technology Consultant. Many Consultants have bachelor's degrees in different fields. Some also have law degrees.

Legal Technology Consultants are generally responsible for their professional development. They do independent study, network with colleagues, participate in conferences, enroll in training and continuing education programs, and so forth.

Experience, Skills, and Personality Traits

Legal Technology Consultants enter this field from different backgrounds—lawyers, paralegals, legal administrators, engineers, economists, and legal technology specialists. Along with having several years of technology expertise, they have an understanding of the way the legal profession works.

Legal Technology Consultants must have the ability to describe technical terms in nontechnical language. They also need excellent interpersonal and communication skills, as they must be able to work well with people of different backgrounds and abilities. In addition, they must have strong writing and presentation skills as well as superior self-management skills—the ability to meet deadlines, prioritize tasks, handle stressful situations, and so on. The self-employed and business owners should also have good small business skills. Successful Legal Technology Consultants share several personality traits such as being patient, friendly, analytical, organized, self-motivated, flexible, and creative.

Licensure and Certification

No professional licensure is required to become a Legal Technology Consultant. However, business owners may be required to obtain appropriate local and state business licenses.

Unions and Associations

Legal Technology Consultants join professional associations to take advantage of networking opportunities, training programs, and other professional services and resources. Some technology associations are the Society for Information Management and LawNet, which is an informal network of legal technology professionals.

Many join local, state, or national bar associations, such as the American Bar Association, participating in the law practice management section or other related sections. Some also join the Association of Legal Administrators, a national professional organization for legal management professions.

Tips for Entry

1. Get basic information technology training in either hardware or software, then obtain legal technology training from consultants in the field.
2. Take basic law courses in college or continuing education programs to become familiar with the needs of lawyers.

3. Many technology consultants enhance their credibility by obtaining product certifications and professional certification in management consulting.

4. Establish a reputation for yourself. Make presentations at conferences for lawyers, legal administrators, and other legal staff. Write articles for legal publications, and even write or contribute to books on the subject of legal technology.

5. You can learn more about the legal technology field on the Internet. One resource is the LawNet web site at *http://www.peertopeer.org*. To find relevant web sites, use keywords such as *legal technology* and *legal technology consultant*.

LITIGATION SUPPORT
PROFESSIONALS

BAIL BOND AGENT

CAREER PROFILE

Duties: Sell bail bonds; interview potential clients; locate and return missing clients; as owners or managers, oversee business operations

Alternate Titles: Bondsman

Salary Range: $20,000 to $92,000

Employment Prospects: Fair

Advancement Prospects: Limited

Prerequisites:

Education/Training—A high school diploma; on-the-job training

Experience—Prior experience may not be needed for entry-level positions

Special Skills and Personality Traits—Customer service, communication, interpersonal, math, writing, computer, and self-management skills; confident, assertive, resourceful, detail-oriented, organized, persistent, professional

Licensure/Certification—Licensure by state department of insurance; appropriate business licenses

CAREER LADDER

```
┌─────────────────────────────────────┐
│   Senior Bail Bond Agent, Manager,   │
│      or Bail Bond Agency Owner       │
└─────────────────────────────────────┘

┌─────────────────────────────────────┐
│           Bail Bond Agent            │
└─────────────────────────────────────┘

┌─────────────────────────────────────┐
│        Bail Bond Agent Trainee       │
└─────────────────────────────────────┘
```

Position Description

For most crimes in the United States, defendants may be released from jail on bail until they are actually convicted. Bail is an amount of money set by judges based on the type of crime that defendants are accused of committing, the defendants' criminal histories, the likelihood of defendants fleeing the area, and other factors. By posting bail, criminal defendants promise to appear at the appointed times and places for their court hearings and trials.

When defendants cannot come up with bail, they or their lawyers, family members, or friends may seek the services of Bail Bond Agents. Also known as Bondsmen, these professional men and women are state-licensed as surety insurance agents. They sell bail bonds in the form of cash bonds or surety bonds, which are underwritten by an insurance company. However, Bail Agents do not hand the bail bonds directly to the defendants, but instead agree to write bail bonds to the courts. These bail bonds are a guarantee to the courts that the Bail Bond Agents will pay the full amount of the bail if defendants skip out of their court hearings.

Bail Bond Agents carefully decide to whom they will sell bail bonds. They interview prospective clients—the defendants—as well as their lawyers, family members, or friends. If agents feel that defendants may flee, the agents won't take them as clients. Many Bail Bond Agents also refuse to take clients who are accused of committing certain crimes.

Agents charge a fee that is usually equivalent to 10 to 15 percent of the bail. For example, if bail is $10,000, an Agent charging 10 percent would receive a $1,000 fee. Many Bail Bond Agents require that clients also put up collateral (such as a car, house, stocks, or money) which would go to the Agents if defendants do not show up in court.

Once agents have posted bail for the clients, the courts release them to the Agents' custody. Many Bail Bond Agents make a point of monitoring their clients and reminding them about court dates. If clients skip out, Bail Bond Agents have the authority to locate and return them to jail. Courts give agents a certain time limit to find their clients.

Bail Bond Agents use various means to find their missing clients, now known as bail fugitives. They talk with family, friends, coworkers, and neighbors to learn about their likely whereabouts. They also check out restaurants, banks, shops, and other businesses that their clients might visit. On occasion, Agents do surveillance work, which may mean sitting for hours or days, waiting for their clients to appear. Agents also conduct research on computer and Internet databases to uncover old home addresses or other useful information. (Many Bail Bond Agents hire the services of bail recovery agents, commonly known as bounty hunters, to help them locate missing clients.)

Apprehending bail fugitives requires following rigid state regulations, which differ from state to state. For example, some states require that Bail Bond Agents first notify the county sheriff that they plan to apprehend a fugitive. Other states require that agents be accompanied by law enforcement officers. When agents locate fugitives in another state, they must follow the regulations governed by that state. Agents may, for example, be required to first register with local law enforcement agencies.

Many Bail Bond Agents are employees or subagents of bail bond companies. A large number of agents are owners of small independent agencies. Company owners and managers are responsible for overseeing business operations on a daily basis. They perform duties such as maintaining records, paying bills and taxes, keeping licenses up to date, generating new business, supervising staff, recruiting and training new staff, and maintaining the office space.

Bail Bond Agents work evening, late night, and weekend shifts. Many are available to the public 24 hours a day, seven days a week.

Salaries

Earnings for Bail Bond Agents vary, depending on factors such as geographical location and the amount of competition in their area.

In general, salaries for Bail Bond Agents are similar to those earned by insurance sales agents. According to the Bureau of Labor Statistics, the estimated annual salary (in 2000) for most insurance sales agents ranged between $20,070 and $91,530.

Employment Prospects

Opportunities for staff positions vary from one locale to the next. Most openings become available as agents retire or resign. Generally, as bail bond companies grow, they create additional positions.

The success rate for company owners depends on factors such as the local demand for bail bond services, the amount of competition, and the ambition and business sense of the individuals.

Advancement Prospects

Advancement prospects are rather limited for Bail Bond Agents. In large companies, they may advance to senior and managerial positions. Those with entrepreneurial ambitions might start their own bail bond companies.

Education and Training

Bail Bond Agents need at least a high school diploma or a general equivalency diploma. Many employers prefer applicants who have college backgrounds.

Entry-level Bail Bond Agents receive on-the-job training.

Experience, Skills, and Personality Traits

Many employers do not require any previous bail bond experience for entry-level positions.

Bail Bond Agents must have strong customer service skills and have a good sense for judging people's character. They also need strong communication and interpersonal skills, as they must meet people from varied backgrounds. Adequate math, writing, and computer skills are also important. Furthermore, they need excellent self-management skills—the ability to follow instructions, handle stressful situations, be independent, make decisions quickly, meet deadlines, and so on.

Some personality traits that successful Bail Bond Agents share are being confident, assertive, resourceful, detail-oriented, organized, persistent, and professional.

Licensure and Certification

Bail Bond Agent licensure is issued by state departments of insurance. Licensure requirements vary from state to state. Such requirements include being a certain age, completing a minimum number of training hours, passing a written examination, passing background checks, and so on. For more information, contact your state department of insurance.

Owners of bail bond companies must also have proper business licenses, permits, and bonds.

Unions and Associations

Bail Bond Agents might join state professional associations to take advantage of networking opportunities and professional services and resources. Many also belong to the Professional Bail Agents of the United States, a national organization devoted to this profession.

Tips for Entry

1. Talk with Bail Bond Agents to learn more about the profession. You might also contact bail bond associations for information.
2. Many Agents have been hired because they were referred by staff members at a bail bond company.
3. You can learn more about the bail bond industry on the Internet. You might start by visiting the Professional Bail Agents of the United States web site (http://www.pbus.com). Or, to find relevant web sites, enter any of these keywords in a search engine: bail bond industry or bail bond agent.

PRIVATE PROCESS SERVER

CAREER PROFILE

Duties: Serve court summons and complaints to defendants; complete proof of service; serve subpoenas; manage business tasks

Salary Range: $30,000 to $80,000

Employment Prospects: Good

Advancement Prospects: Limited

Prerequisites:

Education/Training—A high school diploma; on-the-job training

Experience—No experience required for entry-level positions; business owners should have several years of work experience

Special Skills and Personality Traits—Interpersonal, communication, reading, writing, math, self-management, and business skills; professional, reliable, energetic, self-motivated, friendly, courteous, persistent

Licensure/Certification—State or local license, certification, or registration may be required; state driver's license; business license, permit, or bond may be required

CAREER LADDER

```
┌─────────────────────────────────┐
│   Process Serving Firm Owner    │
│   or Independent Contractor     │
└─────────────────────────────────┘

┌─────────────────────────────────┐
│ Private Process Server (subcontractor) │
└─────────────────────────────────┘

┌─────────────────────────────────┐
│            Trainee              │
└─────────────────────────────────┘
```

Position Description

In the United States, when lawyers file a lawsuit for their clients, they must notify the defendants (the persons being sued) about the court action. Legal papers—court summons and complaint—must be served to defendants. These are court orders for defendants to appear in court and respond to the legal actions against them. To perform the task of serving legal papers, lawyers may hire private Process Servers.

Private Process Servers must follow court procedures for serving processes, which vary with every state and federal jurisdiction. Additionally, they must deliver legal papers in a timely manner.

In general, Process Servers serve the legal papers to the names listed on the processes. They try to serve papers to defendants at their homes or workplaces. Some defendants may be hard to locate; some are trying to avoid being served. On such occasions, Process Servers must come up with creative ways to serve the papers. For example, they might follow persons to restaurants or other public places to serve them their papers. Or, they might go to people's houses early in the mornings and serve them the papers just as they walk out the door for work.

In some jurisdictions, Process Servers may use alternative ways to serve processes when defendants are not available. For example, some courts allow Process Servers to hand legal papers to an adult who lives at a defendant's home with the directions to give it to the defendant.

Process Servers must complete a proof of service for each paper that they serve, which is then returned to the court. The proof may be a court form or an affidavit that states to whom a paper was served, and when and where it was served.

The workload for Process Servers differs from one day to the next. For example, one day they may have 10 processes to deliver in different cities of a county, and on another day they may have 20 processes to deliver within a 10-mile radius.

Lawyers may also hire private Process Servers to serve subpoenas. These are legal papers that order individuals to appear as witnesses at depositions or trials.

Most Private Process Servers are independent contractors. Some own process service companies. Many are self-employed and work on a contractual basis for law firms, private investigation agencies, or process service companies. When Process Servers work for process companies, they are known as subcontractors.

As independent contractors, private Process Servers are responsible for various business tasks. For example, they invoice clients, pay bills and taxes, generate new business, and maintain their offices. If they use subcontractors (other Process Servers), they are responsible for supervising them and paying their fees. They also take care of recruiting and selecting new subcontractors, as well as training them.

Private Process Servers work part time or full time. Their hours are flexible, which may include working evenings and weekends. Because their job requires a lot of travel, they must have dependable and insured cars.

Salaries

Private Process Servers receive a fee for each paper that they serve. Fees vary, depending on the geographical location and competition in an area. According to Alan Crowe, administrator of the National Association of Professional Process Servers, fees generally range from about $25 to $50 nationwide. It is not uncommon for independent contractors to earn between $30,000 and $80,000, depending on their fees, location, personal ambitions, business costs, and other factors.

Employment Prospects

Opportunities for subcontracting positions with process serving companies are generally available as the turnover rate is high.

Process Servers who want to start their own businesses should be highly experienced and already have a strong reputation with attorneys in their area.

Advancement Prospects

Opportunity for advancement is limited to becoming an owner of a process service company.

Depending on their ambitions and interests, Process Servers might pursue other legal-related careers, such as becoming court clerks, law enforcement officers, lawyers, or criminal justice social workers.

Education and Training

Private Process Servers should have at least a high school diploma or a general equivalency diploma. Many professionals have college degrees or college backgrounds. Some Process Servers also have law degrees.

Entry-level Process Servers receive on-the-job training.

Experience, Skills, and Personality Traits

To start a business, Process Servers should have several years of experience, because attorneys prefer to use established professionals. For entry-level positions, many companies hire individuals without any previous experience. (Remember, most companies hire Process Servers as subcontractors rather than as salaried employees.)

Process Servers need strong interpersonal and communication skills, as they must be able to relate well with people from many backgrounds. They also need good reading, writing, and math skills. Additionally, they need excellent self-management skills—the ability to work independently, follow instructions, handle stressful situations, prioritize tasks, meet deadlines, and so on. Furthermore, as independent contractors, they should have adequate business skills.

Some personality traits that successful Process Servers share are being professional, reliable, energetic, self-motivated, friendly, courteous, and persistent.

Licensure and Certification

States or local governments may require that private Process Servers be licensed, certified, or registered. To learn specific requirements for the location where you wish to work, contact a local Process Server or your local sheriff's office.

Private Process Servers may also be required to obtain local business licenses, permits, or bonds.

Unions and Associations

Professional associations for Process Servers are available at the state and national levels. They offer opportunities for networking with colleagues, as well as various professional services and resources. Two national organizations are the National Association of Professional Process Servers and the International Process Servers Association.

Tips for Entry

1. Contact process serving agencies in your area for work.
2. Read business-management books to learn what is needed to be successfully self-employed. You might also check out continuing education programs for class offerings on starting a business.
3. You can learn more about the private process server industry on the Internet. You might start by visiting the National Association of Professional Process Servers web site (*http://www.napps.com*) or the International Process Servers Association (*http://www.ipsaonline.com*). You can also find relevant web sites by entering the keywords *private process server* in any search engine.

PRIVATE INVESTIGATOR

CAREER PROFILE

Duties: Conduct legal investigations for lawyers; gather evidence for civil or criminal litigation cases; perform other litigation support duties as required

Alternate Titles: Private Detective, Legal Investigator, Financial Investigator, or other title that reflects an area of specialization

Salary Range: $16,000 to $52,000

Employment Prospects: Good

Advancement Prospects: Limited

Prerequisites:

Education/Training—A high school diploma; on-the-job training

Experience—Law enforcement or military background with investigative experience is highly desirable

Special Skills and Personality Traits—Interviewing, interrogation, interpersonal, communication, writing, research, computer, and self-management skills; independent, professional, objective, curious, honest, responsible, flexible

Licensure/Certification—A Private Investigator's license, in most states

CAREER LADDER

```
┌─────────────────────────────────────┐
│  Private Investigation Agency Owner  │
└─────────────────────────────────────┘

┌─────────────────────────────────────┐
│        Private Investigator          │
└─────────────────────────────────────┘

┌─────────────────────────────────────┐
│    Private Investigator Trainee      │
│  or Assistant Private Investigator   │
└─────────────────────────────────────┘
```

Position Description

Private Investigators are licensed, trained professionals. They offer various types of investigative services, such as conducting background checks on individuals, finding missing persons, or collecting specific facts about a person's activities. They are often hired by lawyers to search out facts, or evidence, that may help support their clients' cases in civil or criminal trials. Private Investigators who work primarily for lawyers are sometimes known as Legal Investigators.

Conducting a legal investigation involves various tasks. For example, Private Investigators might:

- gather and review appropriate documents and records—for example, police reports, medical charts, driving records, and bank statements
- examine scenes where personal injuries, accidents, or other incidents related to a case had taken place

- conduct research for background information on people, which may involve doing research on computer databases and the Internet
- locate and interview potential witnesses
- conduct surveillance or undercover work

When they gather evidence, Private Investigators must follow certain legal procedures. Otherwise, the evidence may not be admissible in court. They are also responsible for maintaining accurate, well-detailed notes about their investigations, as well as providing lawyers with verbal or written progress reports.

Private Investigators also perform other litigation support tasks. Some Private Investigators, for instance, serve processes to defendants and witnesses. Or lawyers may ask Private Investigators to find appropriate expert witnesses for their cases. On occasion, Private Investigators testify as expert witnesses about facts or issues related to the cases that they have investigated for lawyers.

Many Private Investigators are self-employed or independent contractors, and so are responsible for managing their businesses. They perform duties such as bookkeeping, invoicing clients, paying bills and taxes, supervising and training support staff, and generating business.

Private Investigators travel constantly. Their job sometimes requires traveling to different cities and states. They work irregular hours, including early mornings, late nights, weekends, and holidays, and sometimes work long days to complete their tasks.

Salaries

Annual earnings depend on such factors as experience, fees, number of cases, and geographical location. In addition, independent Private Investigators must factor in the cost of operating a business. According to the Bureau of Labor Statistics, the estimated annual salary (in 2000) for most Private Investigators ranged from $16,210 to $52,200.

Private Investigators' fees generally range between $25 and $150 per hour. Most also receive reimbursements for the expenses they spend on a case.

Employment Prospects

Private Investigators are either employees or owners of private investigation agencies. Legal investigators may be staff members of legal firms.

The Bureau of Labor Statistics reports that opportunities in this field are expected to grow by 21 to 35 percent through 2010. The competition is keen due to the high number of law enforcement and military personnel who retire or resign and wish to start a second career in this field.

Advancement Prospects

Most Private Investigators realize advancement by earning higher wages and through professional recognition. For many, the top goal is to become successful detective agency owners.

Education and Training

Private Investigators should have at least a high school diploma or a general equivalency diploma. Many employers prefer candidates who have a college background. In fact, many Private Investigators have associate or bachelor's degrees in various fields.

Private Investigators receive on-the-job training. Many attend training workshops, continuing education programs, professional conferences, and so forth to develop and improve skills and expertise needed for their work.

Experience, Skills, and Personality Traits

For entry-level positions, most employers prefer or require that candidates have previous experience in law enforcement, military, insurance, private security, or other fields. Having previous experience in conducting investigations is also highly desirable.

Private Investigators need strong interviewing and interrogation skills, as well as excellent interpersonal and communication skills. They must also have strong writing and computer skills. In addition, they must have superior self-management skills, such as the ability to handle stressful situations, prioritize tasks, make sound judgments, and meet deadlines.

Successful Private Investigators share several personality traits such as being independent, professional, objective, curious, honest, responsible, and flexible.

Licensure and Certification

Most states and many cities require Private Investigators to hold a valid license to practice. Licensure requirements vary from one locale to the next. For information on licensing requirements where you wish to practice, contact your state department of public safety or state professional licensing agency. Or call your local or state police headquarters.

Agency owners must maintain the proper business licenses required by their community and state. For more information on business licenses, contact your city hall.

Unions and Associations

Many Private Investigators join local, state, or national professional associations to take advantage of networking opportunities, training programs, and other professional services and resources. Two national organizations are the National Association of Legal Investigators and the National Association of Investigative Specialists.

Tips for Entry

1. Become familiar with the law and court procedures. You might do independent study by reading appropriate legal books and periodicals. You might also take appropriate classes in college or continuing education programs.
2. Contact private investigators in your area about trainee positions.
3. To enhance your professional credibility, you might obtain certification from a professional organization. For example, the National Association of Legal Investigators grants the *Certified Legal Investigator* designation to licensed investigators who work mostly on negligence or criminal defense investigations.
4. Learn more about Private Investigators on the Internet. You might start by visiting the web sites for these two professional associations: the National Association of Investigative Specialists (*http://www.pimall.com/nais/home.html*) and the National Association of Legal Investigators (*http://www.nalionline.org*).

LEGAL VIDEOGRAPHER

CAREER PROFILE

Duties: Videotape depositions of witnesses for civil or criminal trials; may provide lawyers with other legal video services; manage business duties, for independent operators

Alternate Titles: Legal Video Specialist, Forensic Videographer, Court Videographer

Salary Range: $50,000 to $100,000 or more

Employment Prospects: Excellent

Advancement Prospects: Limited

Prerequisites:
  Education/Training—Legal videography training
  Experience—Professional videography experience
  Special Skills and Personality Traits—Interpersonal, communication, self-management skills; business skills for independent contractors; friendly, cooperative, patient, detail-oriented, ethical, professional
  Licensure/Certification—None required

CAREER LADDER

```
┌─────────────────────────────────┐
│   Senior Legal Videographer,    │
│ Supervisor, or Independent Operator │
└─────────────────────────────────┘

┌─────────────────────────────────┐
│      Legal Videographer         │
└─────────────────────────────────┘

┌─────────────────────────────────┐
│           Trainee               │
└─────────────────────────────────┘
```

Position Description

Professional Legal Videographers videotape depositions for civil or criminal cases. Depositions are the sworn testimonies of witnesses that are given before the trials, and which lawyers may enter as evidence during court trials. Until recently, only depositions taken by certified court reporters, who produce typed transcripts, could be admitted as evidence in court trials. Today, federal courts and many state courts allow lawyers to submit videotaped depositions as evidence before judges and jurors.

Legal Videographers use camera operation, lighting, audio, editing, and shot planning—all specialized areas of video production—to provide the most effective visual record for the judge or jury to view. Videotaped depositions, unlike written depositions, allow judges and jurors to see and hear how witnesses deliver their testimony. Lawyers have been known to settle cases before trial based on how well or how poorly witnesses appear in their videotaped depositions.

With each deposition, Legal Videographers first meet with lawyers to discuss what their needs are. If possible, they look at the room where the deposition will be taken.

The specialists then decide what kinds of equipment they will need and whether they may need additional assistance.

On the day of the deposition, Legal Videographers arrive early, set up their equipment, and take a test run to make sure everything is in working order. In taping a deposition, Legal Videographers follow specific court procedures to ensure that the videotaped deposition may be admitted as evidence at the trial. Videographers must videotape a deposition as simply as possible. If it appears that a videographer was using techniques to influence the viewers, the videotaped deposition can be thrown out of court.

Upon completion of a deposition, Legal Videographers make backup copies of the videotaped deposition. They give the original tapes and backup copies to the attorneys, who will submit the original tape as evidence before the court.

In addition to videotaping depositions, Legal Videographers offer other legal video services to lawyers. For example, lawyers may hire videographers to videotape:

- clients who wish to tape their wills
- scenes of incidents, proof of damages, or evidence of insurance fraud

- mock trials, in which lawyers do a practice run of their case before volunteers acting as pretend jurors
- "day-in-the-life" documentaries that show how personal injuries have changed daily routines of persons seeking compensatory damages

Self-employed Legal Videographers are responsible for managing their business operations. This includes buying and maintaining equipment, record keeping, invoicing clients, paying bills and taxes, generating new business, and so forth.

Legal Videographers work irregular hours. Their job also requires that they travel constantly, sometimes to different cities and states.

Salaries

Earnings vary for independent contractors, depending on such factors as experience, fees, services offered, and personal ambition. According to the American Guild of Court Videographers, the average annual income for independent Legal Videographers generally ranges from $50,000 to $100,000 per year. In major markets, Legal Videographers may be able to earn more. From their gross earnings, they must subtract the cost of all equipment, supplies, and other business expenses.

Employment Prospects

The majority of Legal Videographers are independent operators. Staff positions may be found with video services, court reporting firms, and litigation support companies that offer legal video services. Large law firms, usually in major cities, sometimes hire staff Legal Videographers.

The Legal Videographer field has been steadily growing due to the change in court procedures for videotaped depositions. Further, increasingly more lawyers see how videos can be effective tools. In early 2002, the demand for properly trained videographers is greater than the number of qualified Legal Videographers.

Advancement Prospects

Advancement opportunities for employees are limited to openings for lead and managing positions. As independent contractors, Legal Videographers generally pursue advancement by gaining professional recognition, offering additional professional services, and earning higher incomes.

Education and Training

New entrants into this field must be trained in such areas as the basics of legal video (including techniques for videotaping depositions), laws governing legal video, legal procedures and paperwork, and basic legal and technical vocabulary. Legal videography training might be obtained through apprenticeships or internships under professional Legal Videographers, or through completion of training programs offered by professional associations.

Throughout their careers, Legal Videographers enroll in training and continuing education programs to build up their skills and expertise.

Experience, Skills, and Personality Traits

Entry-level Legal Videographers should already be professional videographers.

Along with their videography skills, Legal Videographers need excellent interpersonal and communication skills for their work. They should also have strong self-management skills—the ability to work well with others, prioritize tasks, meet deadlines, and handle stressful situations. Additionally, independent contractors must have good business skills.

Being friendly, cooperative, patient, detail-oriented, ethical, and professional are some personality traits that Legal Videographers share.

Unions and Associations

Legal Videographers join professional associations to take advantage of training programs and other professional services and resources, as well as opportunities to network with colleagues. Some national associations available to Legal Videographers are the American Guild of Court Videographers, the National Legal Video Association, and the National Court Reporters Association.

Tips for Entry

1. Take basic video training courses that are offered at your high school or in community youth programs. You might also find basic courses at local community colleges or continuing education programs.
2. Talk with different Legal Videographers to learn more about their profession. Ask if you might observe them at their work.
3. Many specialists obtain voluntary professional certification that is granted by either the American Guild of Court Videographers (*http://www.agcv.com*) or the National Court Reporters Association (*http://www. verbatimreporters.com*).
4. One way to spread the word about your business is to network with lawyers, Legal Videographers, court reporters, and other litigation support professionals.
5. You can learn more about the legal videography field on the Internet. To find pertinent web sites, enter these keywords in a search engine: *legal video* or *legal videography.*

DEMONSTRATIVE EVIDENCE SPECIALIST

CAREER PROFILE

Duties: Create demonstrative exhibits for lawyers to use in court trials; design solutions that break down complex concepts into a visual that jurors can understand quickly and easily

Alternate Titles: Legal Graphic Artist; Graphic Designer, Medical Illustrator, Animator, or other title that reflects a particular specialty

Salary Range: $30,000 to $75,000

Employment Prospects: Good

Advancement Prospects: Good

Prerequisites:
   Education/Training—A solid formal education in graphic design, illustration, animation, or related field
   Experience—Several years of experience in a particular specialty; familiarity with law is desirable
   Special Skills and Personality Traits—Communication, interpersonal, teamwork, self-management skills; business skills for self-employed specialists; intelligent, patient, calm, organized, hardworking, open-minded, flexible
   Licensure/Certification—None required

CAREER LADDER

```
┌─────────────────────────────────┐
│   Senior Specialist, Manager,   │
│   or Independent Contractor     │
└─────────────────────────────────┘

┌─────────────────────────────────┐
│ Demonstrative Evidence Specialist │
└─────────────────────────────────┘

┌─────────────────────────────────┐
│      Demonstrative Evidence      │
│        Specialist Trainee        │
└─────────────────────────────────┘
```

Position Description

Demonstrative Evidence Specialists are professional graphic designers, illustrators, medical illustrators, photographers, animators, videographers, and other visual artists. They create demonstrative exhibits, or demonstrative evidence, for lawyers to use in court trials. These may include graphs, charts, illustrations, photographs, audiotapes, videotapes, and computer-generated graphics. Demonstrative Evidence Specialists may create one, dozens, or hundreds of demonstrative exhibits for a trial.

A demonstrative exhibit depicts specific facts that have been presented in sworn testimony by witnesses or experts. For example, a lawyer may show a computer animation that recreates the scene of an automobile accident as presented by a key witness. By using oral and visual testimonies together, lawyers believe, jurors can understand abstract concepts better and remember those concepts when they deliberate on a verdict in the jury rooms. Many lawyers also use demonstrative exhibits in their opening and closing statements.

Demonstrative Evidence Specialists work closely with lawyers and with expert witnesses. They create demonstrative exhibits for a wide range of criminal and civil cases. Thus, along with having artistic talents and skills, specialists must be able to break down complex concepts presented by lawyers and experts and translate them into visual aids that communicate the ideas clearly and simply. Specialists help determine what concepts need to be communicated visually and in what form (perhaps an illustration, chart, or animation) they should be presented.

Demonstrative Evidence Specialists create demonstrative exhibits that are based on testimony or physical evidence. Attorneys provide them with witness statements, photographs, accident reports, medical records, and other relevant documents. Specialists must pay close attention to every detail. The details must be accurate and correct, as well as be relevant to the issues involved in the case. Otherwise, the demonstrative evidence may not be admissible in court. In addition, specialists must ensure that their designs do not mislead jurors or judges in any way.

Demonstrative Evidence Specialists may be called to testify at trials. As expert witnesses, they testify that the demonstrative evidence that they created is accurate, unbiased, and represents the actual evidence.

Most Demonstrative Evidence Specialists are independent contractors. Many go by titles of their particular field, such as Graphic Designer, Medical Illustrator, Photographer, or Animator. Depending on the legal market in their areas, they may do projects for other industries. Independent contractors must also handle the tasks of running a business. Their duties include bookkeeping, maintaining project files, invoicing clients, paying bills and taxes, ordering supplies, generating new business, and so forth.

All Demonstrative Evidence Specialists are responsible for maintaining their skills. They accomplish this through independent study, enrolling in continuing education programs, participating in professional conferences, networking with colleagues, and the like.

Demonstrative Evidence Specialists work part time or full time. It is not uncommon for specialists to work nights and weekends to complete projects for lawyers.

Salaries
The annual salary for Demonstrative Evidence Specialists generally ranges between $30,000 and $75,000, depending on factors such as experience, personal ambition, and geographical location. In major markets, such as the Northeast and Pacific Coast region, specialists can expect to earn more.

Employment Prospects
Demonstrative Evidence Specialists may be independent contractors or employees of litigation support firms that offer demonstrative evidence services.

Demonstrative Evidence Specialists are part of a relatively young field, which has been steadily growing since the 1980s. Job opportunities are expected to continue growing as increasingly more lawyers need visual aids as tools for trials, as well as for mediations, arbitrations, and settlements.

The demand for experienced Demonstrative Evidence Specialists is currently high.

Advancement Prospects
In large firms, specialists can advance to project management positions, such as project managers, art directors, and operations directors. The goal of many Demonstrative Evidence Specialists is to own successful firms.

Education and Training
Demonstrative Evidence Specialists come from various backgrounds, including art, advertising, law, and communications.

Generally, specialists have a solid, formal education in graphic design, illustration, animation, or related fields.

Entry-level specialists receive on-the-job training.

Experience, Skills, and Personality Traits
In general, employers look for candidates with several years of professional experience in their particular fields (illustration, graphic design, photography, and so on). They demonstrate the ability to understand complex ideas and to design solutions that can be easily understood by judges and jurors. They should also be familiar with the legal system.

To succeed in this field, Demonstrative Evidence Specialists must have excellent communication skills—the ability to articulate as well as listen to clients. They also need strong interpersonal and teamwork skills. In addition, they must have superior self-management skills—the ability to handle various tasks, meet deadlines, work independently, handle stressful situations, and so on. Self-employed specialists must also have good business skills.

Being intelligent, patient, calm, organized, hard working, open-minded, and flexible are some of the personality traits that Demonstrative Evidence Specialists share.

Unions and Associations
Demonstrative Evidence Specialists join professional associations to take advantage of professional services and resources, as well as opportunities to network with colleagues. One national organization dedicated to this field is the Demonstrative Evidence Specialists Association. The Association of Medical Illustrators, the Evidence Photographers International Council, and the American Guild of Court Videographers are some other professional associations that different specialists might join.

Tips for Entry
1. One way to break into the field is to get an internship with an established Demonstrative Evidence Specialist.
2. Having a variety of competent multimedia skills may enhance your employability.
3. Are you interested in becoming a medical illustrator? Medical illustrators typically complete a bachelor's program with a combination of art courses, as well as science courses of the type required for medical school. Many also go on to earn a master's degree in medical illustration.
4. Before starting your own business, learn how big a market is available for your services. Survey lawyers in the area about their needs for your particular services.
5. You can use the Internet to learn more about the field. This includes learning about various firms and the type of services they offer. To find relevant web sites, enter the keywords *demonstrative evidence* in any search engine.

TRIAL CONSULTANT

CAREER PROFILE

Duties: Assist lawyers in developing the most effective trial strategies for their clients' cases; provide various services, such as conducting pretrial surveys, focus groups, or mock trials, preparing attorneys for trial, assisting with jury selection, and conducting posttrial research

Alternate Titles: Jury Consultant, Jury and Trial Consultant, Litigation Consultant

Salary Range: $50 to $350 or more per hour

Employment Prospects: Good

Advancement Prospects: Limited

Prerequisites:

  Education/Training—Advanced degrees

  Experience—Several years of experience in their area of specialization and familiarity with the law and legal systems; to become independent contractors, several years in the trial consultant field on a full-time basis

  Special Skills and Personality Traits—Analytical, time management, interpersonal, teamwork, communication, interviewing, report-writing, and presentation skills; business skills for self-employed consultants; self-motivated, organized, creative, flexible

  Licensure/Certification—None required

CAREER LADDER

```
┌─────────────────────────────┐
│   Senior Trial Consultant   │
│  or Independent Contractor  │
└─────────────────────────────┘

┌─────────────────────────────┐
│      Trial Consultant       │
└─────────────────────────────┘

┌─────────────────────────────┐
│   Junior Trial Consultant   │
└─────────────────────────────┘
```

Position Description

Trial Consultants help attorneys prepare their clients' cases for trials by providing lawyers with an idea of how jurors may perceive their cases. These consultants are experts in human dynamics, and are trained to observe how jurors react to words, images and sound. Thus, Trial Consultants advise lawyers on matters such as jury selection, credibility of witnesses, and presentation styles. They also help lawyers develop trial strategies that would most effectively influence jurors to deliberate in their clients' favor.

Trial Consultants provide services to lawyers before, during, and after trials. Pretrial services might include conducting surveys to measure the feelings that a community has about issues related to a court case. Another service is developing and coordinating focus groups and mock trials before which lawyers briefly present their arguments. Trial Consultants analyze responses and provide lawyers with a written report that includes profiles of the best and worst type of jurors to have sitting in their trials.

Other pretrial services that Trial Consultants might offer are:

- reviewing the documents, depositions, and other case materials, and providing lawyers with an opinion on how well they may do in a trial
- assisting lawyers in preparing witnesses for depositions and trials
- coaching lawyers on how to present themselves before jurors, as well as how to use exhibits and technology to their advantage in court
- drafting questions to ask potential jurors during the jury selection process in a trial

Many Trial Consultants advise lawyers as trials occur. Lawyers might ask Consultants to help them during the actual jury selection. Trial Consultants sit in the courtroom and provide lawyers with immediate feedback about potential jurors. Lawyers might also hire Trial Consultants to monitor their trials. They provide lawyers with daily feedback so that they can make necessary changes in their presentations.

Some Trial Consultants also offer posttrial research services. They design questionnaires about case themes, exhibits, witnesses, and other aspects of a trial. Then, when the trial is complete, they interview jurors for their feedback.

Different consultants offer different services, depending on their backgrounds and expertise, so it is common for several Trial Consultants to collaborate on a case, each providing services in their particular strengths or areas.

Some Trial Consultants are independent contractors, or self-employed. Others are employees of trial consulting firms or litigation consulting companies that offer various types of litigation support services. Self-employed consultants must handle tasks related to running their businesses, including drafting business contracts, maintaining client records, invoicing clients, paying bills and taxes, and generating new business.

Many Trial Consultants write articles and books about their field, as well as give lectures and presentations at programs, seminars, and conferences. Some Trial Consultants also maintain an academic career as college and university professors or adjunct lecturers.

Trial Consultants work part time or full time. They sometimes travel to different cities and states to work with clients.

Salaries

Trial Consultants generally earn between $50 and $350 or more an hour, depending on their experience, geographical location, and other factors.

Employment Prospects

The Trial Consultant field has been growing steadily in the last 20 years, and in recent years has become more established. Opportunities are expected to grow as increasingly more lawyers require litigation consulting services.

Advancement Prospects

Staff consultants can advance to senior and managing positions, becoming responsible for specific projects, supervising others, and generating new business for their firms. Some consulting firms also offer opportunities for consultants to become principal consultants or partners.

Many Trial Consultants' goal is to have their own successful consulting firms.

Education and Training

Trial Consultants typically have master's and doctoral degrees in social psychology, sociology, communications, marketing, and other related fields. Some Trial Consultants also hold law degrees.

Entry-level consultants receive training on the job. Trial Consultants continually develop their skills and expertise through independent study, networking with colleagues, attending professional seminars and conferences, and so on.

Experience, Skills, and Personality Traits

Generally, employers choose staff consultants who have several years of experience in their area of specialization. They also prefer candidates who are familiar with the law and legal systems.

To become independent contractors, Trial Consultants should have several years in the field on a full-time basis. Lawyers typically are more confident about choosing consultants who have been exposed to a variety of cases.

Trial Consultants need excellent analytical and time management skills as well as interpersonal, teamwork, and communication skills. They also must have strong interviewing, report-writing, and presentation skills. Additionally, self-employed consultants need good business skills.

Personality traits that many Trial Consultants share are being self-motivated, organized, creative, and flexible.

Unions and Associations

Many Trial Consultants are members of the American Society of Trial Consultants and the American Psychology-Law Society, a division of the American Psychology Association. Many Trial Consultants also belong to local, state, and national bar associations. By joining professional organizations, they are able to take advantage of various professional services and resources, as well as opportunities for networking with colleagues.

Tips for Entry

1. Talk with Trial Consultants to learn more about their work and how they got into the field.
2. While in college, obtain internships with trial consulting or litigation consulting firms.
3. Contact trial consulting firms directly about staff positions or contractual positions. (Small firms sometimes hire Trial Consultants on a contractual basis.)
4. You can learn more about the Trial Consultant field on the Internet. To find relevant web sites, enter the keywords *trial consultant* or *jury consultant* in any search engine.

LITIGATION CONSULTANTS AND EXPERT WITNESSES

LITIGATION CONSULTANT

CAREER PROFILE

Duties: Provide various pretrial services that help lawyers prepare for trials; may provide testimony as an expert witness; manage business operations

Alternate Titles: Litigation Specialist, Forensic Examiner, Forensic Consultant, Expert Witness; a title that reflects a profession such as Real Estate Appraiser, Forensic Accountant, or Questioned Document Specialist

Salary Range: $100 to $2,000 per hour

Employment Prospects: Good

Advancement Prospects: Limited

Prerequisites:

　　Education/Training—College degrees and training appropriate to an occupation

　　Experience—Extensive work experience in field

　　Special Skills and Personality Traits—Interpersonal, writing, communication, presentation, and business skills; competent, credible, articulate, positive, calm, fair, objective

　　Licensure/Certification—Professional licensure or certification may be required, depending on occupation

CAREER LADDER

```
┌─────────────────────────────────────┐
│        Litigation Consultant        │
└─────────────────────────────────────┘

┌─────────────────────────────────────┐
│      New Litigation Consultant      │
└─────────────────────────────────────┘

┌─────────────────────────────────────┐
│  Senior, Administrative, or Management  │
│      position (in a workplace)      │
└─────────────────────────────────────┘
```

Position Description

Lawyers handle litigation cases that may involve issues about which they lack sufficient technical knowledge. To ensure that they prepare the best cases for their clients, lawyers may hire one or more Litigation Consultants. These are experts in their particular fields—nursing, family counseling, psychiatry, plastic surgery, criminology, trace evidence examination, pathology, computer forensics, accounting, stock trading, civil engineering, electrical engineering, pilot procedures, crash reconstruction, art restoration, physical security, real estate appraising, and so on.

Litigation Consultants are independent contractors. They offer various pretrial services that help lawyers prepare their civil and criminal cases. For example, they might:

- analyze and evaluate a case to help lawyers determine whether it should be brought to trial
- review a case to help lawyers identify the issues and facts of a case

- educate lawyers about the subject matter so they can fully understand the issues of a case
- help lawyers develop effective strategies for a case
- gather physical evidence
- interview eyewitnesses
- conduct research for additional raw data that may support a case
- conduct tests or experiments to prove or disprove certain facts or issues; for example a criminalist expert tests blood samples to determine if the blood found at a crime site matches the defendant's blood type
- locate and recruit other expert witnesses who would be appropriate for testifying about specific issues of a case
- prepare reports that lawyers would use with motions and other pretrial court proceedings or in settlement negotiations
- formulate a list of questions that lawyers would ask witnesses for the opposing party

- prepare demonstrative evidence (such as diagrams, models, or computer animation) that help juries and judges understand specific issues of a case

Many Litigation Consultants also offer expert witness services. That is, they provide sworn testimony at arbitrations, depositions, or trials. Expert witnesses are used for one of two purposes in court trials. One is to provide technical information so that the judges or juries can better understand the particular issues of a case. The second is to provide an expert opinion on a particular issue or fact in a case. Expert witnesses are expected to explain technical concepts and vocabulary in terms easy to understand.

To be an expert witness, a Legal Consultant must have the appropriate experience, knowledge, skills, education, or training that gives the consultant the expertise to testify about a specific issue. Although they are hired by either the plaintiff or defendant, expert witnesses provide testimony that is impartial and unbiased. They are ethically bound not to support or oppose the arguments of either party.

(Note: Not all expert witnesses are Litigation Consultants. Many professionals—doctors, criminologists, engineers, forensic scientists, researchers, and so on—offer expert witness services as a supplemental activity to their occupation or practice.)

As independent contractors, Litigation Consultants are responsible for managing their business operations. Their tasks include billing clients, paying bills and taxes, maintaining offices and equipment, generating new business, and so on.

Litigation Consultants work flexible hours. Many offer their services statewide as well as nationwide.

Salaries
Annual gross earnings for Litigation Consultants are based on the total number of hours they've worked at an hourly rate. The fees vary, depending on such factors as area of expertise, experience, types of services being offered, fees, demand for services, and geographical location. In general, hourly rates range between $100 to $2,000 per hour.

In addition, many consultants bill clients for out-of-pocket expenses such as photocopying expenses, telephone calls, and travel costs.

Employment Prospects
Most Litigation Consultants are self-employed or owners of litigation consulting firms. Their services may be used by individuals, insurance companies, and corporations, as well as by lawyers.

Opportunities for Litigation Consultants depend on the demand by lawyers for their particular area of expertise, and on the number of similar consultants in their geographical area.

Advancement Prospects
Litigation Consultants realize advancement by earning higher incomes and receiving high accolades for their work.

Many also measure success in terms of being sought out by lawyers for very complex or publicized cases.

Education and Training
Litigation Consultants have completed the appropriate education and training that is required for their particular professions.

Throughout their careers, they enroll in continuing education and training programs to develop and maintain their professional skills and expertise.

Experience, Skills, and Personality Traits
Professionals typically become Litigation Consultants after many years of experience in their fields. Many have retired or resigned from senior, administrative, or management positions to start litigation consulting and expert witness services.

Litigation Consultants need excellent interpersonal skills to work well with lawyers. Additionally, they need strong writing, communication, and presentation skills. As independent contractors, Litigation Consultants also need good business skills.

Personality traits that successful Litigation Consultants share are being competent, credible, articulate, positive, calm, fair, and objective.

Licensure and Certification
Litigation Consultants hold the appropriate licensure and certification that is required for their occupations. For example, physicians have valid medical licenses in the states where they practice.

Unions and Associations
Litigation Consultants join professional associations that serve their particular fields, such as criminology, forensic accounting, heart surgery, psychiatry, aerospace engineering, or recreation.

Tips for Entry
1. Join professional associations and participate in their various activities.
2. Market your services directly to lawyers. For example, you might send professional brochures to law firms, advertise in legal publications, or list yourself in expert witness databases on the Internet.
3. To enhance their credibility, many Litigation Consultants obtain professional designations from recognized professional organizations in their field. Many also teach, give presentations, as well as write articles and books about their subject matter.
4. On the Internet, you can learn more about Litigation Consultants. To get a list of relevant web sites, enter any of these keywords in a search engine: *expert witness, expert witness testimony,* or *expert witness resources.*

CRASH RECONSTRUCTION CONSULTANT

CAREER PROFILE

Duties: Analyze and reconstruct traffic collisions to answer specific questions related to issues in a litigation case; may provide expert witness services

Alternate Titles: Accident Reconstruction Specialist, Collision Reconstructionist

Salary Range: $100 to $200 per hour+

Employment Prospects: Good

Advancement Prospects: Limited

Prerequisites:

    Education/Training—Completion of training programs from recognized institutions; ongoing training and continuing education programs

    Experience—Several years of experience in crash reconstruction units in law enforcement agencies; or engineering background

    Special Skills and Personality Traits—Communication, analytical, report-writing, business skills; problem solver, dedicated, methodical, detail oriented, innovative

    Licensure/Certification—A private investigator license may be required in some states

CAREER LADDER

```
┌─────────────────────────────────────┐
│   Crash Reconstruction Consultant    │
└─────────────────────────────────────┘

┌─────────────────────────────────────┐
│   Crash Reconstruction Specialist    │
│      (law enforcement agency)        │
└─────────────────────────────────────┘

┌─────────────────────────────────────┐
│    Crash Reconstruction Trainee      │
│      (law enforcement agency)        │
└─────────────────────────────────────┘
```

Position Description

Crash Reconstruction Consultants are experts in analyzing traffic accidents and reconstructing what took place during the collisions. (A traffic collision may involve automobiles, trucks, motorcycles, bicycles, as well as pedestrians.) They are also known as *Accident Reconstruction Consultants.* Lawyers hire their consulting services for civil or criminal cases, such as personal injury lawsuits or manslaughter charges, that involve traffic crashes.

Crash Reconstruction Consultants often work on cases in which the accidents may have occurred several months or years ago. They analyze traffic crashes to answer specific questions that are related to the issues of a case. For example: How fast were the drivers going? Did the plaintiff try to avoid the collision? Was the defendant's view of the pedestrian blocked? Were the car headlights on at the time of the crash?

To reconstruct a traffic crash, consultants examine physical evidence, such as skid marks and vehicle parts. They also review police reports, eyewitness testimony, photographs of the accident site, and other sources of information. They carefully piece together the data and rebuild the events of the collision. Their work involves investigative techniques, as well as the use of math formulas and scientific laws and principles. They might also recreate a crash, using similar vehicles, to set a clearer understanding of what took place.

Crash Reconstruction Consultants provide lawyers with detailed reports that include diagrams, models, computer animations, or other visual aids to illustrate their findings. Lawyers often use these reports to negotiate settlements with the opposing side.

Many Crash Reconstruction Consultants also offer expert witness services. They may provide testimony at arbitrations, depositions, and trials. As expert witnesses, Consultants give opinions only on the specific issues that they are being asked. They present technical concepts in nontechnical terms so that the judge or jury can understand the issues. Consultants often use demonstrative exhibits (diagrams, photographs, models, and so forth) to help them explain technical concepts more clearly.

Along with their consulting services, many Crash Reconstruction Consultants write articles or contribute to magazines and books about their discipline. Many also teach courses at universities, conduct training workshops for law enforcement officers, and give presentations at conferences and meetings.

As business owners or independent contractors, Crash Reconstruction Consultants are responsible for overseeing their business operations. They perform tasks such as billing clients, paying taxes and bills, record keeping, maintaining their office space and equipment, and generating new business.

Crash Reconstruction Consultants have flexible hours. They sometimes work long hours to meet deadlines. They may travel to different cities and states to meet with clients, survey traffic scenes, or testify in court.

Salaries
Crash Reconstruction Consultants charge hourly fees, which typically range from $100 to $200 per hour or more. Their fees are based on such factors as experience, the services offered, and geographical location. Many Consultants charge a flat fee for the creation of demonstrative exhibits.

Employment Prospects
Most Crash Reconstruction Consultants are self-employed or owners of consulting firms. Attorneys and insurance companies hire them on a contractual basis.

Advancement Prospects
Crash Reconstruction Consultants realize advancement through the growth of their businesses, by earning higher incomes, and by being recognized for the high quality of their work.

Education and Training
Most Crash Reconstruction Consultants received their training when they were law enforcement officers. They completed several weeks of basic training from nationally recognized institutions such as the Institute of Police Technology and Management, the Traffic Institute (at Northwestern University), or the Texas Engineering Extension Service. This is followed by training in specialty areas such as motorcycles, heavy trucks, applied physics, and pedestrian crashes.

Throughout their careers, Crash Reconstruction Consultants enroll in training and continuing education programs to develop and maintain their skills and expertise.

Experience, Skills, and Personality Traits
The majority of Crash Reconstruction Consultants are former law enforcement officers who served many years in their agencies' traffic crash reconstruction detail. Some consultants come to this field from engineering backgrounds.

Crash Reconstruction Consultants need excellent communication, analytical, and report-writing skills. To succeed in business, they also need adequate business skills. Some personality traits that successful consultants share are being a problem solver, as well as being dedicated, methodical, detail-oriented, and innovative.

Licensure and Certification
No professional licensure is required to become a Crash Reconstruction Consultant. However, some states may require that they hold a private investigator license. For licensure information, contact the business licensing department in the state where you wish to practice.

Unions and Associations
Crash Reconstruction Consultants join state and national professional associations that serve their particular field to take advantage of networking opportunities with colleagues as well as professional services and resources. Some organizations are the:

- American Society of Safety Engineers
- International Association of Accident Reconstruction Specialists
- National Association of Professional Accident Reconstruction Specialists
- National Association of Traffic Accident Reconstructionists and Investigators
- Society of Accident Reconstructionists

Tips for Entry
1. Helpful courses to take in high school are math and physics.
2. To enhance their credibility, many consultants obtain the professional certification granted by the Accreditation Commission for Traffic Accident Reconstruction (ACTAR). For more information about this voluntary certification, write to ACTAR at P.O. Box 5436, Hudson, FL 34674-5436. Or call (800) 809-3818, or visit its website, *http://www.actar.org.*
3. You can learn more about traffic crash reconstruction on the Internet. Two web sites you might visit are the Traffic Accident Reconstruction Origin, *http://www.tarorigin.com,* and the Accident Reconstruction Resource—the ARC Network, *http://www. accidentreconstruction. com.*

CRIMINOLOGIST

CAREER PROFILE

Duties: Conduct research studies in the causes of crime; teach criminology or criminal justice courses; provide expert witness services

Alternate Titles: Professor of Criminology, Professor of Criminal Justice

Salary Range: $34,000 to $87,000

Employment Prospects: Fair

Advancement Prospects: Fair

Prerequisites:

Education/Training—Advanced degree; doctorate required for academic teaching

Experience—Many years of research and teaching experience in a particular area of study

Special Skills and Personality Traits—Analytical, concentration, writing, interpersonal, and communication skills; creative, curious, observant, detail-oriented, objective, open-minded

Licensure/Certification—None required

CAREER LADDER

```
┌─────────────────────────────────┐
│  Criminologist—Expert Witness   │
│    and Litigation Consultant    │
└─────────────────────────────────┘

┌─────────────────────────────────┐
│         Criminologist           │
└─────────────────────────────────┘

┌─────────────────────────────────┐
│        Doctoral Student         │
└─────────────────────────────────┘
```

Position Description

Criminologists are often hired by attorneys to provide expert witness testimony at depositions and trials. As highly trained social scientists, Criminologists study the causes of crime. They research such questions as: What makes people commit a certain kind of crime? Why does crime happen more often in certain neighborhoods? Why would someone join a gang? Their research is used by law enforcement agencies, corrections, social work organizations, government, and others to design more effective crime prevention programs and rehabilitation programs. Criminologists' research also helps law enforcement agents with the apprehension of criminals.

Some people, including many in the media, confuse Criminologists with criminalists, or forensic scientists. Criminalists are part of the criminology discipline; however, their expertise is in the examination of physical evidence that is found at crime scenes. They examine such physical evidence as blood, DNA, bullets, trace evidence, and questioned documents. Having backgrounds in physical or life science, criminalists work in police or private crime labs.

Most Criminologists, on the other hand, are employed as professors in criminology and criminal justice departments in colleges and universities, teaching courses to undergraduate students as well as to graduate and doctoral students. They conduct research projects, often in conjunction with government law enforcement agencies and criminal justice programs.

Criminologists specialize in studying one or a few areas of crime. Some of those areas include violent crime, domestic violence, white-collar crime, cyber crime, youth gangs, race and crime, women and crime, victimization, deviance, prison subcultures, correctional rehabilitation, policing, criminal court system, alternative justice programs, and crime prevention. Some Criminologists devote their time to developing and improving effective research methods for studying clues in the crime lab as well as at the crime scene.

As expert witnesses, Criminologists provide testimony that helps judges and juries determine the truth in the judicial process. In civil or criminal cases, they offer opinions on criminal behavior related to the specific issues of the particular cases. However, they can testify only after the judge has ascertained that they have the required expertise, skills, knowledge, training, or education.

Some Criminologists offer other types of litigation consulting services. For example, they might interview defendants and family members to gather evidence for specific issues. Or they might review all the records of a case to help lawyers develop trial strategies.

Criminologists typically have flexible work hours. They divide their time between teaching, conducting research, writing, giving presentations, and litigation consulting.

Salaries

Salaries for Criminologists vary, depending on experience, education, employer, and geographical location.

Criminologists in academic settings receive salaries according to their rank (instructor, assistant professor, associate professor, or professor). The average salary for full-time faculty in four-year colleges and universities ranged between $33,742 and $87,022, according to a 1999–2000 survey by the American Association of University Professors.

Employment Prospects

Most Criminologists work in colleges and universities as part of the teaching and research staff in the criminology or criminal justice departments. Criminologists are also employed by law enforcement agencies, correctional facilities, criminal justice research institutes, and crime prevention programs.

In general, openings become available as Criminologists retire, resign, or transfer to other positions. Chances for opportunities are higher in academic institutions than in other work settings. The competition is keen for all positions.

Advancement Prospects

As college and university professors, Criminologists can advance through the ranks as instructor, assistant professor, associate professor, and full professor.

Many Criminologists pursue advancement by earning higher incomes and professional recognition. Some also measure success in terms of being sought out to provide expert witness testimony in highly complex or publicized trials.

Education and Training

Criminologists hold a master's or doctorate degree in criminology, criminal justice, sociology, psychology, or other related field. Most practicing Criminologists have earned a doctoral degree, which is a requirement for academic teaching and research positions. In addition, attorneys generally look for Criminologists with doctorates to provide expert witness testimony.

Experience, Skills, and Personality Traits

Attorneys typically choose as expert witnesses Criminologists who have a solid reputation for their expertise in their area of study. They usually have many years of teaching and research experience and have published articles and books in their subject matter. Lawyers also look for Criminologists who have a balance of academic and practical experience.

Along with teaching and researching skills, Criminologists have superior analytical, concentration, and writing skills. They also have excellent interpersonal and communication skills.

Some personality traits that successful criminologists share are being creative, curious, observant, detail-oriented, objective, and open-minded.

Unions and Associations

Many Criminologists belong to professional associations to take advantage of networking opportunities, training programs, professional publications, and other professional resources and services. Some associations that Criminologists join are the American Society of Criminology, the Western Society of Criminology, the Academy of Criminal Justice Sciences, and the American Sociological Association.

Tips for Entry

1. As an undergraduate, talk with criminology professors or an advisor of the criminology or sociology graduate program at your college. Find out what classes you should take to prepare for a graduate program.
2. Gain experience in the field of criminology and criminal justice by obtaining appropriate internships. Talk with your advisor or college career counselor for help finding available opportunities.
3. As a student, begin building up a network of professionals and others whom you can contact about job openings.
4. Learn more about criminology on the Internet. You might start by visiting the web site of the American Society of Criminology (http://www.asc41.com). To find other relevant web sites, use these keywords in a search engine: criminology or criminologist.

FORENSIC PSYCHOLOGIST

CAREER PROFILE

Duties: Vary, depending on the work setting—for example, may provide assessment and treatment services, conduct research, or provide consulting services; provide expert witness testimony; may provide litigation consulting services

Salary Range: $28,000 to $92,000

Employment Prospects: Good

Advancement Prospects: Fair

Prerequisites:

Education/Training—A doctorate in psychology is preferred or required

Experience—To be expert witnesses, several years of experience in area of specialization; familiarity with the law and legal procedures

Special Skills and Personality Traits—Research, communication, interpersonal, teamwork, and presentation skills; patient, adaptable, analytical, compassionate

Licensure/Certification—A psychologist license or certification is required to provide assessment and treatment

CAREER LADDER

```
┌─────────────────────────────────────┐
│ Senior Forensic Psychologist, Program │
│ Director, or Private Practitioner    │
└─────────────────────────────────────┘

┌─────────────────────────────────────┐
│        Forensic Psychologist         │
└─────────────────────────────────────┘

┌─────────────────────────────────────┐
│          Doctoral Student            │
└─────────────────────────────────────┘
```

Position Description

Forensic Psychologists are trained in the areas of psychology and law. They are often retained by lawyers to provide expert witness testimony on psychological issues that are related to their litigation cases. They may testify for civil or criminal cases about such issues as trial competency, sanity, criminal responsibility, domestic violence, drug dependence, psychosocial motivations, child abuse, paranoid disorders, and malingering.

Forensic Psychologists perform different roles in the legal and court systems. Some are clinical psychologists, working in correctional facilities, psychiatric hospitals, and other forensic units. Their primary duty is assessing and treating juvenile and adult criminal offenders. Other clinical Forensic Psychologists have private practices, working with children, adults and families.

Many Forensic Psychologists are researchers and educators, working in universities, medical schools, hospitals, research institutes, and clinics. Others are jury consultants, working independently or with trial consulting firms. Their expertise is in helping lawyers select jurors that may be more sympathetic to their clients.

Some Forensic Psychologists work with law enforcement agencies, helping with criminal investigations. They do criminal profiling, which is creating psychological profiles of typical offenders of certain crimes. Some experts work with court systems, performing various duties, such as evaluating defendants for their ability to stand trial or investigating cases of abused or neglected children.

As expert witnesses, Forensic Psychologists testify only on issues for which the court has qualified them as being experts. Attorneys use Forensic Psychologists for one of two purposes. One is to explain specific psychological concepts so that judges and juries can fully understand the issues of the case. The other is to present their opinions about defendants based on their professional evaluations.

Many Forensic Psychologists offer litigation consulting services as a supplementary activity. However, they are ethically bound to provide either consulting or expert witness services on a case, but not both. This is to prevent a conflict of interest, as well as to ensure that their testimony as expert witnesses is objective and unbiased.

In addition to their primary activity (such as research, clinical work, or trial consulting), many Forensic Psychologists devote time to teaching classes and training workshops. Many also make presentations at conferences and write articles and books.

Salaries

Salaries for Forensic Psychologists vary, depending on factors such as experience, work setting, nature of their work, and geographical location. For example, most clinical psychologists in 2000 earned an estimated salary between $28,090 and $76,840, according to the Bureau of Labor Statistics. The annual salary in 2000 for Forensic Psychologists employed by the Federal Bureau of Prisons ranged from $41,834 to $91,589.

Forensic Psychologists who provide consulting services charge an hourly fee, generally ranging from $75 to $250 per hour.

Employment Prospects

Opportunities are expected to grow steadily for Forensic Psychologists in all work settings, particularly for those holding doctoral degrees. Some experts predict that the highest demand for Forensic Psychologists shall come from attorneys, courts, and lawmakers.

Advancement Prospects

In general, supervisory and management opportunities for Forensic Psychologists are to be found in the various work settings. For example, in a prison, an entry-level staff psychologist can rise up through the ranks to become the psychology department chief or even the top administrator at the prison.

Education and Training

Most employers require or prefer to hire Forensic Psychologists with a doctorate in psychology from an accredited institution.

Formal training for doctoral-level Forensic Psychologists involves several years. Students first earn a bachelor's degree in psychology or other behavioral science field. They then complete a one- or two-year master's program in psychology, followed by a three-year doctorate program. Students wishing to become clinical psychologists usually complete a four-year doctorate program in clinical psychology, followed by a one-year internship.

Experience, Skills, and Personality Traits

To be expert witnesses, Forensic Psychologists normally have several years of experience in their area of specialization. In addition, they are familiar with the law and legal procedures.

Forensic Psychologists must have excellent research, communication, and interpersonal skills. They also need strong teamwork skills, as they work with various professionals in their particular work settings. As expert witnesses, Forensic Psychologists need good presentation skills and must be able to explain psychological concepts in clear and understandable words to nonpsychologists.

Some personality traits that successful Forensic Psychologists share are being patient, adaptable, analytical, and compassionate.

Licensure and Certification

Forensic Psychologists who provide forensic assessment and treatment services must be licensed or certified psychologists in the states where they practice. Licensure or certification is not necessary for those who are primarily consultants, educators, researchers, or policy makers. Having state licensure, however, may enhance a Forensic Psychologist's credibility as an expert witness.

Unions and Associations

Many Forensic Psychologists join state and national professional associations to take advantage of professional resources and services as well as opportunities to network with peers. Two national organizations that serve the interests of Forensic Psychologists are the American Academy of Forensic Psychology and the American Psychology-Law Society, a division of the American Psychological Association.

Tips for Entry

1. Find out if this field is right for you before starting a graduate program. Read about forensic psychology. Also talk with some professionals.
2. As an undergraduate student, talk with psychology professors or a psychology advisor for the graduate program at your college. Find out what classes you should take to prepare yourself for a graduate program.
3. To enhance their credibility, many Forensic Psychologists obtain the *Diplomate in Forensic Psychology* designation, granted by the American Board of Professional Psychology (ABPP). For more information, contact ABPP at 128 North Craig Street, Pittsburgh, PA 15213. Or call (412) 681-3000, or fax (412) 681-1471. Or visit its web site at *http://www. abfp.com.*
4. You can learn more about forensic psychology on the Internet. You might start by visiting the web site for the American Psychology-Law Society *(http://www. unl.edu/ap-ls).*

LEGAL NURSE CONSULTANT (LNC)

CAREER PROFILE

Duties: Provide litigation consulting services in the area of health care; may provide expert witness testimony; as independent consultants, manage business operations

Salary Range: $30,000 to $100,000

Employment Prospects: Good

Advancement Prospects: Limited

Prerequisites:

Education/Training—Legal Nurse Consultant certificate programs are available

Experience—Several years of clinical or surgical experience preferred

Special Skills and Personality Traits—Analytical, research, report-writing, communication, interpersonal, computer, and self-management skills; business skills for independent consultants; organized, detail-oriented, ethical, patient, determined, resourceful

Licensure/Certification—A registered-nurse license

CAREER LADDER

```
┌─────────────────────────────────────┐
│ Independent Legal Nurse Consultant  │
└─────────────────────────────────────┘

┌─────────────────────────────────────┐
│      Staff or Independent Legal      │
│         Nurse Consultant             │
└─────────────────────────────────────┘

┌─────────────────────────────────────┐
│          Registered Nurse            │
└─────────────────────────────────────┘
```

Position Description

Legal Nurse Consultants (LNCs) offer litigation consulting services in the area of health care. As highly experienced registered nurses, LNCs assist lawyers with civil and criminal cases that involve medical issues. They work on a wide range of litigation cases, including personal injury, wrongful death, heart surgery, medical malpractice, negligence, elder abuse, product liability, worker's compensation, and so on.

Legal Nurse Consultants offer various types of pretrial services. Some of these services are:

- reviewing medical records and other documents to determine issues, such as liability and standards of care
- working with financial experts to identify damages and related costs of services
- educating lawyers about health care facts and issues related to their cases
- conducting research to answer questions about health-related issues
- interviewing health care practitioners and patients
- assisting lawyers with writing motions, briefs, interrogatories, demand letters, and other legal documents

- organizing and summarizing medical records and other medical materials needed for litigation
- developing and preparing demonstrative exhibits such as charts and diagrams
- preparing a list of questions that lawyers would ask the expert witnesses for the opposing party
- locating appropriate health practitioners who can provide expert witness testimony for specific issues in a case

Some LNCs also offer expert witness services. They would provide testimony as experts in their nursing specialty (such as intensive care, pediatric nursing, or elder care). When serving in the capacity of a nurse expert, they usually will not provide any other litigation consulting services. This is to prevent a conflict of interest, as well as to ensure that their testimony as expert witnesses is objective and unbiased.

Most LNCs are independent contractors, providing services on a contractual basis. As independent contractors, they must handle various business tasks. They keep records, pay bills and taxes, invoice clients, maintain files, generate new business, and so on.

LNCs work part time or full time. Many Legal Nurse Consultants continue working as registered nurses.

Salaries

Salaries vary significantly for independent and in-house LNCs, depending on factors such as experience, personal ambition, and geographical location. In general, annual salaries can range between $30,000 and $100,000. Hourly rates range between $25 and $100 per hour.

Employment Prospects

The majority of LNCs are independent contractors. They may be self-employed or owners of legal nursing consulting firms. Some LNCs are staff members at law firms, insurance companies, government agencies, or health care institutions.

The Legal Nurse Consultant field has been steadily growing during the last 20 years. The demand for experienced LNCs is predicted to continue growing as increasingly more lawyers see that it is more cost-effective to use the medicolegal services of LNCs than those of medical doctors.

Advancement Prospects

Many LNCs pursue advancement by earning higher incomes and by gaining professional recognition among colleagues and lawyers.

Education and Training

There is no standard educational requirement to become Legal Nurse Consultants. LNCs may have associate, bachelor's, or advanced degrees in nursing.

Prospective LNCs can obtain basic training by enrolling in LNC certificate programs, which are offered by two-year and four-year colleges, universities, private postsecondary schools, and professional associations. These programs provide students with a basic knowledge of law and legal procedures relevant to performing LNC duties. Students also learn practical skills, such as legal research, legal writing, and working with medical records.

Experience, Skills, and Personality Traits

Lawyers prefer hiring LNCs who have several years of clinical or surgical experience, which includes interpreting medical records.

Legal Nurse Consultants need strong analytical, research, and report-writing skills, as well as excellent communication and interpersonal skills. Having good computer skills is also necessary. In addition, they have strong self-management skills, such as the ability to manage multiple tasks, meet deadlines, and work independently. Independent consultants should have good business skills.

Successful Legal Nurse Consultants share several personality traits such as being organized, detail-oriented, ethical, patient, determined, and resourceful.

Licensure/Certification

LNCs generally maintain their registered-nurse licenses, although only those who are practicing nurses are required to hold valid licenses.

Unions and Associations

Legal Nurse Consultants join local, state, and national nursing associations such as the American Nurses Association and the American Association of Legal Nurse Consultants. As members of professional associations, LNCs can take advantage of education programs, networking opportunities, and other professional services and resources.

Tips for Entry

1. Entry into an LNC certificate program may require that an applicant have worked a minimum number of years as a practicing registered nurse.
2. To enhance their employability, many LNCs obtain the professional certification granted by the American Association of Legal Nurse Consultants (AALNC). For more information, write AALNC at 4700 W. Lake Avenue, Glenview, IL 60025-1485. Or call (877) 402-2562, or fax (877) 734-8668. Or visit its web site at *http://www.aalnc.org*.
3. Let lawyers in your area know about your services. Send brochures or flyers about yourself to local lawyers as well as local bar associations. Also prepare press releases to local newspapers and legal publications.
4. You can learn more about the profession on the Internet. To find relevant web sites enter the keywords *legal nurse consultant* in any search engine.

FORENSIC ACCOUNTANT

CAREER PROFILE

Duties: Analyze and interpret financial evidence; provide lawyers with litigation consulting services, which may include expert witness services

Alternate Titles: Forensic Examiner

Salary Range: $28,000 to $74,000

Employment Prospects: Good

Advancement Prospects: Fair

Prerequisites:

Education/Training—A bachelor's degree; on-the-job training

Experience—Accounting and auditing experience

Special Skills and Personality Traits—Analytical, investigative, organizational, communication, report-writing, and interpersonal skills; curious, creative, persistent, discreet, honest, open-minded

Licensure/Certification—Many voluntarily obtain a Certified Public Accountant (CPA) license; many also voluntarily obtain the Certified Fraud Examiner (CFE) and the Certified Insolvency and Reorganization Accountant (CIRA) designations

CAREER LADDER

```
┌─────────────────────────────┐
│  Senior Forensic Accountant,│
│  Department Manager, or     │
│  Independent Contractor     │
└─────────────────────────────┘

┌─────────────────────────────┐
│     Forensic Accountant     │
└─────────────────────────────┘

┌─────────────────────────────┐
│  Assistant Forensic Accountant │
└─────────────────────────────┘
```

Position Description

Forensic Accountants offer litigation consulting services in the area of investigative accounting. They use accounting, auditing, and investigative skills to analyze and interpret financial records. As litigation consultants, Forensic Accountants advise lawyers about financial issues related to civil and criminal litigation cases, such as personal injury, medical malpractice, divorce, contract disputes, product liability claims, fraud, and embezzlement.

Forensic Accountants provide various litigation consulting services. For example, they might:

- analyze financial records to determine specific issues such as the amount of losses or damages, the flow of funds between particular people and organizations, or the accuracy of financial statements
- gather evidence, which requires extensive review of various financial records and business documents
- interview witnesses

- determine what financial documents lawyers should ask the opposing party to provide
- write well-documented reports that lawyers can use as a basis for pretrial motions and proceedings as well as negotiation settlements
- create, or oversee, the development of demonstrative exhibits (such as charts and diagrams)
- educate lawyers on the basic concepts of accounting principles
- provide expert witness testimony at arbitrations, depositions, and trials

Forensic Accountants also offer investigative accounting services to individuals, law enforcement agencies, government agencies, insurance companies, banks, corporations, and other organizations. For example, they might investigate fraud cases (such as securities fraud, insurance fraud, and kickbacks) for law enforcement agencies. Or they might review financial records for businesses to help them determine if they should declare bankruptcy.

Forensic Accountants are self-employed or work for accounting companies, including firms that exclusively provide forensic accounting services. Lawyers hire Forensic Accountants on a contractual basis.

Forensic Accountants often work longer than 40 hours a week to complete their projects for clients.

Salaries

Salaries vary, depending on experience, geographical location, and other factors. According to the Bureau of Labor Statistics, the estimated annual salary in 2000 for most accountants and auditors ranged from $28,190 to $73,770.

Employment Prospects

Since the 1980s, forensic accounting has been one of the fastest-growing disciplines in the field of accounting. The demand for experienced Forensic Accountants is expected to continue, especially in areas such as securities litigation, Securities and Exchange Commission (SEC) investigations, health care fraud, business fraud, intellectual property theft, and computer theft.

Advancement Prospects

In accounting firms, Forensic Accountants can advance to senior and managing positions, and in many firms can become partners. The top goal for some Forensic Accountants is to become successful independent operators or owners of their accounting firms.

Education and Training

Many Employers prefer or require that Forensic Accountants have a bachelor's degree in accounting or have completed general accounting courses.

Entry-level Forensic Accountants are trained on the job. Throughout their careers, accountants enroll in continuing education and training programs to develop and maintain their skills and expertise.

To maintain professional designations, Forensic Accountants are required to complete a minimum of continuing professional education (CPE) credits.

Experience, Skills, and Personality Traits

For entry-level positions, employers look for candidates who have accounting and auditing experience. Candidates demonstrate the ability to make sensible judgments and should be able to visualize the whole picture of a case as well as examine the many fine details.

Forensic Accountants demonstrate strong analytical, investigative, and organizational skills. They also have excellent communication, report-writing, and interpersonal skills. Being curious, creative, persistent, discreet, honest, and open-minded are some personality traits that successful Forensic Accountants share.

Licensure and Certification

No professional licensure is required to become a Forensic Accountant. But many Forensic Accountants voluntarily obtain the *Certified Public Accountant* (CPA) licensure. For licensure information, contact your state board of accountancy.

Many Forensic Accountants also voluntarily obtain professional certifications to enhance their credibility as experts for their skill, knowledge, education, training, and experience. One is the *Certified Fraud Examiner* (CFE) designation, granted by the Association of Certified Fraud Examiners. Another is the *Certified Insolvency and Reorganization Accountant* (CIRA) designation, granted by the Association of Insolvency and Restructuring Advisors.

Unions and Associations

Many Forensic Accountants belong to local, state, and national professional associations to take advantage of networking opportunities as well as professional services and resources. Some professional groups are the Forensic Accountants Society of North America, the Association of Certified Fraud Examiners, the American Institute of Certified Public Accountants, and the Association of Insolvency and Restructuring Advisors.

Tips for Entry

1. Start gaining experience by obtaining internships with firms that offer forensic accounting services.
2. Check out job listings at web sites of professional accounting associations, as well as in professional publications.
3. You can learn more about forensic accounting on the Internet. To find relevant web sites, enter the keywords *forensic accounting* or *forensic accountant* in any search engine.

APPRAISER

CAREER PROFILE

Duties: Provide an opinion on the value of property that is based on well-documented research; provide expert witness services; may provide other litigation consulting services

Alternate Titles: A title that reflects a specialty area, such as Real Estate Appraiser, Jewelry Appraiser, Art Appraiser, Business Appraiser, or Horse Appraiser

Salary Range: Salaries vary, depending on specialty area

Employment Prospects: Good

Advancement Prospects: Fair

Prerequisites:

Education/Training—Apprenticeship or training under professional Appraisers

Experience—Highly experienced and knowledgeable in specialty area

Special Skills and Personality Traits—Interpersonal, communication, writing, research, computer skills; impartial, trustworthy, curious, resourceful

Licensure/Certification—State license or certification required for Real Estate Appraisers

CAREER LADDER

```
┌─────────────────────────┐
│    Senior Appraiser     │
└─────────────────────────┘

┌─────────────────────────┐
│       Appraiser         │
└─────────────────────────┘

┌─────────────────────────┐
│    Appraiser Trainee    │
└─────────────────────────┘
```

Position Description

Appraisers are often retained by lawyers to provide expert witness testimony in litigation cases. Their expertise lies in providing professional opinions on the value of tangible and intangible property—real estate, automobiles, aircraft, machinery, gems, jewelry, artwork, antiques, toys, furniture, quilts, books, businesses, mines, oil fields, public utilities, patents, trademarks, and so on. Appraisers typically specialize in appraising one or several types of property.

Appraisers do not establish the value of property. What they do is complete as well-documented report, or appraisal, that states their opinions of how much a property is currently worth. The appraisal process begins with an inspection or examination of a property. Then appraisers conduct research to find out what the current prices are for similar properties in the local area, as well as regionally, statewide, and nationally. Their research includes reading market reports, searching computer databases, interviewing experts in the specialty area, and so on.

As expert witnesses, Appraisers testify only about issues that are related to the value of the property in question. At the start of their assignment, attorneys give them specific instructions about their tasks and the raw data (such as business documents) that they need to complete their appraisal. Appraisers submit written reports for review by the courts and the lawyers, as well as for questioning by the opposing lawyers in sworn depositions. Sometimes cases are settled before reaching trial.

At trials, they present their information so that judges and juries can easily understand technical concepts and terms. Appraisers sometimes use demonstrative exhibits to illustrate difficult concepts more clearly. Appraisers can expect to be cross-examined by the opposing lawyers who do their best to discredit their testimony.

Many Appraisers also offer litigation consulting services, such as:

- providing technical assistance to lawyers, such as answering questions about the appraisal process

- reviewing cases at the beginning of litigation to provide lawyers with an idea of further research and analysis that may be required
- documenting the value of the property in question
- preparing appraisal reports of the property that lawyers can use for pretrial proceedings and trials, as well as settlement negotiations
- reviewing appraisals presented by opposing parties (Typically, if Appraisers will be providing expert testimony, they may avoid reviewing the opposing appraisals to ensure their objectivity.)
- conducting research for additional new data

Appraisers work full time or part time.

Salaries

Salaries vary, depending on the area of specialization, experience, employer, geographical location, and other factors. For example, annual salaries for Art Appraisers range from $23,000 to $55,000 or more. Estimated annual earnings for Real Estate Appraisers (in 2000) range from $19,970 to $68,230, according to the Bureau of Labor Statistics.

Earnings for Independent Appraisers are based on hourly fees. For example, Personal Property Appraisers generally earn $100 to $200 per hour.

Employment Prospects

Professional Appraisers are employed by government agencies, insurance companies, accounting firms, real estate companies, auction houses, and other organizations. Many Appraisers are independent contractors.

Staff positions usually become available as Appraisers retire, resign, or move on to other positions. The opportunities for independent Appraisers depend on the demand for their specialization in their geographical area and the number of Appraisers locally available.

Advancement Prospects

Many Appraisers seek advancement by achieving professional reputations and earning higher incomes.

Education and Training

Appraisers complete a training period or apprenticeship in their areas of specialization under professional Appraisers. Their training programs also include study in appraisal theory, principles, procedures, ethics, and law.

Experience, Skills, and Personality Traits

Professional Appraisers are highly experienced and knowledgeable in their specialty areas. They are up to date with the latest appraisal standards and are familiar with local, regional, national, and even international markets.

Appraisers need excellent interpersonal and communication skills, as well as strong writing and research skills. Good computer skills are also essential.

Successful Appraisers share personality traits such as being impartial, trustworthy, curious, and resourceful.

Licensure and Certification

Personal property, business, and some other Appraisers do not need a state licensure.

Real estate Appraisers are required to have state licenses or certification. Requirements vary from state to state. Real estate trainees may also be required to obtain a trainee appraisal license before or soon after they are hired. For more information, contact the state regulating board in the state where you wish to work.

Many Appraisers obtain voluntary professional certification from professional associations that serve their disciplines.

Unions and Associations

Appraisers join local, state, and national professional associations that serve their areas of specialization. These associations offer certification programs, training programs, continuing education programs, and other professional services and professional resources. They also provide members with opportunities for networking with colleagues.

Some national associations are

- American Society of Appraisers (general)
- International Society of Appraisers (personal property)
- Appraisers Association of America, Inc. (personal property)
- National Association of Independent Fee Appraisers (real estate)
- National Association of Master Appraisers (real estate)
- National Association of Jewelry Appraisers
- American Society of Farm Managers and Rural Appraisers
- Institute of Business Appraisers

Tips for Entry

1. Talk with professional Appraisers in the discipline in which you wish to work to learn specific information. You may also be able to find someone willing to take you on as a trainee or an apprentice.
2. Network with professional Appraisers in the different disciplines. Most Appraisers refer clients to other Appraisers who can serve their specific needs.
3. Learn more about the appraisal industry on the Internet. Two web sites to visit are: American Society of Appraisers (*http://www.appraisers.org*) and Appraisal Foundation (*http://www.appraisalfoundation.org*).

JUDGES

STATE OR FEDERAL TRIAL JUDGE (GENERAL JURISDICTION)

CAREER PROFILE

Duties: Preside over court trials, ensuring that laws are being applied fairly and without bias; conduct hearings and conferences, research law, review court documents, supervise staff, and perform other duties as required

Alternate Titles: Federal District Court Judge, Superior Court Judge

Salary Range: $77,000 to $137,000 for state Trial Judges; $145,100 for federal Trial Judges (in 2001)

Employment Prospects: Limited

Advancement Prospects: Limited

Prerequisites:

Education/Training—A law degree

Experience—Previous experience as a lawyer

Special Skills and Personality Traits—Case management, interpersonal, and communication skills; patient, courteous, fair, objective, and hardworking

Licensure/Certification—An attorney's license generally required

CAREER LADDER

```
┌─────────────────────────────────────┐
│  Presiding Judge or Judge (in a higher │
│      state or federal court)          │
└─────────────────────────────────────┘

┌─────────────────────────────────────┐
│   Trial Court Judge (state or federal, │
│        general jurisdiction)          │
└─────────────────────────────────────┘

┌─────────────────────────────────────┐
│   Attorney or Judge (in a lower court) │
└─────────────────────────────────────┘
```

Position Description

The United States has two separate levels of court systems—the federal court system and the individual state court systems. Most civil cases (legal disputes between two parties) and criminal cases are tried in either a federal or state trial court. Trial Judges are responsible for ensuring that the law is being applied fairly and without bias throughout court proceedings. They also have the duty to make sure that court trials run smoothly and efficiently.

The various types of courts have the authority to hear specific cases. Trial courts such as federal tax courts or county family courts have limited jurisdiction because Trial Judges can only hear cases that are pertinent to their type of courts. Trial Judges in general jurisdiction trial courts can hear a wide range of cases, generally in such realms as major lawsuits and criminal felony offenses.

At the state level, general jurisdiction Trial Judges preside in superior courts, which might also be called state district courts, circuit courts, or courts of common plea. State

Trial Judges hear cases that involve the laws of their particular states. At the federal level, general jurisdiction Trial Judges preside in U.S. district courts. They hear cases that involve the federal government, constitutional issues, federal law violations, or lawsuits between citizens of different states.

Court trials may take a few days, several weeks, or months to complete. Judges must stay objective throughout the court proceedings. They cannot in any way influence the outcome of trials. They are, nevertheless, responsible for overseeing court proceedings. They make sure that lawyers, witnesses, and others follow court procedures, and that both sides of a dispute or criminal charge have the opportunity to be heard. Trial Judges determine the facts surrounding cases, ruling on the admissibility of physical evidence and witness testimony that is submitted in court.

A trial may be decided by a Trial Judge or by a jury. In other words, either a Trial Judge or a jury determines if an accused party is guilty or not guilty, or who is the wronged party in a civil dispute. A Trial Judge has the power to overrule a jury's verdict, but such instances are rare.

In a jury trial, a Trial Judge oversees the selection process of jury members. The lawyers generally do most of the interviewing and choosing of potential jurors. However, the judge may also question potential jurors, as well as dismiss them from the jury. When the trial begins, the Trial Judge instructs jurors about applicable laws and about their duty to deduce the facts from the evidence that is presented before the bench. During the jury's deliberation, the Trial Judge clarifies any legal questions that the jury may ask him or her.

In federal trial courts and most state trial courts, Trial Judges are responsible for making the formal judgment of punishment in criminal cases. Judges may grant probation or a prison sentence. In some states, Trial Judges can hand down a capital punishment sentence.

Trial Judges also preside over other hearings, such as pretrial hearings (used to determine whether there should be a trial), sentence hearings, and settlement conferences. In addition, they perform other tasks. For example, they research legal issues, review pleadings and motions, and supervise law clerks, secretaries, and other court support staff.

Each court has its own system for assigning Trial Judges to cases. Some courts, for example, make assignments by a random drawing of names; other courts assign judges according to their expertise in certain areas of law.

Trial Judges are either appointed or elected to serve. Federal judges are appointed by the president, with confirmation by the U.S. Senate. They serve a life term. State judges serve limited terms that may be renewed. In some states, Trial Judges may be initially appointed by the governor or state legislature for one term, and then are elected by the voters for additional terms. In other states, Trial Judges run for office on either a partisan (as a proclaimed member of a poltical party) or nonpartisan ballot.

Judges usually work 40 hours a week, and often work additional hours when needed.

Salaries

Salaries vary among the different courts. A 2000 survey by the National Center for State Courts reports that judges serving in state general jurisdiction courts earned an annual salary ranging from $77,439 to $136,700. The annual salary (in 2001) for federal District Court Judges was $145,100.

Employment Prospects

The number of judgeships at the state level are established by state legislatures, and at the federal level, by Congress. Creation of new positions is limited by the availability of state or federal funds. Most opportunities become available as judges retire or resign. The competition for available positions is keen and intense, as it involves being nominated for

candidacy, and then being appointed to the bench or elected by the voters.

Advancement Prospects

Advancement opportunities are limited. Judges may serve as supervisory or presiding judges for their courts, but for limited terms. Trial Judges might seek appointments to higher state and federal courts.

At both the state and federal levels, retired Trial Court Judges may continue as senior judges, assisting with court caseloads when needed.

Education and Training

Judges typically have law degrees.

Newly elected or appointed Trial Judges receive orientation training. Many states require that judges complete continuing education courses throughout their careers on the bench.

Experience, Skills, and Personality Traits

Federal courts and state courts require that general jurisdiction Trial Judges be lawyers. Judges should have strong case management skills, as well as excellent interpersonal and communication skills. They should be able to work well under stress and handle poltical pressure. Being patient, courteous, fair, objective, and hardworking are a few personality traits that successful Trial Judges share.

Licensure and Certification

Trial Judges of state courts may be required to hold current attorney's licenses.

Unions and Associations

Many Trial Judges join professional associations such as the American Judges Association to take advantage of professional services, professional resources, and networking opportunities. Judges are also eligible to join the American Bar Association; federal judges can join the Federal Bar Association.

Tips for Entry

1. Lawyers can contact the courts in which they would like to preside to learn about the application process for judicial positions.
2. Network with judges, lawyers, and others to learn about current or upcoming vacancies.
3. You can learn more about judges and the U.S. court systems on the Internet. You might start by visiting these web sites: the American Judicature Society (*http://www.ajs.org*) and the Federal Judiciary (*http:// www.uscourts.gov/faq.html*).

APPELLATE JUDGE

CAREER PROFILE

Duties: Review petitions to appeal the court decisions made in trial courts; review briefs and motions, conduct legal research, and write opinions; perform other judicial duties as required

Alternate Title: Associate Justice, Chief Justice

Salary Range: $84,000 to $157,000 for state judges (in 2000); $154,000 to $186,000 for federal judges (in 2001)

Employment Prospects: Limited

Advancement Prospects: Limited

Prerequisites:

Education/Training—A law degree

Experience—Previous experience as a lawyer or judge

Special Skills and Personality Traits—Case management, interpersonal, and communication skills; calm, respectful, fair, analytical, hardworking

Licensure/Certification—An attorney's license generally required

CAREER LADDER

```
┌─────────────────────────────────┐
│   Presiding Judge or Judge      │
│ (in a higher state or federal   │
│           court)                │
└─────────────────────────────────┘

┌─────────────────────────────────┐
│     Appellate Court Judge       │
│   (state or federal court)      │
└─────────────────────────────────┘

┌─────────────────────────────────┐
│ Attorney or Judge (in a lower court) │
└─────────────────────────────────┘
```

Position Description

The U.S. court system has two types of courts, each serving a different function. Trial courts determine the facts of criminal and civil cases and make judgments based on the testimony and evidence presented in court. If litigants disagree with the decisions, they can file petitions with the appellate courts.

Appellate Judges do not retry cases or hear new evidence. Their duty is to determine if errors have been made during the trial process which resulted in a miscarriage of justice.

Appellate cases are reviewed by a panel of Appellate Judges. They review lawyers' arguments in the form of legal briefs (written legal statements). They may also listen to brief oral arguments from the lawyers, but limit their time to between 10 and 30 minutes.

The judges make one of three decisions. They may agree with the decision made by a trial judge. They may reverse a trial court's decision. Or they may send a case back to the trial court for a retrial.

If a litigant disagrees with the appellate court's decision, the party can appeal to a higher court. The federal court system and all state court systems have two levels of appeals courts. The higher appeals courts are known as the supreme courts. The U.S. Supreme Court is the highest court in the country. (The judges in these courts are called Supreme Court Justices.)

Appellate Judges spend most of their time in chambers and law libraries, reviewing briefs and motions, researching the law, and writing and editing opinions (decisions). They spend only a few hours each week in the courtroom hearing oral arguments.

In addition to their judiciary duties, many Appellate Judges teach courses at law schools, colleges, and universities, as well as lead workshops and seminars sponsored by professional associations. Many write articles and books about the legal and judicial systems. Some also give presentations to professional associations, schools, community groups, and so on.

Appellate Judges are selected in various ways. Federal Appellate Judges and Supreme Court Justices are appointed by the president with the approval of the U.S. Senate. They serve a lifetime term. They can only be removed from office through impeachment.

At the state level, the selection process varies from state to state. Some states choose their Appellate Judges and Supreme Court Judges in either partisan or nonpartisan elections. (Partisan elections mean that judges run for office as members of a political party.) In other states, the governor appoints Appellate and Supreme Court Judges who have been nominated by a state judicial nominating committee. These state appointments may require confirmation by the state senate. After completing their first term, governor-appointed judges usually face a retention election, in which state, county, or district voters decide whether to keep those judges in office.

In most states, Appellate Judges and Supreme Court Judges serve terms between six to 15 years. A few states allow judges to hold lifetime terms until the age of 70.

Judges usually work 40 hours a week, and often work additional hours when needed.

Salaries

Salaries vary, depending on factors such as experience and geographical location. According to a 2000 survey by the National Center for State Courts, appellate judges generally earned between $85,887 and $146,994. Associate Justices of the highest state courts earned between $83,550 and $153,052, while Chief Justices earned between $84,993 to $156,969.

Salaries for federal judges in 2001 were: $153,900 for Appellate Judges, $178,300 for Associate Chief Justices of the Supreme Court, and $186,300 for the Supreme Court Chief Justice.

Employment Prospects

The competition for judgeships is keen and intense, as it involves being nominated for candidacy and then being appointed to the bench or elected by the voters. Most opportunities become available as Appellate Judges retire or resign.

Advancement Prospects

Appellate Judges may be selected as chief judges of their courts, which are administrative positions for limited terms. At both the state and federal levels, retired Appellate Judges may continue as senior judges, assisting with court caseloads when needed.

Education and Training

New Appellate Judges in federal and state courts complete orientation training. Many states require that judges complete continuing education courses throughout their careers on the bench.

Experience, Skills, and Personality Traits

Most states require that candidates for Appellate Judges be practicing lawyers or have practiced for a minimum number of years. For federal appellate judgeships, candidates are usually lawyers, state court judges, bankruptcy judges, U.S. magistrate judges, and law professors.

Appellate Judges need strong case management skills, as well as excellent interpersonal and communication skills. Successful Appellate Judges share several personality traits, such as being calm, respectful, fair, analytical, and hardworking.

Licensure and Certification

A state may require that its Appellate Judges be members of its state attorney bar association. Some states require that candidates be a bar association member for a minimum number of years.

Unions and Associations

Appellate Judges join professional associations such as the American Judges Association and the American Bar Association to take advantage of professional resources, professional services, and networking opportunities. Many federal judges join the Federal Bar Association.

Tips for Entry

1. To gain experience in appellate courts, you might obtain internships while in law school. You might also apply for law clerk positions with Appellate Judges.
2. You can learn more about appellate courts on the Internet. Many state and federal appellate courts have web pages. To get a list of web pages, enter any of these keywords in a search engine: *appellate court, state appellate court,* or *federal appellate court.*

MUNICIPAL JUDGE

CAREER PROFILE

Duties: Preside over criminal and civil trials in limited jurisdiction courts; perform judicial duties as required

Alternate Titles: City Judge, Town Judge, Village Judge, Police Court Judge

Salary Range: $19,000 to $135,000

Employment Prospects: Limited

Advancement Prospects: Limited

Prerequisites:

Education/Training—Orientation training for new judges; annual completion of continuing education units may be required

Experience—Several years of experience as practicing lawyers

Special Skills and Personality Traits—Case management, interpersonal, and communication skills; patient, courteous, fair, objective, hardworking

Licensure/Certification—Requires an attorney's license in most locations

CAREER LADDER

```
┌──────────────────────────────────────────┐
│        Presiding Judge or Judge          │
│  (in a higher state or federal court)    │
└──────────────────────────────────────────┘

┌──────────────────────────────────────────┐
│            Municipal Judge               │
└──────────────────────────────────────────┘

┌──────────────────────────────────────────┐
│               Attorney                   │
└──────────────────────────────────────────┘
```

Position Description

Municipal Judges are trial judges in limited jurisdiction courts called municipal, or city, courts. The municipal courts are the lowest level of state courts. They are sometimes known as police courts, city courts, township courts, or village courts. The jurisdiction of these courts extends to the boundaries of the municipalities—cities, towns, boroughs, or villages.

Municipal judges preside over both civil and criminal trials. The types of cases vary from court to court. In general, Municipal Judges have the authority to hear any or all of these types of cases:

- civil lawsuits that involve monetary values ranging between $3,000 and $25,000 in property or cash, depending on the municipality
- violations of municipal codes such as in landlord-tenant cases or in cases involving building infractions
- criminal misdemeanors such as disorderly conduct, shoplifting, simple assault, and lewdness
- domestic violence cases
- violations of motor vehicle and traffic laws, including parking tickets, speeding, reckless driving, and driving under the influence of alcohol or drugs

In some courts, Municipal Judges may conduct preliminary hearings for defendants accused of committing felonies.

Municipal Judges conduct jury and nonjury trials as well as pretrial conferences and other hearings. Their duties also include reading motions and pleadings, researching legal issues, and supervising their court staff. Municipal Judges may also handle the issuing of court processes, such as summons, subpoenas, and warrants.

Depending on the municipality, Municipal Judges may be appointed by mayors or city councils or elected by city voters. They serve limited terms, usually four to 10 years.

Municipal Judges may serve on a part-time or full-time basis.

Salaries

Salaries vary, depending on factors such as employer and geographical location. According to the Bureau of Labor

Statistics, the estimated annual salary (in 2000) for most judges, including Municipal Judges, ranged between $19,320 and $134,660.

Employment Prospects

Opportunities are limited, and usually become available as Municipal Judges retire or resign. Competition for positions is typically intense due to the political nature of obtaining appointments or being elected by voters in a municipality.

Advancement Prospects

Municipal Judges can be selected to serve as supervisory or presiding judges in their courts, but these are for limited terms. Many Municipal Judges seek appointments to district courts, other state courts, or federal courts.

Education and Training

Newly elected or appointed Municipal Judges receive orientation training. Some municipal courts require their judges to complete a minimum of continuing education units each year.

Experience, Skills, and Personality Traits

Most Municipal Judges are experienced lawyers who have worked in their communities for several years. Some municipalities require judicial candidates to have been practicing lawyers for a minimum number of years. In some municipalities, candidates are not required to be lawyers, but must meet special training requirements.

Municipal Judges, like all judges, need excellent case management skills, as well as superior interpersonal and communication skills. They should be able to work well under stress and to handle political pressure. Being patient, courteous, fair, objective, and hardworking are a few personality traits that successful Municipal Judges share.

Licensure and Certification

Municipal Judges may be required to hold attorney's licenses.

Unions and Associations

Municipal Judges join professional associations to take advantage of training programs, professional resources, and other professional services. Their membership also provides them with various opportunities to network with judges, lawyers, and other professionals. Many Municipal Judges are members of their local or state municipal court associations and attorney bar associations.

Some national professional associations that Municipal Judges might join are the American Judges Association, the American Judicature Society, and the American Bar Association.

Tips for Entry

1. Observe the proceedings in a municipal court room to get an idea of what Municipal Judges do.
2. You will need to build up a support base in your community to become a Municipal Judge. To start, get involved in community service and social activities. Also network with elected officials, lawyers, and judges, as well as local business people and citizens.
3. Learn more about municipal courts and judges on the Internet. Many municipal courts have web pages. To get a list of web pages, enter the keywords *municipal court* in a search engine.

FAMILY COURT JUDGE

CAREER PROFILE

Duties: Hear cases that involve children and family issues such as divorce, child abuse, domestic violence, and juvenile delinquency; perform judicial duties as required

Alternate Titles: Family Judge, Municipal Judge, District Judge

Salary Range: $19,000 to $135,000

Employment Prospects: Limited

Advancement Prospects: Limited

Prerequisites:

Education/Training—Orientation training for new judges; required or voluntary training throughout career

Experience—Experience as attorneys in family law practice; knowledgeable about psychology, child development and related disciplines

Special Skills and Personality Traits—Case management, writing, analytical, interpersonal, and communication skills; patient, respectful, fair, impartial, decisive, dedicated

Licensure/Certification—An attorney's license may be required

CAREER LADDER

```
┌─────────────────────────────┐
│   Presiding Judge or Judge  │
│     (in a higher court)     │
└─────────────────────────────┘

┌─────────────────────────────┐
│     Family Court Judge      │
└─────────────────────────────┘

┌─────────────────────────────┐
│          Attorney           │
└─────────────────────────────┘
```

Position Description

Family Court Judges are trial judges in special limited-jurisdiction courts. They conduct legal proceedings that focus solely on problems and issues concerning families and children. Family members or social agencies may submit petitions to have their cases heard in family courts.

Family courts are established at the local and state government levels. Their main purpose is to help and protect families whose unity is being threatened and to help families find ways to stay together. These courts also make sure that children are receiving care, guidance, and discipline that is in their best interest. Thus, to achieve their objectives, family courts work closely with social service agencies and other resources in their communities.

Family Court Judges preside over a wide range of family law cases. These can vary from one court to the next. Some family law cases that a Family Court Judge may have the authority to hear are:

- divorce (or dissolution of marriage), legal separation, and annulment
- alimony and child support
- child custody and visitation
- child abuse and neglect
- legal guardianships of children and disabled persons
- paternity
- adoption
- termination of parental rights
- child protection cases, which involves removing children from families and placing them in foster care
- juvenile delinquency, including law violations and status offenses
- domestic violence and other criminal offenses that happen within a family
- commitment of mentally ill family members to hospitals or other health care facilities
- probate of wills as well as the administration of trusts and estates

In family courts, cases are tried only before the Family Court Judges. In other words, the judges hear the testimony and make the final decision. The legal proceedings are called hearings, and are less formal than trials. Family Court Judges conduct unbiased and impartial hearings in an orderly procedure. The opposing parties each have the opportunity to present evidence that supports their case.

After hearing the testimony, Family Court Judges decide if the facts of the case have been proved. If they have not, the case is dismissed. If the facts have been proved as true, then the judges decide what should happen to the parties. For example, in a child custody case, a judge may decide which parent has physical custody of the child. Or, in a juvenile crime case, a judge may decide to send the child to a prison for juveniles or place the child on probation on the condition that the child and family attend weekly counseling sessions.

Generally, family court hearings are open to the public. But on occasion, judges close the courtroom to the public to protect the privacy of the parties. They may also exclude certain people from the courtroom if they feel children are at risk of being harmed.

Family Court Judges also conduct other types of hearings and conferences, such as status hearings and emergency hearings. Their duties also include reviewing motions and pleadings, reading legal documents, researching legal issues, and writing orders and opinions. In addition, they supervise a staff of law clerks, judicial assistants, and other court support staff.

Family Court Judges serve terms that typically vary from four to 12 years depending on the courts. Family Court Judges are selected in one of two ways. They may be appointed initially by state or local executives and then run in a retention election after serving their first term. Or they may be elected by popular vote in partisan or nonpartisan elections. In some localities, they may be elected or appointed specifically to a Family Court Judge position. In other areas, judges are elected or appointed as Trial Judges and then assigned to positions in family court.

Family Court Judges work 40 hours a week, putting in additional hours when needed.

Salaries

Salaries vary, depending on geographical location and other factors. According to the Bureau of Labor Statistics the 2000 estimated annual salary for most judges, including Family Court Judges, ranged between $19,320 and $134,660.

Employment Prospects

Most positions become available when judges complete their terms or when they resign, retire, or leave for other reasons before their terms end. A court may create new positions to meet the demands of increasing caseloads if funds are available.

Advancement Prospects

Family Court Judges may be selected to serve as supervisory or presiding judges for limited terms. As chief judges, they are responsible for overseeing the daily administrative operations of their courts. Retired judges may continue to serve as senior judges, assisting with court caseloads when needed.

Many Family Court Judges pursue appointments for judgeships in higher state courts as well as in federal courts.

Education and Training

New Family Court Judges receive orientation training. Many states require that judges complete annual legal and judicial training and continuing education programs.

Throughout their careers, Family Court Judges voluntarily participate in relevant training and education programs related to juvenile justice, child development, family issues, and so forth.

Experience, Skills, and Personality Traits

Many Family Court Judges are lawyers who have practiced for several years in the area of family law. In addition, they are knowledgeable about psychology, child development, and related disciplines.

Family Court Judges need excellent case management, writing, and analytical skills, as well as strong interpersonal and communication skills. Being patient, respectful, fair, impartial, decisive, and dedicated are a few personality traits that successful Family Court Judges share.

Licensure and Certification

Family Court Judges may be required to hold current attorney's licenses.

Unions and Associations

Many Family Court Judges join professional associations to take advantage of professional services and resources as well as networking opportunities with their colleagues. One organization that specifically serves their profession is the National Council of Juvenile and Family Court Judges. Some other national associations are the American Judges Association and the American Bar Association. Many Family Court Judges also join local and state attorney bars.

Tips for Entry

1. Volunteer with community agencies that serve the different social needs of children, youth, or families. Find out if the area of family law is right for you.

Read about different family issues. Observe family courts in action. Visit community and social agencies that work with children, youth, or families. You might also volunteer or obtain jobs or internships with a social or community agency.

2. You can learn more about family courts and family law on the Internet. To find relevant web pages, enter any of these keywords in a search engine: *family court, family court judge,* or *family law.*

BANKRUPTCY JUDGE

CAREER PROFILE

Duties: Oversee the administration of bankruptcy cases; conduct conferences, hearings, and trials; make final decisions on cases; perform duties as required

Alternate Titles: Chief Bankruptcy Judge

Salary: $133,492

Employment Prospects: Limited

Advancement Prospects: Limited

Prerequisites:

Education/Training—Training and education programs throughout career

Experience—Minimum of five years in active law practice or other acceptable qualifying experience

Special Skills and Personality Traits—Case management, interpersonal, and communication skills; patient, courteous, fair, objective, and hardworking

Licensure/Certification—An attorney's license

CAREER LADDER

```
┌─────────────────────────────┐
│   Chief Bankruptcy Judge    │
└─────────────────────────────┘

┌─────────────────────────────┐
│      Bankruptcy Judge       │
└─────────────────────────────┘

┌─────────────────────────────┐
│         Attorney            │
└─────────────────────────────┘
```

Position Description

In the United States, debtors who are experiencing such deep financial difficulties that they cannot pay their creditors may file for bankruptcy in federal courts. Bankruptcy is a legal procedure that protects debtors so that they can reorganize their finances in order to pay off some or all of their debts. The federal district courts have jurisdiction over bankruptcy cases. Bankruptcy Judges are in charge of overseeing the administration of these cases. They are also responsible for deciding disputes that creditors may have with bankruptcy cases.

Debtors may be persons, businesses, corporations, municipalities, government agencies, and institutions. When debtors file their petitions, the courts automatically place an order, called a stay, on their debts. This order prevents creditors from taking any kind of collections action while the stay is in effect.

There are generally two types of bankruptcy proceedings. In one proceeding, the bankruptcy court sells most of a debtor's property and distributes the cash among the creditors. In the other proceeding, a debtor proposes a financial plan for paying back some or all of his or her debts to the creditors. Bankruptcy Judges do not handle the day-to-day management of individual cases. Instead, they appoint trustees to administer individual cases.

Bankruptcy Judges hold conferences and hearings with debtors and trustees in person or by telephone. They have the authority to make final decisions on bankruptcy cases. For example, they approve or disapprove the petitions that debtors initially file. They approve or disapprove repayment plans. They can also discharge some or all debts in a case. That means a debtor does not have to repay creditors for those debts that a Bankruptcy Judge discharges.

Bankruptcy Judges also conduct trials that involve disputes between the debtors and their creditors. Litigation in bankruptcy courts is conducted the same way as in trial courts. There are pretrial proceedings, settlement conferences, and so on. Cases may be heard before judges or juries.

Bankruptcy Judges handle various tasks in their work. For example, they:

- schedule weekly or monthly calendars
- review motions
- research the law for legal precedents
- write orders and opinions, following specific formats

Bankruptcy judges are appointed for 14-year terms by the judges of the U.S. Court of Appeals. They may be reappointed for unlimited terms.

On occasion, Bankruptcy Judges are temporarily assigned to other bankruptcy courts where judges are handling heavy caseloads.

Salaries

All U.S. Bankruptcy Judges earn the same salary. In 2001, their annual salary was $133,492.

Employment Prospects

There are more than 300 active Bankruptcy Judges. The number of bankruptcy judges is determined by Congress, based on recommendations of the Judicial Conference of the United States.

Opportunities typically become available as judicial terms of Bankruptcy Judges end or as they retire or resign before the end of their terms. Additional positions in a bankruptcy court may be created to meet increasing caseloads.

Advancement Prospects

Advancement opportunities are limited. Bankruptcy Judges may serve as supervisory or presiding judges for their courts, but for limited terms. Retired judges may continue as senior judges, assisting with court caseloads when needed.

Education and Training

Newly appointed Bankruptcy Judges receive orientation training. They also complete training and education programs throughout their careers. Many of these programs are sponsored by the U.S. Judicial Conference's Bankruptcy Judges Education Committee, the Federal Judicial Center, and other organizations.

Experience, Skills, and Personality Traits

Candidates must have actively practiced law for at least five years. They may also qualify by having had experience as:

- a state judge
- a U.S. magistrate judge, bankruptcy referee, or other federal judicial officer
- a government attorney
- a judicial law clerk

Bankruptcy Judges need strong case management skills, as well as excellent interpersonal and communication skills. Some personality traits that successful Bankruptcy Judges share are being patient, courteous, fair, objective, and hardworking.

Licensure and Certification

To become a Bankruptcy Judge, a candidate must be licensed to practice in at least one state, the District of Columbia, or the Commonwealth of Puerto Rico.

Unions and Associations

Many Bankruptcy Judges join professional associations to take advantage of professional services and resources as well as networking opportunities with their colleagues. One organization that serves their profession is the National Conference of Bankruptcy Judges. Some other organizations are the American Judges Association, the American Bar Association, and the Federal Bar Association.

Tips for Entry

1. While in law school, get an idea if bankruptcy law might be an area that suits you. For example, you might obtain an internship with a bankruptcy court or a law firm that specializes in bankruptcy law.
2. Use the Internet to learn more about bankruptcy courts. Many of the courts have their own web sites. To get a list, enter the keywords *bankruptcy court* in a search engine. To learn more about bankruptcy on the Internet, enter the keywords *bankruptcy* or *bankruptcy law.*

ADMINISTRATIVE LAW JUDGE

CAREER PROFILE

Duties: Preside over legal proceedings for federal, state, or local government agencies; perform judicial duties such as conducting conferences, reviewing motions, researching law, and writing opinions

Alternate Titles: Hearing Officer, Hearing Examiner, Adjudicator, Appeals Referee

Salary Range: $32,000 to $112,000 or more

Employment Prospects: Fair

Advancement Prospects: Limited

Prerequisites:

Education/Training—Orientation training; completion of mandatory and voluntary continuing education programs

Experience—Experience as a trial lawyer or other qualifying work experience; knowledgeable about administrative law and procedures and familiar with the subject matter (such as social security) of the legal proceedings

Special Skills and Personality Traits—Analytical, organizational; legal writing, communication, and interpersonal skills; objective, decisive, unbiased, calm, respectful

Licensure/Certification—An attorney's license is generally required

CAREER LADDER

```
┌─────────────────────────────────────┐
│   Chief Administrative Law Judge     │
└─────────────────────────────────────┘

┌─────────────────────────────────────┐
│     Administrative Law Judge         │
└─────────────────────────────────────┘

┌─────────────────────────────────────┐
│             Attorney                 │
└─────────────────────────────────────┘
```

Position Description

Administrative Law Judges (ALJs) conduct legal proceedings, or administrative hearings, for government agencies. They have the authority to make rulings on disputes and complaints that individuals, businesses, or others may have with government agencies. ALJs are more commonly known as Hearing Officers.

In the United States, federal, state, and local government agencies are responsible for administering laws in such areas as health, welfare, tax, environment, labor, professional licensure, workplace safety and public utilities regulations. Government agencies create and enforce the regulations that govern the activities of businesses and industries, as well as the issuance of government benefits (such as Social Security or unemployment benefits). They also establish the regulations for the enforcement of laws, such as environmental, civil rights, and employment laws.

Administrative Law Judges generally preside over various types of cases. For example:

- An individual disputes an agency's decision to deny, limit, or end his or her government benefits.
- A business or corporation disputes an agency's ruling on how it can run its activities or services.
- A government agency claims that an individual, business, or organization has violated a government law or regulation—such as a workplace safety regulation, civil rights law, environmental law, building code, or tax rule.
- An individual claims that a business, licensed by a government agency, has violated the agency's regulations.

Although ALJs are employed by government agencies, they are ethically bound to conduct fair and impartial legal proceedings. They do not discuss cases with the involved parties, including the government agencies.

Administrative hearings are informal, but follow specific procedures. The length of a hearing may be as short as 15 minutes or as long as several weeks. Unlike court trials, administrative hearings do not involve juries. Also, individuals may represent themselves or choose to be represented by lawyers. ALJs do not have the authority to appoint or select attorneys for individuals. Nor can they order the losing party to pay the other party's legal costs.

ALJs may conduct hearings in person as well as by telephone or videoconference. At the hearings, ALJs listen to the arguments of the opposing parties who may present evidence to support their cases. When the hearings are complete, ALJs review the testimony and evidence and make their decisions.

Depending on the type of case, ALJs make either a final decision or a recommended decision. Final decisions are issued to the parties involved in the case. Recommended decisions are sent to the proper officials within the government agency who make the final decisions.

If a party disagrees with the decision, the party can file an appeal with the proper administrative appeals board within the agency. In some states and municipalities, administrative appeals are filed with the courts.

Administrative Law Judges handle a large number of cases each year. In addition to conducting hearings, they perform other duties. They also conduct prehearings and settlement conferences. They review motions, research legal precedents, write decisions, advise agency officials on matters of law, develop procedural rules, and so on.

ALJs might work alone or as members of a hearing board. Some ALJs are required to travel to other locations to conduct hearings.

State Administrative Law Judges work full time or part time. Some state agencies hire ALJs on a contractual basis, paying them on an hourly or daily rate.

Salaries

Salaries for ALJs vary, depending on experience, employer, and geographical location. Earnings are generally higher in metropolitan areas, and federal ALJs typically earn higher salaries than state ALJs. According to the Bureau of Labor statistics, the estimated annual salary for most ALJs (in 2000) ranged between $32,970 and $111,590.

The basic pay in 2001 for federal Administrative Law Judges ranged from $82,100 to $125,700. ALJs who live in metropolitan areas receive additional pay due to the higher cost of living.

Employment Prospects

ALJs are employed by federal, state and local government agencies. As of 2001, about 1,400 ALJs were employed by the federal government. The Social Security Administration, the U.S. Department of Labor, and the National Labor Relations Board employ the largest number of ALJs.

The competition is high for available positions at both the state and federal level. Generally most opportunities become available as ALJs resign or retire. The creation of new positions is limited to the availability of funding.

Advancement Prospects

Advancement opportunities are limited to such positions as supervisory or chief ALJs. Many pursue ALJ positions with other federal or state agencies, which usually means an increase in pay.

Education and Training

New ALJs receive orientation training. Throughout their careers, most ALJs complete mandatory as well as voluntary training and continuing education programs. Along with building up their legal and judiciary skills, they continue to learn more about the topics of the various cases that they handle each day.

Experience, Skills, and Personality Traits

Requirements vary from one administrative agency to the next. In general, agencies require that each candidate have several years' experience as a lawyer that includes trial experience in courts or before administrative agencies. Agencies may substitute other work experience for those who have served as a judge of a court of record, a hearing officer or examiner of an administrative agency, or a similar position. In addition, candidates are knowledgeable about administrative law and procedures, and are familiar with the subject matter (such as workers' compensation or social security) with which they will be working.

ALJs must have excellent analytical, organizational, and legal writing skills. They also need communication and interpersonal skills to work effectively with the general public, attorneys, and agencies.

Some personality traits that successful ALJs share are being objective, decisive, unbiased, calm, and respectful.

Licensure and Certification

Employers require or prefer that ALJs hold current attorney's licenses.

Unions and Associations

Many ALJs join state and national professional associations to take advantage of professional resources, professional services, and networking opportunities. Two national organizations specifically for ALJs are the National Association of Administrative Law Judges and the National Conference of Administrative Law Judges. One organization specifically for federal ALJs is the Federal Administrative Law Judges Conference.

Tips for Entry

1. Contact administrative hearing offices of executive agencies for whom you would like to work. Ask those offices about their requirements for ALJs and their selection process. If possible, talk with ALJs to learn more about their work.

2. Although federal ALJs work in different agencies, they are hired under a program administered by the Office of Personnel Management. To learn more, contact the nearest U.S. Office of Personnel Management, or visit its web site at *http://www.opm.gov.*

3. You can learn more about administrative law and ALJs on the Internet. Enter any of these keywords in a search engine to find pertinent web pages: *administrative law, administrative law judge, administrative law office,* or *administrative law division.*

COURT SUPPORT STAFF

JUDICIAL LAW CLERK

CAREER PROFILE

Duties: Provide legal support to a judge; conduct legal research; provide legal analysis; draft opinions, and other legal documents; perform other duties as required

Salary Range: $35,000 to $95,000 (for federal and states' highest courts)

Employment Prospects: Good

Advancement Prospects: Limited

Prerequisites:

Education/Training—A law degree; on-the-job training

Experience—Knowledgeable about legal principles, statutory and case law, court rules, and court procedures; may require one year of legal experience; for career law clerks, experience as law clerks or practicing attorneys may be required

Special Skills and Personality Traits—Legal research, legal writing, computer, communication, analytical, interpersonal, and teamwork skills; mature, detail-oriented, discreet, impartial, honest, flexible

Licensure/Certification—An attorney's license may be required

CAREER LADDER

```
┌─────────────────────────────────────┐
│  Attorney (in any work setting)     │
│  or Other Law-Related Profession    │
└─────────────────────────────────────┘

┌─────────────────────────────────────┐
│         Judicial Law Clerk          │
└─────────────────────────────────────┘

┌─────────────────────────────────────┐
│            Law Student              │
└─────────────────────────────────────┘
```

Position Description

Judicial Law Clerks provide legal support services to judges, helping them prepare for hearings and trials. They work directly with judges in trial and appellate courts as well as in administrative offices for government agencies.

Conducting legal research is one major responsibility of Judicial Court Clerks. They provide pertinent information for the various cases that are brought before a judge. When judges require additional information to help them decide on a motion or ruling, they assign Law Clerks to research the issues. Law Clerks search for laws, court decisions, briefs, opinions, and so forth that may provide interpretations applicable to the judge's case. Law Clerks conduct their research in law libraries and on computer and Internet databases.

Another responsibility is to provide judges with legal analysis. For example, Judicial Law Clerks prepare bench memorandums for judges to help them decide the proper disposition of cases. A bench memorandum (or bench memo) is a summary of a case that explains and analyzes each party's

position. It includes a statement of the issues involved, and may also include suggestions or recommendations.

Judicial Law Clerks are also involved with drafting opinions, orders, and other legal documents. Judges review and edit these first drafts into their final documents. The Law Clerks must follow specific guidelines and formats for composing the various documents. They make sure that they use formal and precise language and that all citations are correct.

Judicial Law Clerks perform other duties which vary from court to court. For example, they might:

- review drafts of judges' works for errors of fact and law
- proofread legal documents and correct grammar, spelling, punctuation, and typographical errors
- maintain law libraries
- review professional journals and recent opinions to keep themselves and judges up to date on current legal issues
- serve as the judge's contact person for attorneys
- perform clerical and administrative tasks

Judicial clerkships are temporary positions that last one to two years. Judicial Law Clerks are usually recent law graduates or have been practicing law for a short time. They apply for these short-term positions to gain firsthand experience working within the court systems, as well as to gain valuable experience working under the guidance and support of judges.

Law Clerks may be assigned to individual judges or work for several judges.

Salaries

Salaries vary, depending on factors such as employer, experience, and geographical location. Federal courts typically pay higher salaries than state and municipal courts. According to a 2001 survey by the *National Law Journal,* the annual salary for federal law clerks ranged from $43,326 to $94,862; and for first-year clerks in the states' highest courts, $35,206 to $60,888.

Employment Prospects

Judicial Law Clerks are employed by state and federal courts as well as by administrative hearing offices in government agencies. Opportunities are available yearly to replace Law Clerks whose terms are ending. However, the competition for judicial clerkships is keen.

Judicial clerkships are typically temporary positions. On occasion, judges hire Law Clerks on a permanent basis.

Advancement Prospects

In general, Judicial Law Clerks use their experience as the beginning step leading to their attorney careers. Their next step may be in positions as law firm associates, government lawyers, prosecutors, public defenders, corporate lawyers, public interest attorneys, solo practitioners, and so on. Judicial Law Clerks can also pursue other legal-related careers such as becoming legal researchers, legal reporters, or law professors.

Education and Training

Judges require that Judicial Law Clerks be graduates of accredited law schools.

Judicial Law Clerks receive on-the-job training.

Experience, Skills, and Personality Traits

Qualifications vary with the different judges. Generally, candidates must be knowledgeable about legal principles, statutory and case law, court rules, and court procedures. Some judges require or prefer that candidates have at least one year of legal experience. Many judges prefer candidates who have moot court experience, who have worked on their school's law review, or who have had legal articles published.

For career clerk positions, some judges hire only experienced law clerks or practicing attorneys.

Judicial Law Clerks need excellent legal research skills, including the use of CD-ROM and Internet databases. They also must have strong writing and analytical skills. In addition they need good communication, interpersonal, and teamwork skills.

Being mature, detail-oriented, discreet, impartial, honest, and flexible are some personality traits that successful Judicial Law Clerks share.

Licensure and Certification

Judges may require (or strongly prefer) that Judicial Law Clerks hold valid attorney's licenses.

Unions and Associations

Judicial Law Clerks join local, state, and national legal associations to take advantage of networking opportunities and other professional services and resources. Many Law Clerks are members of their local and state bar associations. Many also belong to other legal associations such as the American Bar Association or the National Lawyers Association.

Tips for Entry

1. Contact the judges for whom you would like to work to learn about their specific requirements and application process.
2. Start your research into judicial clerkships in your first year of law school. Some judges offer clerkships to students who are still in their second year of law school. The clerkships would begin right after their graduation.
3. You can learn more about judicial clerkships on the Internet. One web site you might visit is "Welcome to the World of Judicial Clerkships" *(http://www. judicialclerkships.com),* which is maintained by DMS Consulting. To find other relevant web sites, enter these keywords in a search engine: *judicial clerkships* or *judicial law clerk.*

JUDICIAL ASSISTANT

CAREER PROFILE

Duties: Perform various administrative and clerical tasks for judges

Alternate Titles: Judicial Secretary, Secretary to Judge, Legal Secretary

Salary Range: about $22,000 to $51,000

Employment Prospects: Fair

Advancement Prospects: Good

Prerequisites:

Education/Training—A high school diploma; legal secretary or paralegal training is desirable

Experience—One or more years of legal clerical, secretarial, or paralegal experience; familiarity with court functions, court procedures, legal terminology, and legal documents

Special Skills and Personality Traits—Proficiency in business English, grammar, punctuation, and spelling; secretarial, clerical, computer, communication, interpersonal, teamwork, organizational, and self-management skills; positive, tactful, patient, responsible, reliable, detail-oriented

Licensure/Certification—None required

CAREER LADDER

```
┌─────────────────────────────────┐
│    Senior Judicial Assistant    │
│   or Administrative Assistant   │
└─────────────────────────────────┘

┌─────────────────────────────────┐
│       Judicial Assistant        │
└─────────────────────────────────┘

┌─────────────────────────────────┐
│  Court Clerk, Legal Secretary,  │
│          or Paralegal           │
└─────────────────────────────────┘
```

Position Description

Judicial Assistants work directly with judges, performing various administrative and clerical tasks. They also help judges oversee daily judicial activities so that courts work effectively and efficiently.

Their duties vary, depending on their experience and abilities as well as the particular needs of the judges. For example, experienced Judicial Assistants are responsible for supervising and training clerical staff, conducting job performance evaluations, and assisting judges with the preparation of budgets.

Most Judicial Assistants fulfill the role of liaison for judges. They are the judges' contact person for attorneys, law enforcement officers, other judge's offices, court administrators, social service agencies, the general public, the media, and others. Judicial Assistants provide general information about court policies and procedures in person or over the phone. They also give out information about court activities to appropriate personnel. In addition, they notify appropriate professionals, such as social service workers, whom judges are appointing to cases.

Another major duty for Judicial Assistants is the preparation of correspondence, legal documents, administrative reports, and court forms, such as court processes, court orders, and affidavits. Using typewriters, word processors, or computers, they produce final products from written drafts, notes, dictation tapes, or oral instructions. They make sure that their work follows proper formats and guidelines. They also check for completeness and accuracy of facts, as well as for correct grammar, punctuation, and spelling. Many Judicial Assistants are assigned the task of preparing routine reports, forms, and correspondence for judges to review and sign.

Most Judicial Assistants manage the court and professional calendars for judges. Assistants schedule appointments for motions, pretrial hearings, conferences, trials, and so forth, as well as mark the dates for committee meetings, professional events, and other professional conferences. They keep judges current with any date changes and cancellations.

Many Judicial Assistants help judges with case management. They update information in case files. They advise judges, attorneys, or litigants about any lack of information, and may remind them about filing deadlines. Judicial Assistants also review case files before scheduled hearings for accuracy and completeness of information as well as for compliance with required formats.

Here are a few other duties that Judicial Assistants might perform:

- conduct routine research for legal documents, such as finding the appropriate legal codes for judicial reports
- assist with jury management
- prepare the official record of court proceedings that includes judgments, orders, and decrees
- help maintain law libraries
- make travel and lodging arrangements for judges
- receive and process court fines

Judicial Assistants also perform a wide variety of routine clerical tasks. These include distributing mail, photocopying, answering telephones, ordering office supplies, maintaining files, updating databases, and so on.

Judicial Assistants may be assigned to serve one judge or several judges. They typically work 40 hours a week.

Salaries
No salary surveys are available for Judicial Assistants. However, a look at the earnings of legal secretaries (their counterparts) can give a general idea of what Judicial Assistants may earn. According to the Bureau of Labor Statistics, the estimated annual salary for legal secretaries in 2000 ranged between $22,440 and $50,970.

Employment Prospects
Judicial Assistants are hired by state and federal courts. Most opportunities become available as assistants retire, resign, or transfer to other positions. On occasion, courts may create new positions to meet staffing needs, as long as funds are available.

Advancement Prospects
Judicial Assistants generally realize advancement by earning higher wages and being assigned complex responsibilities.

With additional experience and education or training, Judicial Assistants can pursue related careers, by becoming paralegals, lawyers, clerks of courts, or court administrators.

Education and Training
Judicial Assistants must have a high school diploma or a general equivalency diploma. Having additional legal secretarial or paralegal training is considered highly desirable by many employers. For higher-level positions, employers generally prefer candidates with college degrees or college backgrounds.

Judicial Assistants receive on-the-job training. Throughout their careers, they enroll in voluntary and mandatory training and continuing education programs to enhance their skills.

Experience, Skills, and Personality Traits
Employers usually require that entry-level candidates have one or more years of qualifying legal clerical, secretarial, or paralegal work experience. In addition, candidates must be familiar with court functions and procedures, legal terminology, and legal documents. They are also highly proficient in business English, grammar, spelling, and punctuation.

Judicial Assistants must have basic secretarial and clerical skills as well as good computer skills. In addition, they need strong communication, interpersonal, and teamwork skills in order to work well with judges, lawyers, and others of various backgrounds. Furthermore, assistants should have excellent organizational and self-management skills— such as the ability to work independently, prioritize tasks, understand and follow instructions, handle stressful situations, and so on.

Being positive, tactful, patient, responsible, reliable and detail-oriented are some personality traits that Judicial Assistants share.

Unions and Associations
Many Judicial Assistants join local and state professional associations to take advantage of networking opportunities, training programs, and other professional services and resources. Judicial Assistants are also eligible to join NALS . . . the association for legal professionals.

Tips for Entry
1. Some courts have open recruitment for Judicial Assistant positions. Applicants who successfully pass the selection process are placed on an eligibility list, from which candidates are chosen when openings become available.
2. Contact courts directly to learn about job openings and their application processes.
3. Use the Internet to learn more about the court systems. For general information about state courts, visit the National Center for State Courts web site (http://www.ncsc.dni.us). For information about federal courts, visit the Federal Judiciary Home Page (http://www.uscourts.gov), which is maintained by the Administrative Office of the U.S. Courts.

BAILIFF
(LOCAL AND STATE COURTS)

CAREER PROFILE

Duties: Preserve order in courtrooms during trial proceedings; maintain security in courtrooms and surrounding areas; protect judges and jurors; guard criminal defendants; perform other duties as required

Alternate Title: Court Service Officer

Salary Range: $17,000 to $53,000

Employment Prospects: Fair

Advancement Prospects: Limited

Prerequisites:

Education/Training—Completion of bailiff training

Experience—One or more years of law enforcement experience; knowledgeable about court security, court functions, and court proceedings

Special Skills and Personality Traits—Interpersonal, computer, communication, and self-management skills; courteous, tactful, firm, reliable

Licensure/Certification—Peace officer certification

CAREER LADDER

```
┌─────────────────────────┐
│      Senior Bailiff      │
└─────────────────────────┘

┌─────────────────────────┐
│         Bailiff          │
└─────────────────────────┘

┌─────────────────────────┐
│     Bailiff Trainee      │
└─────────────────────────┘
```

Position Description

In municipal and state courts, security duties are performed by Bailiffs. They are responsible for preserving order in courtrooms during trial proceedings, as well as maintaining the security of the courtrooms and the surrounding areas. Bailiffs also provide protection to the judges and jurors, and ensure that criminal defendants are safe and secure.

Sheriff's offices are usually responsible for providing bailiff services to local and district courts. In some municipal courts, police departments handle the bailiff services. State police departments typically provide bailiff services for state supreme courts. (In federal courts, the court security and bailiff duties are provided by the U.S. Marshals Service.)

Bailiffs perform a wide variety of tasks before, during, and after court proceedings. They usually work in teams of two or more. Before each court session, Bailiffs inspect courtrooms for security and cleanliness. They seat witnesses and jurors in specific areas of the courtroom. They open each session of court by announcing the entrance of the judge. Bailiffs swear in witnesses before they testify in court. They escort juries between courtrooms and jury rooms during court proceedings, as well as stand guard outside the jury rooms.

Bailiffs guard criminal defendants throughout court proceedings. They escort defendants between the holding cells and the courtrooms. They also make sure that holding cells at the courts are secure and free of any contraband. Some Bailiffs have the duty of transporting prisoners between the court and the jail.

When juries are making their deliberations, Bailiffs make sure that jurors have no contact with other people besides themselves. They accompany jurors to all meals and remain with them during the meals. If a jury must be sequestered overnight, Bailiffs arrange for meals, lodging, and transportation for the jurors.

Bailiffs work closely with judges and the court staff to make sure that the courts operate efficiently and safely. In some courts, security measures involve screening individuals before they can enter the courtroom. Bailiffs might operate weapon detection devices or perform hand searches. As certified law enforcement officers, Bailiffs have the authority to arrest persons who disturb the court proceedings or break security violations either inside or outside the courtrooms. Bailiffs also take charge during medical emergencies, bomb threats, fire alarms, and other emergencies.

Bailiffs are also responsible for various clerical tasks. For example, they complete security reports, photocopy documents, log information on court forms, or update databases in a computer system. Some Bailiffs are in charge of arranging with the jail staff to make prisoners available for court. Furthermore, Bailiffs may be asked by judges to run such errands as summoning lawyers to judges' chambers, delivering court files, or fetching supplies.

Bailiffs work 40 hours a week, sometimes working additional hours when required.

Salaries

Salaries vary, depending on factors such as job duties, rank, and geographical location. According to the U.S. Bureau of Labor Statistics, the estimated annual salary in 2000 for most Bailiffs ranged from $16,550 to $52,780.

Employment Prospects

Bailiff duty is a voluntary assignment in sheriff's offices and state police departments. Some local police departments also have bailiff units. Opportunities generally become available as Bailiffs retire, resign, or transfer to other positions. Courts may request additional Bailiffs to fit staffing needs as long as funding is available.

Advancement Prospects

As law enforcement officers, Bailiffs can advance in rank as well as in pay scale. Law enforcement officers can stay with this detail as long as they are qualified for the job or until they request transfer to other details.

Education and Training

The minimum education requirement for law enforcement officers is a high school diploma or general equivalency diploma. Some agencies also require that peace officers have an associate degree or some college background.

New Bailiffs typically complete specialized training that includes classes in legal matters, arrest procedures, firearms training, process serving, and security training.

Experience, Skills, and Personality Traits

Depending on the law enforcement agency, candidates generally need one to three years of law enforcement experience. They also are knowledgeable about court security, court functions, and court proceedings. In addition, they demonstrate a professional appearance and demeanor, as well as the ability to make sound judgments.

Bailiffs must have excellent interpersonal and communication skills in order to work well with judges and other court employees. They also need good computer skills. In addition, Bailiffs need strong self-management skills—the ability to understand and follow directions, work independently, handle stressful situations, and so forth

Being courteous, tactful, firm, and reliable are a few personality traits that successful Bailiffs share.

Licensure and Certification

Bailiffs are required to be certified law enforcement officers—sheriff's deputies, local police officers, or state police officers (or state troopers).

Unions and Associations

Bailiffs typically join local, state, and national professional associations to take advantage of professional services, resources, and networking opportunities. Two national associations that serve law enforcement officers are the American Deputy Sheriffs' Association and the Fraternal Order of Police. In addition, many Bailiffs belong to the International Association of Court Officers and Services, Inc.

Tips for Entry

1. Would you like to get an idea of what it may be like to be a Bailiff? Contact the courts in your area to learn about their volunteer programs. Many courts use volunteers to help Bailiffs with some of their more routine duties.
2. As a deputy's sheriff or police officer, talk with the commander in charge of bailiff detail. Let him or her know about your interest, even if you are not yet eligible.
3. Many law enforcement agencies have web sites. To find the web site for a specific agency, enter its name in any search engine. (For example, "Los Angeles County Sheriff's Office," "Seattle Police Department," or "New York State Police.")

COURT INTERPRETER

CAREER PROFILE

Duties: Provide oral translations in court proceedings for witnesses or litigants who have very limited English language skills; translate written materials into English or a second language; perform other tasks as required

Alternate Titles: Judicial Interpreter, Official Court Interpreter, Legal Interpreter

Salary Range: About $30,000 to about $80,000, for staff positions

Employment Prospects: Good

Advancement Prospects: Limited

Prerequisites:

Education/Training—Completion of a voluntary court interpretation program

Experience—Previous court interpreting experience may be required or preferred

Special Skills and Personality Traits—An extensive vocabulary and general knowledge about various subjects; familiarity with legal terminology and court proceedings; highly proficient in English and another language and knowledgeable about the cultures of the non–English speakers; interpersonal, communication, and public speaking skills; business skills for independent contractors; respectful, articulate, sincere, truthful

Licensure/Certification—State or federal certification or registration may be required

CAREER LADDER

```
┌─────────────────────────────────┐
│      Senior Court Interpreter,  │
│       Program Coordinator,      │
│     or Independent Contractor   │
└─────────────────────────────────┘

┌─────────────────────────────────┐
│      Court Interpreter (Staff)  │
│     or Independent Contractor   │
└─────────────────────────────────┘

┌─────────────────────────────────┐
│      Court Interpreter Trainee  │
└─────────────────────────────────┘
```

Position Description

In the U.S. court system, when witnesses or litigants in court trials are unable to communicate effectively in the English language, Court Interpreters may translate for them. Many courts have staff Court Interpreters or use freelancers on a contractual basis. They are fluent in English and one or more other languages—Spanish, American Sign Language, Vietnamese, Thai, Russian, Korean, Mandarin, Japanese, Ilocano, Polish, Arabic, Hindi, Ukrainian, Serbo-Croatian, Tongan, Farsi, Greek, Navajo, Haitian Creole, Portuguese, and so on. Court Interpreters do accurate, word-for-word oral translations. They do not change, nor do they add anything to, what is said by speakers. In addition, Court Interpreters preserve the tone and level of language of the speakers.

Court Interpreters provide their services for various criminal and civil cases. For example, they interpret testimony for witnesses, defendants, or plaintiffs in murder trials, drug trials, domestic violence cases, landlord and tenant disputes, arson trials, child support hearings, and small claims cases. In addition to court trials, Court Interpreters are also used during arraignments, pretrial hearings and conferences, depositions, and probation meetings.

Court interpretation is a difficult task. Court Interpreters must interpret the everyday language of witnesses from various backgrounds. They must deal with the legal terminology of judges and attorneys. They interpret as well as handle the technical vocabulary of police officers, forensic scientists, and various expert witnesses.

Court Interpreters perform three types of court interpreting. One is called consecutive interpreting, in which they orally translate statements into English or the second language after the speaker has finished speaking. Another type is simultaneous interpreting, in which Court Interpreters orally translate a speaker's statements as the person is speaking. The third type is sight interpreting, which is used when Court Interpreters read a document written in one language while translating it orally into another language.

As officers of the court, Court Interpreters must follow court policies as well as an ethical code of professional responsibility. They maintain an impartial attitude at all times. In other words, they do not become emotionally involved with the participants or the cases. In addition, Court Interpreters do not express personal opinions nor act as an advocate for either party in a case.

Staff Court Interpreters perform other duties as required by their employers. For example, they might interpret and translate technical, medical, legal and other documents for judges and court staff. They may also provide interpretation for public inquiries in the clerk offices or over the telephone. They also perform various clerical tasks, such as filing and maintaining records of their interpreting and translating activities.

Freelance Court Interpreters are responsible for managing various business tasks. Such tasks include paying bills and taxes, invoicing clients, generating new business, and so forth. Many independent contractors also offer their services to private attorneys, public defenders, law enforcement agencies, social service agencies, hospitals, health care facilities, and others.

Staff Court Interpreters work a standard 40-hour week. Freelancers are employed on an as-needed basis, and so have flexible work hours.

Salaries

Staff Court Interpreters receive salaries, while freelancers are paid by the hour or per diem (by the day). Earnings vary, depending on factors such as experience, employer, geographical location, and the demand for a particular language. Federal courts generally pay higher wages than local, state, or administrative courts. According to the National Association of Judiciary Interpreters and Translators, the annual salaries for full-time staff positions range from about $30,000 to about $80,000.

Employment Prospects

Court Interpreters are hired or contracted by state and federal courts as well as by administrative boards in government agencies.

Freelance positions are more readily available than staff positions. The demand for qualified Court Interpreters is strong, particularly in cities with large immigrant populations.

Spanish-language interpreters are the most in demand nationally. The demand for other language interpreters vary, depending on the geographical location.

Advancement Prospects

Supervisory and management opportunities for staff Court Interpreters are limited. Generally, Court Interpreters realize advancement by making higher earnings and through professional recognition.

Education and Training

Prospective Court Interpreters typically complete court interpreter training programs that focus on specialized vocabulary and interpreting skills. Enrollment in these programs requires that students already be highly proficient in the second language.

Throughout their careers, Court Interpreters participate in voluntary and mandatory training and continuing education programs to increase their interpreting skills and expertise.

Experience, Skills, and Personality Traits

Many employers require or prefer that candidates have work experience as a staff or freelance interpreter in court or non-court settings. Employers generally look for candidates who possess an extensive vocabulary and have general knowledge about various subjects. Candidates are also familiar with legal terminology and court proceedings.

Court Interpreters must be highly proficient in reading, writing, speaking, and listening for both English and a second language. In addition, they are familiar with various dialects and idiomatic expressions in both languages. They are also knowledgeable about the cultural differences, regionalisms, and issues of the non–English speakers.

Court Interpreters have strong interpersonal and communication skills, as well as good public speaking skills. They also demonstrate a professional demeanor and appearance. Additionally, Independent Contractors should have adequate business skills. Being respectful, articulate, sincere, and truthful are a few personality traits that successful Court Interpreters share.

Licensure and Certification

Court Interpreters may be required to be certified or registered by a federal or state court before they can obtain employment. Requirements vary from court to court. For information about federal Court Interpreter certification, contact a federal court in your area. For information about state court certification, contact your local courts. You can also write to the Consortium for State Court Interpreter Certification, National Center for State Courts, 300 Newport Avenue, Williamsburg, VA 23185. Or call (757) 253-2000, or fax (757) 220-0449. Or visit its web site at *http://www.ncsc.dni.us/research/interp*.

Unions and Associations

Many Court Interpreters are members of local, state, and national professional associations. These organizations offer networking opportunities as well as various professional services and resources. Some national organizations are the Translators and Interpreters Guild, the American Translators Association, and the National Association of Judiciary Interpreters and Translators.

Tips for Entry

1. To find court interpretation programs, check out the colleges and universities in your area. You might also contact local or state court interpreter associations to learn about available training programs.

2. To learn about job opportunities, requirements, and application processes, contact a court interpreter's office directly. If a court has no such office, than ask to talk with the person in charge of hiring court interpreters.

3. You can learn more about court interpreting on the Internet. To find relevant web sites, enter any of these keywords in a search engine: *court interpreting, judiciary interpreting,* or *court interpreter.*

OFFICIAL COURT REPORTER

CAREER PROFILE

Duties: Make a verbatim record of court proceedings; maintain official records of court proceedings; produce official court transcripts

Alternative Titles: Court Reporter, Shorthand Reporter

Salary Range: $19,000 to $69,000 (does not include transcript income)

Employment Prospects: Good

Advancement Prospects: Limited

Prerequisites:

Education/Training—A high school diploma; completion of a court reporting program

Experience—Varies with different employers

Special Skills and Personality Traits—Organizational, computer, English, and self-management skills; honest, patient, disciplined, resourceful

Licensure/Certification—May require state or other professional certification

CAREER LADDER

```
┌─────────────────────────────────────┐
│   Senior Official Court Reporter     │
└─────────────────────────────────────┘

┌─────────────────────────────────────┐
│      Official Court Reporter         │
└─────────────────────────────────────┘

┌─────────────────────────────────────┐
│  Student, Freelance Court Reporter,  │
│  or Court Reporter in other settings │
└─────────────────────────────────────┘
```

Position Description

Official Court Reporters are responsible for creating and producing official records of court proceedings. They work in state and federal courts. To ensure the accuracy of their work, Court Reporters do not become emotionally involved or affected by the civil or criminal cases that they hear.

During court trials, Court Reporters record, word for word, what lawyers, judges, and witnesses say. Court Reporters take shorthand notes at speeds of 175 to 225 or more words per minute on stenotype machines. Unlike typewriters or computer keyboards, reporters press several keys at the same time on the stenotype machine keypad (similar to playing chords on a piano) to record words or phrases phonetically. Their notes are produced on paper tape, as well as an electronic format such as a computer disk. If at any time they have trouble taking notes, they stop the proceedings immediately and request that people speak slower, speak louder, repeat themselves, and so forth.

Some Official Court Reporters do real-time reporting. Their stenotype machines are connected to computers which simultaneously translate their notes into unedited text. The text can be viewed instantly on other computer screens by judges, lawyers, persons with hearing impairments, and others.

Official Court Reporters are responsible for transcribing their notes into formal transcripts, which lawyers typically request to help them with their cases. Producing transcripts usually takes one to three hours for every hour of taking stenotype notes. During busy times or when transcripts must be produced quickly, Official Court Reporters usually hire freelance court reporters and scopists (editors) for assistance.

Most reporters use computer-aided transcription (CAT) software to translate their shorthand notes into the text format that the courts require. The CAT program contains a personalized dictionary of court reporters' stenotype symbols, words, and phrases. The program translates all stenotype symbols that it recognizes into text. The reporters translate unfamiliar symbols and add them to their CAT dictionary.

Official Court Reporters make sure that the transcripts are accurate and clear. They research any items that are vague, check for correct spelling of names and words, make sure that unfamiliar or technical terms and citations were taken down precisely, and so forth. The reporters proofread final transcripts, and have them certified by notary publics as being complete, true, and accurate. If an Official Court Reporter is a notary public, he or she does the certification.

Most Official Court Reporters have a dual status. They are employed by the court systems to make formal records of court trials. However, when they produce transcripts, they are independent contractors. They charge lawyers and others for original transcripts and copies. Many reporters also offer additional services to lawyers. For example, they might provide condensed transcripts, keyword indexes to transcripts, or edited disks of transcripts.

As independent contractors, Official Court Reporters are responsible for the keeping business records. They bill clients, pay bills and freelancers' invoices, and so on. They purchase and maintain their own equipment and supplies. In addition, they hire and train freelance court reporters, scopists, and others who assist with transcript and office tasks.

All Official Court Reporters are responsible for maintaining their skills as well as keeping up with technology updates and new developments in their field. They accomplish this by enrolling in training programs, networking with peers, attending professional conferences, reading professional journals, and so on.

Most Official Court Reporters have a 40-hour work schedule. Reporters often work evenings and weekends to produce court transcripts.

Salaries

The salary for Official Court Reporters depends on such factors as experience and location. According to the U.S. Bureau of Labor Statistics, the estimated annual salary in 2000 for most Court Reporters ranged from $18,750 to $69,000. The United States Court Reporters Association reports that federal Official Court Reporters generally earn between $50,000 to $63,000 per year.

Official Court Reporters earn a separate income for producing transcripts. Transcript income varies among reporters, and earnings also vary from year to year. For example, transcript income for federal Official Court Reporters can range from $5,000 to $80,000 in any given year.

Employment Prospects

Official Court Reporters are hired full time or part time by state and federal courts. Court Reporters are also hired by law firms, court reporting services, government agencies, government legislatures, educational institutions, and others. Furthermore, many court reporters are self-employed.

Staff opportunities generally become available as Official Court Reporters retire or resign. Courts may create new positions when funding is available.

Opportunities are readily available for freelancers as well as permanent employees in other settings. Court Reporters with real-time reporting experience are in demand in all settings.

Advancement Prospects

Senior and supervisory positions are available, but rather limited. Most Official Court Reporters realize advancement through higher pay and professional recognition. Some reporters consider employment with the federal courts or government legislatures as their ultimate career goals. Others strive to become freelancers or owners of court reporting services. Many pursue alternative careers in their field, such as scopists, medical transcriptionists, television closed captionists, or rapid text entry specialists in the business world.

Education and Training

The minimum educational requirement is a high school diploma or general equivalency diploma. Many Court Reporters have associate or bachelor's degrees.

Most court reporters have completed a court reporting program. Court reporting programs are offered by two-year and four-year colleges as well as postsecondary vocational and technical schools. The length of a program varies from two to four years, depending on a student's ability to master court reporting skills and to pass proficiency tests on the stenotype machine.

Experience, Skills, and Personality Traits

Experience requirements for entry-level positions vary from court to court. At the federal court level, entry-level candidates need a minimum of four years experience as state court reporters, freelancers, or a combination of staff and freelance work. They should have prime court reporting experience, such as working on criminal cases or highly-publicized litigation cases.

Court Reporters need strong organizational, computer, and English (grammar, spelling, and punctuation) skills. They also need excellent self-management skills—be self-motivated, work well under pressure, meet deadlines, and so on. Being honest, patient, disciplined, and resourceful are some personality traits that successful Court Reporters share.

Licensure and Certification

Many states require that Official Court Reporters hold state *Certified Court Reporter* (CCR) or *Certified Shorthand Reporter* (CSR) certification. Some states require the *Registered Professional Reporter* (RPR), a nationally recognized certification that is granted by the National Court Reporters Association. Some states require that Official Court Reporters obtain a notary public license. For specific certification and licensure information, contact the state board of examiners of court reporters or a court reporting association in the state where you wish to practice.

Federal courts generally require or prefer that Official Court Reporters have RPR certification.

Unions and Associations

Official Court Reporters join professional organizations to take advantage of networking opportunities, continuing education programs, and other professional services and resources. Along with local and state associations, Official Court Reporters might join the National Court Reporters Association. Official Court Reporters at the federal level might join the United States Court Reporters Association.

Tips for Entry

1. Many employers prefer to hire candidates who have completed court reporting programs accredited by the National Court Reporters Association. For more information, write to the association at 8224 Old Courthouse Road, Vienna, VA 22182-3808. Or call (703) 556-6272. Or visit its website *(http://www. verbatimreporters.com).*

2. Contact local, state, or federal personnel offices directly for information about Official Court Reporter vacancies or requirements.

3. Learn more about official court reporting on the Internet. To get a list of relevant web sites, enter the keywords *official court reporter* in any search engine. To research court reporting in general, use the keywords *court reporting.*

SCOPIST

CAREER PROFILE

Duties: Provide support services to court reporters; edit and produce first drafts of court transcriptions; update court reporters' software dictionaries

Salary Range: $20,000 to $40,000 or more

Employment Prospects: Good

Advancement Prospects: Limited

Prerequisites:

Education/Training—A high school diploma; on-the-job training or completion of a scopist training program

Experience—Familiarity with court reporting procedures, legal terminology, and machine shorthand; knowledge of computer-aided transcription (CAT) software

Special Skills and Personality Traits—Computer, English, communication, and self-management skills; business skills for independent contractors; self-motivated, reliable, flexible, honest, impartial, discreet

Licensure/Certification—None required

CAREER LADDER

```
┌─────────────────────────────────┐
│      Senior Scopist (staff)     │
│    or Independent Contractor    │
└─────────────────────────────────┘

┌─────────────────────────────────┐
│        Scopist (staff) or       │
│     Independent Contractor      │
└─────────────────────────────────┘

┌─────────────────────────────────┐
│   Scopist Trainee, Student (scopist │
│  training program), or Court Reporter │
└─────────────────────────────────┘
```

Position Description

Court reporters are responsible for taking notes of court proceedings and producing those notes into certified court transcripts. When Court Reporters are too busy to transcribe and edit their notes, they use the services of Scopists who are independent contractors or staff members in court reporting firms. The Scopists' job is to produce accurate transcript drafts according to the specifications of the court reporters.

The court reporters take notes on stenotype machines that are attached to a computer system. Court Reporters give Scopists a copy of their files on disks. Some Court Reporters transfer their files directly to Scopists' computers via a modem connection or through e-mail attachments. Court Reporters also provide Scopists with court exhibits, such as audio tapes and documents, for them to use as reference materials.

Scopists work with computer-aided transcription (CAT) software which translates shorthand notes into the English language according to the program's dictionary. Court reporters each have their own personalized CAT dictionaries of stenotype symbols, words, and phrases. Scopists are responsible for updating CAT dictionaries with any new terms or phrases that the court reporters use in their court notes.

Scopists carefully read the software translations and make all necessary edits. They make sure that the proper words are being used. For example, a court reporter may have inputted the word *there,* but the text requires *their.* If any terms or passages are unclear in the drafts, Scopists alert court reporters by placing a note next to those items. Scopists also translate stenotype notes that the CAT program could not.

In addition, Scopists check for and fix typographical errors on the drafts. They make corrections in grammar and punctuation, using the same style as the individual court reporters. Scopists also check the spellings of proper names and technical terms by researching the court exhibits that were provided to them as well as dictionaries, directories, and other resources. Furthermore, Scopists make sure that the drafts follow proper court guidelines and formats.

Scopists return the edited drafts in the form that the court reporter wishes—on disks, as electronic files transferred via modem, or e-mail attachments.

Many Scopists also provide editing services for court reporters who do depositions. Some Scopists also offer editing services for real-time reporting and audio tape transcriptions.

Scopists are responsible for maintaining their skills, as well as keeping up with technology updates and developments in the court reporting profession. They read professional journals, enroll in training and continuing education programs, participate in professional conferences, network with colleagues, and so on.

Self-employed Scopists provide contractual services to official court reporters (those employed by the courts), court reporting firms, and independent court reporters. As independent contractors, Scopists manage various business tasks, such as invoicing clients, paying bills and taxes, keeping records, and generating new business. They are also responsible for buying and maintaining their own computer systems, printers, CAT software, reference materials, and other equipment and supplies.

Scopists often work nights and weekends, putting in long hours to meet deadlines.

Salaries

Earnings vary, depending on factors such as experience, abilities, ambition, and geographical location. Staff Scopists earn a salary, while freelance Scopists are paid an hourly rate, page rate, or a combination of both. In general, earnings for experienced Scopists range from $20,000 to $40,000 or more per year.

Employment Prospects

Most opportunities are available for freelance Scopists. Staff positions typically become available as Scopists resign or transfer to other positions. On occasion, court reporting firms create additional positions to fit staffing needs.

In general, the demand for Scopists parallels the demand for court reporters. In cities and regions where court reporters are in short supply, Scopists can usually expect to find more opportunities. Further, freelance Scopists need not be limited to work only in their local areas. With the capability of transferring computer files electronically, many Scopists are able to work for court reporters in distant cities and states.

Advancement Prospects

Most Scopists realize advancement by earning higher wages and through professional recognition. For many, the top goal is to become successful independent contractors.

Education and Training

Scopists should have at least a high school diploma or general equivalency diploma.

Scopist training can be obtained in either of two ways. One is by on-the-job training in a court reporting firm. The other is by completing a scopist training program. Various scopist training programs are offered by postsecondary vocational and technical schools, community colleges, correspondence or Internet-based programs, and private tutoring programs.

Experience, Skills, and Personality Traits

To enter this field, Scopists must have a background in court reporting or be familiar with court reporting procedures and legal terminology. Scopists must also be familiar with stenotype, or machine shorthand. Additionally, they are able to operate the versions of CAT software used by the court reporters that hire them.

Scopists need excellent computer as well as English-language skills, including vocabulary, word usage, grammar, spelling, and punctuation. Scopists also need strong communication and self-management skills—the ability to meet strict deadlines, work under pressure, work independently, and so forth. Self-employed Scopists should have basic business skills.

Being self-motivated, reliable, flexible, honest, impartial, and discreet are some personality traits that successful Scopists share.

Unions and Associations

Scopists join professional associations, such as the National Court Reporters Association to take advantage of networking opportunities, training programs, and other professional services and resources.

Tips for Entry

1. Join local or state professional associations for court reporters. Network with them at meetings and conferences.
2. Let court reporters in your area know about your services. You might send brochures or flyers to court reporting firms and independent court reporters, as well as court reporting offices at state and federal courts in your area.
3. You can learn more about the scopist field, including available training programs, on the Internet. One web site you might visit is Scopists.com at *http://www. scopists.com*. To get a list of other relevant web sites, enter the keyword *scopist* in any search engine.

COURT CLERK

CAREER PROFILE

Duties: Provide administrative support to courts of law; perform clerical tasks such as typing, filing, distributing mail, and running errands; perform other duties as required

Alternate Titles: Deputy Court Clerk, Court/Legal Clerk; a title that reflects specialized duties, such as Courtroom Clerk, Jury Clerk, or Case Processing Clerk

Salary Range: $17,000 to $42,000

Employment Prospects: Fair

Advancement Prospects: Good

Prerequisites:

    Education/Training—A high school diploma; college background, legal clerical training, or paralegal training for higher-level positions

    Experience—One to three years of general office experience; legal clerk experience for higher-level positions; knowledge of court functions and procedures, legal forms and terminology

    Special Skills and Personality Traits—Reading, writing, and math skills; communication, interpersonal, teamwork, self-management skills; positive, enthusiastic, dependable, cooperative, detail-oriented, flexible

    Licensure/Certification—None required

CAREER LADDER

```
┌─────────────────────────────┐
│   Senior Court Clerk        │
│   or Supervisory Clerk      │
└─────────────────────────────┘

┌─────────────────────────────┐
│   Court Clerk (Journey Level)│
└─────────────────────────────┘

┌─────────────────────────────┐
│   Court Clerk (Entry Level) │
└─────────────────────────────┘
```

Position Description

Court Clerks provide administrative support in a court of law. In general, they are responsible for recording and processing legal documents, legal records, and court forms, as well as keeping legal records and files up to date. They may be assigned to work in court offices or courtrooms, under the general supervision of clerk supervisors, department managers, or judges.

They perform various clerical tasks that include typing correspondence, legal documents, and forms; preparing court letters for mailing; updating records; maintaining files; taking phone messages; distributing mail; running errands; and so on. They operate various office machines such as typewriters, photocopiers, fax machines, tape recorders, 10-key calculators, and multiline telephone systems. Court Clerks also use computers, working with word processing, spreadsheets, databases, and other software programs.

In addition, Court Clerks answer general questions over the phone or in person from the public, lawyers, government offices, and others. When requested by the judges, Court Clerks contact witnesses, attorneys, litigants, and others to obtain specific information for the court.

Depending on the size and needs of a court, the clerical staff may range from one or two clerks to hundreds. Their duties vary, depending on their positions as well as their abilities and experience. Here are just a few duties that Court Clerks perform:

- schedule cases for hearings, conferences, and trials, as well as inform participants when and where they must appear in court
- review case files for all required records and documents, and request lawyers, litigants, or others to supply the missing information

- assist in the jury selection process, which involves tasks such as contacting jurors for service, conducting jury orientation, and recording daily attendance of jurors
- provide courtroom support during court trials—such as recording the court proceedings, administering oaths to witnesses, and acting as custodians of physical evidence
- record rulings and decisions on required forms after court trials are complete, then process the records
- collect and process court fees, fines, and other payments received from defendants and others
- conduct research on criminal justice, FBI, department of motor vehicles, or other related computer databases for specific information
- prepare court processes (such as summonses, subpoenas, warrants, and writs) and secure a judge's signature on them
- supervise other Court Clerks

Some Court Clerks are identified by job titles that describe the duties that they perform. For example, Courtroom Clerks work primarily in the courtrooms, Jury Clerks perform duties related to jury selection, and Civil Processing Clerks specialize in preparing civil processes.

Court Clerks generally work 40 hours a week. In courts where sessions are scheduled during evening hours, Court Clerks may work evenings.

Salaries

Salaries vary, depending on factors such as experience, job duties, and geographical location. According to the Bureau of Labor Statistics, the estimated annual salary in 2000 for Court Clerks ranged between $16,640 and $41,680.

Employment Prospects

Most opportunities become available as Court Clerks retire, resign, or transfer to other positions. On occasion, courts create additional positions to fit staffing needs if funding is available.

Advancement Prospects

Court Clerks can advance to senior and supervisory clerk positions. With additional experience and/or education, they can become judicial assistants, legal secretaries, administrative assistants, paralegals, and lawyers. For those with administration ambitions, courts offer middle management and high-level management positions, such as program managers, deputy clerks (or deputy court administrators), clerks of court, and court administrators.

Education and Training

For entry-level positions, a high school diploma or general equivalency diploma is required. For higher-level Court Clerk positions, employers usually require some college background, legal clerical training, or paralegal training.

Throughout their careers, Court Clerks enroll in training and continuing education programs to develop their skills and expertise.

Experience, Skills, and Personality Traits

Employers generally require one to three years of general office experience, depending on the position for which one is applying. Legal clerk experience is usually required for higher-level positions. In addition, employers prefer candidates who are knowledgeable about court functions, court procedures, legal forms, and legal terminology.

Court Clerks should have adequate reading, writing, and math skills. They also need strong communication, interpersonal, and teamwork skills. Additionally, they must have excellent self-management skills—the ability to perform several tasks at a time, be punctual, handle stressful situations, and so on.

Being positive, enthusiastic, dependable, cooperative, detail-oriented, and flexible are some personality traits that Court Clerks share.

Unions and Associations

Many Court Clerks join local, state, and national professional associations to take advantage of training programs, professional publications, networking opportunities, and other professional services and resources.

Two national organizations available for Court Clerks are NALS ... the association for legal professionals and the International Association of Clerks, Recorders, Election Officials, and Treasurers. Federal clerks might join the Federal Court Clerks Association.

Tips for Entry

1. Enroll in appropriate classes to develop and improve your office skills. Many community colleges offer certificate or degree programs in court operations and legal office practices.
2. Contact courts directly about job vacancies. Many courts have open recruitment for Court Clerk positions.
3. To find job listings for federal Court Clerk positions, visit the U.S. Office of Personnel Management web site at *http://www.usajobs.opm.gov.*
4. You can learn more about courts on the Internet. For information about federal courts, visit the Federal Judiciary Home Page *(http://www.uscourts.gov),* which is maintained by the Administrative Office of the U.S. Courts. For general information about state courts, visit the National Center for State Courts web site *(http://www.ncsc.dni.us).*

COURT ADMINISTRATOR

CAREER PROFILE

Duties: Oversee all nonjudicial administrative functions in an individual court of a state court system; assist judges in defining the court's goals, objectives, policies, and procedures; perform duties as required

Alternate Titles: Court Executive Officer, Court Manager; or a title that reflects the type of court for which they work, such as Criminal Court Administrator, Family Court Administrator, or Municipal Court Administrator

Salary Range: $29,000 to $133,000

Employment Prospects: Good

Advancement Prospects: Good

Prerequisites:

Education/Training—A bachelor's degree; a master's degree or Institute of Court Management Fellow certification, for positions in larger, complex court systems

Experience—Three to eight years court administration experience; two to four years of supervisory experience; experience in (or knowledgeable about) the various court administrative functions

Special Skills and Personality Traits—Leadership, supervisory, management, interpersonal, writing, communication, analytical, and problem-solving skills; composed, organized, analytical, hardworking, creative

Licensure/Certification—None required

CAREER LADDER

```
┌─────────────────────────────────┐
│     Court Administrator         │
│ (in a larger, complex court     │
│          system)                │
└─────────────────────────────────┘

┌─────────────────────────────────┐
│     Court Administrator         │
└─────────────────────────────────┘

┌─────────────────────────────────┐
│   Assistant or Deputy Court     │
│        Administrator            │
└─────────────────────────────────┘
```

Position Description

Court Administrators hold high-level management positions in the individual courts of the state court systems. These include state supreme courts, district courts, trial courts, appellate courts, municipal courts, family courts, and so on. Their duty is to make sure that all nonjudicial functions in the courts are operating in an organized, efficient and effective manner each day. They oversee various administrative functions such as fiscal management, personnel administration, space and equipment management, automation (or information systems), record and information management, jury operations, community relations, and media relations. Depending on the size of their court, Court Administrators directly manage some or all of the administrative functions.

Court Administrators work closely with the judges to define their court's goals and objectives, as well as develop appropriate policies and procedures, which they implement accordingly. They also participate in planning and developing new and improved court services, programs, and activities.

In addition, Court Administrators are responsible for a wide range of duties. Some of these responsibilities include:

- organizing, directing, and coordinating the various court activities, such as court reporting services, court interpreting programs, case processing, and court security
- planning and managing annual budgets
- providing supervision and guidance to nonjudicial employees, including clerks, technicians, law clerks, supervisors, program managers, and others

- hiring and training personnel
- developing and coordinating employee training programs
- directing records management activities such as the creation of court forms
- reviewing and approving (or rejecting) service contracts with vendors
- conducting special studies (as directed by judges), which includes preparing statistical data and analysis as well as writing reports
- obtaining grant funding for new court programs
- monitoring and reviewing state legislation that pertains to the courts
- serving as liaison to other courts, state legislature, local governments, law enforcement agencies, the news media, the general public, and others

Furthermore, Court Administrators are responsible for keeping up with developments in the court administration field, as well as furthering their own professional development. They enroll in training programs, participate in professional conferences, network with colleagues, read professional journals and books, and so on.

Court Administrators work independently, under the supervision of presiding, or chief, court judges. They generally work a 40-hour week, but sometimes work nights and weekends to complete their various tasks.

Salaries

Salaries vary, depending on such factors as experience, job duties, employer, and geographical location. Earnings are typically higher in metropolitan areas.

No formal salary surveys are available for Court Administrators. However, a look at the earnings of other management occupations can give a general idea of what Court Administrators may earn. According to the U.S. Bureau of Labor Statistics, the estimated annual salary in 2000 for most management occupations ranged from $29,220 to $132,710.

Employment Prospects

The field is continually growing, and opportunities are available for Court Administrators in small courts as well as in larger, complex court systems. Most opportunities become available as Court Administrators retire, resign, or transfer to other positions.

Advancement Prospects

Court Administrators pursue advancement by seeking positions with higher salaries and more complex responsibilities. This usually involves transferring from one court to the next. Court Administrators can also advance to top management positions in state administrative offices, which oversee the state court systems.

Education and Training

Employers generally require candidates to have at least a bachelor's degree. Course work in public administration, court management, business administration, law, criminal justice, or related fields is highly desirable.

Educational requirements for Court Administrator positions in complex court systems usually include a master's degree in public administration, court administration, or related field. Many employers also accept candidates who have earned the Fellow designation granted by the Institute for Court Management. For information about this certification, contact the Institute for Court Management by mail at 300 Newport Avenue (23185), P.O. Box 8798, Williamsburg, VA 23287-8798. Or call (800) 616-6160, or fax (757) 220-0449. Or visit its web site at *http://www.ncsc.dni.us/icm*.

Experience, Skills, and Personality Traits

Depending on the employer, Court Administrators need three to eight years of court administration experience with two to four years of supervisory experience. In addition, they have experience in or are knowledgeable about the different areas of court operations, such as human resources, financial management, information systems, facilities management, and customer service practices.

Court Administrators must have excellent leadership, supervisory, and management skills. They also need effective interpersonal skills to work well with judges, court support staff, attorneys, other government agencies, the media, and the public. In addition, they have effective writing and communication skills, as well as strong analytical and problem-solving skills.

Being composed, organized, analytical, hardworking, and creative are a few personality traits that Court Administrators share.

Unions and Associations

Many Court Administrators join local, state, and national associations to take advantage of networking opportunities and other professional services and resources. Two national organizations they might join are the National Association for Court Management and the American Bar Association.

Tips for Entry

1. Talk with Court Administrators to learn more about their jobs.
2. Many Court Administrators worked their way up through the ranks of court clerks, supervisors, and department managers.
3. You can learn more about court administration on the Internet. To find relevant web sites, enter either of these keywords in a search engine: *court administration* or *court administrator*.

CRIMINAL JUSTICE
SOCIAL SERVICES
PROFESSIONALS

PRETRIAL SERVICES OFFICER

CAREER PROFILE

Duties: Assist courts in determining whether criminal defendants should be released before their trials; conduct pretrial investigations; prepare pretrial reports; supervise criminal defendants who are released from jail; perform other duties as required

Alternate Title: Pretrial Release Officer

Salary Range: $29,000 to $68,000, for federal officers

Employment Prospects: Good

Advancement Prospects: Fair

Prerequisites:

    Education/Training—A bachelor's degree; formal and on-the-job training for new officers

    Experience—Previous work experience in court services, probation, criminal justice, or social services required or preferred; knowledge of case management and government and community resources

    Special Skills and Personality Traits—Interviewing, research, communication, writing, computer, teamwork, and interpersonal skills; energetic, self-motivated, analytical, objective, honest, ethical

    Licensure/Certification—None required

CAREER LADDER

```
┌─────────────────────────────────────┐
│   Senior Pretrial Services Officer   │
└─────────────────────────────────────┘

┌─────────────────────────────────────┐
│      Pretrial Services Officer       │
└─────────────────────────────────────┘

┌─────────────────────────────────────┐
│  Pretrial Services Officer Trainee   │
│   or Pretrial Services Assistant     │
└─────────────────────────────────────┘
```

Position Description

In the U.S. criminal justice system, some defendants may be released from jail to await their court trials. It is the responsibility of Pretrial Services Officers to prepare unbiased pretrial reports that help judges determine whether criminal defendants should be detained or released. The pretrial reports provide judges with sufficient information to answer such questions as: If defendants are released, will they show up for their court hearings and trials, and will they stay out of trouble? Would they pose a danger to victims, witnesses, or the general community? Should the courts impose any conditions upon the defendants to decrease their risk fleeing or getting arrested again?

Pretrial Services Officers conduct thorough investigations for all cases that are assigned to them. They gather information about the defendants—their employment histories, criminal records, family relationships, residences, and so on. Pretrial Services Officers conduct research by using various databases from government agencies, law enforcement agencies, credit report companies, and other sources. They also interview the defendants and verify facts by contacting employers, family members, law enforcement agencies, financial institutions, school officials, and so on. Officers may also talk with prosecuting attorneys to find out what the government's position is on releasing or detaining the defendants.

When the Pretrial Services Officers have completed their investigations, they evaluate the data to offer recommendations to the judges. The officers follow specific court guidelines as well as use risk assessment instruments. Pretrial Services Officers recommend whether the defendants should be detained or released from jail to await their trials. They may recommend that the defendants post bail bonds—cash, property, or surety bonds—which they forfeit if they do not show up for their court dates.

Officers may also recommend that the defendants' releases be based on certain conditions. For example, they must obtain mental health evaluations, participate in substance abuse treatment programs, find employment, or avoid the company of certain people. Officers might also recommend that the defendants' freedom of movement be restricted in such forms as curfews or house arrest.

Pretrial investigations and reports must be completed prior to the defendants' first appearance before a judge. Hence, officers must be able to perform their tasks quickly, yet make sure that their work is accurate and complete.

Pretrial Services Officers are also responsible for managing a caseload of criminal defendants who have been released from jail. The officers supervise the defendants until they have been acquitted, they begin their sentences, or when the criminal charges against them have been dropped.

As supervisors, Pretrial Services Officers are responsible for helping the defendants follow the conditions of their release. They provide the defendants with referrals to appropriate resources, such as employment counseling, drug treatment services, health clinics, or school programs. Officers also monitor their activities and movements by keeping regular contact with them in person and by telephone. If the defendants violate any of their conditions, Pretrial Services Officers must inform the courts and prosecuting attorneys.

Pretrial Services Officers are responsible for other duties. For example, they:

- develop community and government resources to whom they can refer criminal defendants for assistance
- conduct background investigations to help courts determine if individuals with first-time or misdemeanor offenses should be placed in diversion programs (such as drug treatment, education, or community service programs) rather than be prosecuted for their crimes
- make presentations about pretrial services to schools, community organizations, and others
- keep up with current criminal justice and social work issues and practices that are relevant to their work

Pretrial Services Officers work 40 hours a week, sometimes putting in additional hours to complete their various tasks.

Salaries

Salaries vary, depending on factors such as experience, education, employer, and geographical location. Federal pretrial services offices typically pay higher wages than state offices. Basic pay for federal Pretrial Service Officers range from about $29,000 to about $68,000.

Employment Prospects

Pretrial Services Officers are employed by state and federal court systems. Most opportunities become available as officers resign, retire, or transfer to other positions. Additional positions are occasionally created to meet staffing needs, as long as funding is available.

Advancement Prospects

Advancements in pretrial services offices are limited to a few supervisory and administrative positions. Most officers realize advancement by earning higher salaries and receiving more complex assignments. Many in state offices seek positions at the federal level.

Depending on their interests, Pretrial Services Officers can pursue other related career paths by becoming probation officers, correctional officers, law enforcement officers, social workers, and lawyers.

Education and Training

Employers generally require that candidates have a bachelor's degree from an accredited college or university. Most prefer a degree (or major course work) in criminal justice, criminology, sociology, social work, psychology, or other behavioral sciences.

New Pretrial Services Officers typically receive formal and on-the-job training.

Experience, Skills, and Personality Traits

In general, employers require (or strongly prefer) that candidates have previous work experience in court services, probation, criminal justice, or social services. In addition, they must be knowledgeable about case management and about available social, legal, and health resources in the government and community.

Pretrial Services Officers need effective interviewing, research, communication, and writing skills. Good computer skills are also important. In addition, they need strong teamwork and interpersonal skills, as they must work well with different people from various backgrounds.

Being energetic, self-motivated, analytical, objective, honest, and ethical are a few personality traits that successful Pretrial Services Officers share.

Unions and Associations

Pretrial Services Officers join local, state, and national professional associations to take advantage of networking opportunities, training programs, and other professional services and resources. One national association that serves pretrial services practitioners is the National Association of Pretrial Services Agencies.

Tips for Entry

1. For federal positions, applicants, must be 36 years old or younger at the time of their appointment.

Applicants who are 37 years old or older may be eligible if they have qualifying law enforcement officer experience.

2. Contact pretrial offices directly to learn about job vacancies, job requirements, and the office's application process.

3. You can learn more about pretrial services on the Internet. One web site you might visit is the Pretrial Services Resource Center web site *(http://www.pretrial.org)*. To find other relevant web sites, enter either of these keywords in a search engine: *pretrial services* or *pretrial services officer.*

U.S. PROBATION OFFICER

CAREER PROFILE

Duties: Supervise probationers and parolees; make recommendations for sentencing offenders; conduct presentence investigations; perform other duties as required

Salary Range: $27,000 to $70,000

Employment Prospects: Fair

Advancement Prospects: Limited

Prerequisites:

Education/Training—A bachelor's degree; a master's degree may be required; formal and on-the-job training for new officers

Experience—One to three years of progressive responsibility in probation, pretrial services, parole, corrections, criminal investigation, substance abuse treatment, or related fields

Special Skills and Personality Traits—Interviewing, research, communication, writing, teamwork, interpersonal, analytical, conflict management, and self-management skills; courteous, honest, respectful, dedicated, realistic, objective

Licensure/Certification—None required

CAREER LADDER

```
┌─────────────────────────────────────┐
│    Senior U.S. Probation Officer     │
└─────────────────────────────────────┘

┌─────────────────────────────────────┐
│       U.S. Probation Officer         │
└─────────────────────────────────────┘

┌─────────────────────────────────────┐
│   U.S. Probation Officer Trainee     │
└─────────────────────────────────────┘
```

Position Description

U.S. Probation Officers are federal law enforcement officers. Their job is to manage a caseload of offenders who have been placed under court supervision by the federal courts, the U.S. Parole Commission, or U.S. military authorities. These criminal offenders are allowed to serve their court sentences in their communities as an alternative to imprisonment. The U.S. Probation Officers are responsible for monitoring their activities and movements to ensure the safety of the communities in which the offenders have been released.

U.S. Probation Officers supervise only offenders who have been convicted of federal crimes. Some are probationers—offenders who receive court supervision sentences instead of prison sentences. Others are parolees—offenders who have been conditionally released from prison before their sentence is complete. Probation Officers provide supervision for probationers and parolees until they have completed their sentences.

All probationers and parolees are released from jail on certain conditions, which are specified in their supervision plans. For example, offenders may be required to obtain employment, finish educational programs, enroll in drug abuse or alcohol treatment programs, or obtain mental health counseling. Offenders may also be restricted as to where they may travel and with whom they may associate.

Probation Officers help offenders meet the terms of their conditions by referring them to proper resources in government and community agencies. They also maintain regular personal contact with the offenders to ensure that they are following their supervision plans. Probation Officers meet with the offenders in their offices, as well as visit the offenders in their homes and at their jobs. Probation Officers also contact employers, family members, and others to see how offenders are doing.

Probation Officers maintain accurate and up-to-date records on their probationers or parolees. They document meetings, the behavior of the offenders, and any significant events. In addition, Probation Officers prepare and submit routine monthly and annual progress reports. They may propose changes to the conditions of the offenders' releases, such as adding or dropping treatment plans. They may also recommend the termination of an offender's supervision if it is appropriate.

If offenders are suspected of having committed a violation of their probation or parole, Probation Officers conduct investigations accordingly. They report any violations to the proper authorities—the court, U.S. Parole Commission, or military authorities.

U.S. Probation Officers also have the major duty of helping federal judges determine the appropriate sentences for offenders. Probation Officers conduct investigations to gather information about the offenders and the circumstances of the offenses that have been committed. They review various documents—court records, criminal history records, pretrial reports, treatment reports, and so on. They interview offenders and verify all facts. In addition, they interview law enforcement officers, attorneys, victims, family members, employers, clergy, community agencies, and others.

Applying appropriate federal laws and federal sentencing guidelines, Probation Officers assess the data and make recommendations for sentencing. Their recommendations may include probation, imprisonment, and fines. Probation Officers submit the data and recommendations in the form of clear and concise reports.

U.S. Probation Officers also perform various other duties as required. For example, they might:

- investigate parole plans for parolees who are under consideration for being released
- assist probation officers in other federal districts to complete investigations
- supervise parolees or probationers transferring between federal districts
- develop community and government resources to whom they can refer offenders
- make public presentations about probation and parole

U.S. Probation Officers sometimes work more than 40 hours per week to complete their various duties and meet deadlines. They may be required to work evenings and on weekends to supervise offenders. Travel is often necessary to visit offenders at their homes and jobs.

Salaries

Salaries vary, depending on factors such as experience, education, and geographical location. Basic annual pay for U.S. Probation Officers ranges from about $27,000 to $70,000.

Employment Prospects

More than 4,000 Probation Officers are employed by the various U.S. Probation Offices in the 94 federal court districts. Most opportunities become available as officers resign, retire, or transfer to other positions. Additional positions

are occasionally created to meet staffing needs, as long as funding is available.

To become U.S. Probation Officers, applicants must be U.S. citizens. They must be under 37 years old upon the time of appointment. (The age requirement may be waived for applicants with qualifying law enforcement experience.) In addition, candidates must pass all steps of the selection process which includes an oral interview, FBI background investigation, medical exam, and drug screening.

Advancement Prospects

Supervisory and administrative positions are available for those interested in management duties. Most Probation Officers realize advancement by earning higher pay and receiving more complex responsibilities.

Education and Training

Employers require that candidates have a bachelor's degree, preferably in a behavioral science discipline. In addition, employers may require that candidates have earned a master's degree, be currently enrolled in a master's program, or have completed a year of graduate-level courses. Some offices may impose a hiring condition in which candidates must earn a master's degree within five years of their appointment.

New U.S. Probation Officers typically receive both formal and on-the-job training. Throughout their careers, Probation Officers enroll in voluntary and mandatory training programs and continuing education classes to develop their skills and expertise.

Experience, Skills, and Personality Traits

In general, employers require one to three years of progressively responsible work in probation, pretrial services, parole, corrections, criminal investigation, substance abuse treatment, or related fields. In addition, candidates should be knowledgeable about the federal court system as well as about policies and procedures for federal probation and parole.

U.S. Probation Officers have excellent interviewing, research, communication, and writing skills. They also have strong teamwork and interpersonal skills as well as effective analytical, conflict management, and self-management skills.

Being courteous, honest, respectful, dedicated, realistic, and objective are a few personality traits that successful U.S. Probation Officers share.

Unions and Associations

Many U.S. Probation Officers are members of professional associations to take advantage of networking opportunities, training programs, and other professional services and resources. Some associations that many join are the American

Probation and Parole Association and the Federal Law Enforcement Officers Association.

Tips for Entry

1. Each U.S. Probation Office is responsible for its own hiring and recruitment. Contact the offices where you wish to work for information about job vacancies and requirements.

2. You can learn more about U.S. Probation Officers on the Internet. One web site that you might visit is the U.S. Probation and Pretrial Services web site at *http://www.uscourts.gov/misc/propretrial.htm.* To find other web sites, enter either of these keywords in a search engine: *U.S. Probation Officer* or *U.S. Probation Office.*

JUVENILE COUNSELOR

CAREER PROFILE

Duties: Provide supervision, counseling, and case management services for the rehabilitation of juvenile offenders; perform other duties as required

Alternate Titles: Juvenile Court Officer, Juvenile Probation Officer, Juvenile Caseworker, Juvenile Probation Counselor

Salary Range: $25,000 to $59,000

Employment Prospects: Good

Advancement Prospects: Fair

Prerequisites:

Education/Training—A bachelor's degree; on-the-job training

Experience—One or more years of experience working with children and teenagers; general knowledge about juvenile laws, juvenile court procedures, human behavior, and adolescent social structures and thinking patterns; familiarity with case management and social, legal, and health resources in the government and community

Special Skills and Personality Traits—Communication, listening, interpersonal, writing, interviewing, analytical, and self-management skills; objective, stable, honest, respectful, concerned, ethical, dedicated

Licensure/Certification—None required

CAREER LADDER

```
┌─────────────────────────────────┐
│      Senior or Supervisory      │
│       Juvenile Counselor        │
└─────────────────────────────────┘

┌─────────────────────────────────┐
│  Juvenile Counselor (Journey Level)  │
└─────────────────────────────────┘

┌─────────────────────────────────┐
│  Juvenile Counselor (Entry Level)  │
└─────────────────────────────────┘
```

Position Description

Juvenile Counselors are employed by juvenile probation departments, which work closely with juvenile courts (or family courts). They provide these courts with supervision, case management, counseling, and other services related to the rehabilitation of juvenile offenders. Juvenile Counselors also go by different titles, such as *Juvenile Counselors, Juvenile Court Officers,* or *Juvenile Caseworkers.*

In the United States, juvenile courts are responsible for conducting legal proceedings against children under the age of 18 who are accused of violating criminal laws, such as vandalism, petty theft, burglary, assault, possession of guns, drug possession, manslaughter, or murder. Juvenile courts also address cases of chronic school truancy as well as cases of undisciplined youth whose parents or guardians are unable to control their disruptive behavior.

Juvenile offenders may be given sentences in juvenile correctional facilities or be placed under probation (or court supervision). The probation usually involves specific conditions, such as agreeing to meet certain expectations such as going to school, avoiding associations with certain persons, and being home by certain times. Their conditions may also include participating in counseling programs, performing community service, attending substance abuse education programs, or enrolling in drug treatment programs. In addition, juvenile offenders may be required to make payments to injured parties.

Juvenile Counselors are responsible for providing supervision to juvenile offenders on probation. Their goals are to ensure the safety of the public, to assist the juveniles and their families in a program of rehabilitation, and to inspire a sense of responsibility in the offenders for their own acts.

Juvenile Counselors usually manage 30 to 40 or more active cases, making personal contact with each juvenile on a regular basis. They help the youth meet the conditions of their probation plan by referring them to appropriate mental health counselors, education programs, community services, and other resources. They also counsel and advise juveniles on their behavior, responsibility, attitudes, goals, and other related concerns or problems. Juvenile Counselors investigate any suspected violations of the juveniles' probation, and when necessary, report violations to the proper authorities.

In addition, Juvenile Counselors monitor their clients' progress by talking with school officials, counselors, parents, and others. They also obtain copies of school records, treatment progress reports, and so forth. Juvenile Counselors maintain accurate and up-to-date records on each of their cases. They are also responsible for submitting weekly or monthly forms and reports about their caseload. When necessary, Juvenile Counselors testify in court about the progress of the youth that they supervise.

Juvenile Courts may also place undisciplined juveniles on protective supervision. In those cases, Juvenile Counselors help the youth secure necessary education, social, and medical services. The counselor also works with the families to make sure the youth are receiving proper supervision and care.

Juvenile Counselors perform other duties, which vary from department to department as well as within a department. Many Juvenile Counselors have the additional duty of helping judges determine the most effective and appropriate sentences for juvenile offenders. Juvenile Counselors conduct investigations, gathering background information about the youth and the offenses they have committed. They provide judges with the facts along with recommendations for probation or commitment to a juvenile correctional facility. In addition, Juvenile Counselors suggest programs appropriate for the offenders' rehabilitation.

Some Juvenile Counselors are also responsible for providing intake duties. They evaluate all juvenile violations and undisciplined behavior complaints to determine if there is enough evidence to warrant court action. Juvenile Counselors interview the juvenile defendants, their families, victims, law enforcement officers, and others who are involved or have relevant information about the juveniles or the juveniles' families.

Juvenile Counselors have daily contact with various professionals, including judges, prosecuting attorneys, community agencies, law enforcement officers, school officials, mental health counselors, and so on. In addition, Juvenile Counselors develop social, mental health, and other resources to which they can refer juveniles.

Many Juvenile Counselors participate in educational and youth programs in schools, community-based organizations, and social services agencies. Some also offer presentations on various juvenile justice topics to parent groups, schools, community organizations, and professional associations.

Juvenile Counselors often work evenings and on weekends to meet with clients and complete their various tasks. Travel may be required to meet with youth, families, school officials, treatment providers, and others.

Salaries

Salaries vary, depending on factors such as experience, education, employer, and geographical location. According to the Bureau of Labor Statistics, the estimated annual salary in 2000 for most Probation Officers (including Juvenile Counselors) ranged between $25,010 and $59,010.

Employment Prospects

Juvenile Counselors are employed by local and state juvenile probation departments. Most opportunities become available as Juvenile Counselors resign, retire, or transfer to other positions. When funding is available, agencies may create additional positions to meet staffing needs.

Advancement Prospects

Supervisory and administrative positions are available within juvenile probation departments.

Depending on their interests, Juvenile Counselors can also pursue other related careers by becoming schoolteachers, school counselors, family therapists, law enforcement officers, or lawyers.

Education and Training

Employers generally require that candidates have a bachelor's degree, preferably in a behavior science discipline.

Entry-level Juvenile Counselors receive on-the-job training. Throughout their careers, Juvenile Counselors enroll in training seminars and continuing education classes to develop and enhance their skills and expertise.

Experience, Skills, and Personality Traits

In general, employers require that candidates have one or more years of experience working with children and teenagers. In addition, candidates must have general knowledge about juvenile laws, juvenile court procedures, and human behavior, as well as adolescent social structures and thinking patterns. Being familiar with social work principles of case management and with the social, legal, and health resources in the government and community is also desirable.

Juvenile Counselors must have excellent communication, listening, and interpersonal skills to work well with young people, judges, and others. They also need effective writing, interviewing, and analytical skills for their work. In addition, they must have exceptional self-management skills—the ability to work independently, handle stressful situations, manage various tasks, meet deadlines, make sound judgments, and so on.

Being objective, stable, honest, respectful, concerned, ethical, and dedicated are a few personality traits that successful Juvenile Counselors share. In addition, they have a good sense of humor and are able to relate well to young people.

Unions and Associations

Juvenile Counselors join local, state, and national professional associations to take advantage of networking opportunities, training programs, professional publications, and other professional services and resources. The American Probation and Parole Association and the American Correctional Association are two national associations that many Juvenile Counselors join.

Tips for Entry

1. Gain experience by interning in juvenile probation departments or volunteering in community-based youth programs that provide support services to juvenile offenders.

2. Many juvenile detention facilities hire temporary or on-call detention counselors to substitute for full-time counselors when they are absent for personal or business reasons. Contact juvenile probation departments for information.

3. You can learn more about juvenile justice on the Internet. One web site that you might visit is for the Office of Juvenile Justice and Delinquency Prevention *(http://ojjdp.ncjrs.org)*. Another is the Juvenile Justice page at the National Criminal Justice Reference Service web site *(http://virlib.ncjrs.org/Juvenile Justice.asp)*. To find other relevant web sites, enter any of these key words in a search engine: *juvenile justice, juvenile probation department,* or *juvenile probation services.*

CHILD PROTECTIVE SERVICES (CPS) CASEWORKER

CAREER PROFILE

Duties: Be advocates for children; provide assessment, counseling, and case management services; ensure that children are receiving protection and proper care in their homes

Alternate Titles: Child Protective Services Specialist, Child Protective Services Investigator

Salary Range: $20,000 to $50,000

Employment Prospects: Good

Advancement Prospects: Good

Prerequisites:

    Education/Training—A bachelor's or master's degree in social work; in-service training

    Experience—Previous experience working with child protective services; knowledgeable about child and adolescent development, as well as family development and dynamics; experience working with people of different cultural, economic, and social backgrounds

    Special Skills and Personality Traits—Communication, listening, interpersonal, conflict management, interviewing, research, and self-management skills; sincere, trusting, discreet, empathetic, resilient, sensitive, patient, flexible, objective

    Licensure/Certification—Being licensed, certified, or registered social workers is required in some states

CAREER LADDER

```
┌─────────────────────────────────────┐
│ Senior or Supervisory Child Protective │
│      Services Caseworker             │
└─────────────────────────────────────┘

┌─────────────────────────────────────┐
│  Child Protective Services Caseworker │
└─────────────────────────────────────┘

┌─────────────────────────────────────┐
│     Child Protective Services        │
│       Caseworker Trainee             │
└─────────────────────────────────────┘
```

Position Description

Child Protective Services (CPS) Caseworkers are social workers who are employed by child welfare government agencies in their communities. As children's advocates, CPS Caseworkers make sure that children have proper protection and care. Their job involves providing assessment, counseling, and case management services to abused and neglected children and their families. They also work with children who are at risk of maltreatment.

CPS Caseworkers are authorized by law to investigate reports of abused and neglected children. Reports come from family members, teachers, law enforcement officers, and others who are concerned that children are being mistreated by their parents or guardians. CPS Caseworkers also receive court orders to look into such reports.

Their investigations involve interviewing children as well as the persons suspected of mistreating the children. Caseworkers also interview others (such as family members, school officials, treatment counselors, and law enforcement officers) to verify information. In addition, caseworkers obtain and review any relevant records pertaining to the children, parents, and other persons living in the home. These include criminal records, medical reports, and mental health records. Caseworkers may request that children be given medical, psychological, or psychiatric examinations to establish whether abuse or neglect has occurred.

Upon completion of their investigations, CPS Caseworkers examine the data and rule whether maltreatment has occured. If abuse or neglect is found, caseworkers may recommend that CPS agencies work with the families to resolve the problems. They may also recommend that petitions be filed in family court to remove children from their homes and place them temporarily in safer environments. In addition, CPS Caseworkers report any suspicions of criminal violations to appropriate law enforcement agencies.

CPS Caseworkers also have the duty to work with families to develop strategies for changing the conditions and behaviors within the homes that resulted in child abuse and neglect. For example, families may need assistance in child care, counseling, or public welfare, or individual family members may need job training, substance abuse treatment, or parenting classes. Caseworkers provide families with the proper services by referring them to the appropriate resources (such as treatment programs, education programs, and community services) in their communities.

CPS Caseworkers meet with the families assigned to their caseload on a regular basis. They provide families with advice and counseling as well as monitor their progress. Caseworkers are responsible for keeping detailed records of their cases and preparing required forms and reports about their cases. If families fail to resolve their problems, CPS Caseworkers may recommend to the court that children be placed permanently with other caregivers. In some cases, they may recommend that parent-child relationships be terminated.

In addition to their investigative and case management duties, CPS Caseworkers are responsible for keeping up with developments in their field. They enroll in continuing education programs, attend professional training workshops, read professional journals and books, participate in professional conferences, network with colleagues, and so on.

CPS Caseworkers work a 40-hour week, but they occasionally work evenings and weekends to meet with clients or to complete their various tasks.

Salaries

Salaries vary, depending on factors such as experience, education, and geographical location. The 2000 estimated annual salary for most child and family social workers ranged from $20,120 to $50,280, according to the Bureau of Labor Statistics.

Employment Prospects

The job outlook for CPS Caseworkers is currently favorable. Because of the difficulty of finding enough qualified applications, many agencies are recruiting outside their region. In addition, many are hiring candidates with bachelor's degrees in social work.

Advancement Prospects

With additional experience and education, CPS Caseworkers can advance to supervisory and administrative positions.

Depending on their interests, CPS Caseworkers can pursue other related careers, becoming child and family therapists, children advocates (in public interest organizations), politicians, child welfare program directors, and family law attorneys.

Education and Training

Depending on the employer, candidates may need either a bachelor's or master's degree in social work (along with qualifying work experience).

CPS Caseworkers receive in-service training. In addition, most enroll in voluntary continuing education and training programs to develop their skills and expertise.

Experience, Skills, and Personality Traits

Employers generally require that candidates have a few years of experience providing child protective services. In addition, candidates must be knowledgeable about child and adolescent development as well as about family development and dynamics. They should also have experience working with people of different cultural, economic, and social backgrounds.

CPS Caseworkers have excellent communication, listening, and interpersonal skills. In addition, they have strong conflict management skills, as well as adequate interviewing and research skills. Furthermore, they have superior self-management skills—the ability to work independently, make sound and timely decisions, handle stressful situations, manage several tasks at the same time, and so forth.

Being sincere, trusting, discreet, empathetic, resilient, sensitive, patient, flexible, and objective are some personality traits that successful CPS Caseworkers share. In addition, they are dedicated and compassionate about child welfare.

Licensure and Certification

In some states, CPS Caseworkers may need to be licensed, certified, or registered social workers. For specific licensure information, contact the regulatory board for social workers in the state where you wish to practice. You can also get information from a local child protective services agency.

Unions and Associations

CPS Caseworkers join local, state, and national professional associations to take advantage of networking opportunities, training programs, educational programs, professional resources, and other professional services. Some national organizations that serve their needs are the American Professional Society on the Abuse of Children, the American Humane Association, and the National Association of Social Workers.

Tips for Entry

1. Gain experience by volunteering or interning with a social service agency, hospital, or therapeutic treatment program that works with abused and neglected children and their families.

2. To get an idea of what it might be like to be a CPS Caseworker, become a Court Appointed Special Advocate (CASA) volunteer. Family court judges assign highly trained CASA volunteers to abuse or neglect cases. For further information, contact a family court.

3. You can learn more about the field of child protective services on the Internet. One web site you might visit is the National Clearinghouse on Child Abuse and Neglect Information *(http://www.calib.com/nccanch/index.htm)*. Along with providing general information, the web site provides links to other relevant web sites.

VICTIM SERVICES SPECIALIST

CAREER PROFILE

Duties: Provide various support services to victims of crimes; assist in the administration and development of victim assistance programs; perform other duties as required

Alternate Title: Victim Advocate

Salary Range: $0 to $53,000

Employment Prospects: Very Good

Advancement Prospects: Limited

Prerequisites:

Education/Training—A bachelor's degree; victim assistance training

Experience—One or more years of experience, for staff positions; familiarity with crime victim laws and court procedures; experience working with people from different cultural, social, and economic backgrounds

Special Skills and Personality Traits—Communication, listening, interpersonal, conflict management, and stress management skills; brave, patient, trusting, respectful, flexible, resourceful, resilient

Licensure/Certification—State certification may be required

CAREER LADDER

```
┌─────────────────────────────┐
│  Victim Assistance Program  │
│  Coordinator or Director    │
└─────────────────────────────┘

┌─────────────────────────────┐
│  Victim Services Specialist │
└─────────────────────────────┘

┌─────────────────────────────┐
│  Volunteer, Intern, or Trainee │
└─────────────────────────────┘
```

Position Description

Victim Services Specialists are advocates of crime victims' rights. In the United States, federal and state laws mandate that victims of crimes have certain rights. For example, crime victims have the right to be informed of the progress of court cases, and to be notified of changes in the status of the suspects or offenders. Victim Services Specialists are trained staff members of victim assistance programs, which are administered by prosecuting attorney's offices, corrections, law enforcement agencies, or community-based organizations. They work with children, teenagers, and adults.

Victim Services Specialists provide various direct services to crime victims, while managing several cases at a time. Some of these services are:

- informing victims about how the criminal justice system works and what their rights are as crime victims

- providing victims with updates about the progress of court cases
- helping victims prepare to testify in court
- escorting victims to court appearances, and providing a safe and secure area for them during court proceedings
- helping victims apply for crime victim compensation programs as well as for restitution from the offenders
- helping victims obtain restraining orders
- notifying victims of the status of the offenders—such as release from custody, eligibility for parole, and escape from custody or prison
- providing victims with emotional support (especially at crime scenes)
- referring victims to services they may require—such as legal assistance, counseling, medical treatment, support groups, and housing services

- acting as liaisons between victims, and their families, and law enforcement agencies, correctional facilities, and other government agencies

Some specialists provide services in one particular area of crime, such as domestic violence, sexual assault, homicide, or gang violence. Some specialists serve particular groups—for example, elderly victims, children, or victims of juvenile offenders.

Victim Services Specialists also perform various other duties. They assist in the administration of grant funds, the development of policies and procedures, the planning of new services and programs, and the creation of public information and training materials. They provide the general public with information about their victim services programs, as well as act as liaisons with other victim assistance agencies.

In addition, specialists continually develop new legal, medical, emotional, and other resources to which they refer victims for help. They also keep up with trends and developments in the victim assistance field. Further, they perform other duties as required.

Victim Services Specialists often work additional hours at night and on weekends to help crime victims.

Salaries

Specific salary information is unavailable for Victim Services Specialists. Many are volunteers, and thus receive no compensation. Paid employees receive salaries comparable to other community and social services occupations. According to the U.S. Bureau of Labor Statistics, the estimated annual salary in 2000 for most community and social services workers ranged from $17,710 to $52,700.

Employment Prospects

Victim assistance services is a young and rapidly growing field. Most opportunities are for volunteer positions, but the number of paid staff positions is gradually increasing.

Most paid positions become available as Victim Services Specialists resign or transfer to other positions. Established programs occasionally create additional positions to meet staffing needs when funding is available. In addition, new victim assistance programs are continually starting throughout the country.

Advancement Prospects

Because the victim services field is so new, advancement opportunities are limited to a few administrative positions.

Education and Training

Employers generally require (or highly prefer) that Victim Services Specialists hold a bachelor's degree in psychology,

social work, criminal justice, or other related field. In some states, specialists must meet minimum training requirements.

Victim services training and continuing education programs are available through colleges, universities, and private organizations. Another source for training programs is the National Victim Assistance Academy (*http://www.nvaa.org*).

Experience, Skills, and Personality Traits

Applicants for paid staff positions are generally required to have one or more years or experience providing victim assistance services. They are familiar with crime victim laws and court procedures. In addition, candidates have experience working with people from different cultural, social, and economic backgrounds.

Victim Services Specialists must have superior communication, listening, and interpersonal skills. They also need excellent conflict management and stress management skills. Successful Victim Services Specialists share several personality traits such as being brave, patient, trusting, respectful, flexible, resourceful, and resilient.

Licensure and Certification

Victim Services Specialists may be required to be state certified. For specific information, contact a victim services agency in the area where you wish to work.

Unions and Associations

Victim Services Specialists join professional associations to take advantage of networking opportunities, training programs, and other professional services and resources. Two national associations that many join are the National Organization for Victim Assistance and the Association of Traumatic Stress Specialists.

Tips for Entry

1. Gain experience by volunteering or interning with victim assistance services programs, such as rape crisis centers, battered women's programs, child protective services agencies, or programs run by law enforcement agencies and prosecuting attorney's offices.
2. Learn more about victim assistance services on the Internet. Here are three web sites that you might visit: U.S. Office for Victims of Crime, *http://www.ojp. usdoj.gov/ovc;* Victim and Victimology Resources, *http://arapaho.nsuok.edu/~dreveskr/victm.html-ssi;* National Organization for Victim Assistance, *http://www.try-nova.org*.

PROFESSIONS IN POLITICS

LEGISLATOR, STATE OR FEDERAL

CAREER PROFILE

Duties: Serve as an elected representative in the U.S. Congress or a state legislature; make federal or state laws; perform duties as required

Alternate Titles: Politician, Elected Official; U.S. Senator, U.S. Representative, State Senator, State Representative

Salary Range: $0 to $157,000

Employment Prospects: Limited

Advancement Prospects: Limited

Prerequisites:

Education/Training—No standard requirements

Experience—Public service and community involvement

Special Skills and Personality Traits—Leadership, organizational, teamwork, interpersonal, communication, public speaking, and debate skills; ability to compromise; outgoing, self-confident, popular, honest, dedicated, energetic, assertive

Licensure/Certification—None required

CAREER LADDER

```
┌─────────────────────────────────┐
│       Federal Legislator        │
└─────────────────────────────────┘

┌─────────────────────────────────┐
│        State Legislator         │
└─────────────────────────────────┘

┌─────────────────────────────────┐
│ Local Elected Official, Legislative │
│     Aide, or Any Occupation     │
└─────────────────────────────────┘
```

Position Description

In the United States, federal and state Legislators are responsible for making laws that govern the nation and the 50 states. They create laws to protect public safety and welfare; protect civil rights; provide for education, affordable health care, and social services; protect the environment; build and repair streets and freeways; assist small business owners; protect people in the workplace; raise or lower taxes; and so forth. As elected officials, federal and state Legislators propose and pass laws that are in the best interests of their constituents, the people whom they represent.

Federal Legislators are elected to serve in the U.S. Congress in Washington, D.C. They work in either one of the two Congressional chambers—the Senate, which is the upper house, and the House of Representatives, which is the lower house. State Legislators work in their state capitals. In 49 states, state Legislators are elected to serve in either one of two legislative chambers. The upper house is also known as the Senate; the lower house is called the House of Representatives, General Assembly, or House of Delegates. In Nebraska, the legislature is made up of only one house.

Along with making laws, state and federal Legislators perform other duties. Some of these responsibilities include:

- planning government budgets
- assessing taxes
- approving official appointments by executive officers
- regulating government activities
- conducting impeachment proceedings
- serving on legislative committees and subcommittees (such as finance, education, or labor) that study prospective legislation

Legislators keep constituents informed about their activities through meetings, press releases, newsletters, web sites, and other methods. They also ask constituents about their opinions regarding issues and proposed bills. In addition, Legislators assist constituents with their requests and questions. Legislators typically have offices in the capital as well as in their local districts. Almost all Legislators maintain a staff that provides office and legislative support.

Legislators work long and varied hours, including evenings and on weekends. Each day is unique. They attend community, social, and charity functions; meet with lobbyists, other legislators, the media, and constituents; make public speeches; research issues; prepare reports; attend meetings; and so on. Legislators often travel back and forth from their home state or district to the capital.

U.S. Senators represent all the people who live in their state, and so are elected by voters statewide. U.S. Representatives are elected by voters in the districts where they live and which they represent. State legislators are elected by voters in the districts that they represent. Legislators are elected to serve terms that usually last from two to six years. They may seek reelection at the end of their terms. In some states, Legislators may run for only a limited number of terms.

At the state and national levels, candidates run for legislative offices as members of a political party—Democrat, Republican, Reform, American Independent, and so on. Candidates begin campaign efforts several months, or even a few years, before an election. They use the television, radio, and print media, as well as distribute materials, to describe their qualifications and reasons for running for office. They make speeches before business, community, and social organizations, as well as meet voters at various public functions and events. Candidates also participate in public debates about issues that concern the communities they would represent. Furthermore, candidates raise money to pay for their political campaigns.

Salaries

Salaries vary widely. In some states, legislators receive no pay but are usually paid a per diem (per day) fee. According to the Bureau of Labor Statistics, the estimated annual salary in 2000 for most legislators ranged from $11,560 to $62,860. In 2001, the annual salary for members of Congress was raised to $145,100. The House and Senate leaders currently receive $157,000.

Employment Prospects

There are 100 U.S. Senate positions, two from each of the 50 states. The number of U.S. Representatives and state legislative positions may increase or decrease depending on the population growth within each district.

Opportunities become available during elections. Any U.S. citizen who meets the age and residence requirements for an office may run for election.

Advancement Prospects

Many Legislators become career politicians, but much of their political success depends on their ability to win elections. Career politicians define their own terms of advancement. Many Legislators pursue a career path of running for higher offices. For example, a state assemblyperson might run for state senate, then after several terms as a state senator run for the U.S. Senate or a state executive office.

Education and Training

There are no standard educational requirements for becoming state or federal Legislators. Most Legislators have bachelor's degrees as well as advanced degrees in various fields. Many Legislators possess law degrees.

Experience, Skills, and Personality Traits

Legislators come from various backgrounds—law, education, business, social services, health care, science, journalism, public advocacy, and so forth. Some Legislators have gained previous experience working as staff members for other politicians, by being legislative aides, chiefs of staffs, political consultants, and so forth.

In general, voters choose candidates who have a track record of being actively involved in their communities. They also select candidates whose political principles and stances on social, economic, and other issues match theirs.

Some basic skills that Legislators need are leadership, organizational, teamwork, interpersonal, communication, public speaking, and debate skills. They also have the ability to make compromises.

Being outgoing, self-confident, popular, honest, dedicated, energetic, and assertive are some personality traits that successful Legislators share. Further, they have a strong commitment to public service and are passionate about making changes for the best interests of the public welfare.

Unions and Associations

As members of their political parties, Legislators actively participate in party meetings, committee work, fund-raising activities, and so on. They also belong to various social, educational, and community organizations, charities, professional associations, and other organizations to take advantage of networking opportunities as well as to continually build a broad base of support.

Tips for Entry

1. Work on political campaigns for candidates as well as for local and state propositions or initiatives in which you believe. Also, get involved in community groups, charities, and public service activities.
2. Gain experience by obtaining internships or fellowships in local, state, or federal government offices.
3. Use the Internet to learn more about how government works. The 50 state governments all have web sites. To find a web site, enter the name of a state and the word *government* (for example, *Florida government*). For information about the U.S. Congress, visit these web sites: U.S. Senate, *http://www.senate.gov,* and the U.S. House of Representatives, *http://www.house.gov.*

LOCAL ELECTED OFFICIALS

CAREER PROFILE

Duties: Serve as elected leaders in city and county governments; make and enforce laws; perform duties as required

Alternate Titles: Mayor; City Council Member; County Commissioner, County Supervisor, County Freeholder (New Jersey)

Salary Range: $0 to $63,000

Employment Prospects: Limited

Advancement Prospects: Limited

Prerequisites:

Education/Training—No standard requirements

Experience—Public service and community involvement

Special Skills and Personality Traits—Leadership, teamwork, interpersonal, public speaking, and debate skills; ability to compromise; outgoing, self-confident, popular, honest, dedicated, energetic, assertive

Licensure/Certification   None required

CAREER LADDER

```
┌─────────────────────────────────────┐
│    State or Federal Elected Office   │
└─────────────────────────────────────┘

┌─────────────────────────────────────┐
│   City Council or County Board of    │
│            Commissioners             │
└─────────────────────────────────────┘

┌─────────────────────────────────────┐
│       Member of a local board        │
│     or commission (such as the       │
│         board of education)          │
└─────────────────────────────────────┘
```

Position Description

In the United States, local government is composed of two levels—county and municipality (city, village, or town). Both levels of local government are created by state governments and are under their authority. But it is the voters within each municipality and county who choose their local government leaders. Heading municipal governments are mayors and council members, while commissioners govern county governments. (In Louisiana, counties are called parishes; in Alaska, boroughs.)

Local Elected Officials are responsible for making and executing laws that provide for the protection, safety, and general welfare of the citizens and the environment. They plan fiscal budgets as well as establish policies, objectives, and goals for running local governments. They also develop public services such as law enforcement, fire services, schools, hospitals, affordable housing, parks, public transportation, and waste treatment systems. In addition, they have the authority to assess and collect taxes. Furthermore,

Local Elected Officials make sure that government operations are running smoothly and effectively each day.

The powers of Local Elected Officials vary, depending on the form of county or municipal government. In most county governments, the governing body consists of a board of one or more commissioners. The board performs both lawmaking and executive duties. In some counties, voters elect an executive officer who shares policy-making decisions with the board of commissioners.

The roles of mayor and city council vary among municipalities. In many city governments, the mayor and city council are two distinct offices. The mayor, as executive officer, determines government policy and runs the government while the city council makes municipal ordinances, or laws. In some municipalities, the mayor has limited powers and shares policy-making decisions with the city council. In other municipalities, the city council is the main governing body. The mayor, who may be elected or appointed, is a member of the council. A city manager is hired by the council to run the city.

Most local elections are nonpartisan. In other words, candidates do not run as members of political parties—Democratic, Republican, Reform, American Independent, and so on. Local Elected Officials usually are elected to serve an office term of two to four years. They may seek reelection at the end of their terms. In some communities, Elected Officials are limited in the number of terms they may serve.

When Elected Officials run for reelection, they must campaign extensively to convince voters that they are still the best candidates for office. They make speeches, meet with voters, participate in public debates, and so forth. They use the television, radio, and print media, as well as distribute materials, to describe their qualifications for office.

City council members and county commissioners work part time or full time in their elected positions. Many continue to hold down part-time or full-time jobs in their primary professions.

Local Elected Officials work irregular hours. They often work evenings and on weekends to attend meetings, review issues, prepare proposals, complete administrative tasks, fulfill official duties at community functions, and so forth.

Salaries

Salaries vary widely. In some local governments, Elected Officials do not receive any salary. According to the Bureau of Labor Statistics, the annual estimated salary in 2000 for most legislators, including local elected officials, ranged from $11,560 to $62,860.

Employment Prospects

Opportunities become available with each local election. Any U.S. citizen who meets age and residence requirements may run for a city council or county board seat. To win, candidates must undertake campaigns that appeal to a broad base of local voters.

Advancement Prospects

Some Local Elected Officials serve for a few terms, accomplishing the goals for which the voters elected them (for example: cutting taxes, adding more social services, or enacting clean air laws). Other officials pursue a political career path, running for elected offices at progressively higher (local, state, and federal) levels.

Education and Training

There are no standard educational requirements for Local Elected Officials. Many hold associate, bachelor's and advanced degrees in various disciplines.

Experience, Skills, and Personality Traits

Local Elected Officials come from different backgrounds—business, community services, law, education, and so forth. However, voters usually choose candidates who have a track record of being actively involved in their communities. They also select candidates whose political principles and stances on social, economic, and other issues match theirs.

Some skills that Local Elected Officials need are leadership, teamwork, interpersonal, communication, public speaking, and debate skills. In addition, they must have the ability to make compromises.

Being outgoing, charming, sincere, honest, dedicated, energetic, creative, and flexible are some personality traits that successful Local Elected Officials share. Further, they have a strong desire to make changes that benefit their communities.

Unions and Associations

Local Elected Officials join state, regional, and national associations that serve city and county governments. Two national organizations are the National League of Cities and the National Association of Counties. These associations offer leadership training programs, opportunities to network with peers, and other professional services and resources.

Tips for Entry

1. Participate in your local government. For example, attend council meetings, apply for voluntary positions on city commissions, or get involved in the political issues that concern your community.
2. Many council members and county supervisors began their political careers by being elected or appointed to local school boards, special district boards, or other local government boards and commissions.
3. Join various community organizations—social, educational, charities, business, and so forth—to gain public service experience and to take advantage of networking opportunities.
4. Use the Internet to learn more about how local government works. Many city and county governments have web sites. To find a web site for a city government, enter the name of the city and the phrase *city government* (for example, *Knoxville city government*). For a county government web site, enter the name of the county and the phrase *county government* (for example, *San Benito county government*).

LEGISLATIVE ASSISTANT

CAREER PROFILE

Duties: Assist legislators with research and decision making for proposed legislation; assist constituents and others with requests for general information; perform public relations duties; perform other duties as required

Alternate Titles: Legislative Aide, Political Aide, District Aide, Field Representative

Salary Range: $15,000 to $60,000

Employment Prospects: Fair

Advancement Prospects: Good

Prerequisites:

Education/Training—A bachelor's degree; many have advanced degrees

Experience—Previous experience as interns, volunteers, or support staff in legislators' offices; knowledge of the legislative process and the issues that concern legislators

Special Skills and Personality Traits—Writing, research, organizational, teamwork, communication, interpersonal, self-management skills; outgoing, energetic, enthusiastic, self-motivated, efficient, ambitious, creative, flexible

Licensure/Certification—None required

CAREER LADDER

```
┌─────────────────────────────────────┐
│  Legislative Director or Chief of Staff │
└─────────────────────────────────────┘

┌─────────────────────────────────────┐
│      Legislative Assistant           │
└─────────────────────────────────────┘

┌─────────────────────────────────────┐
│   Campaign or Legislative Volunteer  │
│          or Staff Member             │
└─────────────────────────────────────┘
```

Position Description

Legislative Assistants provide support to legislators so that they can effectively make laws that are in the best interests of their constituents. Legislative Assistants help legislators in all three levels of government. At the local level, they aid city council members and the county board of supervisors. At the state and federal levels, Legislative Assistants assist senators and representatives who serve in state legislatures or the U.S. Congress.

Legislators, at all levels of government, sponsor legislation as well as vote on proposed bills about funding, social programs, the environment, civil rights, individual rights, education, and other issues. Legislative Assistants are responsible for helping legislators stay on top of each proposed legislation. Some of their duties include:

- conducting research
- meeting with lobbyists, constituents, and others to gather accurate and factual information about the issues

- drafting proposed legislation
- attending legislative committee meetings and preparing reports of the proceedings
- analyzing bills and making recommendations to legislators on the best actions to make
- analyzing the voting records of other legislators
- keeping track of the status of proposed legislation
- keeping legislators informed about the needs and concerns of the legislators' constituents

Legislative Assistants may be assigned to handle several different bills or be in charge of one or more major issues, such as technology, children's rights, or health care.

Legislative Assistants are also responsible for helping constituents and the general public with questions or requests. For example, a constituent may want to know about government programs that help the elderly. Legislative Assistants conduct research and provide the information in person by phone, letter, or e-mail.

Many Legislative Assistants also handle public relations. They maintain relationships with the leaders and constituents in the legislators' home districts. In addition, the assistants keep constituents informed about legislators' activities and accomplishments through press releases, newsletters, web sites, and other forms of communication. Legislative Assistants also set up speaking engagements for legislators at schools, community centers, chambers of commerce, and community organizations, as well as at community events and other functions within their districts.

Many Legislative Assistants are responsible for performing various office and administrative duties. These tasks vary from one office to the next. For example, they might answer phones and e-mail messages, greet visitors to the legislator's office, maintain the legislator's schedule, draft routine correspondence, and supervise interns and volunteers.

Some Legislative Assistants help legislators with their political campaigns. They may plan campaign activities, develop campaign materials, set up fund-raising events, and draft speeches.

At the local and state level, two or more Legislators might share the services of one Legislative Assistant. In some states, legislators are allowed to hire only one assistant. Congress members typically hire several Legislative Assistants for their staffs. Federal and some state legislators have two staffs, one working in their capital offices and the other working in their district offices. District aides are responsible for keeping Legislators up to date with constituents' opinions and addressing constituents' requests.

Legislative Assistants work irregular hours. They often work in evenings and on weekends to complete specific assignments, attend meetings, and participate in social and community events on behalf of the legislators.

Salaries

Salaries vary, depending on experience, job duties, employer, geographical location, and other factors. Congressional assistants generally earn more than state and local legislative aides, and U.S. Senate aides typically receive higher salaries than House aides.

In general, salaries range from about $15,000 to $20,000 for entry-level aides to about $50,000 to $60,000 for those with 10 years experience or more.

Employment Prospects

Opportunities usually become available as Legislative Assistants resign or transfer to other positions. The turnover rate for junior positions is high, but the competition for openings is keen. Legislators occasionally create new positions to help with the increasing complexity of the issues that they must handle.

Advancement Prospects

Legislative Assistants can advance to top staff positions as chiefs of staff and legislative directors. Employers usually appoint individuals with at least 10 years of experience to the top staff positions.

Many Legislative Assistants use their experience as stepping stones to other careers. Some of these careers include being politicians, political consultants, lobbyists, attorneys, journalists, public relations directors, and business executives.

Education and Training

Entry-level Legislative Assistants must have bachelor's degrees, which may be in any field. Legal Assistants who specialize in particular issues, such as the environment, have master's or doctorate degrees in appropriate fields. Some Legislative Assistants hold law degrees.

Experience, Skills, and Personality Traits

Typically, Legislators prefer (or require) that entry-level Legislative Assistants have previous experience working in legislators' offices. They may have been interns or volunteers, or served in such support positions as legal correspondents or researchers. In addition, candidates must be knowledgeable about the lawmaking process as well as the specific issues that concern the legislators.

Legislative Assistants must have excellent writing, research, organizational, and teamwork skills. They also need strong communication and interpersonal skills to effectively handle meetings with constituents, lobbyists, interest groups, media, and others. In addition, they must have superior self-management skills—the ability to meet deadlines, work independently, handle stress, prioritize tasks, and so forth.

Successful Legislative Assistants have several personality traits in common, such as being outgoing, enthusiastic, energetic, self-motivated, efficient, ambitious, creative, and flexible.

Unions and Associations

Legislative Assistants are members of their political parties. Many actively participate in party meetings, events, and fund-raising activities.

Tips for Entry

1. You can begin gaining political experience as a high school or college student. For example, you might participate in student government, attend local government meetings, work on political campaigns, or volunteer in the office of a local, state, or federal legislator.

2. In high school or college, contact your state and congressional legislators to learn about temporary positions as pages or interns.

3. Succeeding in this field requires building and continually developing a network of contacts.

4. Learn more about the legislative process on the Internet. To learn about Congress, visit these web sites: U.S. Senate *(http://www.senate.gov)* or U.S. House of Representatives *(http://www.house.gov)*. To find web sites for state legislatures, enter the name of a state and the word *legislature* in a search engine (for example, *Arizona legislature*).

LOBBYIST

CAREER PROFILE

Duties: Represent the interests of clients on proposed legislation in state and federal legislatures; perform duties as required

Alternate Titles: Legislative Agent, Legislative Advocate, Public Advocate

Salary Range: $0 to $150,000 and more

Employment Prospects: Good

Advancement Prospects: Fair

Prerequisites:

Education/Training—Many have college degrees

Experience—Knowledgeable about the issues, laws, and policies that interest clients; previous work experience in legislative settings or a through understanding of the legislative process

Special Skills and Personality Traits—Writing, communication, interpersonal, organizational, computer, and telecommunications skills; friendly, diplomatic, energetic, persuasive, persistent, flexible, creative

Licensure/Certification—Registration with federal or state legislature is required

CAREER LADDER

```
┌─────────────────────────────────────┐
│      Independent Lobbyist or        │
│  Government Relations Consultant    │
└─────────────────────────────────────┘

┌─────────────────────────────────────┐
│             Lobbyist                │
└─────────────────────────────────────┘

┌─────────────────────────────────────┐
│          Lobbyist Trainee           │
└─────────────────────────────────────┘
```

Position Description

Lobbyists are professional advocates who work in Washington, D.C., and in the 50 state capitals. They provide lobbying services to citizen groups, small businesses, corporations, professional societies, trade associations, labor unions, academic institutions, governments, public-interest organizations, churches, charities, and other organizations. Their job is to persuade lawmakers to sponsor legislation or to pass or oppose bills that would be in the best interests of their clients. For example, one Lobbyist might represent an environmental group that wants federal legislators to vote for certain pollution controls, while another Lobbyist might represent a manufacturer who wants those same legislators to oppose such controls.

Lobbyists handle a wide range of issues reflecting their wide range of clients. These may include education, senior citizens, civil rights, children, health care, the environment, gun control, public safety, scientific research projects, social programs, foreign aid, and so on.

Lobbyists maintain a highly visible presence in federal and state legislatures. They communicate constantly with lawmakers and their staff, by contacting them in person, by phone, letters, faxes, and e-mail. They provide lawmakers with information that supports their clients' positions on specific issues or proposed bills.

In addition, Lobbyists are responsible for keeping tabs on bills that are relevant to their clients. They analyze proposed legislation and educate their clients on the key points. Lobbyists also perform other tasks. For example, they:

- conduct research on the issues that concern their clients
- prepare accurate, correct, and factual reports on issues for both clients and legislators
- collaborate with other organizations and groups to pass or defeat legislation
- attend legislative hearings
- monitor the progress of legislation and keep clients up to date with their status

Lobbyists use the media to generate public interest and awareness of the issues. They write press releases as well as newspaper and magazine articles. They may also appear on radio and TV talk shows. Some lobbyists also do indirect lobbying, which involves organizing people to write or call their legislators on behalf of their clients.

Some Lobbyists provide regulatory advocacy services. That is, they lobby government agencies, such as a state insurance commission or the Environmental Protection Agency, that are proposing regulations which affect the interests of their clients.

Many Lobbyists are independent contractors or employed by lobbying firms or law firms that provide lobbying services. Independent Lobbyists work on a wide range of issues for various groups and organizations; they may be contracted to lobby a specific legislation or be retained to work on an ongoing basis. Other Lobbyists are employed by their clients and work on only those concerns that interest their clients.

Lobbyists work long hours, including nights and weekends, to complete various tasks as well as to meet with legislators and staff. Lobbyists sometimes invite legislators to social functions so that they can interact with them in a more relaxed setting.

Salaries

Salaries vary, depending on such factors as experience, professional contacts, employer, and industry. Lobbyists generally earn higher salaries or fees from the private sector. Volunteer Lobbyists receive no salary. In general, annual salaries for paid Lobbyists range from $20,000 to $150,000 or more. Former politicians who had been highly successful in their legislative or administrative careers, might earn $200,000 or more a year for lobbying services.

Employment Prospects

Lobbying opportunities are generally available at the federal and state levels, but the competition is high.

Advancement Prospects

Most Lobbyists realize advancement by earning higher salaries and gaining reputations as highly effective professionals.

Experienced Lobbyists can pursue careers in other fields such as politics and government, public relations, journalism, education, or in nonprofit organizations.

Education and Training

Most Lobbyists have earned bachelor's degrees in various fields. Many also possess law degrees, master's degrees, and doctoral degrees.

Throughout their careers, Lobbyists participate in training programs to develop their lobbying skills and expertise. They also enroll in continuing education courses and read books and periodicals to learn more about the subjects and issues that they handle.

Experience, Skills, and Personality Traits

Clients hire Lobbyists who are knowledgeable about the issues, laws, and policies that interest the clients. Additionally, they look for candidates who have experience working in legislative settings, or who have a thorough understanding of the legislative process.

Lobbyists need excellent writing and communication skills. In addition, they must have strong interpersonal and organizational skills. They should also have good computer and telecommunications skills.

Some of the personality traits that successful Lobbyists share are being friendly, diplomatic, energetic, persuasive, persistent, flexible, and creative.

Licensure and Certification

Lobbyists are required to register with the proper government office in Congress or the state legislature in which they want to work. Requirements vary with the federal government and the 50 state governments. In addition, Lobbyists must file regular reports on their activities, including information such as their expenses, whom they represent, and what bills they are trying to influence.

Unions and Associations

Many Lobbyists join professional associations to take advantage of training programs, networking opportunities, and other professional resources and services. Two national professional associations that represent lobbyists are the American League of Lobbyists and Women in Government Relations.

Tips for Entry

1. As a high school student, you can learn first hand what is involved in trying to change public policy by getting involved with an issue or cause at your school or in your local community.
2. To gain lobbying experience, obtain intern positions with lobbying firms, public interest organizations, and other groups that have policy advocacy or similar departments.
3. One way to gain an understanding of the legislative process is to work in a legislator's office as a volunteer, intern, or staff member.
4. Positions can be found through networking with other lobbyists.
5. You can learn more about lobbying on the Internet. One web site you might visit belongs to the American League of Lobbyists (*http://www.alldc.org*). To find other relevant web sites, enter any of these keywords in a search engine: *lobbyist, lobbying,* or *lobbying laws.*

PUBLIC INTEREST ADVOCATE

CAREER PROFILE

Duties: Promote public policies and legislation on behalf of the general public; identify issues, develop solutions, conduct research, and organize media events; perform other duties as required

Alternate Titles: A title, such as Transportation Advocate or Environmental Advocate, that reflects a particular area

Salary Range: $0 to $35,000 or more

Employment Prospects: Good

Advancement Prospects: Fair

Prerequisites:

Education/Training—A bachelor's degree required or preferred

Experience—Previous experience working with public-interest organizations; knowledge of specific political issues and the lawmaking process

Special Skills and Personality Traits—Research, writing, computer, organizational, analytical, communication, and teamwork skills; enthusiastic, energetic, persuasive, patient, persistent, creative, flexible, positive

Licensure/Certification—Registration with federal or state legislatures may be required

CAREER LADDER

```
┌─────────────────────────────────────┐
│  Senior Advocate or Program Director │
└─────────────────────────────────────┘

┌─────────────────────────────────────┐
│        Public Interest Advocate      │
└─────────────────────────────────────┘

┌─────────────────────────────────────┐
│  Research Assistant, College Campus  │
│        Organizer, or Volunteer       │
└─────────────────────────────────────┘
```

Position Description

Public Interest Advocates work for public interest organizations, which promote public policies and legislation they believe is in the best interest of the general public. These organizations support specific positions on education, children's issues, the environment, political reform, civil rights, transportation, consumer protection, and other areas. Public Interest Advocates may hold job titles that reflect the particular area in which they are working, such as Consumer Advocate, Water Quality Advocate, Democracy Advocate, or Transportation Advocate.

Public Interest Advocates are responsible for identifying issues that can be presented to state or federal legislatures, government agencies, or other decision makers. They also have the duty of working on the campaigns to advance public policies. They perform a wide range of tasks that include:

• conducting research on issues
• writing comprehensive reports and studies about issues

• drafting proposed legislation
• developing solutions for public policies
• developing political strategies for getting public policies passed
• writing press releases
• organizing press conferences
• testifying in support of solutions at legislative hearings or at administrative hearings in government agencies
• lobbying lawmakers to pass legislation

In addition, Public Interest Advocates build political support. They network with other organizations and groups to create coalitions. Advocates also develop community relations by providing progress reports to local communities as well as by asking for feedback about their campaigns. In addition, they encourage communities to participate in grassroots activities such as having people contact elected officials or putting together peaceful demonstrations.

Public Interest Advocates also perform other tasks. For example, they research and write grant proposals to raise funds for current and future advocacy campaigns. Further, they are responsible for keeping up with current developments in their subject areas.

Public Interest Advocates work long hours to complete their various duties. They sometimes work evenings and on weekends.

Salaries

Salaries vary, depending on factors such as experience, employer, and geographical location. In general, Public Interest Advocates earn an annual salary that ranges from $18,000 to $35,000 or more. Many Public Interest Advocates are volunteers and do not receive any pay.

Employment Prospects

Opportunities for staff positions generally become available as Public Advocates resign or transfer to other positions. In addition, employers create additional positions when they receive funding to maintain current programs or begin new programs. Volunteer positions are readily available.

Advancement Prospects

Advancement Opportunities are limited to program directors (or coordinators) and assistants. Most Public Interest Advocates measure success through the satisfaction of making an impact in social changes.

Public Interest Advocates might choose to pursue related careers by becoming professional lobbyists, elected officials, legislative assistants, and executive officers of nonprofit organizations.

Education and Training

Most Public Interest Advocates have bachelor's or advanced degrees in various disciplines. They typically receive training on the job.

Experience, Skills, and Personality Traits

Employers require (or strongly prefer) that candidates have previous experience working with public interest organizations, especially on advocacy campaigns. In addition, candidates are knowledgeable about the issues that the employers advocate. They also have a thorough understanding of the legislative process.

Public Interest Advocates must have strong research, writing, and computer skills. In addition, they have good organizational and analytical skills as well as excellent communication and teamwork skills.

Being enthusiastic, energetic, persuasive, patient, persistent, creative, flexible, and positive are a few personality traits that successful Public Interest Advocates share. Furthermore, they have a strong passion for and commitment to public interest issues.

Licensure and Certification

Public Interest Advocates may be required to register with the federal government to lobby Congress or with a state government to lobby state legislators.

Unions and Associations

The American League of Lobbyists and Women in Government Relations are two national professional associations that Public Interest Advocates are eligible to join. By joining professional associations, they can take advantage of network opportunities and other professional resources and services.

Tips for Entry

1. Start gaining experience in high school by getting involved in public interest issues that concern you.
2. Some entry-level positions (both paid and volunteer) that are available in public interest organizations are campus organizers, web designers, writers, researchers, and public relations assistants. Many organizations also offer internships.
3. Many public interest employers do not have the budget to advertise widely for job openings. Thus, take the initiative and contact employers for whom you would like to work.
4. Learn more about public interest advocacy on the Internet. Two web sites that you might visit are: State PIRGs (Public-Interest Research Groups) Working Together, *http://www.pirg.org,* and Action Without Borders, *http://www.idealist.org.*

NONPROFIT
ADMINISTRATORS

ASSOCIATION EXECUTIVE

CAREER PROFILE

Duties: Manage a department, such as finance or education, in a professional association; perform duties as required

Alternate Titles: A specific title, such as Director of Finance, that reflects a particular department

Salary Range: $61,000 to $110,000

Employment Prospects: Fair

Advancement Prospects: Limited

Prerequisites:

Education/Training—A bachelor's degree or equivalent

Experience—Several years of executive management experience; knowledge of the trade or profession

Special Skills and Personality Traits—leadership, management, team building, interpersonal, communication, writing, financial management, and public relations skills; hardworking, analytical, organized, flexible, creative

Licensure/Certification—None required

CAREER LADDER

```
┌─────────────────────────┐
│   Executive Director     │
└─────────────────────────┘

┌─────────────────────────┐
│    Program Director      │
└─────────────────────────┘

┌─────────────────────────┐
│     Staff Position       │
└─────────────────────────┘
```

Position Description

Association Executives are responsible for managing the nonprofit organizations that are called associations. In the United States, and throughout the world, thousands of associations serve the interests of professionals and trades. These associations provide their memberships with professional services and resources, such as training and education programs, professional publications, job listings, current information about industry trends, government advocacy, and networking opportunities. Various professional associations (also known as professional societies) represent groups of professionals, such as attorneys, high school teachers, chemists, social workers, or jewelry appraisers. Trade associations represent businesses rather than individuals; for example, a retail trade association would represent a membership made up of retail stores. (Other types of associations represent charitable and philanthropic interests.)

Many professional and trade associations employ several Association Executives to run their operations. The following are some of the typical executive positions.

- *Executive Director* oversees the total operations of an association—program development, human resources, finances, office management, and so on.
- *Director of Finance* manages an association's financial affairs.
- *Director of Communications* manages all communications and public relations activities, such as producing association newsletters and other publications.
- *Director of Education* develops and oversees various education programs that meet the needs of an association's membership.
- *Director of Membership* oversees activities for gaining new members as well as keeping current members.
- *Director of Conventions* oversees the planning and coordination of all convention activities. (Many associations hold a conference for members in a different location each year.)
- *Director of Government Relations* manages the advocacy programs that promote an association's interests in state and federal legislation as well as relations with government agencies.

Depending on the size and budget of an association, Association Executives may manage one or several departments.

All Association Executives are responsible for fulfilling the mission and goals of their associations. They assist in the overall planning and development of their associations' programs and services. Further, all Association Executives perform similar duties for overseeing their particular departments. For example, they supervise and train staff members, plan and manage a departmental budget, and complete required reports.

Association Executives often work long hours, including evenings and weekends.

Salaries

Salaries vary, based on factors such as an individual's experience and education, the position and duties, an association's size, and geographical location. According to a 2001 salary survey by the American Society of Association Executives, the average annual salaries for program directors ranges from $60,732 and $110,162.

Employment Prospects

More than 80,000 national, state, local, regional, and international associations exist today, and new associations become established each year. A large number of associations can be found in the areas of Washington, D.C., New York City, and Chicago.

Opportunities generally become available as Association Executives retire, resign, or transfer to other positions. Associations occasionally create additional positions to meet their growing needs.

Advancement Prospects

Many Association Executives realize advancement through higher salaries, more responsibilities, and job satisfaction. Those aspiring to top positions become Executive Directors. Some executives climb through the ranks within their associations, while others move from one association to the next to attain top positions. Becoming association consultants or owners of association management companies are other career options for Association Executives.

Education and Training

Employers generally require that Association Executives have at least a bachelor's degree or an equivalency in educa-

tion and experience. Association Executives typically hold college degrees that are relevant to the areas in which they work. For example, a Director of Communications might hold a journalism degree, or a Director of Government Relations might possess a juris doctor (J.D.) degree.

Experience, Skills, and Personality Traits

Employers generally require that candidates have several years of executive management experience, particularly in association settings. They also look for candidates who are knowledgeable about the trades or professions that the associations serve.

Being an Association Executive requires excellent leadership, management, and team building skills, as well as superior interpersonal, communication, and writing skills. In addition, they should have adequate financial management and public relations skills. Being hardworking, analytical, organized, flexible, and creative are just a few personality traits that characterize successful Association Executives.

Unions and Associations

Association Executives might join local, state, and national associations that represent their profession, such as the American Society of Association Executives. Many also join professional associations that serve their specific field, such as education or marketing. By joining professional organizations, executives can take advantage of networking opportunities, education and training programs, and other professional resources.

Tips for Entry

1. As a college student, get involved with associations that represent your interests.
2. Many associations offer internships to college students. Contact local associations or talk to college career counselors to learn about intern opportunities.
3. Learn more about the world of associations on the Internet. One web site you might visit belongs to the American Society of Association Executives (*http://www.asaenet.org*). Also check out web sites of different associations to see what they offer. In a search engine, enter the name of a trade or profession that interests you along with the word *association,* for example, *sales association.*

CIVIL LEGAL SERVICES MANAGER

CAREER PROFILE

Duties: Manage the overall operations of nonprofit legal assistance programs; may provide legal services; perform duties as required

Alternate Titles: Executive Director, Deputy Director, Director of Litigation, Managing Attorney

Salary Range: About $65,000 to $100,000

Employment Prospects: Fair

Advancement Prospects: Limited

Prerequisites:

Education/Training—A law degree

Experience—Several years experience providing legal services; legal administrative, management, and supervisory experience

Special Skills and Personality Traits—Leadership, fund-raising, team building, interpersonal, writing, communication, public speaking, and interpersonal skills; organized, resourceful, analytical, sensible, dedicated

Licensure/Certification—An attorney's license generally required

CAREER LADDER

```
┌─────────────────────────────────────┐
│       Legal Services Manager        │
└─────────────────────────────────────┘

┌─────────────────────────────────────┐
│   Senior or Supervising Attorney    │
└─────────────────────────────────────┘

┌─────────────────────────────────────┐
│           Staff Attorney            │
└─────────────────────────────────────┘
```

Position Description

Legal Services Managers are responsible for overseeing the smooth operation of nonprofit legal assistance programs that work with low-income clients. Funded through government grants, foundation grants, and private donations, these programs provide free legal aid in substantive legal matters, such as family law, housing, public benefits, employment, elder law, and disability rights. Many programs provide only civil legal services; some additionally work in specific legal areas or with certain clientele, such as the elderly. Some legal assistance programs also have a government relations component in which they perform lobbying activities in state and federal legislatures.

Legal Services Managers are referred to by different titles, such as *Executive Director* or *Managing Attorney*. They report directly to boards of directors who are responsible for establishing the goals, objectives, and policies for the programs. The Legal Services Managers' job is to assure the successful execution of their board's mission and policies.

Managers also work closely with their boards to develop program policies and fund-raising.

Civil legal services programs range from small offices with a few attorneys to large programs with several different offices in a city, region, or even the country. Regardless of their program size, all civil Legal Services Managers have many of the same duties. For example, they:

- administer office policies and procedures
- manage the various grants for their programs
- prepare and administer budgets
- supervise and support both legal and support staff
- monitor programs for compliance with applicable laws and regulations, as well as with the rules and policies of their different grants
- provide regular written and oral progress reports to the board of directors
- recruit, hire, and train attorneys, paralegals, and support staff
- develop and write grant proposals

- build and maintain relationships with the local bar association, funding sources, and the community

Many Legal Services Managers also provide legal services to clients. Depending on the program, managers may provide direct services to clients or provide leadership counsel on major litigation.

Civil Legal Services Managers often work evenings and weekends to complete reports and other administrative tasks, meet with board members and donors, attend social and community functions, and so forth.

Salaries

Salaries vary, depending on experience, budgets, geographical location, and other factors. Annual salaries generally range from about $65,000 to $100,000.

Employment Prospects

In nonprofit organizations, the creation of new legal services programs is dependent on government grants and fund-raising. In the 1990s, many legal services programs merged, thereby creating fewer management positions. Job openings typically become available as managers resign or transfer to other positions.

Advancement Prospects

Legal Services Managers are the top positions in legal services programs. Further advancement may be measured in any number of ways, such as by earning higher incomes, obtaining management positions in larger programs, or receiving high accolades for the success of their programs.

Education and Training

The majority of Civil Legal Services Managers are law school graduates. Many also hold a bachelor's degree in public administration, business administration, or a related field.

Throughout their careers, they enroll in continuing education and training programs to develop and maintain their professional skills and expertise.

Experience, Skills, and Personality Traits

Requirements vary from employer to employer. Having several years of experience providing legal services is usually required or strongly preferred. In addition, candidates need several years of legal administrative, management, and supervisory experience. Furthermore, they show a strong commitment to providing quality programs to low-income clientele.

Legal Services Managers need excellent leadership, fund-raising, team building, and interpersonal skills, as well as superior writing and public speaking ability. Being organized, resourceful, analytical, sensible, and dedicated are a few personality traits that successful Legal Services Managers share.

Licensure and Certification

Most employers require that Legal Services Managers hold a valid attorney's license in the states where they work.

Unions and Associations

Civil Legal Services Managers join local, state, and national associations to take advantage of professional resources and services. These include opportunities for networking, education programs, publications, job listings, and so on. Some national organizations that managers might join are the Management Information Exchange (MIE), the National Legal Aid and Defender Association, and the American Bar Association.

Tips for Entry

1. In high school and college, you can start getting experience working with low-income clientele. For example, you might volunteer or intern at senior centers, community programs, and social agencies.
2. In law school, obtain internships with legal services programs.
3. You can learn more about legal services programs on the Internet. Enter the keywords *legal services programs* to find relevant web sites.

NONPROFIT ORGANIZATION (NPO) DIRECTOR

CAREER PROFILE

Duties: Provide leadership and direction for a nonprofit organization; work with board of directors; manage all administrative operations; develop fund-raising; promote organization; perform other duties as required

Alternate Titles: Executive Director, Chief Executive Officer

Salary Range: $0 to $114,000 or more

Employment Prospects: Good

Advancement Prospects: Good

Prerequisites:

Education/Training—A college degree in any field

Experience—Experience working in nonprofit settings; supervisory, administrative, and management experience

Special Skills and Personality Traits—Leadership, management, organizational, problem-solving, team building, interpersonal, communication, writing, business, and public relations skills; creative, flexible, optimistic, visionary, self-motivated, diplomatic, dedicated

Licensure/Certification—None required

CAREER LADDER

```
┌─────────────────────────────┐
│     Executive Director       │
└─────────────────────────────┘

┌─────────────────────────────┐
│     Assistant Director       │
└─────────────────────────────┘

┌─────────────────────────────┐
│       Staff Member           │
└─────────────────────────────┘
```

Position Description

Nonprofit Organization (NPO) Directors provide leadership and direction for their public service organizations. Today in the United States, more than 1 million nonprofit organizations exist to promote such social causes as education, the elderly, health issues, animal rights, affordable housing, legal assistance for the poor, consumer rights, and the environment. Religious groups, charities, social services, community-based organizations, public interest organizations, and associations are also examples of nonprofit organizations.

NPO Directors are responsible for several major duties. One duty is to work closely with the boards of directors. They help their boards formulate objectives, strategies, and policies that are best for their organizations. They also keep boards up to date with their organization's progress and activities. Additionally, NPO Directors act as the link between the boards and the staff.

Another major duty is overseeing the development, delivery, and quality of the services, products, and programs that nonprofit organizations offer. For example, a community organization might offer a job training program, legal referral services, and youth counseling to its target clientele. In small organizations, NPO Directors perform some hands-on work. They might, for example, lead workshops, write educational pamphlets, or provide direct services to clients.

Additionally, NPO Directors are responsible for managing the day-to-day operations of their organizations. They work with staff and managers to ensure that fiscal and administrative systems are running smoothly and efficiently. This includes planning and managing budgets, paying salaries, bills, and taxes, completing compliance reports, managing facilities, organizing business meetings, and so forth. In small and mid-size nonprofit organizations, NPO Directors may be responsible for overseeing all administrative duties, while in large organizations NPO Directors work with department managers.

NPO Directors are also responsible for managing human resources. They oversee the recruitment and hiring of paid and volunteer staff, as well as provide for training on an ongoing basis. Directors also establish policies and procedures as required by applicable laws and regulations.

The continuing existence of nonprofit organizations depends on grants and donations. Consequently, fund-raising is a major duty of NPO Directors. They write and submit grant proposals, plan for fund-raising events, meet with prospective donors, and so on.

NPO Directors are the spokespersons for their organizations. Therefore, public relations is another important duty they must handle. In addition, they develop and maintain various external relationships with government officials, donors, the media, other nonprofit organizations, their target clientele, and the community at large.

Each day is unique and challenging for NPO Directors. They continually juggle their various duties, working on multiple tasks and projects at the same time. They often work into the evenings and on weekends.

Salaries

Salaries vary, depending on various factors such as a director's experience and job duties, type and size of organization, an organization's budget, and geographical location. According to the Bureau of Labor Statistics, the estimated 2000 annual salary for most top executives, including nonprofit directors, ranged from $46,390 to $113,810. Some NPO Directors are volunteers, and thus receive no pay.

A 2001 salary survey by *The NonProfit Times* reports average salaries for chief executive directors ranging between $63,351 and $212,587.

Employment Prospects

Job openings typically become available as NPO Directors retire, resign, or transfer to other positions. In general, job opportunities are readily available for highly experienced NPO Directors.

Advancement Prospects

NPO Directors typically realize advancement through professional recognition, higher salaries, the addition of more complex responsibilities, and the success of their organizations.

One career option for NPO Directors is to become nonprofit management consultants.

Education and Training

Employers may require or strongly prefer that NPO Directors have bachelor's or advanced degrees in disciplines related to the services the organizations provide. For example, a family services organization may prefer its director to hold a master's in social services, or a legal services organization may require its director to have a law degree.

Throughout their careers, NPO Directors enroll in continuing education and training programs to develop and maintain their professional skills and expertise.

Experience, Skills, and Personality Traits

Employers generally choose candidates who have extensive experience working in nonprofit settings. Additionally, they should have several years of supervisory, administrative, and management experience in nonprofit settings.

NPO Directors must have excellent leadership, management, organizational, problem-solving, and team building skills. They also need superb interpersonal, communication, and writing skills along with good business and public relations skills. Some personality traits that NPO Directors share are being creative, flexible, optimistic, visionary, self-motivated, diplomatic, and dedicated. Above all, they have a passion and commitment for working in the nonprofit world.

Unions and Associations

NPO Directors join local, state, and national associations to take advantage of networking opportunities, education programs, and other professional resources, and services. One organization that represents nonprofit managers is the Alliance for Nonprofit Management.

Tips for Entry

1. In high school, you can begin gaining experience by joining community youth groups that perform public service projects. Or volunteer with nonprofit organizations in your community that support a cause in which you are interested—such as animal rights, environment, education, or library issues.
2. In college, obtain internships with nonprofit organizations.
3. Talk with NPO Directors for recommendations of college courses that would be helpful in their work.
4. You can learn more about nonprofit management on the Internet. To find relevant web sites, enter the keywords *nonprofit management* in a search engine.

ALTERNATIVE DISPUTE RESOLUTION (ADR) PRACTITIONERS

NEUTRAL

CAREER PROFILE

Duties: Provide alternative dispute resolution (ADR) services, such as mediation, arbitration, and facilitation; help opposing parties resolve their issues and problems; perform duties as required

Alternate Titles: Mediator, Arbitrator, Facilitator, Conciliator, Ombudsperson, Referee, Alternative Dispute Resolution (ADR) Specialist, Conflict Resolution Specialist

Salary Range: $0 to $93,000

Employment Prospects: Good

Advancement Prospects: Fair

Prerequisites:

Education/Training—Dispute resolution training required

Experience—ADR experience; experience in, or knowledgeable about, subject matter of cases being handled

Special Skills and Personality Traits—Negotiation, interpersonal, communication, and listening skills; assimilate and synthesize information and data quickly; impartial, unbiased, patient, courteous, sincere, trusting, flexible

Licensure/Certification—Professional certification or registration may be required

CAREER LADDER

```
┌─────────────────────────────┐
│      ADR Trainer or         │
│    ADR Program Director      │
└─────────────────────────────┘

┌─────────────────────────────┐
│          Neutral            │
└─────────────────────────────┘

┌─────────────────────────────┐
│          Trainee            │
└─────────────────────────────┘
```

Position Description

Neutrals are trained professionals who provide alternative dispute resolution (or ADR) services. They help opposing parties come together voluntarily to agree on a solution to their problems without going through litigation or administrative procedures. Neutrals handle a wide range of disputes in such practice areas as family, personal injury, estates, employment, business, consumer, community, medical, and public policy. They work in various settings such as courts, government agencies, communities, corporations, and educational institutions.

ADR sessions are informal, but confidential. The Neutrals' role is to help the opposing parties define the issues and focus their discussion only on those issues. Neutrals meet with opposing parties both together and separately. Most sessions usually last a few hours. More complex issues may require several sessions over several days.

There are several forms of ADR, and Neutrals specialize in one or more forms. Arbitration and mediation are probably the two most familiar forms of ADR. Arbitration is the one process in which the Neutral decides the outcome for the disputing parties. The neutral (or arbitrator) listens to the evidence and argument offered by each party, and then issues a decision which, in most cases, is enforceable by the courts.

In mediation, Neutrals do not make outcome decisions. The Neutral (or mediator) helps the opposing parties discuss their problems and explore alternatives to resolving them. With a mediator's guidance, the parties decide on the solution that is most agreeable to both parties.

The following are some other forms of ADR.

• Facilitation: A Neutral acts as a guide to keep the discussion between opposing parties on a positive track.

- Conciliation: A Neutral helps conflicting parties restore their relationship to a previous level of trust. The parties can then work on reaching agreements to their problems.
- Neutral evaluation: A Neutral listens to the summaries of opposing parties and offers an opinion on what may happen to their case if it is brought before a trial court or administrative agency.
- Fact-finding: A Neutral gathers information to determine the facts of a dispute in connection with a court case, a corporate internal investigation, or other situation.
- Mini-trial: A Neutral listens to a summary of the evidence and arguments that opposing parties would present at a trial. After that, the Neutral and the parties discuss settlement.
- Private Counseling: A Neutral helps opposing parties explore a conflicting situation; a Neutral generally offers advice on how parties might resolve their problems.

Depending on the nature of a dispute, a Neutral might combine mediation, arbitration, and other ADR forms.

Most Neutrals are independent contractors. Many perform dispute resolution services part time as they work in their primary professions as lawyers, judges, social workers, counselors, professors, executives, and so on. Independent contractors handle small business duties such as invoicing clients, paying bills, marketing their services, and managing office tasks.

Individuals, groups, courts, and others usually choose Neutrals from panels, or rosters, established by professional associations, local attorney bars, community mediation centers, government agencies, universities, private ADR referral services, and other groups. Many Neutrals are part of several panels or rosters. Depending on the organization, Neutrals are nominated to a panel or receive an exclusive invitation from the organization. With some groups, Neutrals may apply for inclusion on a panel if they meet the panel's requirements.

Neutrals are also employed by government agencies, academic institutions, corporations, nonprofit organizations, courts, law firms, and ADR firms. Neutrals in staff positions typically perform other duties. For example, family court mediators may also have counseling duties. Many staff Neutrals, usually called Dispute Resolution Specialists, mostly manage cases. In other words, they review cases to decide if ADR is appropriate and, if so, which form of ADR would work best. They also find appropriate Neutrals for cases, and monitor the cases throughout the process.

Neutrals work full time or part time. Independent Neutrals travel to their sessions, which sometimes are held in distant cities or states.

Salaries

Salaries vary, depending on employer, experience, geographical location, and other factors. Top Neutrals can earn salaries up to six figures or more. Many Neutrals are volunteers, providing services for free. According to the Bureau of Labor Statistics, the estimated 2000 annual salary for most arbitrators, mediators, and conciliators ranged from $23,360 to $93,170.

Independent Neutrals earn an hourly or per-session fee. Rates vary, depending on geographical location, experience, and complexity of cases. Many Neutrals charge between $200 to $500 per hour.

Employment Prospects

The job outlook for Neutrals is positive. The job market is expected to grow gradually in the coming years as more employers in private, nonprofit, and public sectors increasingly use forms of dispute resolution for settling both internal and external problems.

Advancement Prospects

Since this is a relatively new field, Neutrals define their own terms for advancement. For example, Neutrals might measure success in terms of their professional reputation, by earning higher incomes, or by being sought out to handle complex cases.

With additional experience and training, Neutrals may become dispute resolution trainers as well as dispute resolution services consultants. Additionally, administrative opportunities are available for managers and directors of dispute resolution programs in government agencies, corporations, nonprofit organizations, dispute resolution firms, and so on. Some Neutrals start their own firms that provide ADR services.

Education and Training

Neutrals are required to complete a minimum of 20 to 40 hours of dispute resolution training, depending on their employer or on the organization with which they are registered. Many professional associations also set their own training requirements for their memberships. In addition, Neutrals are expected to enroll in education and training programs throughout their careers to maintain and develop their skills and knowledge in ADR as well as in their practice areas.

Neutrals generally have bachelor's and advanced degrees in disciplines that relate to the subject areas in which they practice. Many Neutrals have law degrees.

Experience, Skills, and Personality Traits

Neutrals come from various backgrounds—law, social work, theology, counseling, education, human resources, business, and so on.

Employers and organizations that refer Neutrals generally look for individuals who have several years of ADR experience. Neutrals also have the appropriate experience and knowledge in the practice areas (such as family, business, or employment disputes) in which they wish to handle cases.

Neutrals must have excellent negotiation skills and interpersonal skills as well as superior communication and listening skills. They are able to assimilate and synthesize information and data quickly. In addition, Neutrals can relate to people from various backgrounds and with diverse points of view.

Some personality traits that successful Neutrals share are being impartial, unbiased, patient, courteous, sincere, trusting, and flexible.

Licensure and Certification

All ADR referral services, associations, courts, and others have their own set of certification and registration requirements for Neutrals who wish to be on their rosters or panels. For example, a state court system may require that Neutrals be certified by a court-approved training program, as well as be registered with the state and local court systems.

Unions and Associations

Many Neutrals join local, state, and national associations to take advantage of professional resources and services, such as training programs, publications, job referrals, and opportunities to network with peers. Some national organizations that represent Neutrals are:

- American Arbitration Association
- American Bar Association Dispute Resolution Section
- American College of Civil Trial Mediators
- Association for Conflict Resolution (which recently merged with the Society of Professionals in Dispute Resolution and the Academy of Family Mediators)
- Association of Attorney-Mediators
- National Association for Community Mediation

Tips for Entry

1. Join a professional association and actively participate in its programs.
2. Many Neutrals begin their careers as volunteers in order to gain experience and professional exposure.
3. Contact professional associations, courts, local bar associations, and ADR referral services that have panels of Neutrals. Ask about their requirements and application process.
4. You can learn about the ADR field on the Internet. To find relevant web sites, enter any of these keywords in a search engine: *alternative dispute resolution, mediation,* or *arbitration.*

COURT MEDIATOR

CAREER PROFILE

Duties: Mediate civil and criminal cases referred by state and federal courts; help opposing parties decide on an agreeable settlement; perform duties as required

Alternate Title: Family Court Mediator

Salary Range: $23,000 to $93,000

Employment Prospects: Good

Advancement Prospects: Fair

Prerequisites:

    Education/Training—Appropriate college degrees for profession; completion of court-approved training program

    Experience—Be a lawyer or judge; for nonlawyers, have subject-matter expertise and knowledge of court procedures

    Special Skills and Personality Traits—Interpersonal, listening, communication, and interviewing skills; able to handle people of diverse backgrounds and views as well as manage emotional individuals; objective, unbiased, composed, trustworthy, courteous, flexible, creative

    Licensure/Certification—Court certification and/or registration may be required; a law or other professional license may be required

CAREER LADDER

```
┌─────────────────────────────────┐
│    Court Mediator/Trainer        │
│    or Program Director           │
└─────────────────────────────────┘

┌─────────────────────────────────┐
│    Court Mediator                │
└─────────────────────────────────┘

┌─────────────────────────────────┐
│    Trainee                       │
└─────────────────────────────────┘
```

Position Description

Today many state and federal courts use mediation, a form of alternative dispute resolution (ADR), to resolve many court cases. In the court mediation process, Court Mediators help opposing parties work together to explore possible solutions to their problems and then decide on a solution on which they can both agree. Court Mediators have helped settle disputes of all kinds, including divorce, child custody, small claims, personal injury, employment, environmental, bankruptcy, and appellate cases.

Court mediation does not take the place of litigation. A judge may recommend that a case go into mediation on a voluntary basis. Some courts require certain cases to go through the mediation process before a hearing or trial date is set. Court Mediators do not act as judges nor as arbitrators. They do not hear testimony, make rulings, or render decisions or awards. Any decisions made in a mediation process are by the involved parties.

The mediation sessions are usually conducted in a neutral place, such as at a meeting room in a courthouse. Most mediation sessions last a few hours, but complex cases sometimes continue for a few days.

Court Mediators meet with the parties in joint sessions, as well as with each party in separate private caucuses. They are trained to help both sides identify and analyze the issues of their cases, as well as to get them to generate options for settlement. The mediation process is informal and confidential.

The opposing parties are required to participate fully in the mediation session until a settlement has been reached. When the parties cannot come to any agreement, Court Mediators may declare an impasse to end the session. Court Mediators may also end the process at any time if they determine that the parties are unwilling to cooperate or to achieve a reasonable agreement. Either party may terminate the mediation process at any time as well.

When opposing parties have achieved a settlement, an agreement is written and signed by the participants. The written agreement is like a contract and therefore is enforceable in court. If the parties cannot reach an agreement, the case goes back to the court for litigation.

Some Court Mediators are employed as staff members of the courts, and usually perform additional duties. For example, a Family Court Mediator may also perform counseling duties. Some courts refer mediation cases to ADR programs run by bar associations, nonprofit corporations, or private services. Many courts maintain a roster of eligible Court Mediators to whom cases are referred. Some courts use only qualified volunteers as Court Mediators, while others use independent contractors who are paid an hourly or session fee by either the involved parties or the courts.

Many volunteer and paid Court Mediators offer other ADR services such as arbitration, facilitation, case evaluation, and mini-trials. Many also provide dispute resolution services to government agencies, corporations, academic institutions, community organizations, and other organizations.

Salaries

Salaries for staff mediators vary, depending on such factors as experience, education, job duties, court budget, and geographical location. The Bureau of Labor Statistics reports that the estimated annual salary in 2000 for most arbitrators, mediators, and conciliators ranged between $23,360 to $93,170.

Independent Court Mediators usually receive an hourly or per-session fee. Fees vary widely, depending on a court's fee limit, geographical location, and the complexity of a case. Some Court Mediators provide pro bono, or free, services.

Employment Prospects

The demand for Court Mediators is expected to increase in the coming years due to the growing number of court mediation programs being established in state and federal courts. Some court mediation programs may be authorized by legal mandate, court rule, or administrative order. Other programs may be set up to help reduce the number of trial cases, decrease the cost of litigation, speed the resolution of cases, improve the relationships between opposing parties, and for various other reasons.

Advancement Prospects

Court Mediators generally realize advancement in terms of their professional reputation, by being sought out to handle complex cases, or by earning higher incomes.

Court Mediators can also become program coordinators or directors, ADR trainers, or ADR consultants.

Education and Training

In many jurisdictions, Court Mediators must possess a juris doctor (J.D.) degree. In courts that use nonlawyers for family court mediation services, candidates must have either a bachelor's or master's degree in psychology, social work, or other related field.

Most courts require that Court Mediators complete a court-approved basic mediation training program. Trainees usually complete between 20 and 40 hours of classroom training in addition to supervised mediations and observations. Some states require additional mediation training hours in the practice areas, such as family disputes, in which the Court Mediators will work.

Throughout their careers, Court Mediators enroll in education and training programs to maintain and build their mediation skills.

Experience, Skills, and Personality Traits

State and federal courts each have their own set of eligibility requirements for Court Mediators. Most courts require that Court Mediators be lawyers who have been in practice for several years. Many courts use nonlawyer mediators who have extensive professional experience in their subject matter (such as children and family issues) and are knowledgeable about court procedures.

Court Mediators need excellent interpersonal, listening, communication, and interviewing skills. They are able to handle people from diverse backgrounds and with different views. Additionally, they can manage individuals who become upset, angry, or otherwise emotional. Being objective, unbiased, composed, trustworthy, courteous, flexible, and creative are some personality traits that successful Court Mediators share.

Licensure and Certification

In general, courts require that Court Mediators be certified by the courts, as well as be registered in each court with which they wish to work.

Court Mediators are required to possess an attorney's license or other professional license (such as a counselor's or social work license).

Unions and Associations

Court Mediators join local, state, and national professional associations to take advantage of networking opportunities, training programs, job listings, and other professional resources and services. Some national associations that Court Mediators are eligible to join are the Association for Conflict Resolution, the American College of Civil Trial Mediators, the Association of Attorney-Mediators, the American Bar Association Alternative Dispute Resolution section, and AFCC—an association of family, court, and community professionals.

Tips for Entry

1. Talk with Court Mediators to learn more about their work and what advice they have for entering their field.
2. Contact the individual state and federal courts in which you would like to work for information about their mediation programs.
3. You can learn more about court mediation programs and Court Mediators on the Internet. To find pertinent web sites, enter either of these keywords in a search engine: *court mediators* or *court ADR program.*

ARBITRATOR, LABOR OR EMPLOYMENT

CAREER PROFILE

Duties: Facilitate arbitration cases for either labor-management or employment disputes; make final decisions or awards; perform other duties as required

Alternate Titles: Labor Arbitrator, Employment Arbitrator

Salary Range: $23,000 to $93,000

Employment Prospects: Fair

Advancement Prospects: Limited

Prerequisites:

Education/Training—Complete arbitration training

Experience—Employment Arbitrators need experience in employment law; labor Arbitrators need experience in collective bargaining, labor management relations, and labor law

Special Skills and Personality Traits—Negotiation, problem-solving, interpersonal, communication, and listening skills; impartial, fair, unbiased, patient, courteous, trustworthy, flexible

Licensure/Certification—None required

CAREER LADDER

```
┌─────────────────────────────────┐
│      Full-time Arbitrator       │
└─────────────────────────────────┘

┌─────────────────────────────────┐
│      Part-time Arbitrator       │
└─────────────────────────────────┘

┌─────────────────────────────────┐
│  Lawyer, Law Professor, Business │
│     Executive, Labor Union       │
│  Representative, or Other Profession │
└─────────────────────────────────┘
```

Position Description

Labor and Employment Arbitrators settle labor-management and employment disputes with arbitration, a form of alternative dispute resolution (ADR). The arbitration process allows opposing parties to present their cases in a less formal setting than the courtroom. The Arbitrators have the authority to make the final decisions or awards. In most arbitration cases, the Arbitrators' decisions are final and binding in courts of law.

Labor Arbitrators handle labor-management cases that involve collective bargaining negotiations about wages, working conditions, employee benefits, and other issues between groups of employees and their employers. The employees are often represented by a union or other labor organization. Employment Arbitrators handle employment cases that involve various issues between employees and employers, such as discrimination, breach of employment contracts, wrongful termination, and other workplace grievances.

Parties in a labor-management or employment dispute may voluntarily choose arbitration to settle their differences.

Some cases go into arbitration because of legal mandates, court rule, or contractual agreements. In arbitration, the opposing parties together select one or more Arbitrators. (Either disputant may be represented by a legal counsel or other authorized representative.) Arbitrators are usually selected from rosters maintained by an administrative agency (such as the Federal Mediation and Conciliation Service) or a private nonprofit arbitration administration agency (such as the National Academy of Arbitrators).

Arbitrators conduct prehearing meetings with the disputants to determine when and where the hearing shall take place and how long it will last. Arbitrators also discuss other matters that may help make the proceedings move quickly, including defining the issues to be arbitrated; outlining the laws and rules that will apply to the proceeding; explaining the use of witnesses; and determining whether arguments will be summed up orally or in writing.

Arbitrators have the authority to establish the rules of conduct for the hearings. For example, they may decide whether nonwitnesses may attend a hearing. Arbitrators also have the duty of safeguarding the confidentiality of arbitration hearings.

During the proceedings, the disputants present their case before the Arbitrators. Each side has the equal burden of proof, and so produces physical evidence and witnesses to prove their case. If necessary, Arbitrators may subpoena witnesses or documents that are relevant to a case, as well as conduct any necessary inspections or investigations.

After all the evidence has been submitted and testimony heard, the Arbitrators close the hearings. Usually within 30 days, they make their final decisions or awards. When a board of Arbitrators presides, the majority of Arbitrators must agree on a decision unless the law or court requires an unanimous agreement.

Many Arbitrators also provide other forms of ADR, such as mediation, case evaluation, and mini-trials, to settle labor-management or employment disputes.

Arbitrators provide their services on a part-time or full-time basis. Part-time Arbitrators usually work full time in their principal occupations as lawyers, law professors, and so forth.

Salaries

Labor and Employment Arbitrators generally earn hourly or per diem fees. Rates vary, depending on factors such as experience and geographical location. According to the Bureau of Labor Statistics, the estimated 2000 annual salary for most arbitrators, mediators, and conciliators ranged from $23,360 to $93,170.

Employment Prospects

According to the Bureau of Labor Statistics, employment of labor relations staff, including arbitrators, is expected to grow as businesses become more involved in labor relations and try to resolve disputes out of court.

Advancement Prospects

Arbitrators realize advancement in terms of their professional reputation, by earning higher incomes, or by being sought out to handle complex cases.

Education and Training

Arbitrators are generally required to complete arbitration training programs. In addition, they are expected to enroll in education and training programs throughout their careers to maintain and develop their skills and knowledge in ADR as well as practice areas.

Experience, Skills, and Personality Traits

Labor and Employment Arbitrators come from different backgrounds. Some are lawyers, former judges, and law professors. Others are former labor union representatives or employee relations specialists and directors.

Employment Arbitrators should be experienced in the field of employment law. Labor Arbitrators should have extensive experience in collective bargaining, labor management relations, and labor law.

Arbitrators must have excellent negotiation, problem-solving, and interpersonal skills. Superior communication and listening skills are also needed. Being impartial, fair, unbiased, patient, courteous, trustworthy, and flexible are some personality traits that successful Labor and Employment Arbitrators share.

Licensure and Certification

No professional license is required to become a Labor Arbitrator or an Employment Arbitrator. Lawyers and other professionals who provide arbitration services are expected to maintain their professional licenses.

Unions and Associations

Labor and Employment Arbitrators join local, state, and national associations to take advantage of professional resources and services, such as training programs, publications, job referrals, and opportunities to network with peers. Some national organizations are the National Academy of Arbitrators, American Arbitration Association, Association for Conflict Resolution, and American Bar Association Dispute Resolution Section.

Tips for Entry

1. Learn as much as you can about the arbitration process, as well as other forms of alternative dispute resolution.
2. Use the Internet to learn more about arbitration. To find relevant web sites enter any of these keywords in a search engine: *arbitration, labor arbitration,* or *employment arbitration.*

COMPLIANCE OFFICERS

COMPLIANCE SPECIALIST

CAREER PROFILE

Duties: Ensure that employers are meeting appropriate local, state, and federal laws and regulations; perform duties as required

Alternate Titles: Compliance Officer, Compliance Coordinator; a title that reflects a specific compliance area such as Public Utility Compliance Specialist or ADA (Americans with Disabilities Act) Specialist

Salary Range: $26,000 to $69,000

Employment Prospects: Good

Advancement Prospects: Fair

Prerequisites:

    Education/Training—A bachelor's degree

    Experience—Several years' experience in industry; previous experience in compliance, regulatory affairs, or related field

    Special Skills and Personality Traits—Leadership, interpersonal, communication, project management, organization, and writing skills; independent, fair, ethical, analytical, credible, trustworthy, flexible

    Licensure/Certification—None required

CAREER LADDER

```
┌─────────────────────────────────┐
│  Senior Compliance Specialist or │
│  Compliance Program Manager      │
└─────────────────────────────────┘

┌─────────────────────────────────┐
│     Compliance Specialist        │
└─────────────────────────────────┘

┌─────────────────────────────────┐
│          Trainee                 │
└─────────────────────────────────┘
```

Position Description

In the United States, state and federal laws and regulations govern how employers in the various industries must run their businesses. For example, employers must comply with various employment laws that cover equal opportunity, workplace safety, employee benefits, and other workplace issues. In addition, employers must follow specific laws and regulations that govern their industry. Employers who have government contracts or are receiving government funds must follow certain laws and regulations. Failure to comply with appropriate laws and regulations can result in employers being charged with violations and assessed heavy fines, as well as the possibility of being sued. Consequently, many employers hire one or more Compliance Specialists to ensure that they are properly following the laws and regulations.

Compliance Specialists are employed in many different industries—banks, securities, insurance, education, health care, biotechnology, pharmaceuticals, aviation, engineering, public utilities, municipalities, sports, casinos, retail, and so

on. They usually are responsible for managing compliance programs pertinent to specific laws and regulations. For example, ADA Specialists make sure that employers are in compliance with the Americans with Disabilities Act (ADA), while Environmental Compliance Specialists ensure that employers are meeting the required environmental laws and regulations.

Many duties vary among the different Compliance Specialists. Some responsibilities are the same, regardless of the industry in which they work or the compliance areas they cover. Some of these major responsibilities include:

- interpreting local, state, and federal laws and regulations that pertain to their area
- acting as a resource and consultant to managers and staff
- monitoring assigned projects, programs, contracts, and so on for compliance with appropriate laws and regulations as well as with internal policies and rules

- developing, implementing, and maintaining compliance policies and procedures
- conducting audits to measure the effectiveness of monitoring systems
- developing and coordinating training and education programs to inform employees about current and revised laws and regulations as well as about compliance issues
- conducting investigations of complaints or suspicions that compliance is not being met
- maintaining accurate records
- writing correspondence and completing required reports and forms
- staying up to date with changes in laws and regulations as well as with court decisions and proposed legislation

Compliance Specialists generally work a standard 40-hour week.

Salaries

Salaries vary, depending on various factors such as education, experience, job responsibilities, industry, and geographical location. According to the Bureau of Labor Statistics, the estimated annual salary in 2000 for most compliance officers ranged between $25,970 and $68,520. (This salary data excludes compliance officers in the areas of agriculture, construction, health, and transportation.)

Employment Prospects

Compliance Specialists are employed in all industries. Job openings usually become available as Specialists retire, resign, or transfer to other positions. On occasion, employers create additional positions to meet their growing needs.

Advancement Prospects

Compliance Specialists can advance to supervisory and management positions. The top position in most organizations is the Corporate Compliance Officer, which is usually a senior manager or executive officer.

Compliance Specialists with entrepreneurial ambitions can become independent consultants.

Education and Training

Employers generally require that Compliance Specialists possess bachelor's degrees in related fields.

Throughout their careers, Compliance Specialists enroll in education and training programs to develop their skills and expertise.

Experience, Skills, and Personality Traits

Requirements vary from employer to employer. In general, candidates must have several years of experience working in an industry. Additionally, they should have previous experience working in compliance, regulatory affairs, or related fields. Candidates also are able to demonstrate knowledge about appropriate laws and regulations.

Compliance Specialists must be able to work effectively with employees at every level, thus they must have excellent, leadership, interpersonal, and communication skills. In addition they need superior project management, organization, and writing skills.

Some personality traits that successful Compliance Specialists share are being independent, fair, ethical, analytical, credible, trustworthy, and flexible.

Unions and Associations

Many Compliance Specialists join associations (such as the National Society of Compliance Professionals and the Health Care Compliance Association) that represent compliance professionals in their industry. By joining professional associations, they can take advantage of professional services and resources, such as education programs, certification programs, job listings, and networking opportunities.

Tips for Entry

1. Gain experience in the industry in which you would like to work. You might work with private companies, law firms (if a lawyer), or government agencies that regulate the industry.
2. Actively participate in professional associations that serve the industries in which you would like to work. For example, you might attend conferences, give presentations, write articles about compliance issues for publications, and so on.
3. You can learn more about different Compliance Specialists on the Internet. To find job descriptions about various Compliance Specialists, enter the keywords *compliance specialist* in a search engine.

EQUAL OPPORTUNITY (EO) OFFICER

CAREER PROFILE

Duties: Develop, implement, and administer equal opportunity programs and affirmative action plans; monitor employment practices for compliance with government laws, regulations, and executive orders; investigate complaints, perform other duties as required

Alternate Titles: EO Specialist, EO Coordinator, EO Director, Affirmative Action Officer

Salary Range: $26,000 to $69,000

Employment Prospects: Good

Advancement Prospects: Good

Prerequisites:
    Education/Training—A bachelor's degree
    Experience—Previous experience working with equal opportunity or affirmative action programs
    Special Skills and Personality Traits—Writing, communication, teamwork, interpersonal, and self-management skills; courteous, diplomatic, trustworthy, honest, flexible
    Licensure/Certification—None required

CAREER LADDER

```
┌─────────────────────────────────┐
│        Program Manager          │
└─────────────────────────────────┘

┌─────────────────────────────────┐
│  Equal Opportunity Specialist   │
└─────────────────────────────────┘

┌─────────────────────────────────┐
│     Trainee or Support Staff     │
└─────────────────────────────────┘
```

Position Description

In the United States, the civil rights of all individuals are protected in the workplace. According to federal and state laws, employers are required to provide equal opportunity to employees and job applicants regardless of their race, color, national origin, gender, religion, disability, or age. Employers may also be required to comply with other equal opportunity laws, regulations, and executive orders that cover other statuses of people, such as marital status, political beliefs, sexual orientation, or veteran status. To ensure that they are complying with government laws, employers may establish equal opportunity programs. Employers may also be required to establish affirmative action plans that describe their goals for ensuring that their employment practices (such as job recruitment, hiring, promotion, termination, disciplinary action, and compensation) are not discriminatory.

Equal Opportunity (EO) Officers are responsible for managing equal opportunity programs and affirmative action plans for employers. Some of their major duties include:

- developing policies that reflect employers' commitment to equity and nondiscrimination in the workplace
- designing and implementing training and education programs for all employees about equal opportunity principles and affirmative action policies
- creating internal audit and reporting systems for employment practices
- monitoring employment practices
- investigating and resolving internal complaints of discrimination
- keeping up to date with changes in equal opportunity laws and regulations

EO Officers perform various other duties, depending on their position. Lower-level EO Officers perform more routine tasks, such as conducting research, reviewing data, and preparing reports. They also provide support in developing and implementing programs, monitoring for compliance, and conducting investigations.

EO Specialists are responsible for developing and administering one or more equal opportunity and affirmative action programs. For example, one EO Specialist at a company coordinates the affirmative action plan and equal employment opportunity programs while another oversees the disability and veterans equal opportunity programs.

EO Specialists perform many of the same tasks that lower-level officers perform. In addition, specialists are responsible for developing program guidelines and procedures, evaluating the effectiveness of affirmative action plans and goals, designing and implementing training programs, and providing guidance to department managers and supervisors. They prepare statistical reports, publications, and correspondence as required, as well as interpret state and federal laws and regulations. They also conduct investigations or complaints and counsel employees who believe they are being discriminated against. Further, EO Specialists act as resources to executive officers, department managers, and supervisors.

EO Managers (or EO Directors) are in charge of planning and directing the overall affirmative action plan and equal opportunity programs. They are responsible for ensuring that their employers are in compliance with all the appropriate state and federal laws, regulations, and executive orders. In addition, they act as their employers' liaison with government officials. EO Managers also develop program policies and provide supervision and guidance to all EO Officers.

EO Officers generally work a standard 40-hour week.

Salaries

Salaries vary, depending on such factors as education, experience, and geographical location. According to the Bureau of Labor Statistics, the estimated annual salary in 2000 for most compliance officers (not including executive-level officers) ranged from $25,970 to $68,520.

Employment Prospects

EO Officers are employed by corporations, educational institutions, government agencies, nonprofit organizations, and other institutions.

Job openings generally become available when EO Officers resign or transfer to other positions. Employers may create or cut positions, depending on the growth of their organizations.

Advancement Prospects

EO Officers can advance to management and executive-level positions in equal opportunity, which usually requires obtaining positions with other employers. Individuals with entrepreneurial ambitions may become equal opportunity consultants.

EO Officers can also pursue other careers in human resources, such as becoming labor relations specialists, human resource trainers, or employee benefits specialists.

Education and Training

Employers require that candidates hold bachelor's degrees. Some employers prefer that college degrees be in social science, behavioral science, public administration, or another related field. Many employers accept any college degree as long as candidates have qualifying work experience.

Throughout their careers, EO Officers enroll in training and continuing education programs to develop their skills and expertise.

Experience, Skills, and Personality Traits

Employers typically hire EO Officers who have previous experience working with equal opportunity or affirmative action programs. Additionally, they look for candidates who demonstrate knowledge of civil rights, affirmative action, and fair employment practices, laws, and regulations. Experience requirements vary, depending on the job position, responsibilities, employer, and other factors. For example, an employer may require at least one year of experience working with equal opportunity programs for entry-level positions; three years for specialist positions, and five or more years for program managers.

EO Officers need effective writing and communication skills as well as strong teamwork and interpersonal skills. They also need excellent self-management skills that include the ability to work with minimal supervision, handle stressful situations, take initiative, meet deadlines, and so on.

Being courteous, diplomatic, trustworthy, honest, and flexible are some personality traits that successful EO Officers share.

Unions and Associations

Many EO Officers join local, state, and national professional associations to take advantage of networking opportunities, and other professional resources and services. EO Officers are eligible to join associations, such as the Society for Human Resources Management, that represent human resources professionals. Some EO Officers also belong to professional societies that represent compliance officers, such as the American Association for Affirmative Action.

Tips for Entry

1. While in college, obtain internships or part-time jobs in human resources. Let your supervisor know of your interest in gaining experience working with equal opportunity programs.

2. Obtain information interviews with EO program managers at places where you would like to work. These interviews offer you the chance to learn more about the profession and job opportunities, as well as give employers a chance to meet you.

3. To learn more about equal employment opportunity, visit the web site of the U.S. Equal Employment Opportunity Commission *(http://www.eeoc.gov)*. To find other relevant websites about EO Officers, enter either of these keywords in a search engine: *equal opportunity officer* or *equal employment specialist.*

ETHICS OFFICER

CAREER PROFILE

Duties: Develop and implement policies, procedures, and activities for ethics program; act as resource and consultant for senior managers; perform other duties as required

Alternate Titles: Chief Ethics Officer, Ethics Director

Salary Range: about $175,000 or more (for full-time, executive-level positions)

Employment Prospects: Fair

Advancement Prospects: Limited

Prerequisites:

Education/Training—No standard requirements, but many officers have law degrees

Experience—Extensive experience working within an industry; usually been employed several years in an organization

Special Skills and Personality Traits—Leadership, management, training, listening, communication skills; open-minded, tolerant, sensitive, thoughtful

Licensure/Certification—None required

CAREER LADDER

```
┌─────────────────────────────────┐
│      Chief Ethics Officer       │
└─────────────────────────────────┘

┌─────────────────────────────────┐
│         Ethics Officer          │
└─────────────────────────────────┘

┌─────────────────────────────────┐
│   Ethics Manager or Coordinator │
│ (for corporate divisions or     │
│           agencies)             │
└─────────────────────────────────┘
```

Position Description

Many employers have established ethics programs to promote among their employees the moral values and principles to which the employers are committed in conducting their business. Employers write a code of ethics (or code of business conduct) that states how employees are expected to perform their jobs in an honest and conscientious manner. The code also describes potential ethical problems that employees may face, such as conflicts of interest, noncompliance with government regulations, or witnessing illegal activities.

In charge of managing ethics programs are Ethics Officers. They are responsible for creating and implementing strategies and programs that reinforce the importance of an ethical work culture. Ethics Officers also make sure that contractors, vendors, and others with whom their employers do business are also familiar with their employers' code of ethics.

Ethics Officers perform a wide range of complex duties. For example, they:

- formulate ethics policies and procedures
- draft employers' code of business conduct
- review new government laws and regulations and recommend changes to their employers' ethical codes
- design and coordinate training and education programs to teach employees to understand the code of business conduct
- develop informational brochures, articles, and other print and multimedia material to reinforce awareness of ethical policies and procedures
- design internal reporting systems (such as telephone hot lines) that allow for employees and others to report suspected violations of the ethical code
- conduct or oversee investigations into any possible breaches of conduct

Ethics Officers act as resources and consultants to executive officers, assisting them with decision making. Ethics Officers have the responsibility of being their employers' conscience and pointing out any unethical aspects in business decisions.

In many organizations, Ethics Officers are also responsible for overseeing corporate compliance programs. Some Ethics Officers also address other concerns in the workplace, such as civil rights, environment, privacy, and labor issues.

Ethics Officers typically work closely with other operations, especially if their own office has limited resources. These include legal, human resources, internal audit, and security departments.

Ethics Officers report directly to the general legal counsel, chief executive officer, or an ethics committee. They work full time or part time.

Salaries

Formal salary data is unavailable for Ethics Officers, but according to informal reports, full-time executive level officers may earn annual salaries of about $175,000 or more. Salaries vary for Ethics Officers, depending on experience, education, type of employer, geographical location, and other factors.

Employment Prospects

Ethics Officers are employed in many different industries—banks, securities, insurance, health care, biotechnology, retail, manufacturing, telecommunications, public utilities, education, nonprofit associations, and so forth. In addition, state and federal government agencies and local municipalities hire Ethics Officers.

The position is generally more common in larger organizations, and usually in organizations that are more progressive or socially responsible.

Advancement Prospects

Ethics Officers typically realize advancement through higher incomes and job satisfaction. Some Ethics Officers become business ethics consultants.

Education and Training

Ethics Officers hold, at the minimum, bachelor's degrees. Many have law training and have earned juris doctor (J.D.) degrees. Others hold master's degrees in business administration or other fields. Some Ethics Officers also possess doctoral degrees.

Experience, Skills, and Personality Traits

Ethics Officers usually have had extensive experience working within their industry. In addition, many have worked for their organization several years in responsible positions of management. Ethics Officers come from different backgrounds, in such areas as corporate law, human resources, operations/administration, finance, accounting, and internal audit.

Ethics Officers should have excellent leadership, management, and training skills, as well as effective listening and communication skills. Being open-minded, tolerant, sensitive, and thoughtful are some personality traits that successful Ethics Officers share.

Unions and Associations

Many Ethics Officers join the Ethics Officer Association and other state and national professional associations to take advantage of networking opportunities, education programs, and other professional services and resources.

Tips for Entry

1. Many universities offer graduate programs in business ethics for ethics professionals and consultants who develop and administer corporate ethics programs.
2. Network with ethics officers, compliance officers, and executive-level officers to learn about job opportunities.
3. You can learn more about business ethics on the Internet. To find relevant web sites, enter they keywords *business ethics* or *ethics officer* in a search engine.

ANALYSTS AND EXAMINERS

CONTRACT ADMINISTRATOR

CAREER PROFILE

Duties: Oversee the management of various business agreements; draft, review, negotiate, and maintain contracts; perform other duties as required

Alternate Titles: Contract Manager, Contract Specialist

Salary Range: $43,000 to $76,000

Employment Prospects: Good

Advancement Prospects: Fair

Prerequisites:

Education/Training—Bachelor's degree; a law degree, master's of business administration (MBA), or other advanced degree may be required

Experience—Contract administration experience; legal experience preferred; work experience in industry preferred

Special Skills and Personality Traits—Interpersonal, customer service, communication, negotiation, writing, computer, and self-management skills; analytical, organized, detail-oriented, trustworthy, decisive, flexible

Licensure/Certification—None required

CAREER LADDER

```
┌─────────────────────────────────┐
│  Contract Specialist or Contract │
│             Manager              │
└─────────────────────────────────┘

┌─────────────────────────────────┐
│      Contract Administrator      │
└─────────────────────────────────┘

┌─────────────────────────────────┐
│ Associate Contract Administrator or │
│  Contract Administrative Assistant  │
└─────────────────────────────────┘
```

Position Description

Contract Administrators are responsible for overseeing the management of business agreements for their employers. They administer various contracts, among them sales contracts, purchasing contracts, licensing agreements, service agreements, construction contracts, property leases or mortgages, credit agreements, employment contracts, and insurance policies. Many Contract Administrators are also responsible for administering government contracts, as well as compliance records.

Contract Administrators perform a wide range of duties. They coordinate the contractual process; that is, they make sure that proposed contracts are forwarded to department managers and corporate attorneys for review and approval. Contract Administrators also assist department managers with preparing business agreements, which may include the task of drafting contracts. Contract Administrators also review contracts submitted by vendors, contractors, and others, and identify any business, legal, and financial issues that

may concern their employers. In addition, Contract Administrators negotiate the terms and conditions of contracts with vendors, contractors, and others.

Contract Administrators are also responsible for maintaining contracts. They process and file business agreements accordingly. They check that contractual requirements are being met and make sure that contracts are up to date. Furthermore, Contract Administrators respond to questions about the status of contracts, advise on contractual terms and conditions, and resolve any problems or issues in contracts.

Senior Contract Administrators may have the additional responsibility to act as lead team members. Their duties might include making work assignments to other team members, providing guidance and supervision, and evaluating their work. They may also serve as a primary resource for solving problems.

Contract Administrators work a 40-hour week. On occasion, they work overtime in order to meet deadlines. They may be required to travel to meet with vendors; in large companies, they may travel between their home office and branch offices.

Salaries

Salaries vary, depending on such factors as experience, education, and geographical location. According to *The Affiliates 2001 Salary Guide* (by the Affiliates, a national legal staffing business), the average salary for Contract Administrators ranges between $42,750 and $75,750.

Employment Prospects

Contract Administrators work for construction companies, publishing companies, retail stores, hospitals, financial services, government agencies, educational institutions, and so on. Opportunities generally become available as Contract Administrators resign, advance to other positions, or transfer to other occupations.

Advancement Prospects

Contract Administrators can become specialists, overseeing specific types of contracts such as licensing agreements or government contracts. They can also pursue management positions, which may require moving to other organizations. Those with higher ambitions can follow paths to executive positions, such as vice president of administrative services.

Education and Training

Educational qualifications vary from employer to employer. In general, candidates should possess a bachelor's degree in business, finance, accounting, or a related field, depending on the industry. Employers may accept unrelated degrees if candidates have completed relevant coursework or obtained professional certifications in contract administration. Some employers desire that candidates also hold a master's in business administration, a juris doctor (J.D.) degree, or other advanced degree.

Experience, Skills, and Personality Traits

Employers generally require that candidates have several years of experience in contract administration, purchasing, or another related area. Some employers prefer candidates with legal experience, either as lawyers or senior paralegals. In addition, work experience within an employer's industry is highly preferred.

Contract Administrators need superior interpersonal, customer services, and communication skills, as they must be able to work with diverse groups of people—managers, executives, lawyers, vendors, clients, and so forth. They also need excellent negotiation, writing, and computer skills. Furthermore, they should have strong self-management skills that include the ability to meet deadlines, manage multiple projects, prioritize tasks, handle stressful situations, and demonstrate initiative in their work.

Some personality traits that successful Contract Administrators share are being analytical, organized, detail-oriented, trustworthy, decisive, and flexible.

Unions and Associations

Contract Administrators join professional associations to take advantage of networking opportunities, training programs, and other professional services and resources. One organization that Contract Administrators might join is the National Contract Management Association.

Tips for Entry

1. Many individuals obtain additional training by enrolling in a graduate degree or a professional certificate program in contracts management.

2. To enhance your employability, you might obtain one or both of these professional certifications granted by the National Contract Management Association (NCMA): *Certified Professional Contracts Manager* or the *Certified Associate Contracts Manager* designation. For more information, write to NCMA, 1912 Woodford Road, Vienna, VA 22182. Or phone (800) 344-8096. Or visit its web site, *http://www.ncmahq.org*.

3. Contract Administrators typically advance through the ranks of their organization, holding different positions in contract administration and other administrative departments.

4. Learn more about contract administration on the Internet. To find relevant web sites, enter the keywords *contract administration* in a search engine.

PATENT AGENT

CAREER PROFILE

Duties: Prepare patent applications; prosecute patents in the U.S. Patent and Trademark Office; perform other duties as required

Alternate Titles: Patent Analyst, Patent Engineer, Patent Specialist

Salary Range: $40,000 to $120,000 or more

Employment Prospects: Good

Advancement Prospects: Fair

Prerequisites:

Education/Training—A bachelor's degree

Experience—Strong technical background; scientific or technical work experience is desirable

Special Skills and Personality Traits—Writing, analytical, communication, and interpersonal skills; curious, detail-oriented, organized, flexible

Licensure/Certification—Be registered in the U.S. Patent and Trademark Office

CAREER LADDER

```
┌─────────────────────────────┐
│  Supervisory Patent Agent   │
└─────────────────────────────┘

┌─────────────────────────────┐
│       Patent Agent          │
└─────────────────────────────┘

┌─────────────────────────────┐
│         Trainee             │
└─────────────────────────────┘
```

Position Description

Patent Agents help clients—inventors or others who own inventions—obtain patents for new inventions, such as machines, medications, toys, food processes, plant varieties, shoe designs, and compositions of matter. Patents are legal documents that protect the rights of owners to sell their inventions exclusively. In other words, no one else can make, use, sell, or import patented inventions unless the owners first give their permission. (A patent is valid for a specific number of years.) In the United States, the authority for granting patents is the U.S. Patent and Trademark Office (USPTO), a federal office based in Washington, D.C.

Patent Agents can represent clients in the USPTO. In fact, Patent Agents practice patent law in the USPTO. However, they are not attorneys. It is unlawful for them to provide legal services that are performed by lawyers, such as providing legal advice, negotiating licenses to use patented inventions, representing clients in court litigation, or filing appeals in courts. Further, Patent Agents cannot practice law in federal or state courts.

Patent Agents offer clients two major services. One service is to prepare the patent application, upon which the granting of a patent is based. The application consists of a detailed description of an invention and the explicit claim to the invention. The claim describes the territory of use that belongs exclusively to the inventors. Patent Agents are responsible for drafting the application so that it is both technically and legally clear. To make sure the information is accurate, they consult with the inventors.

The other major service Patent Agents provide is the prosecution of patents. They represent their clients in the patent application process. Patent Agents are responsible for filing patent applications, responding to formal correspondence (called office actions) from the USPTO, meeting with examiners to discuss the merits of their clients' inventions, making sure all deadlines are met, and so forth. Patent Agents also counsel their clients on the progress of their applications.

Patent Agents work a standard 40-hour week, but sometimes put in additional hours to meet deadlines and complete tasks.

Salaries

Salaries vary, depending on factors such as education, experience, and geographical location. Annual salaries generally range from $40,000 to $120,000 or more.

Employment Prospects

Many Patent Agents are employed by law firms as well as by companies and businesses that are involved in research and development. Some Patent Agents are solo practitioners while others are members of firms that offer patent prosecution services.

Intellectual property law has been one of the fastest-growing areas in the 1990s and early 2000s and is expected to continue that growth for a long while. Opportunities for Patent Agents are available, particularly in such major science and technology research areas as New York, Boston, Chicago, Austin, Seattle, and San Francisco.

Advancement Prospects

Opportunities for supervisory and management positions are limited and usually requires obtaining positions with other employers. Many agents realize advancement through job satisfaction and by earning higher incomes.

Some Patent Agents earn juris doctor (J.D.) degrees and become patent attorneys.

Education and Training

Patent Agents must have at least a bachelor's degree in engineering, physics, chemistry, biochemistry, or other physical or natural science. Employers may also require that they possess as advanced degree in a science discipline.

Entry-level Patent Agents typically receive on-the-job training. Some employers provide education programs to help Patent Agents study for the USPTO entrance bar examination.

Experience, Skills, and Personality Traits

Requirements vary among the different employers. In general, candidates should have strong technical backgrounds.

Having work experience in the science or technology fields in which they would be practicing patent law is desirable.

Patent Agents must have superior writing skills, including the ability to use technical and legal language clearly. They also need excellent analytical, communication, and interpersonal skills. Being curious, detail-oriented, organized, and flexible are some personality traits that successful Patent Agents share.

Licensure and Certification

No professional license is required to become a Patent Agent. However, a Patent Agent must register with the USPTO in order to practice law before it. This requires passing an entrance bar examination. For more information, write to: Office of Enrollment and Discipline, USPTO, Crystal Plaza 6, Room 1103, Washington, D.C. 20231. Or call (703) 306-4097. Or visit the USPTO web site (*http://www.uspto.gov*) for information.

Unions and Associations

Many Patent Agents join local, state, and national professional associations in the industries in which they serve. Patent Agents are also eligible to join the National Association of Patent Practitioners. By joining professional associations, Patent Agents can take advantage of networking opportunities and other professional services and resources.

Tips for Entry

1. Some high school classes that may prepare you for this field are science, English composition, public speaking, and business law.
2. Directly contact employers for whom you would like to work. Ask about entry-level positions and their job application process.
3. You can learn more about Patent Agents on the Internet. You might visit these three web sites for information: U.S. Patent and Trademark Office, *http://www.uspto.gov;* Patent Cafe Magazine, *http://www.cafezine.com;* National Association of Patent Practitioners, *http://www.napp.org.*

TITLE EXAMINER, REAL ESTATE

CAREER PROFILE

Duties: Conduct research about the legal history of a property title; analyze legal instruments such as property deeds, wills, and liens; prepare reports of findings; perform other duties as required

Salary Range: $19,000 to $54,000

Employment Prospects: Fair

Advancement Prospects: Fair

Prerequisites:

Education/Training—A high school diploma; on-the-job training

Experience—Previous experience performing title search and abstracting work

Special Skills and Personality Traits—Communication, interpersonal, teamwork, customer service, analytical, and organization skills; meticulous, detail-oriented, decisive, dedicated

Licensure/Certification—May be required

CAREER LADDER

```
┌─────────────────────────────┐
│   Senior Title Examiner or  │
│   Department Supervisor     │
└─────────────────────────────┘

┌─────────────────────────────┐
│       Title Examiner        │
└─────────────────────────────┘

┌─────────────────────────────┐
│ Title Searcher or Title Abstractor │
└─────────────────────────────┘
```

Position Description

Title Examiners are part of the process of buying real estate—homes, land, commercial buildings, and so on. In a real estate sale, the title to a property is formally transferred from the seller to the buyer. (A title is the legal document that states a person's true ownership of a property.) It is the responsibility of Title Examiners to check that the seller of a property is the legal owner. They research the legal history of the title and verify that the title is free and clear to transfer to a new owner.

Conducting title searches requires looking through public records in city and county offices. Title Examiners search through books and file cabinets as well as through computer databases to find required records. They review mortgages, deeds, wills, divorce decrees, court judgments, liens, tax records, land maps, and other legal instruments.

Title Examiners read public records closely and carefully. They make sure that the property being purchased matches the title that would be transferred to the new owner. They also look for any restrictions that may limit the use of a property, or if rights to the property have been already granted to others. In addition, Title Examiners learn if any

mortgages, court judgments, and liens are on the property, and if property taxes or other assessments need to be paid.

After performing a title search, Title Examiners prepare a report, or abstract, of their findings. They summarize the facts and attach a list, or copies, of all the legal instruments that apply to the property.

Title Examiners are often faced with deadlines, as property buyers and sellers want to close sales as quickly as possible. Title Examiners usually work a standard 40-hour week.

Salaries

Salaries vary, depending on various factors such as education, experience, and geographical location. According to the Bureau of Labor Statistics, the estimated annual salary in 2000 for most Title Examiners ranged from $18,920 to $53,570.

Employment Prospects

Most real estate Title Examiners work for title companies. Some are employed by lawyers, banks, and local government offices. Some Title Examiners are independent contractors.

In general, positions become available as Title Examiners resign, retire, or transfer to other positions. Experts expect that fewer examiners may be needed because the increased use of technology will allow examiners to handle a heavier workload.

Advancement Prospects

Title Examiners have any number of career paths to choose, depending on their interests and ambitions. They may advance to supervisory or management positions within the title examination and search department of their company, or they may fill such positions in other organizations. Experienced Title Examiners might pursue freelance careers. With additional training and experience, they may pursue other careers within the title and real estate industry by becoming office managers, escrow officers, attorneys, insurance underwriters, or real estate agents.

Education and Training

Educational requirements vary from employer to employer. Minimally, Title Examiners must have a high school diploma or high school equivalency diploma along with qualifying experience. Employers generally prefer that candidates have completed some college courses.

Experience, Skills, and Personality Traits

Depending on the employer, candidates may be required to have one or more years of experience performing title search and abstracting work. Candidates should be familiar with legal documents, descriptions, and terms relating to land titles and transactions.

Title Examiners must have adequate communication, interpersonal, teamwork, and customer service skills as they interact daily with coworkers and outside contacts (such as realtors, government officials, banks, and home sellers). In addition, they need strong analytical and organization skills.

Being meticulous, detail-oriented, decisive, and dedicated are some personality traits that successful Title Examiners share.

Licensure and Certification

Some states require Title Examiners to be licensed. For specific information, contact the state insurance commission in the state where you wish to work.

Unions and Associations

Many Title Examiners are members of state, regional, or national professional associations, such as the American Land Title Association. By joining professional associations, they can take advantage of such professional resources as training programs and networking opportunities.

Tips for Entry

1. To gain experience, apply for an office support position in a title company or real estate office or law firm that does title examination work. Let your supervisor know of your interest in becoming a title examiner. Show your willingness to learn how to do title searches.
2. Title searchers and title abstractors can advance to the position of Title Examiner.
3. Talk with Title Examiners about their work and how they broke into the field.
4. You can learn more about Title Examiners on the Internet. To find other relevant web sites, enter the keywords *title examiners* or *title industry* in a search engine.

ELIGIBILITY WORKER
(FEDERALLY FUNDED PROGRAMS)

CAREER PROFILE

Duties: Determine eligibility of applicants to receive temporary cash grants and other financial aid from public assistance programs; help clients obtain jobs and become self-sufficient; perform duties as required

Alternate Title: Eligibility Interviewer, Eligibility Specialist, Income Maintenance Worker, Human Services Specialist

Salary Range: $22,000 to $43,000

Employment Prospects: Fair

Advancement Prospects: Limited

Prerequisites:
   Education/Training—A high school diploma; college degree may be required
   Experience—Requirements vary
   Special Skills and Personality Traits—Ability to interpret and apply rules and regulations; knowledgeable about basic principles of human behavior; communication, interpersonal, customer service, organizational, math, writing, and self-management skills; polite, tactful, patient, compassionate, fair, ethical, detail-oriented, analytical
   Licensure/Certification—None required

CAREER LADDER

```
┌─────────────────────────────┐
│   Senior or Supervisory     │
│     Eligibility Worker      │
└─────────────────────────────┘

┌─────────────────────────────┐
│     Eligibility Worker      │
└─────────────────────────────┘

┌─────────────────────────────┐
│          Trainee            │
└─────────────────────────────┘
```

Position Description

Throughout the United States, local and state social service agencies offer public assistance programs that help individuals and families in need. These programs are funded with federal grants and must accomplish certain goals established by the federal government. One goal is to provide poor people with temporary financial assistance, including cash grants and financial aid for basic needs such as food, housing, child care, and health care. The other goal is to help recipients find permanent jobs so that they can support themselves and their families.

Eligibility Workers are responsible for determining if applicants qualify for federally funded public assistance programs. They interview applicants to obtain personal data and information needed to determine eligibility. This data includes documents, such as rent receipts, bank statements, or medical records, that may support applicants' current income status.

Eligibility Workers make sure all information is accurate and complete, then evaluate it according to the rules and regulations that govern the public assistance programs. Depending on the agency, Eligibility Workers may recommend or make the final decision about whether applicants are eligible to receive assistance, along with the type and amount of assistance that would be appropriate.

Eligibility Workers are also responsible for monitoring individual cases. (Many Eligibility Workers carry a caseload of 100 or more clients.) They meet with or call clients regularly, and sometimes conduct home visits. Eligibility Workers review cases routinely to determine if clients are still eligible for assistance, if benefits should be increased or decreased, or if other types of benefits may be needed. Eligibility Workers notify clients of any changes to their benefits.

Many Eligibility Workers are also assigned the role of caseworker. They are responsible for helping clients become employable and self-sufficient and for monitoring their progress. Eligibility Workers assess clients' job skills and refer them to appropriate programs, such as job search training, vocational training, or work experience programs. They also help clients handle problems or obstacles that may keep them from finding work. This may entail getting proper clothing for job interviews, finding affordable child care, or being treated for substance abuse. Eligibility Workers refer clients to the appropriate social agencies and community resources that can help them.

Eligibility Workers perform a wide range of duties and tasks. For example, they prepare correspondence and reports; maintain accurate records and files for individual cases; and provide information about public assistance programs to prospective applicants, social workers, the general public, and the media. Eligibility Workers also keep up with changes in federal and state regulations, eligibility guidelines, program policies and procedures, and so forth.

Eligibility Workers are employed part time or full time. They may be assigned to a flexible work schedule, which includes working evenings and weekends.

Salaries

Salaries vary, depending on various factors such as education, experience, job duties, and geographical location. According to the Bureau of Labor Statistics, the estimated 2000 annual wages for most Eligibility Interviewers ranged between $21,280 and $42,650.

Employment Prospects

In general, openings become available as Eligibility Workers retire, advance to other positions, or transfer to other occupations. Additional positions at an agency are created to meet staffing needs when funding is available.

Advancement Prospects

Eligibility Workers can advance to supervisory and management positions, but opportunities in general are limited.

Many Eligibility Workers pursue such other careers as social workers, rehabilitation counselors, lawyers, paralegals, teachers, or law enforcement officers.

Education and Training

Most employers require or prefer that Eligibility Workers hold bachelor's degrees in social work, human services, or other related fields. Employers may choose candidates who

have associate degrees or who have completed only some college course work, if they have qualifying work experience.

Entry-level Eligibility Workers learn policies, procedures, and regulations through both classroom and on-the-job training.

Experience, Skills, and Personality Traits

Requirements for entry-level positions vary from one employer to the next. For example, an employer may require that entry-level candidates have at least one year of experience determining eligibility for loans, financial assistance, benefits, and so on; or that they have one or more years of office experience that included working with the public and performing basic interviewing tasks.

In general, employers look for candidates who show the ability to interpret and apply rules and regulations to public assistance programs. Good candidates are also knowledgeable about basic principles of human behavior, as they may sometimes encounter clients who are angry, confused, or disoriented.

Eligibility Workers need a variety of strong skills to perform their work well, including communication, interpersonal, customer service, organizational, math, and writing skills. They also need excellent self-management skills, such as the ability to work independently, handle stressful situations, and manage a variety of tasks at the same time.

Being polite, tactful, patient, compassionate, fair, ethical, detail-oriented, and analytical are some personality traits that successful Eligibility Workers share.

Unions and Associations

Eligibility Workers join local, state, or national professional associations to take advantage of networking opportunities, training programs, and other professional services and resources. One such national organization is the National Eligibility Workers Association.

Many Eligibility Workers belong to local unions.

Tips for Entry

1. Contact the local social services offices directly for information about job openings and the job application process. Some offices conduct ongoing recruitment for entry-level positions.
2. In some communities, fluency in a second language may give you an advantage in your job search.
3. Learn more about Eligibility Workers and public assistance programs on the Internet. For information, visit the National Eligibility Workers Association, *http://new.invite.net* or the Administration for Children and Families (the federal agency that administers the state-federal public assistance program), *http://www.acf.dhhs.gov.*

INSURANCE CLAIMS PROFESSIONAL

CAREER PROFILE

Duties: Review insurance claims for validity, accuracy, and thoroughness; conduct investigations; assess claims; make settlements; perform other duties as required

Alternate Titles: Claims Representative, Claims Examiner, Claims Adjuster

Salary Range: $26,000 to $68,000

Employment Prospects: Good

Advancement Prospects: Fair

Prerequisites:

Education/Training—A bachelor's degree required or preferred

Experience—Requirements vary for the different claims positions

Special Skills and Personality Traits—Interpersonal, communication, report-writing, computer, and self-management skills; detail-oriented, observant, analytical, fair, judicious

Licensure/Certification—Licensure for independent adjusters may be required

CAREER LADDER

```
┌─────────────────────────────────┐
│      Senior Claims Examiner      │
└─────────────────────────────────┘

┌─────────────────────────────────┐
│ Claims Examiner or Claims Adjuster │
└─────────────────────────────────┘

┌─────────────────────────────────┐
│   Trainee or Claims Representative   │
└─────────────────────────────────┘
```

Position Description

People buy different types of insurance policies—life, health, property, or liability—to cover the risk of loss or harm to their property and lives. When they experience loss or damage, they submit claims to their insurance companies. Insurance Claims Professionals are responsible for determining if customers' claims are covered by their policies. They also have the duty of assessing the facts and settling insurance claims.

Claims Professionals are assigned several cases at a time. With each claim, they carefully examine the claim forms and supporting documents, such as Medical records, for a disability claim, or estimate reports, for a car accident claim. They make sure that the forms are complete and the information is accurate and correct. They review the claimant's policy to ensure that it is still valid and to learn what losses a policy covers and the amount of insurance coverage that was purchased. In addition, Claims Professionals make sure that claims are not false or fraudulent.

They verify the truth of a claim by contacting the claimant, doctors, employers, and others who may have information about the claim.

If more information is needed, Claims Professionals conduct further investigations. They may perform the investigations themselves or refer them to claims investigators. The investigations include interviewing claimants in person, inspecting sites or property, reviewing police, hospital, and other records, and so on.

Upon completion of a review or investigation of a claim, Claims Professionals decide whether to accept or deny the claim. Furthermore, Claims Professionals have the authority to negotiate the amount of a settlement.

Some Claims Professionals are called *Claims Representatives.* Claims representatives usually handle minor claims and work from claims centers at insurance headquarters, making contact with claimants by telephone or mail. They may perform other roles, such as coordinating information for more complex claims as well as gathering and recording information from claimants or senior Claims Professionals.

Senior Claims Professionals who work for life and health insurance companies are called *Claims Examiners*. These professionals are based in insurance headquarters and are usually assigned more complex claims. Claims examiners conduct further investigations if they feel claims need more intensive review.

Claims Adjusters are senior Claims Professionals in property and liability companies. These professionals examine claims for property damage that result from accidents, fires, natural disasters, or other events. They also investigate claims of injury, illness, death, or liability for harm or loss to other people. Claims adjusters may specialize in property, liability, workers' compensation, or other types of claims.

Claims adjusters are based in branch offices. Some handle and settle claims by phone and mail. Others, called *Field Adjusters*, work many hours outside of their offices. They travel to sites to inspect damaged property, interview claimants and witnesses, read police reports and hospital records, and so on.

Claims examiners and claims representatives typically work a standard 40-hour week. Some insurance companies provide customer services 24 hours a day, seven days a week. In those companies, claims representatives may work shifts that include evenings and weekends. Claims adjusters sometimes put in 50 hours or more a week. Their hours are flexible so that they can meet with clients during the evening or on weekends.

Salaries
Salaries vary, depending on education, experience, job duties, geographical location, and other factors. According to the Bureau of Labor Statistics, the 2000 estimated annual salary for most Insurance Claims Professionals ranged between $25,860 and $68,130.

Employment Prospects
Most job opportunities will become available as individuals transfer to other occupations or leave the labor force.

Advancement Prospects
With additional experience and training, claims representatives can advance to higher positions as claims examiners, claims adjusters, or claims investigators. Many claims examiners and claims adjusters pursue advancement by earning higher incomes and by receiving more complex assignments. Experienced claims adjusters may pursue careers as independent adjusters. Claims Professionals with administrative ambitions may seek opportunities for supervisory and management positions.

Education and Training
Requirements vary for the different Claims Professional positions. Generally, employers prefer candidates with bachelor's degrees in liberal arts, business, or a field that is relevant to the type of claim being performed. For example, an engineering degree is desirable for a position dealing with industrial claims, or legal training may be preferred for a position handling workers' compensation claims.

Insurance companies may provide classroom training, on-the-job training, or both for entry-level positions.

Experience, Skills, and Personality Traits
Requirements vary for the different claims positions. In general, employers prefer that candidates have some experience in claims work. Good candidates also demonstrate the ability to understand federal and state insurance laws. It is also helpful to have practical knowledge in the area of claims. For example, an automobile Claims Adjuster should have knowledge about cars and car repairs.

Insurance Claims Professionals must have excellent interpersonal and communication skills, as well as strong report-writing and computer skills. They also need good self-management skills—such as the ability to handle stressful situations, meet deadlines, work independently, and manage several tasks simultaneously.

Some personality traits that successful Insurance Claims Professionals share are being detail-oriented, observant, analytical, fair, and judicious.

Licensure and Certification
Some states require independent claims adjusters to be licensed. For specific information, contact the insurance commission in the state where you wish to work.

Unions and Associations
Insurance Claims Professionals join state, regional, and national professional associations to take advantage of professional services and resources. Two national associations that represent Claims Professionals are the International Claim Association and the National Association of Independent Insurance Adjusters.

Tips for Entry
1. Contact insurance companies directly for general job information, as well as job openings for trainee or entry-level positions in claims.
2. Many Claims Professionals enhance their employability by obtaining the *Associate in Claims* designation, granted by the Insurance Institute of America (IIA). For information, write IIA at 720 Providence Road, PO Box 3016, Malvern, PA 19335-0716. Or

phone (800) 664-2101, or visit its web site *(http://www.aicpcu.org)*.

3. Many claims representatives started at an insurance company as an office clerk, gradually gaining work experience related to claims.

4. You can learn more about insurance companies and Insurance Claims Professionals on the Internet. To find pertinent web sites, enter any of these keywords in a search engine: *insurance claims professionals, claims examiners,* or *claims adjusters.*

ACTUARY

CAREER PROFILE

Duties: Study the financial risk, uncertainties, and probabilities of future events; perform duties as required

Alternate Titles: Actuarial Assistant, Actuarial Associate, Actuarial Consultant

Salary Range: $37,000 to $128,000

Employment Prospects: Good

Advancement Prospects: Good

Prerequisites:

Education/Training—A bachelor's degree; on-the-job training

Experience—Previous work experience may not be necessary for entry-level positions; completion of one or more actuarial examinations is preferred or required

Special Skills and Personality Traits—Problem-solving, project management, teamwork, communication, interpersonal, and computer skills; enthusiastic, adaptable, flexible, analytical, self-motivated, creative

Licensure/Certification—The Associate credential granted by either the Society of Actuaries or the Casualty Actuarial Society

CAREER LADDER

```
┌─────────────────────────────────────┐
│  Senior Actuary, Department Manager, │
│      or Actuarial Consultant         │
└─────────────────────────────────────┘

┌─────────────────────────────────────┐
│              Actuary                 │
└─────────────────────────────────────┘

┌─────────────────────────────────────┐
│        Actuarial Assistant           │
└─────────────────────────────────────┘
```

Position Description

Actuaries study the financial risk, uncertainties, and probabilities of future events for their employers. Using mathematics, statistics, and financial theory, Actuaries define and analyze problems that may occur during the course of their employers' activities. They also help employers create programs that would be able to handle future financial loss.

Most Actuaries work in the fields of insurance, pension plans, and financial investments. Insurance Actuaries specialize in the different areas of insurance—life, health, property, casualty, or workers' compensation.

Actuaries work on a wide range of projects for their employers. For example, they might:

- determine what price or rate at which a product should be sold
- calculate potential profits and losses for a new product or program
- project the cost of a loss over a number of years
- determine the financial risk involved in a business merger or acquisition
- estimate the financial loss for an employer if a natural or human-made disaster should occur
- determine the amount of reserves needed to cover future losses
- appraise the current value of an organization, a particular program, or specific inventory
- design new products or programs
- establish rating guidelines and risk categories
- estimate future cash flows, earnings, taxes, assets, and liabilities

Actuaries gather data from various sources to analyze. Along with numerical information, they read historical data, appropriate laws and regulations, trends, and so on. They develop mathematical models to help them analyze problems. Actuaries then discuss their findings with executives, attorneys, marketing staff, and other employees. They must be able to explain complex, technical concepts in terms that are clearly understood.

As part of their job, Actuaries keep up with current legislation, economic and social trends, and developments in their industry.

Actuaries sometimes provide expert witness testimony at court trials, depositions, administrative hearings, legislative hearings, and arbitrations. For example, an Actuary might testify at an Environmental Protection Agency (EPA) hearing about how a proposed regulation may affect a corporation's business, or an Actuary might provide testimony about the value of a pension plan in a divorce case.

Actuaries obtain professional status by passing a series of examinations that are administered by professional actuary associations. There are two professional levels. The first level is *Associate,* which takes most Actuaries four to six years to achieve. The second level is *Fellow,* which takes a few more years to complete.

Actuaries work a standard 40-hour week.

Salaries

Salaries vary, depending on experience, the number of actuarial exams that have been passed, job responsibilities, and other factors. According to the Bureau of Labor Statistics, the estimated annual salary in 2000 for most Actuaries ranged between $37,130 and $127,360.

Employment Prospects

Actuaries are employed by insurance companies, actuary consulting firms, banks, financial institutions, corporations, hospitals, government agencies, and other organizations.

Job opportunities generally become available as Actuaries resign, retire, or advance to other positions. Employers create additional positions to meet growing needs.

Advancement Prospects

Actuaries can advance to supervisory and management positions, based on their experience, job performance, and professional status (Associate or Fellow). Actuaries can also follow a career path as solo consultants or firm owners that provide actuarial services.

Education and Training

Many Employers require or prefer that Actuaries hold a bachelor's degree in mathematics, actuarial science, statistics, or other related field. Employers may hire candidates with nonmath degrees if they have passed one or more actuarial examinations.

Employers provide on-the-job training for entry-level positions.

Many employers have education programs to help Actuaries study for their actuarial examinations.

Experience, Skills, and Personality Traits

Requirements vary from employer to employer for entry-level positions. Employers often hire college graduates with little or no experience, if they can demonstrate good business sense as well as show strong mathematical and technical aptitudes. Many employers prefer (or require) that candidates have completed one or more actuarial examinations.

Actuaries must have excellent problem-solving, project management, and teamwork skills. They also need superior communication and interpersonal skills. In addition, they have strong computer skills, with the ability to use word processing programs, spreadsheets, statistical analysis programs, database manipulation, and so forth.

Successful Actuaries have several personality traits in common, such as being enthusiastic, adaptable, flexible, analytical, self-motivated, and creative.

Licensure and Certification

No professional license is required to become an Actuary. However, to gain professional status, an Actuary must obtain the *Associate* credential. The Casualty Actuarial Society grants the professional credential to those in the property and casualty practices. The Society of Actuaries grants the credential to those who practice in life insurance, health insurance, finance, investments, or pension plans. (Contact information may be found in Appendix 3.)

Actuaries who practice in pension plans governed by federal laws must be licensed by the Joint Board for the Enrollment of Actuaries. (This board is composed of members from the U.S. Department of the Treasury and the Bureau of Labor Statistics.) For further information, write to the Joint Board for the Enrollment of Actuaries, Internal Revenue Service, N:C:SC:DOP, 1111 Constitution Avenue, NW, Washington, DC 20224. Or call (202) 694-1891, or fax (202) 694-1876. You can find information at its web page (*http://www.irs.gov/bus_info/tax_pro/actuary.html*).

Unions and Associations

Most Actuaries are members of one or more professional associations, such as the American Academy of Actuaries, American Society of Pension Actuaries, Casualty Actuarial Society, Conference of Consulting Actuaries, and Society of Actuaries. By joining professional associations, Actuaries can take advantage of various professional services and resources, such as networking opportunities, job listings, and education programs.

Tips for Entry

1. As a college student, obtain internships to see if the actuarial field is right for you. Visit your college career center for help in finding internships.

2. Many Actuaries recommend that students take courses in economics, business, computer science, and liberal arts in addition to mathematics courses.

3. You can learn more about Actuaries on the Internet. Two pertinent web sites are Actuary.com, *http://www.actuary.com* and Be an Actuary, *http://www.BeAnActuary.com.*

EDUCATORS

LAW PROFESSOR

CAREER PROFILE

Duties: Teach law theory, practical skills, or clinical courses in law schools; prepare course outlines, course materials, and class lessons; research and write scholarly legal work; provide school and community service; perform duties as required

Alternate Titles: Instructor, Assistant Professor, Associate Professor, Professor

Salary Range: $30,000 to $136,000

Employment Prospects: Fair

Advancement Prospects: Fair

Prerequisites:

Education/Training—A law degree

Experience—Attorney experience required or preferred

Special Skills and Personality Traits—Communication, presentation, interpersonal, organizational, and management skills; enthusiastic, flexible, inspirational, independent, self-motivated, dedicated

Licensure/Certification—None required

CAREER LADDER

```
┌─────────────────────────────┐
│      Law School Dean        │
└─────────────────────────────┘

┌─────────────────────────────┐
│         Professor           │
└─────────────────────────────┘

┌─────────────────────────────┐
│  Attorney, Judicial Law Clerk, │
│      or Law Student         │
└─────────────────────────────┘
```

Position Description

Law Professors are educators and scholars who have the duty of teaching law students essential knowledge of the law and basic lawyering skills, such as legal research and legal writing. As role models and mentors, they also have the duty of impressing on their students the responsibility they must uphold as future professionals to promote individual justice as well as social justice.

Most Law Professors are lawyers with experience in private practice, the court systems, public interest organizations, corporations, government agencies, and other institutions. Many Professors continue practicing law throughout their careers as legal educators.

Generally, most Law Professors teach doctrinal, or theory, courses. These are courses in substantive areas, such as contracts, torts, civil procedure, constitutional law, criminal law, property law, family law, estate planning, intellectual property, commercial law, and environmental law. Some Law Professors focus their education careers in the teaching of practical lawyering skills, such as legal research, legal

writing, or negotiation. Other Law Professors teach in clinical programs that provide students with hands-on experiences. Clinical professors closely supervise students as they handle cases of family disputes, employment issues, criminal defense, appeals, and so forth.

Professors who teach doctrinal courses usually have the freedom to design their own courses. Skills and clinical professors usually follow an established curriculum that is designed by program directors and senior faculty.

All Law Professors are responsible for preparing the courses that they teach. They prepare their course syllabi, outlines of what will be taught in the course. They also assemble course materials, which may include the use of technology, such as the Internet. In addition, they plan for each class session, preparing lecture notes and designing exercises and assignments to reinforce students' learning. Other teaching tasks include creating examinations, evaluating students' assignments, providing students with feedback on their work, and so on.

Law Professors teach in various settings, depending on the nature of their courses. For example, they may lecture about constitutional law to large groups of first-year students in lecture halls, work one-on-one with second-year students in legal writing workshops, or lead small groups of third-year students in discussion about commercial law.

Most Law Professors are required to hold formal office hours so students can meet with them individually. Professors are available to answer questions about class assignments, as well as to advise students about career options and opportunities.

Along with their teaching, Law Professors are expected to contribute to legal scholarship by authoring academic articles, student textbooks, court opinions, and so forth. Many professors are involved in one or more research projects on legal subjects that interest them. They sometimes solicit the help of students for their projects.

Law Professors are also expected to provide school and community service. They serve on faculty committees for both the law school and the university. They get involved in boards and committees for professional legal associations at the local, state, and national level. Many give presentations at lawyer and nonlawyer conferences. Law Professors who continue to practice law often perform pro bono (free) work for public interest groups and other non-profit organizations.

Furthermore, Law Professors are responsible for keeping up with developments in their legal areas. They read journals and books in their field, network with colleagues, participate in professional conferences, and so forth.

Law Professors may be hired for tenure-track or non–tenure track positions. Doctrinal professors are usually hired for tenure-track positions. When professors become tenured they are assured a job until they retire or resign. They cannot be fired from their job without just cause and due process. Non–tenure track professors (usually skills and clinical instructors) are hired on a contractual basis. They receive limited-term contracts, usually for three years. The contracts are often renewable.

Salaries

Salaries vary, depending on experience, tenure, school, geographical location, and other factors. According to the Bureau of Labor Statistics, the estimated annual salary in 2000 for most law teachers ranged between $29,540 and $135,840.

Employment Prospects

Law Professors work for law schools that are part of public or private university systems. Job opportunities at law schools typically become available as Law Professors retire, resign, or transfer to administrative positions.

Advancement Prospects

Law Professors on tenure tracks can advance through the ranks as assistant professors, associate professors, and full professors. Those with administrative ambitions can become assistant and associate deans, and eventually become deans of law schools. Such positions can lead further to executive positions in the university administration.

Education and Training

Minimally, Law Professors possess juris doctor (J.D.) degrees. Many also hold master of law (L.L.M.) degrees, which they earn after being practicing attorneys for several years.

Experience, Skills, and Personality Traits

Law schools typically choose candidates who have excellent academic credentials. Many schools also require or strongly prefer experienced attorneys. They prefer that candidates have a specialty in the substantive areas that the law schools emphasize. In addition candidates show a commitment to teaching.

Law Professors need excellent communication and presentation skills, as well as strong interpersonal skills to work well with students, faculty members, administrators, and others. Additionally, they should have good organizational and management skills.

Being enthusiastic, flexible, inspirational, independent, self-motivated, and dedicated are some personality traits that successful Law Professors share.

Licensure and Certification

No professional license is required to become a Law Professor.

Many Law Professors maintain their attorney's license, especially if they plan to continue to practice law.

Unions and Associations

Law School Professors join different professional associations to take advantage of networking opportunities and other professional services and resources. Two organizations that represent legal educators are the Society of American Law Teachers and the Clinical Legal Education Association. Some higher education associations that Law Professors may join are the American Association for Higher Education and the American Association of University Professors.

Many Law Professors join local and state bar associations, as well as national bar associations such as the American Bar Association. In addition, many belong to special-interest associations such as the Association of Trial Lawyers of America, the National Asian Pacific American Bar Association, or the National Association of Women Lawyers.

Tips for Entry

1. One way to obtain teaching experience is to become an adjunct instructor. Many law schools hire part-time teachers to teach legal research and legal writing classes or practical skills courses such as trial advocacy classes.

2. Representatives from most law schools attend a hiring convention sponsored by the Association of American Law Schools (AALS) to interview and hire candidates for entry-level teaching positions. For more information, write to AALS at 1201 Connecticut Avenue, NW, Suite 800, Washington, D.C. 20036-2605. Or phone (202) 296-8851. Or visit the AALS web site *(http://www.aals.org)*.

3. Learn more about Law Professors on the Internet. Two web sites that are helpful are Jurist: The Legal Education Network *(http://jurist.law.pitt.edu)* and Teachlaw *(http://teachlaw.law.uc.edu)*.

LEGAL WRITING INSTRUCTOR

CAREER PROFILE

Duties: Teach the basics of legal writing, legal research, legal reasoning, and legal analysis; prepare course syllabi and create course materials; critique students' assignments; perform duties as required

Alternate Titles: Legal Writing Professor, Professor of Legal Research and Writing, Lecturer

Salary Range: $30,000 to $130,000

Employment Prospects: Good

Advancement Prospects: Limited

Prerequisites:

Education/Training—A law degree

Experience—Law practice or judicial clerkship experience; teaching experience is preferred

Special Skills and Personality Traits—Interpersonal, listening, communication, teamwork skills; tactful, patient, caring, dedicated, flexible, creative

Licensure/Certification—None required

CAREER LADDER

```
┌─────────────────────────────────────┐
│   Legal Writing Program Director     │
└─────────────────────────────────────┘

┌─────────────────────────────────────┐
│       Professor on a tenure or       │
│          non-tenure track            │
└─────────────────────────────────────┘

┌─────────────────────────────────────┐
│         Adjunct Instructor           │
└─────────────────────────────────────┘
```

Position Description

The ability to write about the law clearly, accurately, and concisely is a necessary skill for lawyers. Thus, many law schools hire Legal Writing Instructors who are experienced attorneys as well as legal educators who specialize in teaching legal writing. Legal Writing Instructors are sometimes called Legal Research and Writing Instructors because they teach more than legal writing skills. Their instruction also includes the basics of legal research, legal analysis, and legal reasoning skills. Through progressive lessons, students learn to research topics, analyze cases and statutes, reason and argue the facts, apply the law, and write their legal analysis in court briefs, office memorandums, and other legal documents. In addition, students learn about common legal writing formats and presentation styles.

Legal Writing Instructors usually follow a curriculum designed by the legal writing program director and senior legal writing faculty. The instructors, however, are responsible for preparing their course syllabi and designing course materials. Because theirs is a required course, Legal Writing Instructors may be assigned from 30 to 70 students each semester. Full-time instructors usually teach two or more sessions each semester.

Instructors typically teach and demonstrate new skills, then assign students research and writing exercises to practice the skills. Instructors critique and evaluate their students' work. They also hold individual sessions with students to discuss their assignments and provide them with additional help.

Along with teaching, many Legal Writing Instructors conduct research projects and produce scholarly work about their field. They write books and articles about legal writing, teaching methodology, and other topics. Some law schools provide grants to support them with their research.

Many Legal Writing Instructors are adjunct, or part-time, instructors. They are typically practicing attorneys. They usually teach one legal writing course and spend only a few hours on campus. They generally are not given offices and rarely have a voice in school policies.

Some full-time instructors are hired as assistant or associate professors on a tenure track. When professors become tenured they are assured a job until they retire or resign.

They cannot be fired without just cause and due process. Other full-time Legal Writing Instructors are hired on a contractual basis. Entry-level instructors receive one- to three-year contracts which may be renewable. Some law schools limit the number of years that Legal Writing Instructors may teach on their campus.

Salaries

Salaries for Legal Writing Instructors are generally lower than doctrinal professors in many law schools. Salaries vary, depending on experience, rank, geographical location, and other factors. According to a 2001 survey by the Legal Writing Institute and the Association of Legal Writing Directors, the annual salaries for full-time legal research and writing faculty ranged from $30,000 to $130,000.

Employment Prospects

The legal writing field is a young but growing one. Typically, adjunct and contractual positions are more available than tenure-track positions. Some in the field expect that more law schools will begin appointing Legal Writing Instructors to tenure track so as to keep experienced teachers.

Advancement Prospects

Advancement opportunities are limited to legal writing program directorships. Most Instructors pursue advancement by being appointed on tenure track, by earning higher incomes, and by gaining professional reputations in their field.

Education and Training

Legal Writing Instructors hold juris doctor (J.D.) degrees; many also possess master of law (L.L.M.) degrees.

Instructors usually learn on the job as well as through mentoring with senior faculty members. Throughout their careers, Legal Writing Instructors enroll in training and education programs to develop their teaching skills and stay current with legal subjects.

Experience, Skills, and Personality Traits

Law schools generally look for candidates who have strong academic credentials as well as practice or judicial clerkship experience. Many schools require or prefer that Legal Writing Instructors have teaching experience.

Legal Writing Instructors need excellent interpersonal, listening, and communication skills to work well with students, fellow teachers, and others. They also need good teamwork skills. Being tactful, patient, caring, dedicated, flexible, and creative are some personality traits that successful Legal Writing Instructors share.

Unions and Associations

Many Legal Writing Instructors are eligible to join different associations to take advantage of networking opportunities and other professional resources and services. For example, they might join the Society of American Law Teachers, which represents law professors. They might also join the Association of Legal Writing Specialists, which represents professionals who work within legal writing programs. In addition, Legal Writing Instructors might belong to professional associations that serve the interests of all professors, such as the American Association for Higher Education or the American Association of University Professors.

Tips for Entry

1. While you are in law school, obtain a teaching assistant position in the legal writing program to gain experience.
2. Openings for adjunct positions in legal writing programs are often filled by word of mouth. Therefore, talk with current adjuncts to learn about current or future openings.
3. For information about job openings, contact the legal writing programs or faculty at the law schools where you would like to work.
4. You can learn more about legal writing and the profession on the Internet. To find relevant web sites, enter the keywords *legal writing* in a search engine.

LAW SCHOOL DEAN

CAREER PROFILE

Duties: Act as both chief academic and administrative leader of law schools; perform duties as required

Alternate Title: Dean of School of Law

Salary Range: $33,000 to $109,000

Employment Prospects: Fair

Advancement Prospects: Fair

Prerequisites:

    Education/Training—On-the-job training

    Experience—Be a law professor; experience in academic administration required or highly preferred

    Special Skills and Personality Traits—Leadership, management, administrative, fund-raising, listening, communication, interpersonal, and team building skills; respectful, humble, appreciative, confident, positive, energetic, dedicated

    Licensure/Certification—None required

CAREER LADDER

```
┌──────────────────────────────────────┐
│   University Provost or President     │
└──────────────────────────────────────┘

┌──────────────────────────────────────┐
│          Law School Dean             │
└──────────────────────────────────────┘

┌──────────────────────────────────────┐
│   Law Professor or Associate Dean    │
└──────────────────────────────────────┘
```

Position Description

Deans provide vision and leadership to law schools, which are generally part of public and private university systems. Their job is complex and challenging as they perform various duties and tasks each day.

Law School Deans serve two roles. As chief academic officers, they oversee the development of academic programs, curriculum, services, and activities. Unlike other academic deans, Law School Deans work directly with faculty members. (In other schools, academic deans work with department chairs.) They are responsible for providing supervision and guidance to faculty, motivating them to excel in teaching and scholarship.

The other role that Law School Deans play is that of head administrative officer. They ensure that all operations are running smoothly and effectively. Law schools have many departments and services that are separate from the universities. For example, law schools have their own admissions and financial aid departments, libraries, and career centers. Assisting Deans with their administrative duties are such managers as associate and assistant deans, admissions officers, financial officers, and law library directors.

Law School Deans perform many administrative duties, such as:

- provide guidance and supervision to their administrative staff
- supervise support staff in their offices
- manage and develop budgets
- oversee the recruitment, hiring, retention, and firing of faculty, administrative staff, and other support staff
- provide for the professional development of academic and administrative staffs
- oversee the recruitment and selection of law students

Deans also actively lead in the role of development, or fund-raising for their schools. For example, they meet with prospective donors in business and social meetings. They also participate in fund-raising activities, such as special alumni events. Furthermore, they motivate and assist faculty in writing proposals for research grants.

In addition, Law School Deans serve on university administrative councils and committees. As part of the university administration, Deans help in the development of university policies.

Law School Deans are expected to be the primary spokespersons for their schools. They interact with local, state, and national attorney bars, as well as with alumni, businesses, community leaders, government agencies, media, and others. Additionally, they participate in legal, community, social, and other types of functions and events as representatives of their schools.

Deans often travel to other cities and states to attend conferences, meet with school supporters, make public presentations, and so forth. They can be expected to work evenings and weekends to complete their many routine tasks, attend meetings or functions, and handle various matters that need immediate attention.

Salaries

Salaries vary, depending on experience, school budget, geographical location, and other factors. According to the Bureau of Labor Statistics, the estimated annual salary in 2000 for most postsecondary educational administrators (including deans) ranged between $32,650 and $109,280.

Employment Prospects

Opportunities generally become available as Deans resign, retire, or transfer to other positions.

Advancement Prospects

Some Deans choose to return to teaching after one or two years because they dislike the pace of administrative work. Those who have further administrative ambitions can advance to such executive positions in a university as assistant provost, provost, and, eventually, president. Some Deans pursue deanships in other law schools that offer additional challenges, higher wages, or more professional prestige.

Education and Training

Deans typically learn their duties and tasks on the job. Many enroll in training workshops and education programs for deans, which are sponsored by professional associations such as the American Bar Association or the Association of American Law Schools.

Experience, Skills, and Personality Traits

Law schools usually choose Deans who are tenured law professors with a distinctive record of teaching, scholarship, and service. Previous experience in academic administration may be required or highly preferred.

Law Deans must have strong leadership abilities and effective management skills, as well as excellent administrative and fund-raising skills. They also need superior listening, communication, interpersonal, and team building skills to work well with professors, administrators, donors, and others.

Being respectful, humble, appreciative, confident, positive, energetic, and dedicated are a few personality traits that successful Law Deans have in common.

Licensure and Certification

No professional licensure is required to become a law school Dean.

Many Deans maintain their attorney's licenses, but that is not a requirement for the position.

Unions and Associations

Law School Deans join various professional and bar associations to take advantage of networking opportunities and other professional resources and services. Some organizations that they join, either as individuals or as school representatives, are:

- Association of American Law Schools
- American Bar Association—Section of Legal Education and Admissions to the Bar
- National Association for Law Placement
- Society of American Law Teachers
- American Association of University Administrators
- American Association for Higher Education
- American Conference of Academic Deans

Tips for Entry

1. Enroll in management classes or training programs to develop strong managerial skills.
2. Volunteer to serve on administrative committees at your law school, as well as at your university.
3. You can learn more about Law Deans on the Internet. To find relevant web sites, enter *law school dean* into a search engine.

PARALEGAL EDUCATOR

CAREER PROFILE

Duties: Teach basic legal knowledge and skills in formal paralegal education programs; prepare course outlines and materials; perform duties as required

Alternate Titles: Paralegal Instructor, Legal Assistant Instructor, Legal Studies Professor

Salary Range: $30,000 to $136,000

Employment Prospects: Fair

Advancement Prospects: Limited

Prerequisites:

    Education/Training—Many have bachelor's degrees along with law degrees or other advanced degrees

    Experience—Several years of lawyering or paralegal experience; experience being paralegals or working with paralegals; have teaching experience or ability

    Special Skills and Personality Traits—Communication, interpersonal, organizational, and self-management skills; patient, inspiring, versatile, resourceful, creative

    Licensure/Certification—Community college teaching credential may be required; attorney license for lawyers

CAREER LADDER

```
┌─────────────────────────────────┐
│      Professor (tenured)         │
└─────────────────────────────────┘

┌─────────────────────────────────┐
│      Instructor or Assistant     │
│      Professor (tenure track)    │
└─────────────────────────────────┘

┌─────────────────────────────────┐
│       Adjunct Instructor         │
└─────────────────────────────────┘
```

Position Description

Paralegal Educators are experienced attorneys and paralegals who train legal assistants, or paralegals, in formal paralegal education programs. They teach courses that provide students with basic legal knowledge and skills to succeed in entry-level paralegal positions. (Paralegals help lawyers with routine legal tasks, such as conducting legal research, interviewing clients, drafting legal documents, and maintaining legal records.)

There are different types of paralegal programs. Some are college degree programs (associate, bachelor's or master's), while others are professional certificate programs. A program's curriculum typically covers legal research and writing, litigation, ethics, technology, contracts, and torts. Many programs include basic courses in real property, wills, estate planning, and family law as part of their core curriculum. In addition, most programs specialize in a few substantive courses (such as criminal law, elder law, immigration law, intellectual property law, and employment law), which

depend on the requirements of the legal markets in their communities. Furthermore, most paralegal programs require students to complete an internship or other clinical experience.

Paralegal Educators are assigned to teach one or more courses. They are responsible for developing a class outline or syllabus for each course, as well as for creating daily lesson plans, class assignments, and examinations. They check students' completed assignments and exams in a timely matter and provide them with feedback. They use various teaching methods to present their lessons, such as lecture, seminar, and role playing. They also use various forms of technology, including the Internet, to supplement their teaching.

Paralegal Educators evaluate and report student performance and progress as required by their programs. They also meet with students individually to provide assistance with class work as well as to counsel students about career opportunities. Paralegal Educators also complete administrative tasks such as marking attendance, filing grades, and completing required paperwork. Some educators are responsible for supervising student interns.

Paralegal Educators typically work independently, but are expected to work together as a team with the program director and other faculty members. They assist with the development of the paralegal program, which includes making decisions about curriculum, class schedules, annual budgets, student recruitment, and so forth. Many Paralegal Educators also assist with fund-raising activities and grant proposal writing.

Paralegal Educators may be hired as adjunct, or part-time, instructors. Some are hired full time but on limited-term contracts. Others are hired for a tenure-track position, usually at an assistant professor level. Tenured educators have job security. They cannot be fired without just cause and due process.

Many Paralegal Educators, whether full-time or part-time instructors, continue working as attorneys and paralegals.

Salaries

Salaries vary, depending on factors such as experience, education, type of employer, and geographical location. According to the Bureau of Labor Statistics, the estimated annual salary in 2000 for most postsecondary teachers who teach law subjects ranged between $29,540 and $135,840.

Employment Prospects

Paralegal Educators are hired by paralegal programs in public and private colleges, universities, and other postsecondary schools. Over 600 paralegal programs are currently available across the United States, according to the American Bar Association.

The paralegal profession is projected to increase by 21 to 35 percent through 2010, according to the Bureau of Labor Statistics. In addition, some experts report that increasingly more employers are hiring paralegals who have completed formal paralegal education programs.

Advancement Prospects

For those interested in administrative duties, Paralegal Educators can become program coordinators or directors. Many Paralegal Educators measure their success through any or all of the following—job satisfaction, professional recognition, and higher incomes.

Education and Training

Most Paralegal Educators have bachelor's degrees, along with law degrees or other advanced degrees in education, paralegal studies, or related fields.

Throughout their careers, Paralegal Educators enroll in education and training programs to build their skills and knowledge for training future legal assistants.

Experience, Skills, and Personality Traits

Requirements vary from employer to employer. In general, candidates must be practicing lawyers or paralegals with several years of experience in their practice areas. Lawyers must have experience working with paralegals. In addition, candidates have teaching experience or are able to demonstrate teaching ability.

Paralegal Educators need excellent communication and interpersonal skills to work well with students, faculty and others. They also must have excellent organizational skills along with strong self-management skills—the ability to work independently, handle several projects and tasks at the same time, meet deadlines, and so forth.

Successful Paralegal Educators share several personality traits such as being patient, inspiring, versatile, resourceful, and creative. Furthermore, they are strongly committed to providing quality paralegal education programs.

Licensure and Certification

To teach in community college systems, Paralegal Educators may be required to obtain a state teaching credential. For specific information, contact the community colleges where you would like to teach.

Employers may require that lawyers be licensed to practice law in the states where they teach.

Unions and Associations

Many Paralegal Educators belong to the American Association for Paralegal Education and the American Bar Association Standing Committee on Legal Assistants (SCOLA). These organizations, and other local and state professional societies, specifically represent the needs of Paralegal Educators. They offer professional resources and services, such as training programs, current research data, publications, and networking opportunities.

Tips for Entry

1. As a paralegal or lawyer, you might offer your services as a guest lecturer to local paralegal programs in order to gain teaching experience.
2. Because there are hundreds of different paralegal programs in different settings, learn more about a paralegal program before taking a teaching position. For example: Is the setting one in which you wish to work? Do the program's mission and goals match yours? Does the program meet the standards of quality set by local and national paralegal associations?
3. You can use the Internet to explore the various types of paralegal programs available. To find pertinent web sites, enter either of these keywords in a search engine: *paralegal program* or *legal assistant program.*

JUDICIAL BRANCH EDUCATOR

CAREER PROFILE

Duties: Develop and manage continuing education programs for judges and court support staff; perform duties as required

Alternate Titles: Judicial Educator, Judicial Education Specialist, Judicial Education Coordinator, Judicial Education Manager

Salary Range: about $34,000 to $69,000

Employment Prospects: Fair

Advancement Prospects: Limited

Prerequisites:

    Education/Training—A bachelor's degree in education, court administration, or related field; a law degree or other advanced degree may be required

    Experience—Experience developing adult training programs is desirable; experience working in the legal field or court systems

    Special Skills and Personality Traits—Communication, teamwork, interpersonal, writing, project planning and computer skills; Self-motivated, determined, organized, dedicated, creative

    Licensure/Certification—None required

CAREER LADDER

```
┌─────────────────────────────────┐
│   Program Manager or Director    │
└─────────────────────────────────┘

┌─────────────────────────────────┐
│  Senior Judicial Branch Educator │
└─────────────────────────────────┘

┌─────────────────────────────────┐
│     Judicial Branch Educator     │
└─────────────────────────────────┘
```

Position Description

Judicial Branch Educators are responsible for providing educational services in the federal, state, and local courts. They develop and administer educational programs for judges and other court staff, including attorneys, public defenders, social workers, juvenile officers, bailiffs, interpreters, administrators, clerks, and so on. The programs provide participants with basic knowledge and skills that help them perform their duties effectively and efficiently. For example, Judicial Branch Educators have developed orientation programs for entry-level court judges, in-service workshops for court mediators, court interpreter training programs, jury management classes, and diversity workshops. They also develop seminars on issues that judges and other court staff handle, such as child abuse and neglect, domestic violence, and developments in science.

Judicial Branch Educators fulfill roles as curriculum developers, instructional designers, and program managers. They continually develop new programs, classes, and seminars as well as update current ones. They perform a wide range of duties that vary from court to court, as well as among staff members. Some major duties include:

- conducting assessments to determine the educational needs of judges and court staff
- assisting in planning overall delivery of education services
- developing curriculum, courses, and instructional materials in collaboration with instructors, subject-matter experts, and project managers
- managing education projects, which includes such tasks as finding instructors and vendors, negotiating contracts, coordinating logistics, handling registration, and ensuring that courses comply with laws, regulations, and rules
- developing and conducting course evaluations
- conducting training sessions for trainers

- maintaining a library of tapes, books and other judicial education and training materials
- serving as a resource on trends, research, teaching methodologies, and so forth
- creating newsletters or web pages to provide judges, court staff, and the public with information about current court decisions, laws, and other legal developments

Senior educators have additional supervisory duties, while managers (or coordinators) are also responsible for the leadership and administration of the judicial education programs as a whole.

All Judicial Branch Educators are responsible for staying up to date with trends in judicial education, as well as with emerging issues (social, technology, professional, and so forth) that are relevant to the judges and court support staff.

Judicial Branch Educators generally work a 40-hour week.

Salaries

Salaries vary, depending on such factors as education and experience, the size and budget of the judicial education program, and geographical location. Judicial Branch Educators with supervisory and management responsibilities can expect to earn higher wages.

Formal salary information for this profession was unavailable. Below are examples of salaries for Judicial Branch Educators in 1999 and 2000. (Information is from the National Center for State Courts [NCSC] web site, *http://www.ncsc.dni.us/is/clrhouse/ jobdeda/sect13.htm).*

- Education Manager, Oregon Judicial Division, $49,116 to $65,808 (1999)
- Judicial Educator, Vermont Court Administrator, $50,000 to $55,000 (1999)
- Education Specialist II, California Administrative Office of the Courts, San Francisco, $56,868 to $69,120 (2000)
- Education Specialist, Nevada Administrative Office of the Courts, $33,742 to $45,643 (2000)
- Senior Educator, Washington Office of the Administrator of the Courts, $43,128 to $55,212 (2000)

Employment Prospects

Most opportunities become available as Judicial Branch Educators resign or transfer to other positions. As judicial education programs are established and expand throughout the states and federal court systems, additional positions will be created. Opportunities, in general, are dependent on the availability of funding.

Advancement Prospects

Judicial Branch Educators can advance to management and administrative positions, which may require transferring from one judicial education program to another.

Education and Training

Minimally, Judicial Branch Educators must possess bachelor's degrees in education, court administration, or related fields. In addition, employers may require or strongly prefer that Judicial Branch Educators hold law degrees or master's degrees in education or related fields.

Judicial Branch Educators enroll in training and education programs throughout their careers to further develop their skills and knowledge.

Experience, Skills, and Personality Traits

In general, employers require or strongly prefer candidates who have previous experience developing training programs for adults. Additionally, some employers require that candidates have experience working in the legal field or within the court systems.

Judicial Branch Educators need excellent communication, teamwork, and interpersonal skills to work well with judges, court administrators and staff, and others. They also need strong writing and project planning skills as well as competent computer skills. Being self-motivated, determined, organized, dedicated, and creative are some personality traits that characterize successful Judicial Branch Educators.

Unions and Associations

Judicial Branch Educators join professional societies, such as the National Association of State Judicial Branch Educators, to take advantage of professional resources and services. For example, professional associations generally offer opportunities for networking with colleagues, in addition to training programs and reports of current research projects.

Tips for Entry

1. Enroll in courses about adult education theory and instruction.
2. Learn as much as you can about the court systems.
3. To learn more about judicial education programs on the Internet, visit JERITT: The Judicial Education Reference, Information and Technical Transfer Project *(http://jeritt.msu.edu).* To find other relevant web sites, use any of these keywords in a search engine: *judicial education, judicial educators,* or *judicial branch educators.*

CAREER SERVICES
PROFESSIONALS

LAW SCHOOL CAREER COUNSELOR

CAREER PROFILE

Duties: Provide career counseling and job search advice to law students and alumni; coordinate programs and activities as assigned; perform duties as required

Alternate Title: Career Services Counselor

Salary Range: $24,000 to $67,000

Employment Prospects: Fair

Advancement Prospects: Limited

Prerequisites:

Education/Training—A bachelor's degree; a law degree or master's degree in counseling strongly preferred

Experience—Previous experience in career counseling, student services, or law firm recruitment; lawyering experience preferred

Special Skills and Personality Traits—Organizational, interpersonal, writing, communication, and computer skills; patient, objective, friendly, supportive, tactful, trustworthy, flexible, creative

Licensure/Certification—None required

CAREER LADDER

```
┌─────────────────────────────┐
│   Assistant Director or Director │
│   of Career Services Center  │
└─────────────────────────────┘

┌─────────────────────────────┐
│   Law School Career Counselor │
└─────────────────────────────┘

┌─────────────────────────────┐
│   Career Counselor or Attorney │
└─────────────────────────────┘
```

Position Description

Most, if not all, law schools have career services centers that help law students (and alumni) with planning their careers and with finding employment. Career Counselors provide law students with career development counseling. They advise students of the various traditional and alternative legal careers that are available to them. They help students identify career options and develop their career plans. Career Counselors work with students in individual or group counseling sessions.

Career Counselors also have the duty of helping students find employment. They help students find part-time or summer employment as well as internships. They also assist graduating students and alumni with their searches for attorney positions, judicial clerkships, and nonlawyer positions.

Furthermore, Career Counselors advise students of ways to develop their job search strategies and techniques. Career Counselors plan, organize, and lead workshops on different job search skills, such as writing a résumé, networking, and organizing a job hunt. They also work with students individually to help them develop their résumés or to build their job interviewing techniques. In addition, they counsel students about various employment issues and concerns, such as salary negotiation, career satisfaction, and what to expect on their jobs as attorneys.

Career Counselors perform other duties, which vary from one counselor to the next. For example, they might:

- help develop their center's career and job reference library, which usually includes both print and electronic resources
- create print and nonprint materials about alternative careers, practice areas, job search techniques, and so on
- coordinate recruitment programs, job fairs, career conferences, and other similar programs
- help in the development and implementation of new and ongoing services, programs, and activities
- maintain working relationships with students, faculty, alumni, legal employers, legal recruiters, and others
- represent the law school at professional conferences

Career Counselors in law schools work part time or full time. They may be required to work evening hours to accommodate students who work and attend classes during the day.

Salaries

Salaries vary, depending on such factors as experience, education, job duties, and geographical location. According to the Bureau of Labor Statistics, the estimated annual salary in 2000 for most education and vocational counselors ranged between $23,560 and $67,170.

Employment Prospects

Job openings usually become available as counselors retire, resign, or transfer to other positions. The creation of additional positions depends on the need for more counselors at a school, along with the availability of funds.

Advancement Prospects

Law school Career Counselors with administrative and executive ambitions can pursue positions as program directors as well as deans of career services departments. This career path may require moving from one school to the next. They can also pursue other career paths by becoming private career counselors or law firm recruiters.

Education and Training

Most law schools strongly prefer that their Career Counselors have a juris doctor (J.D.) degree or a master's degree in counseling, student personnel, or related field. Schools sometimes choose candidates without advanced degrees if they have extensive experience in legal career counseling.

Throughout their careers, Career Counselors enroll in education and training programs to keep up with career development trends as well as to build their skills.

Experience, Skills, and Personality Traits

Law school Career Counselors generally have previous experience in career counseling, student services, or law firm recruitment. Many law schools prefer that candidates have previous legal experience, such as working in law firms or serving in judicial clerkships.

Career Counselors need excellent organizational and interpersonal skills, as well as superior writing and communication skills. Additionally, they should have strong computer skills, including the ability to use the Internet. Being patient, objective, friendly, supportive, tactful, trustworthy, flexible, and creative are a few personality traits that successful Career Counselors in law schools share.

Unions and Associations

Career Counselors join local, state, and national professional associations to take advantage of education programs, networking opportunities, and other professional services and resources. Some national groups that represent Career Counselors are the National Career Development Association and the American Counseling Association. As representatives of their law schools, Career Counselors might belong to the National Association for Law Placement. Many law school Career Counselors also join and actively participate in bar associations.

Tips for Entry

1. As a high school or college student, find out if counseling is the right profession for you. You might, for example, participate in a peer counseling program.
2. Gain experience in the career counseling field by volunteering or working in school career centers, community job search training programs, or government employment offices.
3. You can learn more about law school career centers on the Internet, as many centers maintain web pages. To find a list of web pages, enter the keywords *law school career services* or *law school career development* in a search engine.

LEGAL SEARCH CONSULTANT

CAREER PROFILE

Duties: Find qualified attorney candidates for legal employers; perform duties as required

Alternate Titles: Headhunter, Job Recruiter

Salary Range: Salaries vary based on commission

Employment Prospects: Good

Advancement Prospects: Limited

Prerequisites:

Education/Training—A bachelor's degree; many possess a law degree

Experience—Lawyer, job recruiter, or career counselor experience preferred; experience in, or knowledgeable about, the legal industry

Special Skills and Personality Traits—Interpersonal, interviewing, communication, and listening skills; can handle rejections; have good instincts; reliable, honest, ethical, persistent, enthusiastic, trustworthy, self-motivated

Licensure/Certification—None required

CAREER LADDER

```
┌─────────────────────────────────────┐
│  Principal Legal Search Consultant   │
└─────────────────────────────────────┘

┌─────────────────────────────────────┐
│      Legal Search Consultant         │
└─────────────────────────────────────┘

┌─────────────────────────────────────┐
│       Law Firm Recruiter or          │
│       Legal Search Associate         │
└─────────────────────────────────────┘
```

Position Description

Legal Search Consultants offer recruiting services to law firms, corporate law departments, and other legal employers. They are also known as headhunters or legal recruiters. Their expertise is finding the best attorney candidates that match their clients' requirements for associate, partner, or general counsel positions.

Legal Search Consultants generally receive job orders from their clients which state specific information about their job openings, such as type of position, job duties, salaries, and advancement prospects. To get a better sense of the best candidates for a client, Legal Search Consultants research the employer. They learn as many details as they can—the employer's mission and goals, areas of practice, types of clients, work values, working styles, and so on. The headhunters also provide this information to prospective candidates so that they can decide whether they might be compatible with an employer.

Legal Search Consultants begin their search by first producing a list of potential candidates that is often made up of 100 names or more. However, at the end of the screening process, they usually present résumés of only the top candidates to their clients. To find qualified candidates, headhunters go through databases and contacts of attorneys, law firms, corporations, and so on. Their initial search may include candidates from all over the state, country, and world. They also list potential candidates who are not actively searching for new positions.

Headhunters go through résumés and choose attorneys who best match the requirements of their clients. They call up these individuals and find out if they may be interested in the job openings. Most headhunters meet with interested individuals to learn more about them as well as to provide them with more information about the job opening and the employer.

Legal Search Consultants work closely with candidates whom they will be presenting to their clients. They review candidates' résumés and help revise résumés if necessary. They prepare prospective candidates for their interviews and coach them on their interviewing techniques. When their candidates are offered a job, Legal Search Consultants may assist them with salary and benefits negotiations.

Legal Search Consultants typically conduct attorney searches for several job openings at a time. In small and mid-size firms, they generally perform all aspects of an attorney search. In large firms, researchers and associates assist with the research and initial screening process.

Many Legal Search Consultants specialize in the type of attorney searches that they conduct. For example, they may recruit for certain positions (such as lateral transfers or partners), certain practice areas (for example, intellectual property), or only for law firms or corporations.

Performing legal search work usually requires long hours. Travel to other cities or states may be necessary to meet with clients and potential candidates.

Salaries

Most Legal Search Consultants work on a commission basis. They are paid a fee for every successful placement that they make. The commission is generally between 20 and 30 percent of a position's gross annual salary during the first year.

A headhunter's annual earnings vary yearly, depending on a headhunter's ambition, the total number of successful placements, the annual salary earned by each position, and other factors. Hardworking and dedicated headhunters can earn annual incomes of six figures and higher.

Employment Prospects

Most Legal Search Consultants work in small firms with one to five headhunters. Consultants of different firms typically compete with each other for placement of attorneys. Most legal employers work with several firms, paying a fee to the firm that presented the candidate they hired.

During the 1990s, the legal recruiting field grew broadly as an increasing number of legal employers realized the advantages of using third party recruiters. In general, the legal recruiting field is highly competitive and changes constantly, following the market trends for attorneys.

Advancement Prospects

Advancement opportunities are limited. Legal Search Consultants may become principal (or lead) search consultants or legal recruiting firm owners.

Most Legal Search Consultants measure success by gaining professional reputations and by earning higher incomes.

Education and Training

Legal Search Consultants hold bachelor's degrees; many also possess law degrees.

Typically, novices learn on the job, receiving supervision and mentoring from senior headhunters.

Experience, Skills, and Personality Traits

Legal Search Consultants usually have years of experience as lawyers, job recruiters, or career counselors. They have solid experience in, or knowledge about, the legal industry.

To succeed in this field, headhunters must have superior interpersonal and interviewing skills, as well as excellent communication and listening skills. They also can handle rejections. Furthermore, they have an instinct for making matches between candidates and clients that are highly compatible.

Some personality traits that successful consultants share are being reliable, honest, ethical, persistent, enthusiastic, trustworthy, and self-motivated.

Unions and Associations

Many Legal Search Consultants join local, state, and national professional associations to take advantage of networking opportunities, education programs, publications, and other professional resources and services. One such national organization is the National Association of Legal Search Consultants.

Tips for Entry

1. Obtain work as a researcher or an internship with a legal recruiting firm to see if it is a field that might interest you.
2. To find reputable recruiting firms for whom you'd like to work, ask for recommendations from law firm recruiting coordinators.
3. Many Legal Search Consultants observe the professional code of ethics established by the National Association of Legal Search Consultants, whether they are members or not.
4. Use the Internet to learn more about legal recruiting. To find relevant web sites, enter any of these phrases into a search engine: *legal recruiting, legal headhunter,* or *legal search consultants.*

LIBRARIANS

ACADEMIC LAW LIBRARIAN

CAREER PROFILE

Duties: Develop and maintain library collections in law schools; provide user services, technical services, and administrative services as required by their particular position

Alternate Titles: Reference Librarian, Technical Services Librarian, or other title that reflects a specialized area

Salary Range: $36,000 to $67,000

Employment Prospects: Fair

Advancement Prospects: Fair

Prerequisites:

Education/Training—A master's degree in library science; a law degree may be required

Experience—Experience in law libraries or academic settings; knowledgeable about the legal system and familiar with legal materials; have appropriate qualifications for specific positions, such as research librarians

Special Skills and Personality Traits—Customer service, interpersonal, communication, teamwork, management, and organizational skills; diplomatic, efficient, adaptable, versatile, detail-minded, creative

Licensure/Certification—None required

CAREER LADDER

```
┌─────────────────────────────┐
│   Assistant or Associate    │
│     Director of Library     │
└─────────────────────────────┘

┌─────────────────────────────┐
│   Senior Law Librarian or   │
│       Department Head       │
└─────────────────────────────┘

┌─────────────────────────────┐
│   Academic Law Librarian    │
└─────────────────────────────┘
```

Position Description

Academic Law Librarians are responsible for running the law school libraries in public and private universities. These librarians serve the needs of law students and faculty as well as law school alumni, the local legal communities, and the general public.

Staffs of trained Academic Law Librarians develop and manage diverse collections of print and nonprint materials that support the various legal courses taught at their law schools. In addition, Academic Law Librarians are involved in the scholarly process. For example, many assist law professors with research and teach law students the basics of legal research. Many Academic Law Librarians also produce their own scholarly work.

Law school library staffs are composed of various types of librarians. Academic Law Librarians who are responsible for user services deal directly with patrons. They are typically called Reference Librarians and Public Services Librarians. They provide reference services to library users, manage the circulation and reserve rooms, and oversee computer facilities. They also teach classes and workshops, as well as provide individual instruction on the use of print and electronic research tools, such as CD-ROMs and electronic databases. In addition, they provide faculty with help on their research projects. In many law schools, reference librarians also have the duty of teaching legal research courses to students.

Other Academic Law Librarians provide technical services for their libraries. They are responsible for acquiring new print and electronic materials, processing and cataloguing materials, and maintaining present collections. They also implement and maintain automated circulation systems as well as online systems that allow access to library catalogs at other library systems. In addition, they perform various other duties as required of their specific job title, such as

Acquisition Librarian, Catalog Librarian, or Computer Services Librarian.

Academic Law Librarians also provide administrative services to their libraries. Some librarians, such as library directors and department heads, perform administrative duties exclusively. They are responsible for developing library plans, policies and procedures, and budgets. Their many duties include coordinating library activities, negotiating contracts for services, materials, and equipment, supervising and training library staff, performing public relations duties, writing grant proposals, and so forth.

Many Academic Law Librarians, particularly reference librarians, hold faculty rank and tenure. (Tenure is job security; they cannot be fired without just cause and due process.) Like other academic faculty members, they are expected to conduct research projects, publish scholarly work, and participate in faculty and community service activities.

Academic Law Librarians have flexible work schedules that may include working some evenings and weekends.

Salaries

Salaries vary, depending on experience, job duties, geographical location, and other factors. According to the 2000–01 salary survey by the Association of Research Libraries, the average annual salary for Academic Law Librarians ranged between $36,330 and $67,008.

Employment Prospects

In addition to academic settings, Law Librarians work in law firms, private practices, corporate law departments, courts, and government agencies.

Opportunities usually become available as librarians retire, resign, or advance to higher positions.

Advancement Prospects

Academic Law Librarians can advance to such administrative positions as department heads and library directors within law schools. Academic Law Librarians have also been known to be appointed to deanships and other middle management positions in law schools. Law degrees are usually required to obtain such positions.

Law Librarians who are on tenure tracks receive promotional rankings as assistant professors, associate professors, or full professors.

Education and Training

Law schools generally require that Law Librarians possess master's degrees in library science, preferably from institutions accredited by the American Library Association. Reference librarians may be required to also hold a law degree.

Experience, Skills, and Personality Traits

Generally, employers look for candidates who have professional experience in law libraries or academic settings. They also are knowledgeable about the legal system and familiar with legal materials. In addition, candidates have the appropriate qualifications for the specific position for which they are applying. For example, teaching and legal research experience are typical requirements for Research Librarians.

Regardless of their position, Academic Law Librarians should have strong customer service, interpersonal, communication, and teamwork skills, as they must work well with students, faculty, staff, and others. In addition, they need excellent management and organizational skills.

Successful Academic Law Librarians share several personality traits, such as being diplomatic, efficient, adaptable, versatile, detail-minded, and creative.

Unions and Associations

Many Law Librarians join local, state, and national associations to take advantage of networking opportunities, training programs, professional publications, and other professional resources and services. The American Association of Law Libraries, the Association of Research Libraries, and the American Library Association are a few national organizations that Academic Law Librarians join.

Tips for Entry

1. Law Librarians who are willing to relocate may have better chances of finding the positions that they want.
2. Use the Internet to find job openings. Some web sites that post jobs for Academic Law Librarians are the American Association of Law Libraries, *http://www.aallnet.org,* the American Library Association, *http://www.ala.org,* and the Career Network of the Chronicle of Higher Education, *http://chronicle.com/jobs.*
3. You can learn more about law libraries on the Internet. To find a list of web pages, enter the keywords *law school library* in a search engine.

LAW FIRM LIBRARIAN

CAREER PROFILE

Duties: Manage libraries in private law firms; provide information support to attorneys and other staff; conduct training workshops; perform other duties as required

Alternate Titles: Information Resources Manager, Legal Information Specialist, Legal Researcher; a title, such as Reference Librarian or Electronic Services Librarian, that reflects a specialized area (usually in large firms)

Salary Range: $25,000 to $63,000

Employment Prospects: Fair

Advancement Prospects: Limited

Prerequisites:

　Education/Training—A master's degree in library science required or preferred

　Experience—Law library, business library, or legal experience; strong foundation in technology

　Special Skills and Personality Traits—Research, organization, writing, communication, customer-service, interpersonal, teamwork, and self-management skills; enthusiastic, positive, resourceful, creative, flexible

　Licensure/Certification—None required

CAREER LADDER

```
┌─────────────────────────────────┐
│        Library Director          │
└─────────────────────────────────┘

┌─────────────────────────────────┐
│       Law Firm Librarian         │
└─────────────────────────────────┘

┌─────────────────────────────────┐
│  Assistant Law Firm Librarian    │
│  or Academic Law Librarian       │
└─────────────────────────────────┘
```

Position Description

Law Firm Librarians are employed by private practices to provide library services to attorneys, paralegals, and other law firm staff members. They oversee private libraries that include collections of books, journals, and other printed materials as well as CD-ROMs, electronic databases, and legal-oriented web sites. Law Firm Librarians may work alone or be part of a team of librarians and library technicians.

In most law firms, librarians are expected to manage all library operations—that is, to provide reference services, conduct research, catalog books, develop and maintain book collections and electronic sources, plan budgets, negotiate vendor and services contracts, and so forth. In large law firms, Law Librarians may specialize in specific types of services, such as reference services or electronic services.

A major responsibility of Law Librarians is providing information support to their law firms. Because they are

more familiar with the available resources in their libraries, Law Firm Librarians are able to quickly direct attorneys and others to the materials or databases that provide them with the information they need.

Law Firm Librarians also conduct legal and nonlegal research for attorneys, which the attorneys may incorporate into legal briefs, memorandums, and other legal documents.

Typically, librarians must deliver requests for information promptly, and they must ensure that their information is correct and accurate. Librarians use both traditional sources (printed materials) and electronic sources (computer and online databases) in their research. They might also contact other law, special, academic, or public librarians, as well as subject-matter experts.

Many Law Librarians also provide nonlegal research to other departments in a law firm. For example, they may be asked to gather information about prospective clients or estimate the costs of research services on business proposals.

Law Firm Librarians have the responsibility of planning training programs so law firm employees can use the library resources more effectively. They may put together a library orientation for summer interns, for example; or conduct a workshop on the use of new reference publications for legal support staff. Librarians provide one-on-one instruction as well as conduct group workshops on the use of CD-ROM technology and the World Wide Web.

Furthermore, Law Librarians promote the library services within their firms. They might develop brochures to describe databases and services. They might write newsletters to inform employees about new acquisitions and services, as well as about new research techniques. Many also create handbooks for using the various library resources.

Law Firm Librarians work part time or full time. Most have a flexible work schedule, adapting to the demands of attorney deadlines.

Salaries

Salaries vary, depending on experience, education, job duties, geographical location, and other factors. According to the Bureau of Labor Statistics, the estimated annual salary in 2000 for most librarians ranged from $25,030 to $62,990.

Employment Prospects

Law firms add or reduce staff positions to meet their needs and demands. In general, opportunities in law firms become available as librarians resign or transfer to other positions.

Advancement Prospects

Advancement opportunities for Law Firm Librarians are limited to supervisory and administrative positions, which may require moving to other law firms. Most Law Firm Librarians realize advancement through job satisfaction and higher incomes.

Some Law Firm Librarians have pursued entrepreneurial paths, offering legal research services, law library management services, or consulting services to law firms.

Education and Training

Some Law Firm Librarians do not have formal training, but instead learned on the job. They were originally paralegals and attorneys who increasingly took on more legal research and library responsibilities. However, most law firms today require or prefer that candidates hold master's degrees in library science from schools accredited by the American Library Association. Law degrees are usually not required, though many Law Firm Librarians have juris doctor (J.D.) degrees.

Throughout their careers, Law Firm Librarians enroll in training and education programs to increase their legal knowledge and maintain their professional skills.

Experience, Skills, and Personality Traits

In general, employers look for candidates who have law library, business library, or legal experience, or are at least familiar with legal research terminology, techniques, and materials. In addition, candidates should have strong foundations in technology, including the ability to use hardware, software, networks, legal and nonlegal databases, and so forth.

Law Firm Librarians need excellent research, organization, writing, and communication skills to do their work effectively. Having customer-service, interpersonal, and teamwork skills is also essential to their job, as they must work well with lawyers, legal staff, vendors, and others. Further, they must possess strong self-management skills—the ability to prioritize tasks, meet deadlines, handle stress, work independently, and so on.

Being enthusiastic, positive, resourceful, creative, and flexible are a few personality traits that successful Law Firm Librarians share.

Unions and Associations

Many Law Firm Librarians join local, state, and national professional associations to take advantage of networking opportunities, training programs, professional publications, and other resources and services. The American Association of Law Libraries, the American Library Association, and the Special Libraries Association are a few organizations that represent librarians in law firms.

Tips for Entry

1. Enroll in a few courses in paralegal studies to familiarize yourself with the law, legal research, legal terminology, and so forth.
2. Build a portfolio to present at your job interviews. Some items you might include are letters of recommendation, work or school projects, and published work.
3. You can learn more about law librarianship on the Internet. To find a list of relevant web sites, enter the keywords *law librarianship* or *law firm librarian* in a search engine.

LAW LIBRARY TECHNICIAN

CAREER PROFILE

Duties: Assist librarians with providing user and technical services in law libraries; perform duties as required

Alternate Titles: Library Assistant, Library Associate

Salary Range: $14,000 to $36,000

Employment Prospects: Good

Advancement Prospects: Limited

Prerequisites:

Education/Training—A high school diploma; an associate degree may be required

Experience—Previous experience working in libraries; familiarity with legal terminology and legal systems; ability to operate computers and standard office equipment

Special Skills and Personality Traits—Customer service, interpersonal, teamwork, communication, writing, and self-management skills; flexible, detail-oriented, organized, calm, patient

Licensure/Certification—None required

CAREER LADDER

```
┌─────────────────────────────────┐
│  Senior Law Library Technician  │
└─────────────────────────────────┘

┌─────────────────────────────────┐
│     Law Library Technician      │
└─────────────────────────────────┘

┌─────────────────────────────────┐
│   Trainee or Library Assistant  │
│     in other library settings   │
└─────────────────────────────────┘
```

Position Description

Law Library Technicians are paraprofessionals who provide assistance in law libraries. They may work in law schools, law firms, courts, or government agencies. Technicians work under the supervision of law librarians as they perform various user and technical services.

Their duties vary, depending on their work settings and positions. Some of their duties might include:

- maintaining library stacks and reading rooms
- moving and arranging books
- answering general questions about reference materials
- teaching patrons on how to access data on computers
- maintaining computer databases
- retrieving information from computer databases
- receiving and processing books and other library materials
- helping with cataloging and coding of library materials
- handling interlibrary loan requests
- preparing materials for binding
- assisting librarians with producing brochures, newsletters, and other publications about the library
- transporting boxes of books

Law Library Technicians also perform routine office tasks. For example, they might file papers, sort and distribute incoming mail, operate office machines, and monitor inventory of office supplies.

Technicians in private firms and government agencies may assist in conducting legal and nonlegal research as well as in preparing bibliographies.

Those working in law schools may specialize in helping librarians with either user services or technical services. They may also be assigned to supervise student employees.

Law Library Technicians work part time or full time.

Salaries

Salaries vary, depending on factors such as education, experience, type of employer, and geographical location.

According to the Bureau of Labor Statistics, the estimated annual salary in 2000 for most library technicians (in all work settings) ranged from $13,810 to $35,660.

Employment Prospects

According to the Bureau of Labor Statistics, job growth is expected to increase among library technicians due to advances in technology. Many routine tasks done by librarians have been computerized and are being assigned to technicians.

Advancement Prospects

With additional experience and education, Law Library Technicians can advance to supervisory and administrative positions. Some library technicians earn library degrees and become librarians.

Many career technicians realize advancement by earning higher wages, being assigned complex responsibilities, and enjoying job satisfaction and professional recognition.

Education and Training

Law Library Technicians must have at least a high school diploma or a high school equivalency diploma. Some employers require that technicians also have an associate degree, preferably in library science.

Technicians are usually trained on the job. Many enroll in continuing education programs throughout their careers to develop their skills and expertise in librarianship further.

Experience, Skills, and Personality Traits

In general, employers look for candidates who have previous experience working in libraries. Candidates should also be familiar with legal terminology and legal systems, and be able to operate computers and standard office equipment.

Law Library Technicians need strong customer service, interpersonal, teamwork, communication, and writing skills. In addition, they must have excellent self-management skills, such as being able to work independently, follow directions, prioritize tasks, meet deadlines, and so forth.

Some personality traits that successful Law Library Technicians share are being flexible, detail-oriented, organized, calm, and patient.

Unions and Associations

Many library technicians join local, state, and national associations to take advantage of networking opportunities, training programs, professional publications, and other professional resources and services. Many Law Library Technicians belong to the Council on Library/Media Technicians and the American Library Association.

Tips for Entry

1. As a high school student, volunteer or obtain a part-time job in your school or public library. If your school has a work experience program, try to get a placement in a law office to see what it is like to work in such a setting.
2. Enroll in computer classes as well as in general courses at community colleges to expand your knowledge and skills. Also take courses in paralegal studies to familiarize yourself with the law and terminology.
3. Consider enrolling in an associate of arts degree program in library technology, if a local community college offers such a program.
4. You can learn more about library technicians on the Internet. To find relevant web sites, enter any of these keywords in a search engine: *library technicians, library paraprofessionals,* or *law library technician.*

PUBLISHING
PROFESSIONALS

LEGAL REPORTER

CAREER PROFILE

Duties: Provide objective and accurate reports about people, events, issues, and other happenings in the legal community; perform duties as required

Alternate Titles: Legal Journalist, Legal Affairs Reporter, Legal Correspondent

Salary Range: $17,000 to $69,000

Employment Prospects: Fair

Advancement Prospects: Fair

Prerequisites:

    Education/Training—A bachelor's degree; a law degree may be required or preferred

    Experience—Several years of journalism experience; legal experience is desirable

    Special Skills and Personality Traits—Writing, organization, research, communication, listening, interpersonal, computer, and self-management skills; energetic, detail-oriented, patient, persistent, impartial, resourceful, composed, adaptable, creative

    Licensure/Certification—None required

CAREER LADDER

```
┌─────────────────────────────────┐
│   Principal Reporter or Editor   │
└─────────────────────────────────┘

┌─────────────────────────────────┐
│            Reporter             │
└─────────────────────────────────┘

┌─────────────────────────────────┐
│         Novice Reporter          │
└─────────────────────────────────┘
```

Position Description

Legal Reporters provide the news about people, events, issues, and other things that are happening in the legal community. They report on court trials, court decisions, proposed bills, new regulations, legislative meetings, lawmakers, judges, attorneys, professional conferences, legal-related professions, and so on. Their job is to gather the facts and to summarize them clearly and comprehensively in a limited number of words. The stories may take place at the local, state, or national level.

Many Legal Reporters write for trade publications (newspapers, magazines, and newsletters) that cover only legal topics and events in the legal community. The audience for these publications consists of attorneys and other legal professionals. Trade publications are available in printed or electronic formats. Some publications are nationwide, while others serve a particular state or region. Smaller publications usually specialize in a specific practice area such as employment, immigration, or public interest law.

Legal Reporters also write for the general daily newspapers as well as alternative weekly or monthly newspapers. They are usually known as *Legal Affairs Reporters*. A few Legal Reporters work for radio and TV stations and read their news reports on the air. Some Legal Reporters are freelance journalists.

Legal Reporters keep their eyes and ears open at all times for leads and tips for breaking news. They read press releases and announcements. They observe legislative meetings and court trials, as well as attend press conferences and other special events. In addition, they routinely talk with public relations staff and other sources in courthouses, legislatures, government agencies, professional associations, law firms, and so forth.

Legal Reporters are constantly under pressure to meet their deadlines. Thus, they gather details efficiently, yet thoroughly. They interview eyewitnesses as well as those who are directly involved in the events. Some Legal Reporters may take photographs in addition to taking notes.

They also conduct research for background information. They talk with subject-matter experts, read books and articles, search for information on the Internet, and so on.

Legal Reporters are able to organize their notes quickly and decide on the best structure for their stories. They write their stories so people can see, hear, smell, and feel as if they were there. They double-check dates and figures, the spelling of names and places, the correct professional titles of people, and other facts.

All journalists are responsible for reporting the news objectively, and for making sure that facts are accurate. Reporters and their publications can be sued for any untrue or libelous statements that they make. Thus, reporters find persons, documents, or other reliable sources that can verify information for them.

With the smaller legal publications, reporters may also be assigned to the editor role. As editors, they are responsible for putting together each issue. They decide what stories should be covered, when stories are due, where stories should be placed in an issue, what headlines should be, and so on. Editors also review stories to make sure they are newsworthy and accurate. They copyedit stories for clarity and length as well as for grammar, spelling, and punctuation errors.

Legal Reporters have different work schedules, depending on their newspapers' deadlines. For example, they may work nights for daily papers that are distributed in the mornings. Regardless of their work schedule, reporters work long and irregular hours in order to follow up on story ideas or to meet deadlines.

Salaries

Salaries vary, depending on various factors such as experience, personal ambition, type and size of employer, and geographical location. According to the Bureau of Labor Statistics, the estimated annual salary in 2000 for most news reporters and correspondents ranged between $16,540 and $69,300.

Employment Prospects

In general, Legal Reporter positions become available as individuals retire, transfer to other papers, or advance to other positions. Occasionally, opportunities open when legal newspapers add another news bureau or when legal newsletters are created.

Advancement Prospects

Legal Reporters generally realize advancement by earning higher incomes, receiving more complicated assignments, and being recognized for the high quality of their work.

Depending on their ambitions and interests, Legal Reporters may become columnists, special correspondents, legal analysts, and book authors, as well as editors, news bureau directors, and legal publishers. Legal Reporters might pursue other careers, becoming educators, attorneys, politicians, public relations professionals, or novelists.

Education and Training

Requirements vary, depending on the employer. Ideally, Legal Reporters should have training in both journalism and the law. Legal Reporters must have at least a bachelor's degree in journalism or other field. Many legal trade publications require or prefer that reporters have law degrees.

Experience, Skills, and Personality Traits

Employers generally require that applicants have several years of journalism experience. Having legal experience is desirable. Some employers are willing to hire lawyers without journalism experience if they demonstrate a willingness and an aptitude for reporting.

Legal Reporters need excellent writing skills as well as strong organization and research skills. Their job also requires that they have excellent communication, listening, and interpersonal skills. In addition, Legal Reporters should have adequate computer skills. Further, they need good self-management skills, such as the ability to handle stressful situations, meet deadlines, work independently, take initiative, and juggle various tasks.

Being energetic, detail-oriented, persistent, impartial, resourceful, composed, adaptable, and creative are some personality traits that successful Legal Reporters share.

Unions and Associations

Many Legal Reporters join professional associations to take advantage of networking opportunities and other professional services and resources. The Society of Professional Journalists is one association that Legal Reporters might join. Independent journalists are eligible to join the National Writers Union or the American Society of Journalists and Authors.

Tips for Entry

1. Some courses that you might take in high school or college to prepare for a reporting career are journalism, English, and social studies.
2. As a college student, obtain internships or part-time jobs with local newspapers or other news organizations.
3. Build a portfolio of your published work, as publishers will want to see your writing samples.
4. Contact the publications where you would like to work about their job opportunities. Ask about both permanent and freelance positions that may be available.
5. Many legal publications have web sites on the Internet. To find relevant web sites, enter the keywords *legal newspaper* in a search engine.

BOOK EDITOR

CAREER PROFILE

Duties: Develop and acquire new legal titles for legal publishers, general book publishers, university presses; develop and edit manuscripts; maintain relationships with authors; perform other duties as required

Alternate Titles: Acquisition Editor, Development Editor; Legal Editor, Case Law Editor, Attorney Editor

Salary Range: $23,000 to $73,000

Employment Prospects: Fair

Advancement Prospects: Good

Prerequisites:

   Education/Training—A bachelor's degree; a law degree may be required or preferred

   Experience—Book publishing experience; legal experience or background required or highly preferred

   Special Skills and Personality Traits—Writing, research, interpersonal, communication, teamwork, and self-management skills; tactful, creative, flexible, organized, detail-oriented, decisive, adaptable

   Licensure/Certification—None required

CAREER LADDER

```
┌─────────────────────────────┐
│       Senior Editor         │
└─────────────────────────────┘

┌─────────────────────────────┐
│           Editor            │
└─────────────────────────────┘

┌─────────────────────────────┐
│  Assistant Editor; for Case Law │
│  Editors, Attorney or Law Student │
└─────────────────────────────┘
```

Position Description

Hundreds of new titles about law and legal topics are published each year by legal publishers as well as by general book publishers and by university presses. These include biographies, scholarly monographs, self-help legal books, law textbooks, legal manuals, practice guides, case reporters, code books, and so forth. Many publishers also publish non-print materials such as CD-ROMs, audiotapes, and online resources.

Book Editors are responsible for acquiring and developing new titles that meet their publishing house's mission and goals. They review proposals and manuscripts submitted by authors and agents, and recommend those that Book Editors think are publishable to editorial committees, which accept or reject them. Book Editors also propose ideas for new titles and seek legal experts to develop book proposals and manuscripts.

Book Editors are responsible for overseeing the development of manuscripts. They work closely with authors as they first develop content outlines and later write their manuscripts. Editors review drafts and provide authors with suggestions and comments to improve the manuscripts. They might point out gaps in logic, lack of focus, organizational problems, unclear language, and so forth. Editors monitor authors' progress to ensure that deadlines are being met.

Book Editors edit finished manuscripts for content and clarity. They also edit manuscripts so they meet their publishing house's formats and standards. Some Editors also copyedit and prepare manuscripts for production. Book Editors release final manuscripts to production departments, where manuscripts are turned into book pages for printing.

Editors usually manage several titles simultaneously, which requires working with several authors at a time. In addition, Editors perform a variety of related duties. They may:

- monitor the progress of manuscripts through the production and printing stages
- prepare editorial costs and schedules for individual titles

- help sales and marketing departments plan and develop promotions and publicity for new titles
- conduct research on markets, competition, legal trends, developments in the legal publishing industry, and so on
- provide legal expertise and knowledge in product content as well as design and development of products

In some publishing houses, different Book Editors fill separate roles. *Acquisitions Editors* are in charge of acquiring new titles and maintaining relationships with authors. They also review manuscripts and may perform content editing. *Development Editors* are responsible for editing manuscripts and overseeing their progress through the editorial and production stages.

Editors of case reporters are commonly called Legal Editors or Attorney Editors. (A case reporter is the published compilation of a court's decisions and opinions, also known as court reports.) They are responsible for all legal content. They provide legal analysis and interpretation, as well as write and edit case law summaries, notes, and headings.

Editors sometimes travel to professional conferences to give presentations and workshops. They may also work in publishers' booths to answer questions about the various products. Editors sometimes meet prospective authors at these conferences.

Editors often put in additional hours on evenings and weekends to meet deadlines.

Salaries

Salaries vary depending on factors such as education, experience, size of publisher, and geographical location. According to the Bureau of Labor Statistics, the estimated annual salary in 2000 for most editors ranged between $22,460 and $73,330.

Employment Prospects

Editors of law and legal-related books are hired by legal publishers as well as by legal professional associations, such as the American Bar Association, which have publishing units. Many general book publishers and university presses also hire Editors to manage and oversee their line or division of legal titles.

Generally, opportunities become available as Book Editors advance to other positions or transfer to other publishing houses.

Advancement Prospects

Editors can advance to supervisory and management positions, such as managing editors, editorial directors, vice pres-

idents, and publishers. Advancing through the ranks generally requires moving from one publishing house to the next.

Education and Training

Requirements vary among the different employers. Minimally, Editors must hold bachelor's degrees in any field. Most legal publishers typically require or prefer that Editors hold law degrees. They may hire candidates without law degrees if they have qualifying experience.

Experience, Skills, and Personality Traits

Acquisitions and Developmental Editors generally come up through the ranks of editorial assistants and assistant editors. To become Editors of law and legal-related books, candidates should have legal experience or training. Employers may hire nonattorneys or those with no legal training if they have qualifying experience in legal publishing.

Editors need excellent writing and research skills for their jobs. They also need strong interpersonal, communication, and teamwork skills, as they must work well with authors, editorial staff, and other departments. In addition, they need strong self-management skills, such as being able to meet deadlines, juggle several tasks at the same time, work independently, handle stress, and so on.

Some personality traits that successful Editors share are being tactful, creative, flexible, organized, detail-oriented, decisive, and adaptable.

Unions and Associations

Many Editors join professional associations to take advantage of networking opportunities and various professional services and resources. Legal Editors are eligible to join the Association for Continuing Legal Education.

Tips for Entry

1. Contact publishing houses directly for information about job openings and job requirements.
2. Publishers sometimes hire development and legal editors for part-time and temporary (or freelance) positions.
3. Many legal publishers have web sites on the Internet. To find relevant web sites, enter the keywords *legal publishers* in a search engine.

APPENDIXES

APPENDIX I
EDUCATION AND TRAINING RESOURCES

Listed below are sources for education and training programs for some of the occupations that are discussed in this book. To learn about education and training programs for other occupations, talk with school or career counselors as well as with professionals in the field. You can also look up schools in college directories produced by Peterson's or other publishers, which can be found in school or public libraries.

Note: All street, mailing, and web site addresses were current at the time this book was being written. If you come across a URL that no longer works, enter the name of the institution or organization in a search engine to find its new web site.

INTERNET SOURCES
Below are three web sites where you can search for information about specific colleges and universities as well as about undergraduate and graduate programs.

Peterson's Home Page
http://www.petersons.com

The Princeton Review
http://www.review.com/index.cfm

Graduate School Information
Educational Directories Unlimited, Inc.
http://www.gradschools.com

ACTUARIAL SCIENCE
For information about actuarial science programs, contact:

Society of Actuaries
475 N. Martingdale Road, Suite 800
Schaumburg, IL 60173
Phone: (847) 706-3500
Fax: (847) 706-3599
http://www.soa.org
http://www.soa.org/academic/schoollist.ht
  ml (a list of recommended programs
  can be found at this link)

ALTERNATIVE DISPUTE RESOLUTION
A list of mediation training programs can be found at the following web sites:

Association for Conflict Resolution
http://www.acresolution.org

Association of Attorney-Mediators
http://www.attorney-mediators.org/train.
  html

Mediation Information and Resource Center
http://www.mediate.com/training

COURT INTERPRETING
Court interpreting programs are offered by two-year and four-year colleges, as well as by postsecondary vocational and training schools. For a list of suggested court interpreting training programs, contact:

American Translators Association
225 Reinekers Lane, Suite 590
Alexandria, VA 22314
Phone: (703) 683-6100
Fax: (703) 683-6122
http://www.atanet.org
http://www.atanet.org/bin/view.pl/30472.
  html (the list of schools can also be
  found at this link)

COURT REPORTING
Court reporting programs are offered by two-year colleges, four-year colleges, and postsecondary vocational and technical schools. The National Court Reporters Association (NCRA) maintains a list of schools that meet their general requirements and minimum standards. The schools also are accredited by agencies recognized by the U.S. government. For more information, contact:

National Court Reporters Association
8224 Old Courthouse Road
Vienna, VA 22182-3808
Phone: (800) 272-6272 or (703) 556-6272
Fax: (703) 556-6291;
  TTY: (703) 556-6289
http://www.ncraonline.org
http://www.verbatimreporters.com/pd/
  schools.htm (the list of schools can
  also be found at this link)

COURT MANAGEMENT
The Institute for Court Management offers two court management training programs. For more information, contact:

Institute for Court Management
National Center for State Courts
300 Newport Avenue
Williamsburg, VA 23185
Phone: (800) 616-6160
Fax: (757) 220-0449
http://www.ncsc.dni.us/ICM/index.html
Court Management Program
http://www.ncsc.dni.us/ICM/national/cmp
  .html
Court Executive Development Program
http://www.ncsc.dni.us/ICM/cedp/
  program.html

CRIMINOLOGY—GRADUATE PROGRAMS
For a list of graduate programs in criminology, as well as J.D./Ph.D. joint degree programs, visit:

Western Society of Criminology
http//www.sonoma.edu/cja/wsc/wscmain.
    html or
http://www.westernsocietyofcriminology
    .org

FORENSIC PSYCHOLOGY— GRADUATE PROGRAMS

For a list of graduate programs in forensic psychology, as well as J.D./Ph.D. joint degree programs, visit the following web pages:

The American Psychology-Law Society
http://www.unl.edu/ap-ls
http://www.unl.edu/ap-ls/gradp.htm (the
    list of programs can also be found at
    this link)

PsycLAW.org
http://www.psyclaw.org
http://www.psyclaw.org/grad.html (the
    list of programs can also be found at
    this link)

LAW—JURIS DOCTOR PROGRAMS

Most employers require or strongly prefer as candidates attorneys who have graduated from law schools accredited by the American Bar Association. This association publishes a guide that describes the approved law schools. For more information about the directory, contact:

American Bar Association
Service Center
541 N. Fairbanks Court
Chicago, IL 60611
Phone: (800) 285-2221 or (312) 988-5522
http://www.abanet.org
http://www.abanet.org/legaled/
    approvedlawschools/approved.html
    (the list of schools can also be found
    at this link)

Other Internet sources of links to U.S. law schools are:

Association of American Law Schools
http://www.aals.org/members.html

FindLaw for Students
http://stu.findlaw.com/schools/fulllist.html

Hieros Gamos
http://www.hg.org/schools.html

Jurist: The Legal Education Network
http://jurist.law.pitt.edu

Law School Admission Council
http://www.lsac.org

LEGAL VIDEO TRAINING

American Guild of Court Videographers
1628 East Third Street
Casper, WY 82601
Phone: (800) 678-1990 or (307) 472-3547
Fax: (307) 472-5048
http://www.agcv.com
http://www.agcv.com/seminar.html
    (information about their legal
    videography seminars can be found at
    this link)

National Court Reporters Association
8224 Old Courthouse Road
Vienna, VA 22182-3808
Phone: (800) 272-6272 or (703) 556-6272
Fax: (703) 556-6291;
    TTY: (703) 556-6289
http://clvs.ncraonline.org
http://clvs.ncraonline.org/Cert.htm
    (information about their Certified
    Legal Video Specialist Program can be
    found at this link)

LIBRARY AND INFORMATION SCIENCE— MASTER'S PROGRAMS

Most employers prefer that Law Librarians hold master's degrees from schools that are accredited by the American Library Association. For a list of those schools, contact:

American Library Association
50 East Huron Street
Chicago, IL 60611
Phone: (800) 545-2433
Fax: (312) 440-9374; TDD: (888) 814-
    7692 or (312) 944-7298
http://www.ala.org
http://www.ala.org/alaorg/oa/lisdir.html
    (the list of schools can also be found
    at this link)

For specific information about law librarianship programs, including joint J.D. and Master's in library science programs, contact:

American Association of Law Libraries
53 West Jackson Boulevard, Suite 940
Chicago, IL 60604
Phone: (312) 939-4764
Fax: (312) 431-1097
http://www.aallnet.org
http://www.aallnet.org/committee/tfedu/
    list_1.html (a list of suggested schools
    can be found at this link)

LIBRARY TECHNOLOGY

For a list of postsecondary schools that offer degree programs in library technology, contact:

Council on Library/Media Technicians
Cuyahoga Community College Library,
    Room 400
2900 Community College Avenue
Cleveland, OH 44115
Phone: (216) 987-4655
 Fax: (216) 987-4404
http://library.ucr.edu/COLT
http://library.ucr.edu/COLT/
    ltprograms.html (a list of schools can
    be found at this link)

NONPROFIT MANAGEMENT—MASTER'S PROGRAMS

Listed below are a few schools which offer master's degrees in nonprofit management programs. To learn about other schools, go to the following web sites:

The Internet Nonprofit Center (by the Evergreen State Society, Seattle, Washington)
http://www.nonprofits.org/misc/acad.html

The Chronicle of Philanthropy (The Newspaper of the Nonprofit World)
http://www.philanthropy.com/free/
    resources/general/academic.htm

PARALEGAL STUDIES/TRAINING

More than 600 paralegal programs are available in the United States. These include associate, bachelor's, and master's degree programs as well as professional certificate programs. The following professional associations each provide a list of suggested programs.

American Association for Paralegal Education

2965 Flowers Road South, Suite 105
Atlanta, GA 30341
Phone: (770) 452-9877
Fax: (770) 458-3314
http://www.aafpe.org
http://www.aafpe.org/programs.html (a list of the suggested programs can be found at this link)

American Bar Association Standing Committee on Legal Assistants

541 N. Fairbanks Court
Chicago, IL 60611
Phone: (800) 285-2221 or (312) 988-5522
http://www.abanet.org/legalassts/home.html
http://www.abanet.org/legalassts/directory.
html (a list of suggested programs can be found at this link)

National Federation of Paralegal Associations

P.O. Box 33108
Kansas City, MO 64114
Phone: (816) 941-4000
Fax: (816) 941-2725
http://www.paralegals.com
http://www.paralegals.com/Choice/School/home.html (Paralegal Education Program Directory)
http://www.paralegals.com/Choice/home.html (For a discussion about choosing a program, go to this link.)

PUBLIC ADMINISTRATION

For a list of colleges and universities that offer associate, bachelor's, masters, and doctoral degrees in public administration, contact:

National Association of Schools of Public Affairs and Administration

1120 G Street, NW, Suite 730
Washington, DC 20005
Phone: (202) 628-8965
Fax: (202) 626-4978
http://www.naspaa.org/degrees.htm

APPENDIX II
BAR ADMISSION OFFICES

Attorneys are required to be properly licensed and registered in each state and federal court that they plan to practice. In this appendix, you will find contact information for the appropriate office that handles applications for attorney licensure in the state, territory, or federal court in which you wish to practice.

NOTE: All contact information and web site addresses were current when the book was being written. If you come across a URL that no longer works, you may be able to find an organization's new web site by entering its name in a search engine.

A. STATE COURTS

In each of the 50 states (as well as the District of Columbia and the U.S. territories), attorneys must be first admitted to the bar of a state Supreme Court, the highest state court, before they can practice in the state. Requirements for entry vary from state to state, and usually entail passing an examination by the State Board of Law Examiners and a background investigation.

Listed below are the offices where you can get information about bar admissions in the 50 states, the District of Columbia, and the U.S. territories.

ALABAMA

Admissions Department
Alabama State Bar
415 Dexter Avenue
Montgomery AL 36104
Phone: (334) 269-1515
http://www.alabar.org

ALASKA

Admissions Department
Alaska Bar Association
P.O. Box 100279
Anchorage, AK 99510-0279
Phone: (907) 272-7469
http://www.alaskabar.org/2.cfm

ARIZONA

Committee on Examinations and Character and Fitness
Arizona Supreme Court
1501 W. Washington, Suite 104
Phoenix, AZ 85003-3231

Phone: (602) 364-0369
http://www.supreme.state.az.us/admis

ARKANSAS

Board of Law Examiners
State of Arkansas
625 Marshall Street
120 Justice Boulevard
Little Rock, AR 72201
Phone: (501) 374-1855
Fax: (501) 374-1853
http://www.courts.state.ar.us/courts/
    ble.html

CALIFORNIA

Office of Admissions
State Bar of California
555 Franklin Street
San Francisco, CA 94102
Phone: (415) 561-8303
http://www.calbar.org/admissions

COLORADO

Board of Law Examiners
Colorado Supreme Court
600 17th Street, Suite 520-S
Denver, CO 80202
Phone: (303) 893-8096
http://www.courts.state.co.us/ble/ble.htm

CONNECTICUT

Bar Examining Committee
State of Connecticut
80 Washington Street
Hartford, CT 06106-4424

Phone: (860) 756-7900; (800) 842-9710,
    for hearing and speech-impaired
    applicants
http://www.jud.state.ct.us/faq/barexcom.
    htm

DELAWARE

Board of Bar Examiners
Supreme Court of Delaware
200 W. Ninth Street, Suite 300-B
Wilmington, DE 19801
Phone: (302) 577-7038
Fax: (302) 577-7037
http://courts.state.de.us/bbe

DISTRICT OF COLUMBIA

Committee on Admissions
District of Columbia Court of Appeals
500 Indiana Avenue, NW, Room 4200
Washington, DC 20001
Phone: (202) 879-2710
http://www.dcbar.org/about_bar/
    admissions.html

FLORIDA

Florida Board of Bar Examiners
1891 Eider Court
Tallahassee, FL 32399-1750
Phone: (850) 487-1292
http://www.barexam.org/florida

GEORGIA

Office of Bar Admissions
Supreme Court of Georgia
244 Washington Street, Suite 440
Atlanta, GA 30334

Phone: (404) 656-3490
http://www2.state.ga.us/Courts/bar/
    barhome.htm

GUAM

Board of Law Examiners
Supreme Court of Guam
Suite 300
Guam Judicial Center
120 West O'Brien Drive
Hagatna, GU 96910
Phone: (671) 475-3180
Fax: (671) 475-3181
http://www.Justice.gov.gu/supreme

HAWAII

Board of Law Examiners
Supreme Court of Hawaii
Ali'iolani Hale
417 South King Street
Honolulu, HI 96813
Phone: (808) 539-4907

IDAHO

Admissions Department
Idaho State Bar
P.O. Box 895
Boise, ID 83701
Phone: (208) 334-4500
http://www.state.id.us/isb/admission_
    information.htm

ILLINOIS

Illinois Board of Admissions to the Bar
625 South College Street
Springfield, IL 62704
Phone: (217) 522-5917
Fax: (217) 522-3728
http://www.ibaby.org

INDIANA

Board of Law Examiners
State of Indiana
South Tower, Suite 1070
115 W. Washington Street
Indianapolis, IN 46204-3417
Phone: (317) 232-2552
Fax: (317) 233-3960
http://www.IN.gov/judiciary/attorneys/
    admissions.html

IOWA

Iowa Board of Law Examiners
Clerk of Supreme Court
Statehouse
Des Moines, IA 50319
Phone: (515) 281-5911
http://www.judicial.state.ia.us/regs/barinfo

KANSAS

Kansas Attorney Admissions
Kansas Judicial Center
301 SW 10th Avenue, Room 374
Topeka, KS 66612
Phone: (913) 296-8410
http://www.kscourts.org/attnyadmit.htm

KENTUCKY

Kentucky Office of Bar Admissions
1510 Newtown Pike, Suite X
Lexington, KY 40511
Phone: (859) 246-2381
Fax: (859) 246-2385
http://www.kyoba.org

LOUISIANA

Admissions Department
Louisiana State Bar Association
601 St. Charles Avenue
New Orleans, LA 70130
Phone: (800) 421-5722, extension 122 or
    (504) 619-0122
Fax: (504) 528-9154
http://www.lsba.org/Bar_Admissions/bar_
    admissions.html

MAINE

Board of Bar Examiners
State of Maine
P.O. Box 30
Augusta, ME 04332
Phone: (207) 623-2464
http://www.maine.bar.org/examiners.html

MARYLAND

Board of Law Examiners
State of Maryland
251 Rowe Boulevard, Room 307
Annapolis, MD 21401
Phone: (410) 260-1975
http://www.courts.state.md.us/ble/index.
    html

MASSACHUSETTS

Massachusetts Board of Bar Examiners
77 Franklin Street
Boston, MA 02110
Phone: (617) 482-4466
Fax: (617) 542-5943
http://www.state.ma.us/bbe/bbe.index.htm

MICHIGAN

Board of Law Examiners
State of Michigan
P.O. Box 30104
Lansing, MI 48909
Phone: (517) 334-6992
http://michbar.inherent.com/admission

MINNESOTA

**Minnesota State Board of Law
    Examiners**
25 Constitution Avenue, Suite 110
St. Paul, MN 55155
Phone: (651) 297-1800 or (800) 627-3529
Fax: (651) 296-5866;
    TTY: (651) 297-5353
http://www.ble.state.mn.us

MISSISSIPPI

Mississippi Board of Bar Admissions
P.O. Box 1449
Jackson, MS 39215
Phone: (601) 354-6055
Fax: (601) 354-6054
http://www.mssc.state.ms.us/
    BarAdmissions/default.asp

MISSOURI

**Missouri State Board of Law
    Examiners**
P.O. Box 150
Jefferson City, MO 65102
Phone: (573) 751-4144
Fax: (573) 751-7514
http://www.osca.state.mo.us/sup/index.nsf

MONTANA

Bar Admissions Administrator
State Bar of Montana
46 N. Last Chance Gulch, Suite 2A
P.O. Box 577
Helena, MT 59624

Phone: (406) 442-7660
Fax: (406) 442-7763
http://www.montanabar.org

NEBRASKA

Nebraska State Bar Commission
635 South 14th Street, Suite 200
Lincoln, NE 68508
Phone: (402) 475-7091 or (800) 927-0117
Fax: (402) 475-7098
http://www.nebar.com/memberinfo/nsbc/
    index.htm

NEVADA

Admissions Department
State Bar of Nevada
600 E. Charleston
Las Vegas, NV 89104
Phone: (800) 254-2797 or (702) 382-2200
http://www.nvbar.org

NEW HAMPSHIRE

**New Hampshire Board of Bar
    Examiners**
Supreme Court Clerk's Office
1 Noble Drive
Concord, NH 03301
Phone: (603) 271-2646
http://www.nhbar.org

NEW JERSEY

New Jersey Board of Bar Examiners
P.O. Box 973
Trenton, NJ 08625-0973
http://www.njbarexams.org

NEW MEXICO

Board of Bar Examiners
State of New Mexico
9420 Indian School Road NE
Albuquerque, NM 87112
Phone: (505) 271-9706
Fax: (505) 271-9768
http://www.nmexam.org

NEW YORK

**New York State Board of Law
    Examiners**
1 Executive Centre Drive, Suite 202
Albany, NY 12203-5195

Phone: (800) 342-3335 or (518) 452-8700
Fax: (518) 452-4729
http://www.nybarexam.org

NORTH CAROLINA

Board of Law Examiners
State of North Carolina
One Exchange Plaza, Suite 700
Raleigh, NC 27601
Phone: (919) 828-4886
Fax: (919) 828-2251
http://www.ncble.org

NORTH DAKOTA

Board of Law Examiners
State of North Dakota
Judicial Wing, First Floor
600 East Boulevard Avenue
Bismarck, ND 58505-0530
Phone: (701) 328-4201
Fax: (701) 328-4480;
    TDD: (701) 328-2884
http://www.court.state.nd.us/Court/
    Committees/BarBd/Board.htm

COMMONWEALTH OF THE NORTHERN MARIANA ISLANDS

Bar Administrator
Supreme Court, Commonwealth of the
    Northern Mariana Islands
P.O. Box 502165
Saipan, MP 96950
Phone: (670) 236-9800
Fax: (670) 236-9702
http://www.cnmilaw.org/htmlpage/
    hpg34.htm

OHIO

Board of Bar Examiners
Supreme Court of Ohio
Rhodes State Office Tower
30 East Broad Street, Second Floor
Columbus, OH 43215-3414
Phone: (614) 466-1541 or (614) 466-1540
Fax: (614) 995-4024
http://www.sconet.ohio.gov/Admissions

OKLAHOMA

Oklahoma Board of Bar Examiners
1901 N. Lincoln
P.O. Box 53036
Oklahoma City, OK 73152-3036

Phone: (405) 416-7000 or
    (800) 522-8065
http://www.okbar.org/publicinfo/
    admissions

OREGON

Oregon State Board of Bar Examiners
5200 SW Meadows Road
P.O. Box 1689
Lake Oswego, OR 97035-0889
Phone: (503) 620-0222, extension 310,
    311, 316, or 410
Fax: (503) 684-1366
http://www.osbar.org/Programs/
    admissions/home.html

PENNSYLVANIA

**Pennsylvania Board of Law
    Examiners**
5070A Ritter Road, Suite 300
Mechanicsburg, PA 17055-4879
Phone: (717) 795-7270
http://www.pable.org

PUERTO RICO

Board of Bar Examiners
Supreme Court of Puerto Rico
P.O. Box 902-2392
San Juan, PR 00902-2392
Phone: (787) 289-0170
http://www.tribunalpr.org/indexfrm3.html

RHODE ISLAND

Rhode Island Board of Bar Examiners
Clerk of the Supreme Court
250 Benefit Street
Providence, RI 02903
Phone: (401) 222-4233
Fax: (401) 222-3599
http://www.courts.state.ri.us/supreme/bar/
    baradmission.htm

SOUTH CAROLINA

Office of Bar Admissions
Supreme Court of South Carolina
P.O. Box 11330
Columbia, SC 29211
Phone: (803) 734-1080
Fax: (803) 734-0394; TTY: (803) 734-6365
http://www.judicial.state.sc.us/bar

SOUTH DAKOTA

South Dakota Board of Bar Examiners
500 East Capitol
Pierre, SD 57501-5070
Phone: (605) 773-4898
Fax: (605) 773-6128
http://www.state.sd.us/state/judicial/
    sdbbe/board_of_bar_examin.htm

TENNESSEE

Tennessee Board of Law Examiners
706 Church Street, Suite 100
Nashville, TN 37243-0740
Phone: (615) 741-3234
Fax: (615) 741-5867
http://www.state.tn.us/lawexaminers

TEXAS

Texas Board of Law Examiners
205 West 14th Street
Austin, TX 78701
Phone: (512) 463-1621
Fax: (512) 463-5300
http://www.ble.state.tx.us

UTAH

Admissions Department
Utah State Bar
645 South 200 East
Salt Lake City, UT 84111-3834
Phone: (801) 531-9077
http://www.utahbar.org/public/html/
    admissions_policies.html

VERMONT

Board of Bar Examiners
State of Vermont
109 State Street
Montpelier, VT 05609-0702
Phone: (802) 828-3281
http://www.vermontjudiciary.org/

VIRGIN ISLANDS

Virgin Islands Bar Examiner's Office
Territorial Court
P.O. Box 70
St. Thomas, VI 00804
Phone: (340) 774-6680
http://www.vibar.org

VIRGINIA

Virginia Board of Bar Examiners
Suite 225, Shockoe Center
11 South 12th Street
Richmond, VA 23219-4009

Phone: (804) 786-7490
http://www.vbbe.state.vs.us/index.html

WASHINGTON

Admissions Department
Washington State Bar Association
2102 Fourth Avenue, Fourth Floor
Seattle, WA 98121-2330
Phone: (206) 727-8209
http://www.wsba.org/licensing.htm

WEST VIRGINIA

**West Virginia Board of Law
Examiners**
910 Quarrier Street
Suite 212, Davidson Building
Charleston, WV 25301
Phone: (304) 558-7815
Fax: (304) 558-0831
http://www.state.wv.us/wvsca

WISCONSIN

Board of Bar Examiners
110 East Main Street, Suite 715
Madison, WI 53703-3328
Phone: (608) 266-9760
http://www.courts.state.wi.us/bbe

WYOMING

Board of Law Examiners
Clerk of the Wyoming Supreme Court
123 Capitol Building
Cheyenne, WY 82002
Phone: (307) 777-7316
http://www.wyomingbar.org/
    admissions.asp

B. FEDERAL COURTS

In the federal court system, attorneys must be admitted into every federal court in which they wish to practice. Each federal court has its own admission procedures; entry generally requires meeting certain requirements. Below is contact and admissions information for learning more about the different federal courts.

U.S. COURTS

The U.S. Courts are made up of district courts, courts of appeals, and bankruptcy courts. General information about the courts can be found at the address below.

**Administrative Office of the U.S.
Courts**
Office of Public Affairs
Washington, DC 20544
Phone: (202) 502-2600
http://www.uscourts.gov
(Links to many federal courts can be accessed at this office's web site.)

U.S. Supreme Court
Admissions Office
Clerk, Supreme Court of the United States
One First Street, NE
Washington, DC 20543-0001
Phone: (202) 479-3387
http://www.supremecourtus.gov/bar/
    baradmissions.html

**U.S. Court of Appeals for the Federal
Circuit**
717 Madison Pl., NW
Washington, DC 20439
Phone: (202) 633-6550
http://www.fedcir.gov

U.S. Tax Court
Admissions Clerk
United States Tax Court
400 Second Street, NW
Washington, DC 20217
Phone: (202) 606-8736
http://www.ustaxcourt.gov

U.S. Court of International Trade
One Federal Plaza
New York, NY 10278-0001
Phone: (212) 264-2800
http://www.uscit.gov

**U.S. Court of Appeals for Veterans
Claims**
625 Indiana Avenue, NW, Suite 900
Washington, DC 20004-2950
http://www.vetapp.uscourts.gov

**U.S. Court of Appeals for the Armed
Forces**
Clerk of the Court
450 E Street, NW
Washington, DC 20442-0001
Phone: (202) 761-1448
http://www.armfor.uscourts.gov

U.S. Court of Federal Claims
Clerk's Office
717 Madison Place, NW
Washington, DC 20005
Phone: (202) 219-9657
http://www.law.gwu.edu/fedcl

APPENDIX III
PROFESSIONAL ASSOCIATIONS

Listed below are the main offices or contacts for the professional organizations that are mentioned in this book. You can contact these groups or visit their web sites to learn about professions, career opportunities, training programs, professional certification programs, and so on. Many of these organizations have branch offices throughout the United States. Contact an organization's headquarters or contact person to find out if a branch is in your area.

Other local, state, regional, and national professional organizations also represent many of the professions discussed in this book. To learn about other relevant professional associations and unions, contact local professionals.

NOTE: All contact information and web site addresses were current when the book was being written. If you come across a URL that no longer works, you may be able to find an organization's new web site by entering its name in a search engine.

ATTORNEYS

American Academy of Appellate Lawyers
15245 Shady Grove Road, Suite 130
Rockville, MD 20850-3222
Phone: (301) 258-9210
Fax: (301) 990-9771
http://www.amappacad.org

American Bar Association
740 15th Street, NW
Washington, DC 20005-1019
Phone: (800) 285-2221 or
   (312) 988-5522
http://www.abanet.org

American Corporate Counsel Association
1025 Connecticut Ave, NW, Suite 200
Washington, DC 20036-5425
Phone: (202) 293-4103
http://www.acca.com

American Immigration Lawyers Association
918 F Street, NW
Washington, DC 20004
Phone: (202) 216-2400
Fax: (202) 371-9449
http://www.aila.org

American Intellectual Property Law Association
2001 Jefferson Davis Highway, Suite 203
Arlington, VA 22202
Phone: (703) 415-0780
Fax: (703) 415-0786
http://www.aipla.org

Association of Federal Defense Attorneys
8350 Wilshire Boulevard, Suite 404
Beverly Hills, CA 90211
Phone: (301) 397-1001
http://www.afda.org

Association of Trial Lawyers of America
The Leonard M. Ring Law Center
1050 31st Street, NW
Washington, DC 20007
Phone: (800) 424-2725 or
   (202) 965-3500
http://www.atlanet.org

Copyright Society of the USA
1133 Avenue of the Americas
New York, NY 10036
Phone: (212) 354-6401
http://www.copyright-society.org

Federal Bar Association
2215 M Street, NW
Washington, DC 20037
Phone: (202) 785-1614
Fax: (202) 785-1568
http://www.fedbar.org

International Trademark Association
1133 Avenue of the Americas
New York, NY 10036
Phone: (212) 768-9887
Fax: (212) 768-7796
http://www.inta.org

Judge Advocates Association
6800 Chapins Road
Bloomsburg, PA 17815-8751
Phone: (570) 752-2027

Fax: (570) 752-2097
http://www.jaa.org

Licensing Executive Society
1800 Diagonal Road, Suite 280
Alexandria, VA 22314-2840
Phone: (703) 836-3106
Fax: (703) 836-3107
http://www.usa-canada.les.org

Minority Corporate Counsel Association
1400 L Street NW, 10th Floor
Washington, DC 20005
Phone: (202) 371-5909
Fax: (202) 371-5950
http://www.mcca.net

National Academy of Elder Law Attorneys
1604 North Country Club Road
Tucson, AZ 85716
Phone: (520) 881-4005
Fax: (520) 325-7925
http://www.naela.org

National Asian Pacific American Bar Association
1341 G Street, NW, Fifth Floor
Washington, DC 20005
Phone: (202) 626-7693
Fax: (202) 628-6327
http://www.napaba.org

National Association of Criminal Defense Lawyers
1025 Connecticut Avenue, NW, Suite 901
Washington, DC 20036
Phone: (202) 872-8600
Fax: (202) 872-8690

http://www.nacdl.org or
http://www.criminaljustice.org

**National Association of Patent
Practitioners**
4680-181 Monticello Avenue
PMB 101
Williamsburg, VA 23188
Phone: (800) 216-9588
Fax: (757) 220-3928
http://www.napp.org

**National Association of Women
Lawyers**
750 North Lake Shore Drive
Chicago, IL 60611
Phone: (312) 988-6186
Fax: (312) 988-6281
http://www.abanet.org/nawl

**National Criminal Justice
Association**
444 N. Capitol Street, NW, Suite 618
Washington, DC 20001
Phone: (202) 624-1440
Fax: (202) 508-3859
http://www.ncja.org

**National District Attorneys
Association**
99 Canal Center Plaza
Alexandria, VA 22314
Phone: (703) 549-9222
Fax: (703) 836-3195
http://www.ndaa.org

**National Employment Lawyers
Association**
44 Montgomery Street, Suite 2080
San Francisco, CA 94104
Phone: (415) 296-7629
Fax: (415) 677-9445
http://www.nela.org

National Lawyers Association
City Center Square
P.O. Box 26005
Kansas City, MO 64196
Phone: (800) 471-2994 or
        (816) 471-2994
Fax: (816) 471-2995
http://www.nla.org

National Lawyers Guild
126 University Place, Fifth Floor
New York, NY 10003

Phone: (212) 627-2656
Fax: (212) 627-2404
http://www.nlg.org

**National Legal Aid and Defender
Association**
1625 K Street, NW, Suite 800
Washington, DC 20006-1604
Phone: (202) 452-0620
Fax: (202) 872-1031
http://www.nlada.org

LEGAL SUPPORT PROFESSIONALS

American Bar Association
740 15th Street, NW
Washington, DC 20005-1019
Phone: (800) 285-2221 or
        (312) 988-5522
http://www.abanet.org

**American Bar Association Law
Practice Management Section**
http://www.abanet.org/lpm/default.
shtml

**American Bar Standing Committee
on Legal Assistants**
http://www.abanet.org/legalassts/
home.html

American Marketing Association
311 S. Wacker Drive, Suite 5800
Chicago, IL 60606
Phone: (800) AMA-1150 or
        (312) 542-9000
Fax: (312) 542-9001
http://www.marketingpower.com

Association for Computing Machinery
1515 Broadway
New York, NY 10036
Phone: (800) 342-6626 or (212) 626-0500
http://www.acm.org

Association of Legal Administrators
175 East Hawthron Parkway, Suite 325
Vernon Hills, IL 60061-1428
Phone: (847) 816-1212
Fax: (847) 816-1213
http://www.alanet.org

Association of Support Professionals
66 Mt. Auburn Street
Watertown, MA 02472
Phone: (617) 924-3944, extension 14
Fax: (617) 924-7288
http://www.asponline.com

LawNet, Inc.
2110 Slaughter Lane, Suite 115
PMB 149
Austin, TX 78748
Phone: (512) 280-7172
Fax: (512) 280-7479
http://www.peertopeer.org

Legal Marketing Association
1926 Waukegan Road, Suite 1
Glenview, IL 60025
Phone: (847) 657-6717
Fax: (847) 657-6819
http://www.legalmarketing.org

Legal Secretaries International, Inc.
8902 Sunnywood Drive
Houston, TX 77088-3792
Phone: (281) 847-9754
Fax: (281) 847-2121
http://www.legalsecretaries.org

**NALS . . . the association for legal
professionals**
314 East Third Street, Suite 210
Tulsa, OK 74120
Phone: (918) 582-5188
Fax: (918) 582-5907
http://www.nals.org

**National Association of Legal
Assistants**
1516 South Boston Avenue, Suite 200
Tulsa, OK 74119
Phone: (918) 587-6828
Fax: (918) 582-6772
http://www.nala.org

National Paralegal Association
Box 406
Solebury, PA 18963
Phone: (215) 297-8333
Fax: (215) 297-8358
http://www.nationalparalegal.org

**Society for Human Resource
Management**
1800 Duke Street
Alexandria, VA 22314
Phone: (703) 548-3440
Fax: (703) 535-6490
http://www.shrm.org

Society for Information Management
401 N. Michigan Avenue
Chicago, IL 60611-4267
Phone: (800) 387-9746 or (312) 527-6734
Fax: (312) 245-1081
http://www.simnet.org

LITIGATION SUPPORT PROFESSIONALS

American Guild of Court Videographers
1628 East Third Street
Casper, WY 82601
Phone: (800) 678-1990 or (307) 472-3547
Fax: (307) 472-5048
http://www.agcv.com

American Psychology-Law Society
Department of Psychology
University of Nebraska—Lincoln
209 Burnett Hall
Lincoln, NE 68588-0308
http://www.unl.edu/ap-ls

American Society of Trial Consultants
Phone: (410) 560-7949
Fax: (410) 560-2563
http://www.astcweb.org

Association of Medical Illustrators
2965 Flowers Road South, Suite 105
Atlanta, GA 30341
Phone: (770) 454-7933
Fax: (770) 458-3314
http://medical-illustrators.org

Demonstrative Evidence Specialists Association
1512 North Woodlawn Avenue
Metairie, LA 70001
Phone: (504) 455-8674
Fax: (504) 888-3263
http://www.desa.org

Evidence Photographers International Council
600 Main Street
Honesdale, PA 18431
Phone: (800) 356-3742 or (570) 253-5450
Fax: (570) 253-5011
http://www.epic-photo.org

International Process Servers Association
P.O. Box 40653
Rochester, NY 14604
Phone: (888) 232-8590
Fax: (716) 546-3463
http://www.ipsaonline.com

National Association of Investigative Specialists
P.O. Box 33244
Austin, TX 78764
Phone: (512) 719-3595

Fax: (512) 719-3594
http://www.pimall.com/nais/home.html

National Association of Legal Investigators
6109 Meadowwood
Grand Blanc, MI 48439
Phone: (800) 266-6254
Fax: (810) 694-7109
http://www.nalionline.org

National Association of Professional Process Servers
P.O. Box 4547
Portland, OR 97208-4547
Phone: (800) 477-8211 or (503) 222-4180
Fax: (503) 222-3950
http://www.napps.com

National Court Reporters Association
8224 Old Courthouse Road
Vienna, VA 22182-3808
Phone: (800) 272-6272 or (703) 556-6272
Fax: (703) 556-6291;
    TTY: (703) 556-6289
http://www.ncraonline.org or
http://www.verbatimreporters.com
http://clvs.ncraonline.org (Certified Legal
    Video Specialists section)

National Legal Video Association
41 Watchung Plaza, Suite 385
Montclair, NJ 07042
Phone: (973) 655-1997
Fax: (973) 655-1612
http://www.nlva.com

Professional Bail Agents of the United States
444 N. Capitol Street, NW, Suite 805
Washington, DC 20001
Phone: (800) 883-7287
Fax: (202) 783-4125
http://www.pbus.com

LITIGATION CONSULTANTS AND EXPERT WITNESSES

Academy of Criminal Justice Sciences
7319 Hanover Parkway, Suite C
Greenbelt, MD 20770
Phone: (800) 757-2257 or (301) 446-6300
Fax: (301) 446-2819
http://www.acjs.org

American Academy of Forensic Psychology
128 North Craig Street
Pittsburgh, PA 15213

Phone: (800) 255-7792 or
    (412) 681-3000
Fax: (412) 681-1471
http://www.abfp.com

American Association of Legal Nurse Consultants
4700 West Lake Avenue
Glenview, IL 60025-1485
Phone: (877) 402-2562
Fax: (847) 375-6313
http://www.aalnc.org

American Institute of Certified Public Accountants
1211 Avenue of the Americas
New York, NY 10036-8775
Phone: (212) 596-6200
Fax: (212) 596-6213
http://www.aicpa.org

American Nurses Association
600 Maryland Avenue, SW
Suite 100 West
Washington, DC 20024
Phone: (800) 274-4262 or
    (202) 651-7000
Fax: (202) 651-7001
http://www.nursingworld.org

American Psychology-Law Society
Department of Psychology
University of Nebraska—Lincoln
209 Burnett Hall
Lincoln, NE 68588-0308
http://www.unl.edu/ap-ls

American Society of Appraisers
555 Herndon Parkway, Suite 125
Herndon, VA 20170
Phone: (703) 478-2228
Fax: (703) 742-8471
http://www.appraisers.org

American Society of Criminology
1314 Kinnear Road
Columbus, OH 43212-1156
Phone: (614) 292-9207
Fax: (614) 292-6767
http://www.asc41.com

American Society of Farm Managers and Rural Appraisers
950 South Cherry Street, Suite 508
Denver, CO 80246-2664
Phone: (303) 758-3513
Fax: (303) 758-01090
http://www.asfmra.org

American Society of Safety Engineers
1800 East Oakton Street
Des Plaines, IL 60018
Phone: (847) 699-2929
Fax: (847) 768-3434
http://www.asse.org

American Sociological Association
1307 New York Avenue, NW, Suite 700
Washington, DC 20005
Phone: (202) 383-9005
Fax: (202) 638-0882;
    TDD: (202) 872-0486
http://www.asanet.org

Appraisers Association of America, Inc.
386 Park Avenue South, Suite 2000
New York, NY 10016
Phone: (212) 889-5404
Fax: (212) 889-5503
http://www.appraisersassoc.org

**Association of Certified Fraud
    Examiners**
716 West Avenue
Austin, TX 78701
Phone: (800) 245-3321 or (512) 478-9070
Fax: (512) 478-9297
http://www.cfenet.com

**Association of Insolvency and
    Restructuring Advisors**
132 West Main Street
Medford, OR 97501
Phone: (541) 858-1665
Fax: (541) 858-9187
http://www.airacira.org

**Forensic Accountants Society of North
    America**
8712 West Dodge Road, Suite 200
Omaha, NE 68114
Phone: (402) 397-9433
Fax: (402) 397-8649
http://www.fasna.org

Institute of Business Appraisers
P.O. Box 17410
Plantation, FL 33318
Phone: (954) 584-1144
Fax: (954) 584-1184
http://www.instbusapp.org

**International Association of Accident
    Reconstruction Specialists**
1036 Gretchen Lane
Grand Ledge, MI 48837-1873
Phone: (517) 622-3135
http://www.iaars.org

International Society of Appraisers
Riverview Plaza Office Park
16040 Christensen Road, Suite 102
Seattle, WA 98188-2929
Phone: (206) 241-0359
Fax: (206) 241-0436
http://www.isa-appraisers.org

**National Association of Independent
    Fee Appraisers**
7501 Murdoch Avenue
St. Louis, MO 63119
Phone: (314) 781-6688
Fax: (314) 781-2872
http://www.naifa.com

**National Association of Jewelry
    Appraisers**
P.O. Box 6558
Annapolis, MD 21401-0558
Phone: (301) 261-8270

**National Association of Master
    Appraisers**
303 West Cypress Street
P.O. Box 12617
San Antonio, TX 78212
Phone: (800) 229-6262
Fax: (210) 225-8450
http://www.masterappraisers.org

**National Association of Professional
    Accident Reconstruction Specialists**
P.O. Box 65
Brandywine, MD 20613-0065
http://www.napars.org

**National Association of Traffic
    Accident Reconstructionists and
    Investigators**
P.O. Box 398
Chadds Ford, PA 19317
Phone: (610) 558-5146
http://www.natari.org

Society of Accident Reconstructionists
4891 Independence Street, Suite 140
Wheat Ridge, CO 80033
Phone: (303) 403-9045
Fax: (303) 403-9401
http://www.accidentreconstruction.com/
    SOAR/index.asp

Western Society of Criminology
Administration of Justice Division
Portland State University
P.O. Box 751
Portland, OR 97207-0751
http://www.sonoma.edu/cja/wsc/
    wscmain.html

JUDGES

American Bar Association
740 15th Street, NW
Washington, DC 20005-1019
http://www.abanet.org

**American Bar Association/Judicial
    Division**
http://www.abanet.org/jd/home.html

American Judges Association
300 Newport Avenue
P.O. Box 8798
Williamsburg, VA 23187-8798
Phone: (800) 616-6165 or
    (757) 259-1841
Fax: (757) 259-1520
http://aja.ncsc.dni.us

American Judicature Society
180 N. Michigan Avenue, Suite 600
Chicago, IL 60601
Phone: (312) 558-6900
Fax: (312) 558-9175, ext. 107
http://www.ajs.org

**Federal Administrative Law Judges
    Conference**
2000 Pennsylvania Avenue, NW,
    Suite 260
Washington, DC 20006
Phone: (202) 675-3065
http://www.faljc.org

Federal Bar Association
2215 M Street, NW
Washington, DC 20037
Phone: (202) 785-1614
Fax: (202) 785-1568
http://www.fedbar.org

**National Association of Administrative
    Law Judges**
P.O. Box 418
Glenview, IL 60025-0418
Phone: (847) 562-0783
Fax: 562-0783
http://www.naalj.org

**National Conference of Administrative
    Law Judges**
c/o American Bar Association/Judicial
    Division
541 N. Fairbanks Court
Chicago, IL 60611
Phone: (800) 238-2667, ext. 5705 or
    (312) 988-5705
http://www.abanet.org/jd/ncalj/home.html

National Conference of Bankruptcy Judges
235 Secret Cove Drive
Lexington, SC 29072
Phone: (803) 957-6226
Fax: (803) 957-8890
http://www.ncbj.org/ncbjhomepage/index.htm

National Council of Juvenile and Family Court Judges
P.O. Box 8970
Reno, NV 89507
Phone: (775) 784-6012
Fax: (775) 784-6628
http://www.ncjfcj.unr.edu

COURT SUPPORT STAFF

American Bar Association
740 15th Street, NW
Washington, DC 20005-1019
http://www.abanet.org

American Deputy Sheriffs' Association
702 S. Grand Street
Monroe, Louisiana 71201
Phone: (800) 937-7940
Fax: (318) 398-9980
http://www.deputysheriff.org

American Translators Association
225 Reinekers Lane, Suite 590
Alexandria, VA 22314
Phone: (703) 683-6100
Fax: (703) 683-6122
http://www.atanet.org

Federal Court Clerks Association
Room 128, U.S. Courthouse
400 South Phillips Avenue
Sioux Falls, SD 57108
Phone: (605) 330-4447
http://www.id.uscourts.gov/fcca.htm

Fraternal Order of Police
1410 Donelson Pike, Suite A-17
Nashville, TN 37217
Phone: (615) 399-0900
Fax: (615) 399-0400
http://www.grandlodgefop.org

International Association of Clerks, Recorders, Election Officials, and Treasurers
Membership: Jeanne McNamara
Board of Elections
P.O. Box 1087
Wheaton, IL 60189-1087

Phone: (800) 890-7368
http://www.iacreot.com

International Association of Court Officers and Services, Inc.
Phone: (703) 838-5322
Fax: (703) 683-6541
http://www.sheriffs.org/iacos.htm

NALS ... the association for legal professionals
314 East Third Street, Suite 210
Tulsa, OK 74120
Phone: (918) 582-5188
Fax: (918) 582-5907
http://www.nals.org

National Association for Court Management
300 Newport Avenue
Williamsburg, VA 23185
Phone: (757) 259-1841
Fax: (757) 259-1520
http://www.nacmnet.org

National Association of Judiciary Interpreters and Translators
551 Fifth Avenue, Suite 3025
New York, NY 10176
Phone: (212) 692-9581
Fax: (212) 687-4016
http://www.najit.org

National Court Reporters Association
8224 Old Courthouse Road
Vienna, VA 22182-3808
Phone: (800) 272-6272 or (703) 556-6272
Fax: (703) 556-6291; TTY: (703) 556-6289
http://www.ncraonline.org or
http://www.verbatimreporters.com

National Lawyers Association
City Center Square
P.O. Box 26005
Kansas City, MO 64196
Phone: (800) 471-2994 or (816) 471-2994
Fax: (816) 471-2995
http://www.nla.org

The Translators and Interpreters Guild
2007 North 15th Street, Suite 4
Arlington, VA 22201-2621
Phone: (800) 992-0367 or (703) 522-0881
Fax: (703) 522-0882
http://www.ttig.org

United States Court Reporters Association
P.O. Box 465
Chicago, IL 60690-0465

Phone: (800) 628-2730
http://www.uscra.org

CRIMINAL JUSTICE SOCIAL SERVICES PROFESSIONALS

American Correctional Association
4380 Forbes Boulevard
Lanham, MD 20706-4322
Phone: (800) 222-5646
http://www.corrections.com/aca

American Humane Association
63 Inverness Drive East
Englewood, CO 80112-5117
Phone: (800) 227-4645 or (303) 792-9900
Fax: (303) 792-5333
http://www.americanhumane.org

American Probation and Parole Association
2760 Research Park Drive
Lexington, KY 40511-8410
Phone: (859) 244-8203
Fax: (859) 244-8001
http://www.appa-net.org

American Professional Society on the Abuse of Children
940 NE 13th Street
Oklahoma City, OK 73104
Phone: (405) 271-8202
Fax: (405) 271-2931
http://www.apsac.org

Association of Traumatic Stress Specialists
7338 Broad River Road
Irmo, SC 29063
Phone: (803) 781-0017
Fax: (803) 781-3899
http://www.atss-hq.com

Federal Law Enforcement Officers Association
P.O. Box 5402
Huntington Station, NY 11746-0997
http://www.fleoa.org

National Association of Pretrial Services Agencies
P.O. Box 280808
San Francisco, CA 94128-0808
Phone: (650) 588-0212
Fax: (650) 588-5752
http://www.napsa.org

National Association of Social Workers
750 First Street, NE, Suite 700
Washington, DC 20002-4241
Phone: (800) 638-8799 or (202) 408-8600
http://www.naswdc.org

National Organization of Victim Assistance
1730 Park Road, NW
Washington, DC 20010
Phone: (202) 232-6682
Fax: (202) 462-2255
http://www.try-nova.org

PROFESSIONS IN POLITICS

American League of Lobbyists
P.O. Box 30005
Alexandria, VA 22310
Phone: (703) 960-3011
Fax: (703) 960-4070
http://www.alldc.org

National Association of Counties
440 First Street, NW, Suite 800
Washington, DC 20001
Phone: (202) 393-6226
Fax: (202) 393-2630
http://www.naco.org

National League of Cities
1301 Pennsylvania Avenue, NW,
    Suite 550
Washington, DC 20004
Phone: (202) 626-3000
http://www.nlc.org

Women in Government Relations, Inc.
801 North Fairfax Street, Suite 211
Alexandria, VA 22314-1757
Phone: (703) 299-8546
Fax: (703) 299-9233
http://www.wgr.org

NONPROFIT ADMINISTRATORS

Alliance for Nonprofit Management
1899 L Street, NW, Sixth Floor
Washington, DC 20036
Phone: (202) 955-8406
Fax: (202) 955-8419
http://www.allianceonline.org

American Bar Association
740 15th Street, NW
Washington, DC 20005-1019
http://www.abanet.org

American Society of Association Executives
1575 I Street, NW
Washington, DC 20005-1103
Phone: (202) 626-2723
Fax: (202) 371-8825;
    TDD: (202) 626-2803
http://www.asaenet.org

Management Information Exchange
515 Washington Street, Third Floor
Boston, MA 02111-1759
Phone: (617) 556-0288
http://www.m-i-e.org

National Academy of Elder Law Attorneys
1604 North Country Club Road
Tucson, AZ 85716
Phone: (520) 881-4005
Fax: (520) 325-7925
http://www.naela.org

National Employment Lawyers Association
44 Montgomery Street, Suite 2080
San Francisco, CA 94104
Phone: (415) 296-7629
Fax: (415) 677-9445
http://www.nela.org

National Legal Aid and Defender Association
1625 K Street, NW, Suite 800
Washington, DC 20006-1604
Phone: (202) 452-0620
Fax: (202) 872-1031
http://www.nlada.org

ALTERNATIVE DISPUTE RESOLUTION (ADR) PRACTITIONERS

AFCC—an association of family, court, and community professionals
6515 Grand Teton Plaza, Suite 210
Madison, WI 53719-1048
Phone: (608) 664-3750
Fax: (608) 664-3751
http://www.afccnet.org

American Arbitration Association
335 Madison Avenue, 10th Floor
New York, NY 10017-4605
Phone: (800) 778-7879 or
    (212) 716-5800

Fax: (212) 716-5905
http://www.adr.org

American Bar Association Section of Dispute Resolution
740 15th Street, NW
Washington, DC 20005-1009
Phone: (202) 662-1690
Fax: (202) 662-1683
http://www.abanet.org/dispute

American College of Civil Trial Mediators
200 East Robinson Street, Suite 500
Orlando, FL 32801
Phone: (407) 843-5880
Fax: (407) 425-7905
http://www.acctm.org

Association for Conflict Resolution
1527 New Hampshire Avenue, NW,
    Third Floor
Washington, DC 20036
Phone: (202) 667-9700
Fax: (202) 265-1968
http://www.acresolution.org

Association of Attorney-Mediators
P.O. Box 741955
Dallas, TX 75374-1955
Phone: (800) 280-1368 or
    (972) 669-8101
Fax: 972-669-8180
http://www.attorney-mediators.org

National Academy of Arbitrators
403 Lower Building
College of Business
Auburn University, AL 36849-5260
Phone: (334) 844-2817
Fax: (334) 844-1498
http://www.naarb.org

National Association for Community Mediation
1527 New Hampshire Avenue, NW
Washington, DC 20036-1206
Phone: (202) 667-9700, extension 213
http://www.nafcm.org

COMPLIANCE OFFICERS

American Association for Affirmative Action
1600 Duke Street, Suite 700
Alexandria, VA 22314

Phone: (800) 252-8952 or
    (703) 299-9285
Fax: (703) 299-8822
http://www.affirmativeaction.org

Ethics Officer Association

30 Church Street, Suite 331
Belmont, MA 02478
Phone: (617) 484-9400
Fax: (617) 484-8330
http://www.eoa.org

Health Care Compliance Association

1211 Locust Street
Philadelphia, PA 19107
Phone: (888) 580-8373
Fax: (215) 545-8107
http://www.hcca-info.org

National Society of Compliance Professionals

22 Kent Road
Cornwall Bridge, CT 06754
Phone: (860) 672-0843
Fax: (860) 672-3005
http://www.nscp.org

Society for Human Resource Management

1800 Duke Street
Alexandria, VA 22314
Phone: (703) 548-3440
Fax: (703) 535-6490
http://www.shrm.org

ANALYSTS AND EXAMINERS

American Academy of Actuaries

1110 17th Street, NW, Seventh Floor
Washington, DC 20036
Phone: (202) 223-8196
Fax: (202) 872-1948
http://www.actuary.org

American Land Title Association

1828 L Street, NW
Washington, DC 20036-5104
Phone: (800) 787-ALTA
Fax: (888) FAX-ALTA
http://www.alta.org

American Society of Pension Actuaries

4245 N. Fairfax Drive, Suite 750
Arlington, VA 22203
Phone: (703) 516-9300
Fax: (703) 516-9308
http://www.aspa.org

Casualty Actuarial Society

1100 N. Glebe Road, Suite 600
Arlington, VA 22201
Phone: (703) 276-3100
Fax: (703) 276-3108
http://www.casact.org

Conference of Consulting Actuaries

1100 West Lake Cook Road, Suite 235
Buffalo Grove, IL 60089-1968
Phone: (847) 419-9090
Fax: (847) 419-9091
http://www.ccactuaries.com

International Claim Association

1255 23rd Street, NW, Suite 200
Washington, DC 20037
Phone: (202) 452-0143
Fax: (202) 833-3636
http://www.claim.org

National Association of Independent Insurance Adjusters

300 West Washington Street
Chicago, IL 60606
Phone: (312) 853-0808
Fax: (312) 853-3225
http://www.Claims-Portal.com/naiia/
    index.cfm

National Association of Patent Practitioners

4680-181 Monticello Avenue
PMB 101
Williamsburg, VA 23188
Phone: (800) 216-9588
Fax: (757) 220-3928
http://www.napp.org

National Contract Management Association

1912 Woodford Road
Vienna, VA 22182
Phone: (800) 344-8096
http://www.ncmahq.org

National Eligibility Workers Association

P.O. Box 1254
Nixa, MO 65714-1254
Phone: (888) 283-6392
http://new.invite.net

Society of Actuaries

475 N. Martingale Road, Suite 800
Schaumburg, IL 60173
Phone: (847) 706-3500
Fax: (847) 706-3599
http://www.soa.org

EDUCATORS

American Association for Higher Education

One Dupont Circle, Suite 360
Washington, DC 20036-1110
Phone: (202) 293-6440
Fax: (202) 293-0073
http://www.aahe.org

American Association for Paralegal Education

2965 Flowers Road South, Suite 105
Atlanta, GA 30341
Phone: (770) 452-9877
Fax: (770) 458-3314
http://www.aafpe.org

American Association of University Administrators

2602 Rutford Avenue
Richardson, TX 75080-1470
Phone: (972) 248-3957
Fax: (972) 713-8209
http://www.aaua.org

American Association of University Professors

1012 Fourteenth Street, NW, Suite 500
Washington, DC 20005-3465
Phone: (202) 737-5900
Fax: (202) 737-5526
http://www.aaup.org

American Bar Association

740 15th Street, NW
Washington, DC 20005-1019
http://www.abanet.org

American Bar Association Standing Committee on Legal Assistants

http://www.abanet.org/legalassts/
    home.html

American Bar Association—Section of Legal Education and Admissions to the Bar

750 N. Lake Shore Drive, Seventh Floor
Chicago, IL 60611
Phone: (312) 988-6738
Fax: (312) 988-5681
http://www.abanet.org/legaled/home.html

American Conference of Academic Deans

1818 R Street, NW
Washington, DC 20009
Phone: (202) 387-3760
Fax: (202) 265-9532
http://www.acad-edu.org

Association of American Law Schools
1201 Connecticut Avenue, NW, Suite 800
Washington, DC 20036-2605
Phone: (202) 296-8851
Fax: (202) 296-8869
http://www.aals.org

Association of Legal Writing
   Specialists
Seattle University School of Law
900 Broadway
Seattle, WA 98122-4340
Phone: (206) 398-4022
Fax: (206) 398-4036
http://lawschool.lexis.com/faculty/lwi/
   specialists.htm

Association of Trial Lawyers of
   America
The Leonard M. Ring Law Center
1050 31st Street, NW
Washington, DC 20007
Phone: (800) 424-2725 or
   (202) 965-3500
http://www.atlanet.org

Clinical Legal Education Association
Contact: Suzanne Jamie Levitt,
   Secretary/Treasurer
Drake University Law School
27th & Carpenter
Des Moines, IA 50311
Phone: (515) 271-3851
Fax: (515) 271-4100
http://clinic.law.cuny.edu/clea/clea.html

National Asian Pacific American Bar
   Association
1341 G Street, NW, Fifth Floor
Washington, DC 20005
Phone: (202) 626-7693
Fax: (202) 628-6327
http://www.napaba.org

National Association for Law
   Placement
1025 Connecticut Avenue, NW,
   Suite 1110
Washington, DC 20036-5413
Phone: (202) 835-1001
Fax: (202) 835-1112
http://www.nalp.org

National Association of State Judicial
   Educators
Supreme Court of Virginia
100 N. Ninth Street
Richmond, VA 23219

Phone: (804)786-7589
Fax: (804) 786-4542
http://nasje.unm.edu

National Association of Women
   Lawyers
750 North Lake Shore Drive
Chicago, IL 60611
Phone: (312) 988-6186
Fax: (312) 988-6281
http://www.abanet.org/nawl

Society of American Law Teachers
Washington College of Law
American University
4801 Massachusetts Avenue, NW
Washington, DC 20016
Phone: (202) 274-4168
Fax: (202) 274-0659
http://www.scu.edu/law/salt

CAREER SERVICES
PROFESSIONALS

American Counseling Association
5999 Stevenson Avenue
Alexandria, VA 22304
Phone: (703) 823-9800
Fax: (703) 823-0252
http://www.counseling.org

National Association for Law
   Placement
1025 Connecticut Avenue, NW,
   Suite 1110
Washington, DC 20036-5413
Phone: (202) 835-1001
Fax: (202) 835-1112
http://www.nalp.org

National Association of Legal Search
   Consultants
11 East Hubbard Street, Suite 5A
Chicago, Illinois 60611
Phone: (312) 755-0635
Fax: (312) 431-8697
http://www.nalsc.org

National Career Development
   Association
10820 East 45th Street, Suite 210
Tulsa, OK 74146
Phone: (866) 367-6232 or (918) 663-
   7060
Fax: (918) 663-7058
http://www.ncda.org

LIBRARIANS

American Association of Law
   Libraries
53 West Jackson Boulevard, Suite 940
Chicago, IL 60604
Phone: (312) 939-4764
Fax: (312) 431-1097
http:/www.aallnet.org

American Library Association
50 East Huron Street
Chicago, IL 60611
Phone: (800) 545-2433
Fax: (312) 440-9374; TDD:
   (888) 814-7692 or (312) 944-7298
http://www.ala.org

Association of Research Libraries
21 Dupont Circle
Washington, DC 20026
Phone: (202) 296-2296
Fax: (202) 872-0884
http://www.arl.org

Council on Library/Media Technicians
Cuyahoga Community College Library,
   Room 400
2900 Community College Avenue
Cleveland, Ohio 44115
Phone: (216) 987-4655
Fax: (216) 987-4404
http://library.ucr.edu/COLT/

Special Libraries Association
1700 Eighteenth Street, NW
Washington, DC 20009-2514
Phone: (202) 234-4700
Fax: (202) 265-9317
http://www.sla.org

Special Libraries Association, Legal
   Division
11311 Cornell Park Drive
Cincinnati, OH 45242
http://www.slalegal.org

PUBLISHING
PROFESSIONALS

American Society of Journalists and
   Authors
1501 Broadway, Suite 302
New York, NY 10036
Phone: (212) 997-0947
Fax: (212) 768-7414
http://www.asja.org

Association for Continuing Legal Education
P.O. Box 4646
Austin, TX 78765
Phone: (512) 453-4340
Fax: (512) 451-2911
http://www.aclea.org

National Writers Union
National Office East
113 University Place, Sixth Floor
New York, NY 10003

Phone: (212) 254-0279
Fax: (212) 254-0673

National Office West
337 17th Street, Suite 101
Oakland, CA 94612
Phone: (510) 839-0110
Fax: (510) 839-6097
http://www.nwu.org

Society of Professional Journalists
3909 N. Meridian Street
Indianapolis, IN 46208

Phone: (317) 927-8000
Fax: (317) 920-4789
http://www.spj.org

APPENDIX IV
STATE BAR ASSOCIATIONS

Below is a list of attorney bar associations for the 50 states as well as for the District of Columbia and the territories of the United States. In some locations, membership in the state attorney bar is required in order to practice law in that state.

Note: All contact information and web site addresses were current when the book was being written. If you come across a URL that no longer works, you may be able to find an organization's new web site by entering its name in a search engine.

Alabama State Bar
415 Dexter Avenue
Montgomery, AL 36104
Phone: (334) 269-1515
Fax: (334) 261-6310
http://www.alabar.org

Alaska Bar Association
510 L Street, Suite 602
Anchorage, AK 99501
Phone: (907) 272-7469
Fax: (907) 272-2932
http://www.alaskabar.org

State Bar of Arizona
111 W. Monroe Street, Suite 1800
Phoenix, AZ 85003-1742
Phone: (602) 252-4804
Fax: (602) 271-4930
http://www.azbar.org

Arkansas Bar Association
400 West Markham
Little Rock, AR 72201
Phone: (800) 609-5668 or
     (501) 375-4606
http://www.arkbar.com

State Bar of California
180 Howard Street
San Francisco, CA 94105-1639
Phone: (415) 538-2000
http://www.calbar.org

Colorado Bar Association
1900 Grant Street, Ninth Floor
Denver, CO, 80203
Phone: (800) 332-6736 or
     (303) 860-1115
Fax: (303) 894-0821
http://www.cobar.org

Connecticut Bar Association
30 Bank Street
New Britain, CT 06050-0350
Phone: (860) 223-4400
Fax: (860) 223-4488
http://www.ctbar.org

Delaware State Bar Association
301 North Market Street
Wilmington, DE 19801
Phone: (302) 658-5279 or (800) 292-7869
Fax: (302) 658-5212
http://www.dsba.org

The District of Columbia Bar
1250 H Street, NW, Sixth Floor
Washington, DC 20005-5937
Phone: (202) 737-4700
Fax: (202) 626-3471
http://www.dcbar.org

The Florida Bar
650 Apalachee Parkway
Tallahassee, FL 32399-2300
Phone: (850) 561-5600
Fax: (850) 561-5826
http://www.flabar.org

State Bar of Georgia
800 The Hurt Building
50 Hurt Plaza
Atlanta, GA 30303-2934
Phone: (800) 334-6865 or (404) 527-8700
Fax: (404) 527-8717
http://www.gabar.org

Guam Bar Association
259 Matyr Street, Suite 201
Hagatna, GU 96910
Phone: (671) 477-7010
Fax: (671) 477-9734
http://www.guambar.org

Hawaii State Bar Association
1132 Bishop Street, Suite 906
Honolulu, HI 96813
Phone: (808) 537-1868
Fax: (808) 521-7936
http://www.hsba.org

Idaho State Bar
P.O. Box 895
525 West Jefferson
Boise, ID 83701
Phone: (208) 334-4500
Fax: (208) 334-4515
http://www2.state.id.us/isb

Illinois State Bar Association
Illinois Bar Center
Springfield, IL 62701-1779
Phone: (217) 525-1760 or (800) 252-8908
Fax: (217) 525-0712
http://www.illinoisbar.org

Indiana State Bar Association
230 E. Ohio, Fourth Floor
Indianapolis, IN 46204
Phone: (800) 266-2581 or (317) 639-5465
Fax: (317) 266-2588
http://www.inbar.org

Iowa State Bar Association
521 East Locust, Third Floor
Des Moines, IA 50309
Phone: (515) 243-3179
http://www.iowabar.org

Kansas Bar Association
1200 Harrison Street
Topeka, KS 66612-1806
Phone: (785) 234-5696
Fax: (785) 234-3813
http://www.ink.org/public/cybar

Kentucky Bar Association
514 West Main Street
Frankfort, KY 40601-1883
Phone: (502) 564-3795
Fax: (502) 564-3225
http://www.kybar.org

Louisiana State Bar Association
601 St. Charles Avenue
New Orleans, LA 70130-3404
Phone: (800) 421-5722 or (504) 566-1600
http://www.lsba.org

Maine State Bar Association
124 State Street
P.O. Box 788
Augusta, ME 04332-0788
Phone: (207) 622-7523
Fax: (207) 623-0083
http://www.mainebar.org

Maryland State Bar Association
520 West Fayette Street
Baltimore, MD 21201
Phone: (800) 492-1964 or (410) 685-7878
Fax: (410) 685-1016
http://www.msba.org

Massachusetts Bar Association
20 West Street
Boston, MA 02111
Phone: (617) 338-0500
http://massbar.org

State Bar of Michigan
306 Townsend Street
Lansing, MI 48933-2083
Phone: (800) 968-1442 or (517) 346-6300
Fax: (517) 482-6248
http://www.michbar.org

Minnesota State Bar Association
600 Nicollet Mall, #380
Minneapolis, MN 55402
Phone: (800) 882-6722 or (612) 333-1183
http://www.mnbar.org

The Mississippi Bar
P.O. Box 2168
643 North State Street
Jackson, MS 39225-2168
Phone: (601) 948-4471
Fax: (601) 355-8635
http://www.msbar.org

The Missouri Bar
P.O. Box 119
Jefferson City, MO 65102
Phone: (573) 635-4128

Fax: (573) 635-2811
http://www.mobar.org

State Bar of Montana
46 N. Last Chance Gulch, Suite 2A
P.O. Box 577
Helena, MT 59624
Phone: (406) 442-7660
Fax: (406) 442-7763
http://www.montanabar.org

Nebraska State Bar Association
635 South 14th Street
Lincoln, NE 68508
Phone: (402) 475-7091
http://www.nebar.com

State Bar of Nevada
600 East Charleston Boulevard
Las Vegas, NV 89104
Phone: (702) 382-2200
Fax: (702) 385-2878
http://www.nvbar.org

New Hampshire Bar Association
112 Pleasant Street
Concord, NH 03301
Phone: (603) 224-6942
Fax: (603) 224-2910
http://www.nhbar.org

New Jersey State Bar Association
New Jersey Law Center
One Constitution Square
New Brunswick, NJ 08901-1500
Phone: (732) 249-5000
Fax: (732) 249-2815
http://www.njsba.com

State Bar of New Mexico
State Bar Center
5121 Masthead Street, NE
Albuquerque, NM 87109
Phone: (505) 797-6000
Fax: (505) 828-3765
http://www.nmbar.org

New York State Bar Association
1 Elk Street
Albany, NY 12207
Phone: (518) 463-3200
http://www.nysba.org

North Carolina Bar Association
P.O. Box 3688
Cary, NC 27519
Phone: (919) 677-0561
Fax: (919) 677-0761
http://www.barlinc.org

State Bar Association of North Dakota
515¹/₂ East Broadway, Suite 101
Bismarck, ND 58501
Phone: (701) 255-1404
Fax: (701) 224-1621
http://www.sband.org

Northern Mariana Islands Bar Association
P.O. Box 2145
Saipan, MP 96950

Ohio State Bar Association
1700 Lake Shore Drive
Columbus OH 43204
Phone: (800) 282-6556 or (614) 487-2050
Fax: (614) 487-1008
http://www.ohiobar.org

Oklahoma Bar Association
P.O. Box 53036
1901 N. Lincoln
Oklahoma City, OK 73152-3036
Phone: (405) 416-7000
Fax: (405) 416-7001
http://www.okbar.org

Oregon State Bar
5200 SW Meadows Road
Lake Oswego, OR 97035
Phone: (800) 452-8260 or (503) 620-0222
http://www.osbar.org

Pennsylvania Bar Association
100 South Street
P.O. Box 186
Harrisburg, PA 17108-0186
Phone: (717) 238-6715
Fax: (717) 238-1204
http://www.pabar.org

Puerto Rico Bar Association (Colegio de Abogados de Puerto Rico)
P.O. Box 9021900
San Juan, PR 00902-1900
Phone: (787) 721-3358
http://www.capr.org

Rhode Island Bar Association
115 Cedar Street
Providence, RI 02903
Phone: (401) 421-5740
Fax: (401) 421-2703;
    TTY: (401) 421-1666
http://ribar.com

South Carolina Bar
950 Taylor Street
Columbia, SC 29202

Phone: (803) 799-6653
Fax: (803) 799-4118
http://www.scbar.org

State Bar of South Dakota
222 East Capitol Avenue
Pierre, SD 57501-2596
Phone: (800) 952-2333 or (605) 224-7554
http://www.sdbar.org

Tennessee Bar Association
221 Fourth Avenue North, Suite 400
Nashville, TN 37219
Phone: (615) 383-7421
Fax: (615) 297-8058
http://www.tba.org

State Bar of Texas
1414 Colorado
Austin, TX 78701
Phone: (800) 204-2222 or (512) 463-1463
Fax: (512) 463-1475
http://www.texasbar.com

Utah State Bar
645 South 200 East
Salt Lake City, UT 84111
Phone: (801) 531-9077

Fax: (801) 531-0660
http://www.utahbar.org

Vermont Bar Association
35-37 Court Street
Montpelier, VT 05602
Phone: (802) 223-2020
Fax: (802) 223-1573
http://www.vtbar.org

Virgin Islands Bar Association
P.O. Box 4108, Christiansted
St. Croix, VI 00822-4108
Phone: (340) 778-7497
Fax: (340) 773-5060
http://www.vibar.org

Virginia State Bar Association
707 E. Main Street, Suite 1500
Richmond, VA 23219-2800
Phone: (804) 775-0500
http://www.vsb.org

Washington State Bar Association
2101 Fourth Avenue, Fourth Floor
Seattle, WA 98121-2330
Phone: (800) 945-WSBA or (206) 443-
  WSBA

Fax: (206) 727-8320
http://www.wsba.org

West Virginia State Bar
2006 Kanawha Boulevard East
Charleston, WV 25311-2204
Phone: (304) 558-2456
Fax: (304) 558-2467
http://www.wvbar.org

State Bar of Wisconsin
5302 Eastpark Boulevard
Madison, WI 53718-2101
Phone: (800) 728-7788 or (608) 257-3838
Fax: (608) 257-5502
http://www.wisbar.org

Wyoming State Bar
500 Randall Avenue
Cheyenne, WY 82001
Phone: (307) 632-9061
Fax: (307) 632-3737
http://www.wyomingbar.org

APPENDIX V
BIBLIOGRAPHY

A. PERIODICALS

The following are some periodicals that various professionals read. You may be able to find copies at a school, law, academic, or public library. These periodicals may come in print or electronic form, or in both versions.

Note: All contact information and web site addresses were current when this book was being written. For a web site address that no longer works, try this: Enter the name of the organization or the web page title in a search engine. You may be able to find its new address.

ATTORNEYS

ABA Journal
http://www.abanet.org/journal

Criminal Justice
http://www.abanet.org/crimjust/cjmag/
   home.html

Labor and Employment Law
http://www.abanet.org/labor/home.html

American Bar Association
Publication Orders
P.O. Box 10892
Chicago, IL 60610-0892
Phone: (800) 285-2221
Fax: (312) 988-5568
http://www.abanet.org

The American Lawyer
Subscription Department
345 Park Avenue South
New York, NY 100010
Phone: (800) 755-2773
http://www.americanlawyer.com

Corporate Legal Times
656 West Randolph Street
Suite 500 East
Chicago, IL 60661
Phone: (312) 654-3500
http://www.cltmag.com

*IDEA—The Journal of Law and
   Technology*
Franklin Pierce Law Center
2 White Street
Concord, NH 03301
Phone: (603) 228-1541
Fax: (603) 224-3342
http://www.idea.fplc.edu

The Internet Lawyer
The Daily Record Company
11 East Saratoga Street
Baltimore, MD 21202-2199

Phone: (800) 296-8181
Fax: (410) 752-2894
http://www.internetlawyer.com

Lawyers Weekly USA
Phone: (800) 451-9998
http://www.lawyersweekly.com (online
   version)

Legal News and Commentary (online)
FindLaw.com
http://news.findlaw.com

The Military Advocate
Judge Advocates Association
6800 Chapins Road
Bloomsburg, PA 17815-8751
Phone: (570) 752-2027
Fax: (570) 752-2097
http://www.jaa.org/mil_advoc.htm

The National Law Journal
Phone: (800) 274-2893
http://www.nlj.com (online version)

The NLA Review
National Lawyers Association
City Center Square
P.O. Box 26005
Kansas City, MO 64196
Phone: (800) 471-2994
Fax: (816) 471-2995
http://www.nla.org

The Journal of Elder Law and Policy
http://www.sunflower.com/~eclecto/
   jelp.html

LEGAL SUPPORT PROFESSIONALS

LAW
NALS Resource Center
314 East Third Street, Suite 210
Tulsa, OK 74120

Phone: (918) 582-5188
Fax: (918) 582-5907
http://www.nals.org/html/atlaw.htm

Law Office Computing
James Publishing, Inc.
P.O. Box 25202
Santa Ana, CA 92799-5202
Phone: (800) 394-2626 or (714) 755-5450
http://www.lawofficecomputing.com

Legal Assistant Today
James Publishing, Inc.
P.O. Box 25202
Santa Ana, CA 92799-5202
Phone: (800) 394-2626 or (714) 755-5450
http://www.legalassistanttoday.com

Legal Management
Association of Legal Administrators
175 East Hawthorn Parkway, Suite 325
Vernon Hills, IL 60061-1428
Phone: (847) 816-1212
Fax: (847) 816-1213
http://www.alanet.org/periodicals/
   printcenter.html

National Paralegal Reporter
National Federation of Paralegal
   Associations
P.O. Box 33108
Kansas City, MO 64114-0108
Phone: (816) 941-4000
Fax: (816) 941-2725
http://www.paralegals.org/Reporter/
   home.html

LITIGATION SUPPORT PROFESSIONALS

The Legal Investigator
P.O. Box 905
Grand Blanc, MI 48439
Phone: (810) 603-0608
http://www.nalionline.org/nalipublications.
   html

P.I. Magazine
755 Bronx
Toledo, OH 43609
Phone: (419) 382-0967
http://pimall.com/pimag

LITIGATION CONSULTANTS/EXPERT WITNESSES

Criminologist

Crime Times (online)
Wacker Foundations
http://www.crime-times.org

Criminology: An Interdisciplinary Journal
American Society of Criminology
1314 Kinnear Road, Suite 212
Columbus, OH 43212-1156
Phone: (614) 292-9207
Fax: (614) 292-6767
http://www.asc41.com/publications.html

Forensic Psychologist

Behavioral Science and the Law
John Wiley and Sons, Inc.
Attn: Subscription Department
605 Third Avenue
New York, NY 10158
Phone: (800) 825-7550 or (212) 850-6021

Psychology, Public Policy, and Law
American Psychological Association
Subscription Department
750 First Street, NE
Washington, DC 20002-4242
Phone: (202) 336-5600
Fax: (202) 336-5568
http://www.apa.org/journals/law.html

Legal Nurse Consultant

Journal of Legal Nurse Consulting
American Association of Legal Nurse
    Consultants
Publication Orders
4700 West Lake Avenue
Glenview, IL 60025-1485
Phone: (847) 375-6313
http://www.aalnc.org/journsub.htm

JUDGES

APBnews.com
65 Broadway, 17th Floor
New York, NY 10006
Phone: (646) 636-5400
http://www.apbnews.com

The Federal Courts Law Review (online)
Federal Magistrate Judges Association
http://www.fclr.org

The Judges' Journal
American Bar Association
Publication Orders
P.O. Box 10892
Chicago, IL 60610-0892
Phone: (800) 285-2221
Fax: (312) 988-5568
http://www.abanet.org/jd

Judicature
American Judicature Society
180 N. Michigan Avenue, Suite 600
Chicago, IL 60601
Phone: (312) 558-6900, extension 147
Fax: (312) 558-9175
http://www.ajs.org/judicature1.html

The Third Branch Newsletter
Administrative Office of the U.S. Courts
Office of Public Affairs
One Columbus Circle, NE
Washington, DC 20544
Phone: (202) 502-2600
http://www.uscourts.gov/ttb

COURT STAFF

Court Interpreter

Proteus
National Association of Judiciary
    Interpreters and Translators
551 Fifth Avenue, Suite 3025
New York, NY 10176
Phone: (212) 692-9581
Fax: (212) 687-4016
http://www.najit.org/proteus/proteus.html

Court Reporter

Court Technology Bulletin
National Center for State Courts
P.O. Box 8798
Williamsburg, VA 23187-8798
Phone: (804) 253-2000, extension 506

http://www.ncsc.dni.us/ncsc/bulletin/
    bulletin.htm

Journal of Court Reporting
National Court Reporters Association
8224 Old Courthouse Road
Vienna, VA 22182-3808
Phone: (703) 556-6272
Fax: (703) 556-6291
http://www.verbatimreporters.com/jcr

CRIMINAL JUSTICE SOCIAL SERVICES PROFESSIONALS

Corrections Today
The American Correctional Association
4380 Forbes Boulevard
Lanham, MD 20706-4322
Phone: (800) 222-5646
http://www.corrections.com/aca/cortoday/
    index.html

The Pretrial Reporter
Pretrial Services Center
1010 Vermont Avenue, NW, Suite 300
Washington, DC 20005
Phone: (202) 638-3080
Fax: (202) 347-0493
http://www.pretrial.org/the_pretrial_
    reporter.htm

NONPROFIT ADMINISTRATORS

The Chronicle of Philanthropy
1225 23rd Street, NW
Washington, DC 20037
Phone: (800) 728-2803
http://www.philanthropy.com

The NonProfit Times
120 Littleton Road, Suite 120
Parsippany, NJ 07054-1803
Phone: (973) 394-1800
Fax: (973) 394-2888
http://www.nptimes.com

Pulse! (online)
Alliance for Nonprofit Management
http://www.allianceonline.org/pulse.html

Association Executive

Association Management
American Society of Association
    Executives
1575 I Street, NW
Washington, DC 20005-1103

Phone: (202) 626-2723
Fax: (202) 371-8825;
    TDD: (202) 626-2803
http://www.asaenet.org/magazine

Legal Services Manager

Management Information Exchange Journal
515 Washington Street, Third Floor
Boston, MA 0211
Phone: (617) 556-0288
http://www.m-i-e.org

ALTERNATIVE DISPUTE RESOLUTION PRACTITIONERS

ADR World.com
1929 37th Street, NW
Washington, DC 20007
Phone: (800) 584-5791 or
    (202) 965-7900
http://www.adrworld.com

The Alternative Newsletter (online)
Mediation Information and Resource
    Center
http://www.mediate.com/tan

Dispute Resolution Magazine
American Bar Association
Publication Orders
P.O. Box 10892
Chicago, IL 60610-0892
Phone: (800) 285-2221
Fax: (312) 988-5568
http://www.abanet.org/dispute/magazine/
    home.html

COMPLIANCE OFFICERS

Ethics Management
P.O. Box 1849
Port Townsend, WA 98368
Phone: (360) 379-3070
http://www.ethicalmanagement.com

Profiles in Diversity Journal
P.O. Box 45605
Cleveland, OH 44145-0605
Phone: (800) 573-2867
http://www.diversityjournal.com

ANALYSTS/EXAMINERS

Contract Administrator

Contract Management
National Contract Management
    Association
1912 Woodford Road
Vienna, VA 22182
Phone: (800) 344-8096
http://www.ncmahq.org/pubs/cm/
    cm.html

Patent Agent

The Disclosure
National Association of Patent
    Practitioners
4680-181 Monticello Avenue
PMB 101
Williamsburg, VA 23188
Phone: (800) 216-9588
Fax: (757) 220-3928
http://www.napp.org/newsletter/
    newsletter.html

Insurance Claims Professional

Claims Magazine: Covering the Business of Loss
The National Underwriter Company
United Airlines Building, Suite 917
2033 Sixth Avenue
Seattle, WA 98121
Phone: (206) 624-6965
Fax: (206) 624-5021
http://www.claimsmag.com

Claims People Magazine
P.O. Box 1406
Roseville, CA 95678-1406
Phone: (916) 783-0100, extension 275
http://www.claimspeople.com

Actuary

The Actuary
The Future Actuary
Society of Actuaries
P.O. Box 95668
Chicago, IL 60694
http://www.soa.org/bookstore/index.asp

EDUCATORS

Law Professor

The Chronicle of Higher Education
1225 23rd Street, NW
Washington, DC 20037
Phone: (800) 728-2803
http://chronicle.com

The Law Teacher (online)
Institute for Law School Teaching
http://law.gonzaga.edu/ilst/newsltr.htm

Syllabus
American Bar Association
Publication Orders
P.O. Box 10892
Chicago, IL 60610-0892
Phone: (800) 285-2221
Fax: (312) 988-5568
http://www.abanet.org/legaled/
    publications/syllabus.html

Paralegal Educator

The Journal of Paralegal Practice and Education
The Paralegal Educator
American Association for Paralegal
    Education
2965 Flowers Road South, Suite 105
Atlanta, GA 30341
Phone: (770) 452-9877
Fax: (770) 458-3314
http://www.aafpe.org

Judicial Branch Educator

JERITT Bulletins
The Judicial Education Reference,
    Information and Technical Transfer
    Project
Michigan State University
Suite 330 Nisbet
1407 South Harrison
East Lansing, MI 48823-5239
Phone: (517) 353-8603
Fax: (517) 432-3965
http://jeritt.msu.edu/bulletins.asp

CAREER SERVICES PROFESSIONALS

The Career Development Quarterly
American Counseling Association
Subscriptions
P.O. Box 2513
Birmingham, AL 35201-2513
Phone: (800) 633-4931

LIBRARIANS

Law Librarians

Law Library Journal
American Association of Law Libraries
53 West Jackson Boulevard, Suite 940
Chicago, IL 60605
Phone: (312) 939-4764
Fax: (312) 431-1097
http://www.aallnet.org/products/
    pub_journal.asp

Legal Division Quarterly (online)
Special Libraries Association
http://www.slalegal.org/Newsletter

Library Technician

*Associates: The Electronic Library
Support Staff Journal* (online)
http://raven.cc.ukans.edu/%7Eassoc

Library Mosaics
P.O. Box 5171
Culver City, CA 90231
Phone: (310) 410-1573
http://www.librarymosaics.com

PUBLISHING PROFESSIONALS

Quill
Society of Professional Journalists
3909 N. Meridian Street
Indianapolis, IN 46208
Phone: (317) 927-8000, extension 204
Fax: (317) 920-4789
http://www.spj.org/quill_list.asp

B. BOOKS

Listed below are some book titles about career information and about some of the different professions that are discussed in this book. To find other books, ask a librarian for help. You might also ask professionals to recommend titles for you to read.

CAREER INFORMATION

Arron, Deborah. *What Can You Do with a Law Degree?* Seattle, Wash.: Niche Press, 1999.

Bureau of Labor Statistics. *Occupational Outlook Handbook 2002–2003.* Washington, D.C.: Bureau of Labor Statistics, 2002.

Camenson, Blythe. *Careers for Legal Eagles and Other Law-and-Order Types.* Lincolnwood, Ill.: VGM Career Horizons, 1998.

———. *Real People Working in Law.* Lincolnwood, Ill.: NTC/Contemporary Publishing Company, 1997.

Davis, Mary L. *Working in Law and Justice.* Minneapolis, Minn.: Lerner Publications Co., 1999.

Editors of Ferguson Publishing Company. *The Top 100: The Fastest Growing Careers for the 21st Century.* Chicago, Ill.: Ferguson Publishing Company, 1998.

Farr, J. Michael. *America's Fastest Growing Jobs.* 5th ed. Indianapolis, Ind.: JISTWorks, Inc., 1999.

Fins, Alice. *Opportunities in Paralegal Careers.* Lincolnwood, Ill.: VGM Career Horizons, 1999.

Greenburg, Hindi. *The Lawyer's Career Change Handbook: More Than 300 Things You Can Do with a Law Degree.* New York: Avon, 1998.

Krannich, Ronald L., and Caryl Rae Krannich. *The Complete Guide to Public Employment.* 3rd ed. Manassas Park, Va.: Impact Publications, 1995.

Law School Admission Council. *So You Want to Be a Lawyer: A Practical Guide to Law as a Career.* New York: Broadway Books, 1998.

Munneke, Gary. *Careers in Law.* Lincolnwood, Ill.: NTC/Contemporary Publishing Company, 1997.

———. *Opportunities in Law Careers.* Lincolnwood, Ill.: VGM Career Horizons, 1994.

Schrayer, Robert M. *Opportunities in Insurance Careers.* Lincolnwood, Ill.: VGM Career Horizons, NTC Publishing Group, 1993.

Seidman, David. *Exploring Careers in Journalism.* New York: Rosen Publishing Group, Inc., 2000.

Southard, JoLynn. *Paralegal Career Starter.* New York: LearningExpress, 1998.

Strausser, Jeffrey. *Judgment Reversed: Alternative Careers for Lawyers.* Hauppauge, N.Y.: Barron's, 1997.

U.S. Department of Labor Employment and Training Administration. *Dictionary of Occupational Titles. Vol. 1. 4th ed.* Washington, D.C.: U.S. Department of Labor Employment and Training Administration, 1991.

LAW STUDENT

Deaver, Jeff. *The Complete Law School Companion: How to Excel at America's Most Demanding Post-Graduate Curriculum.* 2nd ed. New York: John Wiley & Sons, 1992.

Feinman, Jay M. *Law 101: Everything You Need to Know About the American Legal System.* New York: Oxford University Press, 2000.

Turow, Scott. *One L: The Turbulent True Story of a First Year at Harvard Law School.* New York: Warner Books, 1997.

ATTORNEYS

Criminal Law

Baker, Mark. *D.A.: Prosecutors in Their Own Words.* New York: Simon and Schuster, 1999.

Bergman, Paul, and Sara J. Berman-Barrett. *The Criminal Law Handbook: Know Your Rights, Survive the System.* 3rd ed. Berkeley, Calif.: Nolo Press, 2000.

Hewett, Joan. *Public Defender: Lawyer for the People.* New York, N.Y.: Lodestar Books, 1991.

Wormser, Richard. *Defending the Accused: Stories from the Courtroom.* New York: Franklin Watts, Inc. 2001

Elder Law

Sabatino, Charles P., et al. *The American Bar Association Legal Guide for Older Americans: The Law Every American Over Fifty Needs to Know.* New York: Times Books, 1998.

Strauss, Peter J., and Nancy M. Lederman. *The Elder Law Handbook: A Legal and Financial Survival Guide for Caregivers and Seniors.* New York: Facts On File, 1996.

Employment and Labor Law

Fick, Barbara J., and the American Bar Association. *The American Bar Association Guide to Workplace Law: Everything You Need to Know About Your Rights as an Employee or Employer.* New York: Times Books, 1997.

Steingold, Fred S. *The Employer's Legal Handbook.* 4th edition, Berkeley, Calif.: Nolo Press, 2001.

Intellectual Property

Pressman, David. *Patent It Yourself.* 8th ed. Berkeley, Calif.: Nolo Press, 2000.

U.S. Dept. of Commerce. *Patents and How to Get One: A Practical Handbook.* Mineloa, N.Y.: Dover Publications, 2000.

LEGAL SUPPORT STAFF

Anderson, Austin G., ed. *Merriam-Webster's Legal Secretaries Handbook.* 2nd ed. Springfield, Mass.: Merriam Webster, 1996.

Davis, Mary L. *Working in Law and Justice.* Minneapolis, Minn.: Lerner Publications Co., 1999.

De Vries, Mary Ann. *Legal Secretary's Complete Handbook.* 4th ed. Englewood Cliffs, N.J.: Prentice Hall Trade, 1992.

Gilmore, Diane M. *Legal Office: Document Processing.* Cincinnati, Ohio: South-Western Educational Publishing, 1997.

Jonathon, Lynton, Terri Mick Lyndall, and Donna Masinter. *Law Office Management.* 2nd ed. Albany, N.Y.: Delmar Publishers, 1996.

Morton, Joyce. *Legal Office Procedures.* 5th ed. Upper Saddle River, N.J.: Prentice Hall, 2000.

Roper, Brent D. *Using Computers in the Law Office.* Albany, N.Y.: West Legal Studies/Thomson Learning, 2000.

Weisbord, Ellen, Bruce H. Charnov, and Jonathan Lindsey. *Managing People in Today's Law Firm: The Human Resources Approach to Surviving Change.* Westport, Conn.: Quorum Books, 1995.

Paralegals

Estrin, Chere B. *Everything You Need to Know About Being a Legal Assistant.* Albany, N.Y.: Delmar Publishers, 1995.

Larbalestrier, Deborah E. *Paralegal Practice and Procedure: A Practical Guide for the Legal Assistant.* 3rd ed. Englewood Cliffs, N.J.: Prentice Hall Press, 1994.

Southard, JoLynn. *Paralegal Career Starter.* New York: LearningExpress, 1998.

Statsky, William P. *Introduction to Paralegalism: Perspectives, Problems, and Skills.* 5th ed. St. Paul, Minn.: West Publishing, 1997.

Wagner, Andrea. *How to Land Your First Paralegal Job: An Insider's Guide to the Fastest Growing Profession of the New Millennium.* 3rd ed. Upper Saddle River, N.J.: Prentice Hall, 2000.

LITIGATION CONSULTANTS/EXPERT WITNESSES

Feder, Harold A. *Succeeding as an Expert Witness: Increasing Your Impact and Income.* Glenwood Springs, Colo.: Tageh Press, 1993.

Poynter, Dan. *Expert Witness Handbook: Tips and Techniques for the Litigation Consultant.* Santa Barbara, Calif.: Para Publishing, 1997.

Appraisers

Miles, Michele G. *The Business Appraisers and Litigation Support.* New York: John Wiley & Sons, 2001.

Criminologists

Barlow, Hugh D., and David Kauzlarich. *Introduction to Criminology.* 8th ed. Upper Saddle River, N.J.: Prentice Hall, 2001.

Purpura, Philip. *Criminal Justice: An Introduction.* Boston, Mass.: Butterworth-Heinemann, 1997.

Forensic Accounting

Manning, George A. *Financial Investigation and Forensic Accounting.* Boca Raton, Fla.: CRC Press, 1999.

Forensic Psychology

Deyoub, Paul L., and Gretchen V. K. Douthit. *A Practical Guide to Forensic Psychology.* Northvale, N.J.: Jason Aronson, 1996.

Wrightsman, Lawrence S. *Forensic Psychology.* Belmont, Calif.: Wadsworth Publishing Co., 2000.

Legal Nurse Consulting

Bogart, Julie Brewer, ed. *Legal Nurse Consulting: Principles and Practice.* Boca Raton, Fla.: CRC Press, 1997.

JUDGES

Guide to the Federal Courts: An Introduction to the Federal Courts and Their Operation. Know Your Government Series. Washington, D.C.: WANT Publishing Co., 1985.

Bianchi, Anne. *Everything You Need to Know About Family Court.* New York: Rosen Publishing Group, 2000.

Burns, Robert P. *A Theory of the Trial.* Princeton, N.J.: Princeton University Press, 1999.

Neubauer, David W. *Judicial Process: Law, Courts, and Politics in the United States.* Fort Worth, Tex.: Harcourt Brace College and School Division, 1997.

O'Brien, David M., ed. *Judges on Judging: Views from the Bench.* Chatham, N.J.: Chatham House Publishers, 1997.

Satter, Robert. *Doing Justice, A Trial Judge at Work.* New York: American Lawyer Books, Simon & Schuster, 1990.

Tobin, Robert W. *Creating the Judicial Branch: The Unfinished Reform.* Williamsburg, Va.: National Center for State Courts, 1999.

COURT SUPPORT STAFF

Court Interpreters

De Jongh, Elena M. *An Introduction to Court Interpreting: Theory and Practice.* Lanham, Md.: University Press of America, 1992.

Court Reporters

Knapp, Mary H., and Robert W. McCormick. *The Complete Court Reporter's Handbook.* 3rd ed. Upper Saddle River, N.J.: Prentice Hall, 1999.

Fatooh, Audrey, and Barbara Mauk. *Style and Sense: For the Legal Profession: A Handbook for Court Reporters, Transcribers, Paralegals and Secretaries.* Rev. ed. Palm Springs, Calif.: ETC Publications, 1995.

Reily, John R. *'Read That Back, Please!': Memoirs of a Court Reporter.* Santa Barbara, Calif.: Fithian Press, 1999.

Saari, David J. *The Court and Free-Lance Reporter Profession.* N.Y.: Quorum Books, January 1988.

Scopists

Sober, W. Charley, and Linda Knipes-Sober. *Scopistry.* 2nd ed. Humble, Tex.: Logical Resources, 2000.

CRIMINAL JUSTICE SOCIAL SERVICES PROFESSIONALS

Berg, Insoo Kim, and Susan Kelly. *Building Solutions in Child Protective Services.* New York: W. W. Norton & Company, 2000.

Dubowitz, Howard, and Diane DePanfilis, eds. *Handbook for Child Protection Practice.* Thousand Oaks, Calif.: Sage Publications, 2000.

Humes, Edward. *No Matter How Loud I Shout: A Year in the Life of Juvenile Court.* New York: Simon and Schuster, 1996.

PROFESSIONS IN POLITICS

Davidson, Roger H., and Walter Oleszek. *Congress and Its Members.* 7th ed. Washington, D.C.: CQ Press, 2000.

Price, David Eugene. *The Congressional Experience.* 2nd ed. Boulder, Colo.: Westview Press, 2000.

McDonough, John E. *Experiencing Politics: A Legislator's Stories of Government and Health Care.* Berkeley, Calif.: University of California Press, 2000.

Wood, Len. *Elected Official's Little Handbook: A Portable Guide for Local Government Legislators.* Rancho Palos Verdes, Calif.: Training Shoppe, 1994.

Lobbyists

Guyer, Robert L., and Laura K. Guyer. *Guide to State Legislative Lobbying.* Gainesville, Fla.: Engineering the Law, Inc., 1999.

Rosenthal, Alan. *The Third House: Lobbyists and Lobbying in the States.* Washington, D.C.: CQ Press, 1993.

Wolpe, Bruce C., and Bertram J. Levine. *Lobbying Congress: How the System Works.* Washington, D.C.: Congressional Quarterly, 1996.

NONPROFIT ADMINISTRATORS

Drucker, Peter Ferdinand. *Managing the Non-Profit Organization: Principles and Practices.* New York: HarperCollins, 1990.

Wolf, Thomas. *Managing a Nonprofit Organization in the Twenty-First Century.* 3rd ed. New York: Simon & Schuster, 1999.

ALTERNATIVE DISPUTE RESOLUTION PRACTITIONERS

Dunlop, John Thomas, and Arnold M. Zack. *Mediation and Arbitration of Employment Disputes.* San Francisco, Calif.: Jossey-Bass, 1997.

Goodman, Allan H. *Basic Skills for the New Arbitrator.* Rockville, Md.: Solomon Publications, 1993.

———. *Basic Skills for the New Mediator.* Rockville, Md.: Solomon Publications, 1994.

Kolb, Deborah M. *When Talk Works: Profiles of Mediators.* San Francisco, Calif.: Jossey-Bass, 1997.

Nolan-Haley, Jacqueline M. *Alternative Dispute Resolution in a Nutshell.* 2nd ed. St. Paul, Minn.: West Information Publishing Group, 2001.

COMPLIANCE OFFICERS

Seglin, Jeffrey L., and Norman R. Augustine. *The Good, The Bad, and Your Business: Choosing the Right When Ethical Dilemmas Pull You Apart.* New York: John Wiley & Sons, 2000

Ciulla, Joanne B., ed. *Ethics, the Heart of Leadership.* Westport, Conn.: Quorum Books, 1998.

CAREER SERVICES PROFESSIONALS

Figler, Howerad, and Richard Nelson Bolles. *The Career Counselor's Handbook.* Berkeley, Calif.: Ten Speed Press, 1999.

Gurney, Darrell W. *Headhunters Revealed! Career Secrets for Choosing and Using Professional Recruiters.* Los Angeles, Calif.: Hunter Arts Publishing, 2000.

Jupina, Andrea A. *The Recruiter's Research Blue Book: A How-To Guide for Researchers, Search Consultants, Corporate Recuiters, Small Business Owners, Venture Capitalists and Line Executives.* 2nd ed. Fitzwilliam, N.H.: Kennedy Information, 2000.

PUBLISHING PROFESSIONALS

Alexander, S. L. *Covering the Courts: A Handbook for Journalists.* Lanham, Md.: University Press of America, 1998.

Cappon, Rene J. *The Associated Press Guide to Newswriting.* Foster City, Calif.: IDG Books Worldwide, 2000.

Garner, Bryan A. *The Elements of Legal Style.* New York: Oxford University Press, 1991.

Sharpe, Leslie T., and Irene Gunther. *Editing Fact and Fiction: A Concise Guide to Book Editing.* New York: Cambridge University Press. 1994.

APPENDIX VI
RESOURCES ON THE WORLD WIDE WEB

Listed below are some web sites that can help you learn more about many of the professions that are discussed in this book. You will also find some resources that offer career information.

Note: All contact information and web site addresses were current when this book was being written. For a web site address that *no longer works, try this: Enter the name of the organization or the web page title in a search engine. You may be able to find its new address.*

CAREER AND JOB INFORMATION

2002–03 Occupational Outlook Handbook
Bureau of Labor Statistics
http://stats.bls.gov/oco/home.htm

America's Job Bank
http://www.ajb.dni.us

CareerJournal
from *The Wall Street Journal*
http://careerjournal.com

JobStar: Job Search Guide
http://jobstar.org

Law.com Law Jobs
Career Center
http://www.lawjobs.com

LEGAL AND NONLEGAL CAREER LINKS

Office of Career Services
Rutgers School of Law—Camden
http://www.camlaw.rutgers.edu/cservices/
    links.html

Monster.com
(an online career center)
http://www.monster.com

The Next Step Magazine: For High School Students Who Want More
http://www.nextstepmagazine.com

USAJOBS
United States Office of Personnel Management
http://www.usajobs.opm.gov

Wetfeet.com
(an online career center)
http://www.wetfeet.com

ATTORNEYS

Career Library
LexisNexis
http://lawschool.lexis.com/career

The 'Lectric Law Library
http://www.lectlaw.com

FindLaw for Legal Professionals
http://library.lp.findlaw.com

Hieros Gamos
Law and Legal Resource Center
http://www.hg.org

Law.Com
http://www.law.com

The Law Forum
http://www.lawforum.net

Law Library Resource Xchange
http://www.llrx.com

Law School Admission Council
http://www.lsac.org

The Professional Development Center
http://profdev.lp.findlaw.com

The Role of the Internet in Your Legal Job Search
Career Development Office, Shephard Broad Law Center, Nova Southeastern University, Fort Lauderdale, Florida
http://www.nsulaw.nova.edu/career/
    internet_job_search.htm

Government Lawyer

American Bar Association Government and Public Sector Lawyers Division
http://www.abanet.org/govpub

Attorneys in the Federal Service
http://www.usajobs.opm.gov/EI24.htm

Executive Office for United States Attorneys
U.S. Department of Justice
http://www.usdoj.gov/usao/eousa/
    index.html

National Association of Attorneys General
http://www.naag.org

Office of Attorney Recruitment and Management
Department of Justice
http://www.usdoj.gov/oarm

U.S. Attorneys Office
U.S. Department of Justice
http://www.usdoj.gov/usao/eousa/usaos.
    html

Military Lawyer

U.S. Air Force JAG
http://www.jagusaf.hq.af.mil

U.S. Army JAG
http://www.jagcnet.army.mil

U.S. Navy JAG
http://www.jag.navy.mil

U.S. Marine Corps JAG
http://www.mcrc.usmc.mil/section/o/
    index(ol).htm

U.S. Coast Guard Direct Commission Lawyer Program
http://www.uscg.mil/legal/recruit/dclinterinfo.htm

Public Interest Lawyer

Equal Justice Works
http://www.napil.org

Public Interest Law
New Jersey Law Network
http://www.njlawnet.com/public.html

Office of Public Interest Advising
Harvard Law School
http://www.law.harvard.edu/students/opia

Public Interest Clearinghouse
http://www.pic.org

Elder Law Attorney

AARP
http://www.aarp.org

American Bar Association Commission on Legal Problems of the Elderly
http://www.abanet.org/elderly

American College of Trust and Estate Counsel
http://www.actec.org

Kansas Elder Law Network
http://www.keln.org

National Senior Citizens Law Center
http://www.nsclc.org

Seniors Resource Guide: Helping Seniors Find Their Way
http://www.SeniorsResourceGuide.com

Employment Lawyer

American Bar Association Section of Labor and Employment Law
http://www.abanet.org/labor/home.html

Labor and Employment Law Resources on the Internet
LLRX.com
http://www.llrx.com/features/labor.htm

Labor and Employment Links
FindLaw for Legal Professionals
http://www.findlaw.com/01topics/27labor

Environmental Lawyer

Earthjustice Legal Defense Fund
http://www.earthjustice.org

Environmental Law Institute
http://www.eli.org

National Association of Environmental Professionals
http://www.naep.org

National Resource Defence Council
http://www.nrdc.org

U.S. Environmental Protection Agency
http://www.epa.gov

Intellectual Property Attorney

American Bar Association Section of Intellectual Property Law
http://www.abanet.org/intelprop

The Intellectual Property Law Server
http://www.intelproplaw.com

The Intellectual Property Mall
Franklin Pierce Law Center
http://www.ipmall.fplc.edu

U.S. Copyright Office
http://www.loc.gov/copyright

Criminal Lawyer/ Prosecutor/Public Defender

American Bar Association, Section of Criminal Justice
http://www.abanet.org/crimjust/home.html

American Prosecutors Research Institute
http://www.ndaa.org/apri/Index.html

The Defender Association
Public Defense in Seattle-King County, Washington
http://www.defender.org

First Judicial Circuit Public Defender Corporation
http://publicdefender.com

International Association of Prosecutors
http://www.iap.nl.com

Appellate Attorney

American Bar Association Section of Litigation
http://www.abanet.org/litigation/committee/appellate/home.html

The Appellate Law Webpage
Law Office of Bruce Adelstein
http://www.appellatelaw.net

A Client's Primer on Appeals
Hartley & Hartley
http://www.hartley.com/appeals.htm

Solicitor General's Office
http://www.usdoj.gov/osg/aboutosg/function.html

Standards for Appellate Defender Offices
National Legal Aid & Defender Association
http://www.nlada.org/standards/sedado.htm

LEGAL SUPPORT PROFESSIONALS

HR.com
http://www3.hr.com

International Association of Administrative Professionals
http://www.iaap-hq.org

Lawyer Marketing
http://marketing.lp.findlaw.com

The Legal Secretaries Alliance
http://www.legalsecretarymaryland.com

Legal Secretaries, Inc.
http://lsi.org

Legal Technology Resources
NetTech, Inc.
http://www.nettechinc.com/lawtech.htm

Links for Legal Support Personnel
NALS . . . the association for legal professionals
http://www.nals.org/dmy/lkindex.htm

Paralegal

American Association for Paralegal Education
http://www.aafpe.org

The Independent Paralegal Network
http://www.themisintl.com/tipn/index.html

Legal Assistant Management Association
http://www.lamanet.org

National Federation of Paralegal Associations
http://www.paralegals.org

Paralegal Links
Central Texas College
http://www.ctc-pac.com/r_lega.htm

LITIGATION SUPPORT PROFESSIONALS

Bail Bond Agent

Bail Enforcement Agents
Hi Tek's Investigative Resources
http://www.hitekinfo.com/links/
Bail_Enforcement_Agents

Bounty Hunters Online
http://www.onworld.com/BHO/index.html

California Bail Agents Association
http://www.cbaa.com

National Association of Bail Insurance Companies
http://www.nabic.net/welcome.htm

Process Server

Process Servers on the Net
http://www.411law.com/index2.htm

Service of Process Resource Center
http://www.pimall.com/nais/processr.
html

Private Investigator

Infoguys—The Private Investigators Portal
http://www.infoguys.com

Investigator Links
National Association of Legal
Investigators
http://www.nalionline.org/
investigativelinks.html

Trial Consultant

An Interesting Career in Psychology: Trial Consultant
http://www.apa.org/science/ic-stapp.html

Trial Consulting and Forensic Psychiatry
http://www.forensic-psych.com/
articles/catTrialCons.html

LITIGATION CONSULTANTS AND EXPERT WITNESSES

American Academy of Certified Consultants and Experts
http://www.aacce.org

American Academy of Forensic Sciences
http://www.aafs.org

American College of Forensic Examiners
http://www.acfe.com

American Institute for Expert Witnesses
http://www.expertwit.com

ExpertLaw
http://www.expertlaw.com

ExpertPages.com
Directory of Expert Witnesses and
Consultants
http://expertpages.com

Expert Witness Network Home Page
http://www.witness.net/experts.asps

Crash Reconstruction Consultant

Accident Reconstruction and Investigation Center
http://www.aiexperts.com

Accreditation Commission for Traffic Accident Reconstruction
http://www.actar.org

ARC Network
http://www.accidentreconstruction.com

National Academy of Forensic Engineers
http://www.nafe.org/car.htm

TARO: The Traffic Accident Reconstruction Origin
http://www.tarorigin.com

Criminologist

Academy of Criminal Justice Sciences
http://www.acjs.org

Criminal Justice Links
School of Criminology and Criminal
Justice, Florida State University,
Tallahassee, Florida
http://www.criminology.fsu.edu/cjlinks

Criminal Justice Resources: Periodicals on the Web
Michigan State University Libraries
http://www.lib.msu.edu/harris23/crimjust/
per.htm

Forensics Links
Criminal Justice Department
University of North Texas, Denton, Texas
http://www.unt.edu/cjus/forensic.htm

Forensic Psychologist

The American Board of Forensic Psychology
http://www.abfp.com

Careers and Training in Psychology and Law
American Psychology-Law Society
http://www.unl.edu/ap-ls/CAREERS.htm

Forensic Psychiatry and Psychology
Carpenter's Forensic Science Resources
http://www.tncrimlaw.com/forensic/
f_psych.html

Forensic Psychiatry Resource Page
University of Alabama
http://bama.ua.edu/~jhooper

Psych.com, The Internet Psychology Resource
http://www.thepsych.com

The Ultimate Forensic Psychology Database
http://flash.lakeheadu.ca/~pals/
forensics

Legal Nurse Consultant

American Academy of Nursing
http://www.nursingworld.org/aan/index.htm

Legal Nurse Consultant
http://www.psna.org/Career/
legalnurse.htm

National Alliance of Certified Legal Nurse Consultants
http://www.legalnurse.com

Welcome to the Nurse Entrepreneur, Legal Nurse Consultants, Nursing Entrepreneurs
http://www.nursefriendly.com/nursing/ymedlegal.htm

Forensic Accountant

Forensic Accounting Defined
http://www.cris.com/~dfillmer/forensic.htm

Forensic Accounting Demystified
http://www.forensicaccountant.com

National Association of Forensic Accountants, Inc.
http://www.claimssupport.com/nafanet.com/page4.html

Appraiser

The Appraisal Foundation
http://www.appraisalfoundation.org

Appraisal Institute
www.appraisalinstitute.org

JUDGES

American Bar Association Judicial Division
http://www.abanet.org/jd

Bureau of Justice Statistics
U.S. Department of Justice
http://www.ojp.usdoj.gov/bjs

Courts.Net
The Nation's Court Directory
http://www.courts.net

Courts of Law
http://www.lawforum.net/resources/courts.htm

The Federal Courts Law Review
http://www.fclr.org

Family Court
http://www.courtinfo.ca.gov/reference/guide-family.htm

The Family Court and You
Guide to the New York State Family Court
http://www.nysba.org/public/famcourtandu.html

Federal Judicial Center
http://www.fjc.gov

The Federal Judiciary Homepage
http://www/uscourts.gov/faq.html

Federal Magistrate Judges Association
http://www.fedjudge.org

The Future of Children: The Juvenile Court
http://www.futureofchildren.org/juv

Justice Web Collaboratory
Chicago-Kent College of Law
http://judgelink.org

National Association of Women Judges
http://www.nawj.org

National Center for State Courts
http://www.ncsc.dni.us

The National Judicial College
http://www.judges.org

The State Court Locator
Villanova University School of Law
http://vls.law.vill.edu/Locator/statecourt/index.htm

Supreme Court Law Library
http://www.superiorcourt.maricopa.gov/lawlibrary/Oircrts.asp

Supreme Court of the United States
http://www.supremecourtus.gov

Understanding Juvenile and Family Court
http://www.bcm.tmc.edu/cta/Juv_Fam_Ct.htm

COURT SUPPORT STAFF

Job Description Database
Information Resource Center
National Center for State Courts
http://www.ncsc.dni.us/is/clrhouse/jobdeda/main.htm

JUDICIAL LAW CLERK

Judicial Clerkships
http://www.bu.edu/law/careers/clerkships.html

Welcome to the World of Judicial Clerkships
http://www/judicialclerkships.com

Court Interpreter

California Court Interpreter's Association
http://www/ccia.org/index.htm

Court Interpretation homepage
National Center for State Courts
http://www/ncsc.dni.us/RESEARCH/interp

Court Interpreters
California Courts
http://www.courtinfo.ca.gov/programs/courtinterpreters/infopack.htm

The National Center for Interpretation Testing, Research and Policy
http://nci.arizona.edu/ncitrp.htm

Court Reporter

About Court Reporting
http://www.depo.com/abtcrng.htm

The Court Reporting Store
http://www.thecourtreportingstore.com

Machine Shorthand Information Site
http://www.machineshorthand.com

OfficialCourtReporter.com
http://www.officialcourtreporter.com

Scopist

Scopists.com
http://www.scopists.com

Court Administrator

Conference of State Court Administrators
http://cosca.ncsc.dni.us

Institute for Court Management
National Center for State Courts
http://www.ncsc.dni.us/icm

CRIMINAL JUSTICE SOCIAL SERVICES PROFESSIONALS

U.S. Department of Justice
http://www.usdoj.gov

U.S. Department of Health and Human Services
http://www.dhhs.gov

Pretrial Services Officer/U.S. Probation Officer

The Corrections Connection
http://www.corrections.com

National Criminal Justice Reference Service
http://www.ncjrs.org

Pretrial Services Resource Center
http://www.pretrial.org

U.S. Parole Commission
U.S. Department of Justice
http://www.usdoj.gov/uspc

U.S. Probation and Pretrial Services
http://www.uscourts.gov/misc/
propretrial.htm

U.S. Sentencing Commission
http://www.ussc.gov

Juvenile Counselor

The Children's Defense Fund
http://www.childrensdefense.org

Juvenile Justice
National Criminal Justice Reference
Service
http://virlib.ncjrs.org/JuvenileJustice.asp

National Juvenile Detention Association
http://www.njda.com

Office of Juvenile Justice and Delinquency Prevention
http://ojjdp.ncjrs.org

Child Protective Services Caseworker

Child Abuse Prevention Network
http://child-abuse.com

Child Welfare League of America
http://www.cwla.org

National Clearinghouse on Child Abuse and Neglect Information
U.S. Dept of Health and Human Services
http://www.calib.com/nccanch

Victim Services Specialist

Office for Victims of Crime
U.S. Department of Justice
http://www.ojp.usdoj.gov/ovc/welcome.
html

Victim Assistance Online
A Comprehensive Resource Center
http://www.vaonline.org

Victims of Crime
National Criminal Justice Reference
Service
http://virlib.ncjrs.org/VictimsOfCrime.asp

PROFESSIONS IN POLITICS

Association for Political & Public Affairs Professionals
http://www.theaapc.org/what.html

The Council of State Governments
http://www.csg.org

Federal Election Commission
http://fecwebl.fec.gov

County Elected Officials
Municipal Research and Services Center
of Washington, Seattle, Washington
http://www.mrsc.org/localgov/
locgov17.htm

FirstGov
Official site for the U.S. Government
http://www.firstgov.gov

League of Women Voters of the United States
http://www/lwv.org

National Association of State Election Directors
http://www.nased.org

National Conference of State Legislatures
http://www.ncsl.org

Project Vote Smart
http://www.vote-smart.org/ce

Stennis Center for Public Service
http://www.stennis.gov

Thomas
Legislative Information on the Internet
http://thomas.loc.gov

U.S. Association of Former Members of Congress
http://www.usafmc.org

U.S. House of Representatives
http://www/house.gov

U.S. Senate
http://www.senate.gov

Public Interest Advocate

Action Without Borders
http://www.idealist.org

Advocacy Institute
Washington, D.C.
http://www.advocacy.org

Political Links: Advocacy Groups
Robertson School of Government
Regent University, Virginia Beach, Virginia
http://www.regent.edu/acad/schgov/
polinet/advocacy.html

State PIRGS (Public Interest Research Groups) Working Together
http://www.pirg.org

NONPROFIT ADMINISTRATORS

Internet Nonprofit Center
http://www.nonprofit-info.org

National Council of Nonprofit Associations
http://www.ncna.org

Nonprofit Career Network
http://www.nonprofitcareer.com

Nonprofit Links
Center of Nonprofit Management
University of St. Thomas
Minneapolis, Minnesota
http://www.gsb.stthomas.edu/nonprofit/
links.htm

Nonprofit Nuts and Bolts
http://www/nutsbolts.com

Public Service Web Sites

Office of Career Services, Harvard University
http://www/ocs.fas.harvard.edu/html/
nfplink.html

Association Executive

Careers in Associations
American Society of Association
Executives
http://www/asaenet.org/career

Legal Services Manager

Equal Justice Network
http://www/equaljustice.org

Legal Services Corporation
http://www.lsc.gov

National Center on Poverty Law
http://www.povertylaw.org

ALTERNATIVE DISPUTE RESOLUTION (ADR) PRACTITIONERS

American Bar Association Section of Dispute Resolution
http://www.abanet.org/dispute

ADR Resources
http://adrr.com

Center for Applied Conflict Management
Kent State University
http://www.kent.edu/cacm

CPR Institute for Dispute Resolution
http://www/cpradr.org

Institute of Conflict Resolution
School of Industrial and Labor Relations, Cornell University and the Foundation for the Prevention and Early Resolution of Conflict
http://www.ilr.cornell.edu/ICR

Mediate.com
Mediation Information and Resource Center
http://www.mediate.com

Federal Mediation and Conciliation Service
http://www.fmcs.gov

National Arbitration Forum
http://www.arb-forum.com

U.S. Institute for Environmental Conflict Resolution
http://www/ecr/gov/r_faw.htm

COMPLIANCE OFFICERS

Equal Opportunity Officer

American Civil Liberties Union
http://www/aclu.org

Americans with Disabilities Act
U.S. Department of Justice
http://www.usdoj.gov/crt/ada/adahoml.htm

Equal Employment Opportunity Commission
http://www/eeoc.gov

Ethics Officer

Association for Practical and Professional Ethics
http://ezinfo.ucs.indiana.edu/~appe/aims.html

Business for Social Responsibility
http://www.bsr.org

Center for Business Ethics
Bentley College, Waltham, Massachusetts
http://ecampus.bentley.edu/dept/cbe

The Ethics Center
Ethics Clearinghouse on the Web
http://www/taknosys.com/ethics

U.S. Office of Government Ethics
http://www/usoge.gov/home.html

EDUCATORS

Law Professor

American Bar Association Section of Legal Education and Admissions to the Bar
http://www.abanet.org/legaled/home.html

Chronicle of Higher Education: **Career Network**
http://chronicle.com/jobs

Council on Law in Higher Education
http://www.clhe.org

Institute for Law School Teaching
Gonzaga University School of Law, Spokane, Washington
http://law.gonzaga.edu/ilst/ilst.htm

Jurist: The Legal Education Network
University of Pittsburgh School of Law
http://jurist.law.pitt.edu

"So You Want to be a Law Professor?"
University of Miami School of Law
http://www/law.miami.edu/~froomkin/wannable.htm

Teachlaw: Resources for Lawyers Who Want to be Law Professors
http://teachlaw.law.us.edu

Legal Writing Instructor

Association of Legal Writing Directors
http://www.alwd.org

Barger on Legal Writing
University of Arkansas at Little Rock School of Law
http://www.ualr.edu/~cmbarger/Index.html

Legal Writing Institute
http://www.lwionline.org

Judicial Branch Educator

Institute for Court Management
National Center for State Courts
http://www.ncsc.dni.us/ICM

The JERITT Project
Michigan State University
http://jeritt.msu.edu

Judicial Education Center
Institute of Public Law
University of New Mexico
Albuquerque, New Mexico
http://jec.unm.edu

The National Judicial College
University of Nevada
Reno, Nevada
http://www/judges.org

CAREER SERVICES PROFESSIONALS

Advice for the Lawlorn
http://www.nylawyer.com/lawlorn

How to Use a Legal Recruiter
The Counsel Network
http://www.headhunt.com/usearecruiter.htm

Jobs for Recruiters

Wisnik Enterprises
http://www.jobsforrecruiters.com

Research—National Association of Law Placement
http://www.nalp.org/nalpresearch/index.htm

National Board for Certified Counselors, Inc.
http://www.nbcc.org

LIBRARIANS

Law Librarian

**Choosing Law Librarianship:
Thoughts for People Contemplating
a Career Move**
http://www.llrx.com/features/librarian.htm

**Education for a Career in Law
Librarianship**
American Association of Law Libraries
http://www.aallnet.org/committee/tfedu/
education.html

Law Library Technician

Library Support Staff.com
Resources for Library
Mary Niederlander
http://www.librarysupportstaff.com

Library Support Staff Resource Center
maintained by Highline Community
College Library
http://flightline.highline.ctc.edu/lssrc

PUBLISHING PROFESSIONALS

Ask a Reporter Archive
The New York Times on the Web
Learning Network/Student Connections
http://www.nytimes.com/learning/
students/ask_reporters/archives.html

**Legal Newspapers and Legal
Magazines (links)**
Palidan Legal Resources
http://www.palidan.com/legal6.htm

Legal Media Directory
D. M. Freedman Company, 2000
http://www.newstips.org/MRC2/
dir-legal.html

A Legal Publisher's List
University of Colorado Law Library
http://www.colorado.edu/Law/lawlib/ts/
legpub.htm

Newspaper Careers Links
Detroit Free Press
http://www.freep.com/jobspage

INDEX